The Big Book of NLP Expanded

350+ Techniques, Patterns & Strategies
of Neuro Linguistic Programming

5th Edition (2010)

Dedicated to the memory and legacy of

Dr. Milton H. Erickson

Disclaimer

This book makes no medical, psychiatric, or psychological diagnoses, treatments, or recommendations. It is only for informational purposes. This information is not intended to be a substitute for professional medical advice or clinical training. Never disregard professional clinical advice or put off seeking it because of anything you read in this book. It is the reader's responsibility to obtain competent consultation regarding their fitness to use the techniques described in this book for any purpose, as well as what training, certification, or licensure the reader may require for any application of the techniques.

The author has attempted to accurately represent the opinions and techniques expressed by NLP trainers, as well as their documentation, in a useful manner. However, the author provides the material "AS-IS." The author expressly disclaims any and all warranties, express or implied, including fitness for a particular purpose. The author makes no warranty that this book will be completely accurate or applicable to any purpose or situation, including those similar to those listed as typical applications for any given technique.

Although this material is believed to accurately reflect the techniques of the NLP community at the time of publication, due to the possibility of human error and changing standards for the use of such techniques, the individuals involved in the production of this book do not warrant that the information contained herein is in every respect accurate or complete, and are thus not responsible for any errors or omissions, or for the results obtained from the use of such information. The author makes no express or implied representations or warranties.

In no event shall the author, any contributors or editors, or anyone cited as a source or authority be liable for any claims or damages (including, without limitation, direct, incidental, and consequential damages, personal injury or wrongful death, lost profits) arising from the use or inability to use this book, whether based on warranty, contract, tort, or any other legal theory, and whether or not the author is advised of the possibility of such damages. The author will not be held liable for any personal injury, including death, resulting from your use or misuse of this book.

We apologize in advance for any errors or omissions regarding the individuals responsible for the NLP patterns. Because of the large community of NLP developers and the rapid rate of development of the techniques, determining who created a specific pattern can be difficult. We relied on documentation from various dates as well as community members who were familiar with the work of many developers.

The Big Book of NLP, Expanded: 350+ Techniques, Patterns & Strategies of Neuro Linguistic Programming

For additional copies/bulk purchases of this book in the U.S. or internationally, please contact us at www.ericks.org

ISBN: 9657489083

Manufactured in the United States of America.

The Big Book of NLP Expanded

350+ Techniques, Patterns & Strategies of Neuro Linguistic Programming

5th Edition (2010)

Erickson Institute
Shlomo Vaknin

Additional Resources

If you bought this book and you're new to NLP, you're entitled to a **free** six-hour **audio-course** specifically for beginners, focusing on the essentials- contact Ben at *help@ericks.org*

Training: We no longer provide seminars on NLP, as our mission is to help private practitioners build skills, and help their clients, over time and not via short bursts of motivation. However, if you do feel you need to study via the structural NLP seminars, the one training organization we can honestly recommend is the Tad James Company in Australia.

Mentoring: Although we no longer offer short seminars, we do have a personal mentoring program with a limited number of seats. We may be able to assist you if your primary goal is to build or enhance a private practice in therapy or coaching. Please contact our office manager, Ben Schwartz, at help@ericks.org to inquire on availability or with any questions you may have.

NLP: The 57 Meta-Programs
Erickson Institute | ISBN - 8087518071 | 256 pages
The Meta-Programs model is essential for understanding and applying the effective communication patterns of NLP. Learn how to recognize your own and other people's habitual thinking patterns. In a concise and clear language, this book shows you practical ways to use the meta-programs for persuasion and rapport.

Advanced NLP Techniques for Therapists & Coaches
Erickson Institute | ISBN 808751811X | 200 pages
This is an advanced, modern NLP manual for therapists and coaches who want to expand and update their skills. You'll find advise about resistance, preparation for change work, and we cover a few dozens of new and powerful methods such as Vision-Down Stream, Targeting, Body Scan, Echo Events.

Fear of Rejection: NLP Tools You Can Use

Erickson Institute | ISBN - 8087518144 | 220 pages

A practical workbook to help you to take practical steps to overcome your fear of rejection and pursue your goals with courage and determination.

A Short Guide to Self-Motivation

Erickson Institute | ISBN - 8087518152 | 128 pages

Find your own unique path to taking deliberate action and making positive changes in your life, regardless of how you "feel" about it.

Other Recommended Books:

Uncommon Therapy: The Psychiatric Techniques of Milton H. Erickson, M.D.

Jay Haley | ISBN - 978-0393310313 | 320 pages

A must-read for every single professional therapist. The case studies covered in this book will open your eyes and teach you the inner workings of evidence-based therapy procedures. Prof. Haley is a remarkable teacher as well.

The Structure of Magic, Vol. 1: A Book About Language and Therapy

Richard Bandler, John Grinder | ISBN - 978-0831400446 | 225 pages

While it is a somewhat challenging book to read, it is still essential for any learner of NLP. This is the starting point of this field—the ideas that started the revolution in therapy.

Persuasion Mastery: 500 Lessons On The Psychology Of Influence

Stephan Thieme | ISBN - 9788087518106 | 400 pages

This massive book provides 500 practical lessons in an easy-to-read manual that will teach you everything you need to know to move forward in life, influence the people around you, and notice if and how anyone is attempting to manipulate or take advantage of you.

What Matters Most: Living a More Considered Life

James Hollis | ISBN - 978-1592404995 | 288 pages

In a poetic and highly approachable language, the director of the Jung Educational Center offers a glimpse into the unconscious mind and brings to light some of Jung's most difficult to grasp concepts. We buy this book for every professional we collaborate with.

Content

Preface

Being alive means also being vulnerable to the common forms of human suffering. Certainly, there are traumatic events and disastrous tragedies. There is an underworld of suffering that is often transparent to the surrounding. Consider: Pain. Shame. Anxiety. Lethargy. Self-doubt. Guilt. Suicidal ideation. Jealousy. Helplessness. Addictions. Idiopathic diseases. The list goes on and on. You can find clues for these forms of suffering, whenever a statement begins with "I should have..." or "If only I was / could / would / had...".

The purpose of this book in particular, and my life's work at the Erickson Institute in general, is to alleviate a very special breed of human suffering. As Mark Twain said, "I am an old man and have suffered through a great many troubles, most of which never actually happened." Anxiety, psychosomatic pain, and all sorts of emotional pains are troubles that exist only in the mind, and for no valid reasoning. They never actually happen, in any person's objective external reality, only within the confinements and torturous realms of their internal subjective experience of life.

Why does it happen? Well, we humans tend to suffer unnecessarily mostly because we stubbornly think, and often downright believe, that we can overcome all sorts of problems with cognitive reasoning alone. How often did you manage to reason yourself into doing, effectively and with satisfying results, something you're extremely afraid of, such as bungee jumping or giving a speech to a crowd of 1,000 bored and impatient dentists?

Our minds do not change their processes naturally based on linguistic logic and reasoning, and the proof to this is simple: you had to learn your mother's tongue in order to communicate properly. Without the knowledge of language, you would not be able to create rationalizations in a coherent manner. We take our native language for granted, and that's where we get it all wrong. You were born with a clean slate mind. You were not born an English speaker or a Spanish orator. Language dictates the meaning of our subjective experience by forcing its intrinsic limitations on verbal interpretation of external and internal stimuli.

When applied correctly, NLP is purely practical and realistic. That's why we chose to focus this book on what matters most: actions you can take right now to enable you or your client to make the mental shifts required to achieve your goals and dreams. I'm guessing that's why you picked up this book in the first place, rather than just out of curiosity, isn't it?

Everyone who learns Neuro Linguistic Programming knows the power of the patterns and strategies that employ the skills and knowledge of NLP. Whether you have just been introduced to the basics, or you have mastered advanced material and patterns, this work provides you with many techniques and practical concepts in a concise reference format. I have selected each pattern for its value and relevance. If you know the pattern, you can refresh your memory; if you want to learn it, you can do it without wading through fluff, such as long explanations of NLP terms or magical stories of healing and success. This is a 'fluff-free' book.

This book contains a listing of over 350 NLP patterns, techniques, and strategies. You should not aim to memorize them all, and frankly, you don't need to. When you've decided on a pattern to work with, go over the steps thoroughly to ensure you understand the process. Every procedure in NLP is based on sound reasoning. The steps are organized in a logical manner. Attempt to uncover and comprehend that logic.

This publication is not the last word on NLP patterns. It is a work in progress, just as NLP is an evolving body of theory and knowledge. It is also where your involvement and contributions can be seen. While you read this book, practice the concepts and methods, applying them to yourself and others. Keep an open mind, discover what works best, and write to us about your insights, ideas and questions.

I hope you find this book to be one of your most valuable resources. Our email address is help@ericks.org and we'd love to hear from you.

All the best to you and yours!

Shlomo Vaknin, C.Ht
Director
Erickson Institute - www.ericks.org

NLP Briefly Explained

—

NLP is a model of the vast and ephemeral world of human attitudes and interaction derived from the study of perception and behavior components that enable our subjective and unique experiences. In our view, all human beings encode, translate, direct, and alter their behavior through evolutionary mental filters. The study and purposeful usage of these filters is NLP.

Here we introduce the word "**state**", which in NLP refers to your physiological and mental condition at any given moment. Note that this has nothing to do with "positive thinking" or "mindfulness". Recognition of a state, whether desirable or undesirable, has nothing to do with it being positive or negative. Sadness is as valid a state as joy. Apathy is not less important than love. Judgement of any specific state's value depends on context alone and not on spiritual or esoteric wishes. In other words, the reason we're able to feel apathy is because there are times in which it is a useful state to be in. The same goes for anxiety, grief, and pain.

Most people notice consciously only a small portion of what is going on in their own minds at any given time. When our awareness is so limited, we have so little authority over our behavior and feelings. A state is the conscious "felt" consequence of the intentional or unintentional activation of unconscious strategies. It's how you find yourself feeling and behaving in the moment.

You can't change limiting beliefs or resolve painful emotions if you don't know what they are, exactly. You may be feeling down in general, oblivious to the fact that you are angry, sad, or afraid underneath. Alternatively, you may be anxious, oblivious to the fact that, beneath your anxiety, you are alone, overwhelmed, or uncertain. Worse yet, you may be so emotionally exhausted and numb to the point of being unable or unwilling to feel anything at all.

In therapy sessions, we tell our clients that their emotional reactions are in fact within their realm of responsibility. Supposedly, someone else said something, and shortly after, you felt anger bubbling up inside of you. You react with annoyance and spite. If your reasoning for feeling angry is: "It's your fault, you made me angry!", the meaning is "what you said made me angry" (as it was not the mere fact that this person exists that made you angry, but his words) and it can be represented as:

Input → Output

"What you said" → "My angry reaction" =

Words → Feelings

That gives quite a lot of power to entities outside your nervous system, does it not? In reality, though, that is too simplistic and far from what goes on within your organism. The actual process looks more like this:

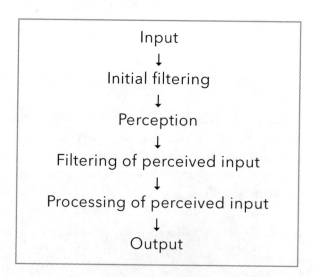

Input
↓
Initial filtering
↓
Perception
↓
Filtering of perceived input
↓
Processing of perceived input
↓
Output

Input - the sensory stimuli in current reality - everything that happens around and within you at any given moment.

Initial filtering - of all stimuli that is entering your five senses.

Perception - the result of the initial filtering, which means transforming the stimuli from the environment into cognitive data for further processing.

Filtering of perceived input - This process prioritizes the available stimuli (now cognitive data) that entered the system according to what seems more important and requires conscious attention. For example, a sudden horrific crash from a car down the street would take precedence over the birds singing on the tree right next to you or even a conversation you're emerged in with another person.

Processing of perceived input - here we have a complex of many sophisticated processes, below conscious level, that in the simplest terms answer the questions "what does it mean for me?", and "how do I respond?".

Output - the resulting behavior or kinesthetic reaction (emotions).

We'll get into all these processes soon enough. What's important to notice here is that the stimulus (the words that person uttered) has to go through several very sophisticated processes before it is eventually synthesized as an angry feeling. Therefore, there are variable decision points, albeit mostly unconscious, between the input (hearing the sounds of the words) and the output (habitual reaction). The filtering stage is when your mind decides whether or not that input is of any importance or relevance to your survival, first of all, and then your well-being, as a secondary priority. The processing stage involves many different levels and simultaneous mental protocols to finally initiate the kinesthetic reaction as a feeling or behavior or both. The point here is that, because there are a lot of decision variables within the operation stage, you do have a choice as to whether you end up feeling angry and upset or not.

Another person cannot make you angry; he can only remind your critical mind to unconsciously activate the strategy that results in an angry state. The proof of that notion is that another person in your situation may not get angry at all and be apathetic towards the whole scenario. Therefore, it is not the other person who made you angry. There is another factor at work between the sensory input you received and the emotional reaction you experienced. That factor is a learned strategy that was programmed within your unconscious mind that gets activated with certain stimuli. The essence of NLP is becoming aware of that program and having the skills to change it, if you wish to do so. Apathy is neither good nor bad; it is either useful or not-useful, depending on the context and its relevance to your desired outcome.

Because of the type of intelligence we possess – our self-reflexive awareness – the "meta" component emerges in the human mind. That is, as we think and feel about everything and anything in the world (called a primary state), such as excitement, worry, compassion, frustration, fatigue, etc., we can step back and explore new (secondary state) thoughts and feelings regarding our experience. When we are worried about our own anxiety, we produce a meta-state. We can appreciate our excitement, dread our resentment, be embarrassed by our suspicion, and be disheartened by our mistakes. The secondary state is connected with the first. Awareness gets immensely sophisticated here. Not merely another thought or sensation about something, but rather a new way of thinking and feeling about that thing itself. We go "meta" to a higher level of cognitive analysis.

NLP as a *meta-model* implicitly includes a wide variety of practical applications. Behavioral parameters can be recognized, structured, and coded to achieve desired outcomes in any type of interaction, including interpersonal, group, organizational, and system dynamics. As life experiences are sorted, analyzed, and unpacked, what is left is a simple, clear collection of behavioral aspects and principles that can be easily comprehended.

Through our senses, we are in contact with the world around us. Only five senses are available to us, and they are limited by nature. More or less, we can only see what is right in front of our eyes. Between 20 and 20,000 Hz is the human hearing range. The sting of the mosquito on our elbow is not kinesthetically perceived until it is too late.

The world bombards us with stimuli at all hours of the day and night, and our brain's limited processing capacity can only handle a fraction of it. Our brain, like a computer's processor, must filter data coming in through the senses in order to keep up with the necessary functions of life. According to Broadbent's Filter Theory of

Attention, this type of filtering occurs early in the process, before the meaning of the input is examined. Even data that you don't consciously pay attention to is processed to some extent, such as when you hear your name mentioned by someone far away in a crowded social event, for example. Both NLP and hypnotherapy are concerned with uncovering and modifying the mental processes stashed in the unconscious in order to promote healing and relieve the brain of unnecessary over-processing.

Over time, human beings have developed a variety of frameworks for categorizing and evaluating the world around them. Culture, religion, art, psychology, and philosophy are only a few of the labels given to the various models for organizing and classifying the interactions of individuals in their surroundings. Like in science and technology, each model has its own set of sub-models nested within it, just as each model intersects with other models and may include smaller sub-models within itself.

This means that each model is unique in terms of what it represents and prioritizes, as well as in how it organizes and utilizes its selected representations. In the end, they're all interested in the results of human behavior.

Each model's mission is to find patterns in the way humans interact with their circumstances so that the actions of individuals can be systematized within the chosen context in order to achieve intended and adaptive results more efficiently, consistently, and predictably.

From this perspective, behavior is programmed by the combination and sequencing of visual, auditory, kinesthetic, and olfactory stimuli. A certain behavioral outcome is formed by processing a given input stimulus through a series of internal representations.

Because it comes from the Greek word "neuron," the term "**neuro**" refers to the idea that all behavior is a byproduct of neurological processes, not only certain types of movements or reactions.

The term "**linguistic**", from the Latin word lingua, meaning "language", refers to the way in which neurological events are represented, arranged, and sequenced into models, patterns and functional strategies by various modes of communication, both verbal and nonverbal.

"**Programming**" is the process of arranging the components of the system - sensory modalities representations - to achieve certain objectives.

The acronym NLP was coined by the field's primary co-founders, Richard Bandler and John Grinder, in the late 1970's. Since then, a whole lot of advances and evolutions have occurred in this field. Many trainers and therapists have done research and contributed practical concepts and methodologies to the NLP community, among which are Dr. Tad James (originator of Timeline Therapy), Robert Dilts (who introduced the Logical Levels model), L. Michael Hall, Steve and Connirae Andreas, as well as ourselves at the Erickson Institute.

The paradigms and procedures provided by NLP show us how to unpack and repackage behavior into efficient and communicative sequences that can be explained to any other human being.

When it comes to dealing with current reality, we don't actually interact with it directly; rather, we use our sensory representational systems to understand the world around us. The mind serves as our central processing "hub," receiving, organizing, consolidating, and transmitting data from our surroundings as well as our constantly changing physiological states (biological and chemical processes). This data is then transformed using internal processing protocols that each person has developed unconsciously starting at age 0. Habitual thoughts, instincts, and behaviors are the end result of this process.

In NLP, behavior is defined as any sensory representation experienced and exhibited internally and/or externally for which data is accessible from the subject (the person expressing the behavior) and/or an observer (who can calibrate, or detect, the components of the behavior in the other person). In the framework of NLP, both the actual reality of bungee jumping from a hot air balloon and the imagination or visualizing oneself doing so are considered actions.

Naturally, our neural networks are responsible for programming both macro-behavior and micro-behavior. Overt and obvious activities such as driving a car, speaking in public, fighting, eating, becoming sick, or riding a bike constitute macro-behavior. Purer but equally important phenomena such as heartbeat, accent intensity, facial feature changes, pupil dilation, and events such as mental imagery or internal dialogue are examples of micro-behavior.

Models like this—as well as the behavior that results from them—indicate something important about the minds of the people who use them as organizing strategies for their behaviors. To put it another way, we can learn a lot about how our brains are wired by looking at the variety and breadth of human behavior. A look at these models today shows how they've evolved over time and how our predecessors' intelligence has endured. The utility or adaptiveness of a model as a reference for the behavior of the species is ultimately decided upon after the cacophony of economic, religious, and ideological conflicts has passed. The adoption or rejection of these models, as well as their development and expansion, show how human thought and conduct have evolved over time.

Identifying and representing a collection of structural elements, as well as a syntax, are prerequisites to the development of all models. In a model, the structural elements are its "building bricks." a set of rules or directives describing the possible combinations of basic components.

Typical structural elements in linguistic models are words, either written or spoken. In a sentence, syntax is the set of linguistic rules that govern how the individual words fit together to convey specific meanings.

Even though a native English speaker has a vocabulary of roughly 20,000 words, countless different phrases have been authored and countless thoughts have been put into words over the centuries in the English language. There are a variety of ways in which the words might be arranged in different circumstances to elicit distinct connotations and associations. The same twenty-six letters of the alphabet appear in every book ever written in the English language, even though the words are arranged differently at different times.

The complexity of human behavior, like the infinite number of possible well-formed sentences in a language, may be distilled to a finite number of structural elements and syntax courtesy of NLP. All of our behaviors, from studying, memorizing, and reasoning to coming to a conclusion, communicating, and influencing, are the result of sensory representations that are systematically organized. The NLP model can help behavioral

scientists understand, predict, and modify many of the issues and occurrences that have stumped them in the past.

Because some portions of each model's structural elements and syntax are perceived (or stated) as being within or beyond a person's control, each model incorporates another behavioral model that describes the possibilities and constraints of human behavior in terms of desired outcomes and objectives.

The axis of behavioral control in NLP is placed in the person, thereby extending the constraints of the present scientific paradigm. The purpose of NLP is to investigate the relationships between what we perceive as the outer world and our internal representations of that reality. NLP depends on several recent breakthroughs in neurology, psycholinguistics, linguistics, cybernetics, cognitive science, and bio-informatics.

NLP is a new process of thinking—a new model—that involves the use of changing patterns that are based on contextual factors and feedback within and across behaviors that may be observed in your continuous experience. The NLP method is held strictly responsible for the evidence of sensory experience—yours or anyone else's who uses the process—while it is both formal and systematic. In its role as a template in the modeling process, it is always evolving and growing as a result of its own breakthroughs.

Behavioral patterns like eating a banana or riding a bike, as well as large-scale municipal and business transactions involving thousands of civilians, are all governed by laws, principles, and preconceptions encoded in the brains of individuals. If the neural pattern is lacking, the behavior is nonexistent; if the behavior is ineffective or unsuitable, the neural pattern is not appropriately structured to elicit a functional or appropriate behavior. The overt and implied laws, principles, and preconceptions of any model operate as codes or symbols for diverse patterns of neural organization geared toward creating a certain set of behavioral responses.

The Big Book of NLP

Because NLP is concerned with form rather than content, we can extract strategies for efficient and appropriate behaviors from any model and apply them to any other model of our choosing. An uninspired industrial designer confronted with a difficult technical issue, for example, can benefit from a filmmaker's creative strategy. Alternatively, the practical motivational strategy of a super-efficient private company may be transferred to a slow regulatory body. Except for demonstration reasons, referring to the nomenclature or contents of the models from which particular forms, structural interrelationships, and outcomes have been generated is superfluous because NLP is exclusively concerned with representations of experience at the neurological level. We don't care if the source of the modeled behavior is attributed to luck or inborn talent, as long as the same neuronal strategy sequence results in the same behavioral outcomes.

Similar to how behavioral strategies are transferred from one individual to another, one person can adapt a successful approach from one element of their experience (such as aiming a golf swing) to another aspect (such as a challenge in social interactions). In general, people have a wide range of life experiences from which to draw, and they can use the methodologies discovered with NLP to apply strategies they've learned in more successful areas to less successful ones.

The intention of NLP is to expand the number of outcomes that can be achieved by a given behavior; in other words, it is a method for converting additional contextual information into input values. In layman's terms, NLP is highly useful for people who want to accomplish their desired outcomes while also enjoying the journey. In order to attain new outcomes, behavior modification can be described as a three-point procedure that can be applied to individuals, groups, or organizations:

1. Current representation of the state.

2. Recognition of the desired outcome or state.

3. Accessing and deploying resources.

Internal resources are accessed and deployed to assist a person, team, or organization in achieving their goals or desired state.In order to truly understand behavior, one must first understand how the person interacts with their environment through the five senses: the three primary ones are visual (seeing), auditory (hearing), and kinesthetic (body sensations). The two secondary senses are gustatory (tasting) and olfactory (smelling).

Neurolinguistic programming assumes that the distinctions we can make between our internal and external environments, as well as our behavior, can be meaningfully described in terms of these systems, which is the premise of the model. The structures of subjective experience can be broken down into these perceptual classes.

According to NLP, all of our continuous experiences can be appropriately categorized as a combination of these sensory classifications. We use the **4-tuple model** to depict and abbreviate our continuing sensory experience.

The following are abbreviations for the key sensory classes or representational systems we employ to build our models of the world:

$V_{e,i}$ = Vision/Sight

$A_{e,i}$ = Auditory/Hearing.

$K_{e,i}$ = Kinesthetic/Body Sensations.

$O_{e,i}$ = Olfactory/Gustatory

The superscripts "e" and "i" signify whether the representations are external ("e") to us, such as when you are looking at, hearing, or sensing a physical input by touching or on your skin, smelling, or tasting something, or internal ("i"), such as when we are recalling or visualizing an image, sound, feeling, scent, or flavor.

There are three components in each representational system: input, processing, and output. The first stage, input, entails collecting data and receiving feedback from the environment, both internal and external.

The mapping of the environment and the construction of behavioral strategies like learning, judgment, forming memories, noticing patterns and so on are all examples of representation or processing.

Output is the result of the representational mapping process's informal translation. Any action within a representational system dynamic at any of these levels can be referred to as "behavior" in NLP. Behavior includes the actions of seeing, hearing, and sensing. It's also "thinking," which may be split down into sensory-specific processes like visualizing, hearing one's own thoughts, experiencing one's own emotions, and so on. Even the smallest actions, such as sideways eye movements, voice pitch changes, and breathing changes, are examples of behavior, as are larger ones, such as uncontrollable rage, swinging a golf club, or developing a psychosomatic illness.

The structural elements of our own behavioral models are derived from our **representational systems**. Humans' "behavioral lexicon" is made up of all we've learned and experienced through our senses over the course of our lives. This arranging of experience into predictable sequences or "behavioral phrases" develops the maps or models that control our behavior. These sequences of representations are referred to as "strategies" in NLP because of the formal patterns they follow.

The significance of a particular representation in human behavior is determined by the way we sequence representations through our strategies, much as the sequencing of words in a sentence determines the meaning of words or phrases. A single depiction is of little value in and of itself. What matters is how a person's behavior is influenced by the way their mental representations work together.

When you read this sentence, you are unwittingly employing a technique for deciphering the strange patterns of black writing on this white sheet. Like the other visual occurrences already described, these letter sequences have no significance unless you attach sensory experiences from your own past to them. Written and spoken words are nothing more than codes that set off our brain's fundamental sensory representations. It's impossible for us to understand the meaning of a word we've never seen or heard before since we lack the necessary sensory input. If you walk in Italy and a young boy runs towards you and screams "fuoco! fuoco!", you may get upset because it sounds similar to a curse word in English. What if the boy also grabs you and turns you around, pointing towards a cloud of smoke nearby and continues shouting "fuoco! fuoco!"? The word now has a completely different meaning than you had previously interpreted.

The visual patterns generated by the letters in this paragraph may, for example, make you hear yourself uttering the words in your mind as you read. It's possible that the words printed here sound familiar from something else you've encountered. You may have felt a sense of satisfaction or recognition as a result of these visual patterns.

While reading our description of the young boy screaming "Fire!," you may have noted how your own visualizations of the text were ignited by the representation of the words, even if you do not speak Italian. Each of us has the power to make meaning by transforming textual symbols into mental images, into auditory representations, and into feelings, tastes, and odors. In some situations, certain tactics are more effective than others in establishing meaning, whereas in others, the opposite is true. This method of interpreting exterior visual symbols into internal auditory dialogue would not be effective for talking to your landlord or listening to your favorite music.

One of NLP's greatest assets is its adaptability. This method can be applied to a wide range of contexts, from individual human beings to large-scale systems, from circumstances involving therapeutic change (cognitive flexibility) to contexts involving dynamic changes, expanding the domain of decision variables beyond the existing state for an individual or system presently functioning effectively. The representational systems of an individual and the internal organization of an organizational structure can both benefit from the use of NLP. A system's probable outcomes and its ability to secure those results will be determined by the formal sequencing and timing of activities among its structural components. The presence of strategies necessitates the existence of interconnected networks of activity in the brain.

Synesthesia in NLP refers to interconnections between representational system structures that allow action in one system to trigger activity in another.

An example of auditory-kinesthetic synesthesia is being bothered by a harsh tone of voice. A visual-kinesthetic synesthesia would involve seeing a celebrity behind you in line and feeling nervous or joyful. A kinesthetic–auditory synesthesia would involve feeling frustrated and hearing a self-condemnation monologue inside your mind. An auditory–visual synesthesia occurs when you hear the neighbor screaming at his wife and you imagine how they act out the argument.

The method by which humans construct their own sense of meaning is heavily reliant on synesthesia structures. Representational system activities play a critical role in complex processes like understanding, decision-making, and communication. The crossover inter-connections between neuronal representational structures are directly responsible for human development in all domains, fields, and expertise. Synesthesia correlations are the primary source of the variances between people of various skills, characteristics, and strengths.

By making these cognitive patterns explicit, NLP provides a workable paradigm and an applied methodology for the intentional use of correlated patterns to achieve any behavioral outcome. We can, in effect, reproduce any behavior—of anyone who does something well—by discovering synesthetic sequences that lead to specific outcomes and making them accessible to people who want to attain those outcomes.

All of our outward actions are influenced by our internal strategies for interpreting data. Getting out of bed every morning, managing tasks effectively, teaching, engaging in group discussions, and so on are all areas in which each of you has developed a unique set of methods for achieving your objectives. Nonetheless, our cultural models do not clearly teach us the exact procedures required to fulfill the behavioral outcomes articulated or inferred by every paradigm. This was nearly entirely left to personal trial and error prior to the emergence of NLP.

The TOTE (Test-Operate-Test-Exit) model created by George Miller, Eugene Galanter, and Karl Pribram is the basic framework we will use to define a specific sequence of behavior.

Our sensory representational systems have developed into functional units of behavior known as TOTEs, which are normally executed in the shadows of the unconsciousness, below the level of conscious awareness.

A TOTE's behavioral sequence might be as basic or sophisticated as desired. One shape may be all that a beginner painter can handle in terms of complex behavior. But when a painter's talent grows, they may be able to perform a sophisticated design with the movement of the brush as a single unit of behavior, albeit one that is a complicated series of behaviors that have been included as a TOTE.

The test denotes the criteria that must be met before the reaction occurs.

If the test phase conditions are met (a comparison between the current state and the desired state), the stimulus-initiated action moves on to the next step in the behavior chain. If not, there is a feedback stage in which the system works to change some element of the stimulus or the individual's internal state in order to meet the criteria of the test, but it doesn't always succeed. In order for the test to be passed and the action to be performed, the test-operate feedback loop must be repeated numerous times.

The TOTE will also exit if, after many tries, its operating phase fails to have any substantial effect on the test outcome, albeit not with the same behavior as if it had passed the test.

Until the "incongruity" between the organism's state and the state being tested for is eliminated, the action will continue. A reflex's overall pattern therefore involves testing the input energy against some requirements established in the organism, reacting if the test results show an incongruity, and responding until the incongruity disappears, at which point the reflex is discontinued. To put it another way, there is a feedback loop between doing something and estimating how it turns out.

TOTE's simplicity and incorporation of feedback and outcomes make it a better model for examining behavioral units than other approaches. A tote of this type is what you're doing when you adjust the level on your television or sound system. As you adjust the volume dial, you listen to the sound to determine whether it's loud enough. If the level is too low, simply crank the knob clockwise to increase the volume. If you overshoot and the volume becomes excessively loud, you can lessen the intensity of the music by twisting the knob counterclockwise. When you have set the volume on the stereo system to the right level, you exit the TOTE and stop adjusting the knob.

The TOTE model has a unique feature that allows several TOTEs to be nested within each other in the operating phase of a single TOTE. Consequently, there may be a hierarchical structure among TOTEs.

Representational systems and strategies are used to refine the TOTE paradigm in the NLP model. A central tenet of NLP is that all of our human behavior, even cognitive functions, can be conceptualized as taking place via our representational systems. In this way, you can easily and quickly assign all of the steps of the TOTE to one of many different types of representational systems or to a group of representations.

One of the representational systems will additionally capture the sensation of "congruence" (the exit point in the TOTE) and "incongruence" (the operating point in the TOTE) as a function of the test. The individual may imagine the very next action with regard to the feedback, hear an inner voice that tells them whether or not the feedback resolves the tension generated by the incongruence, or even have a sensation or gut feeling associated with the feedback loop.

It is important to keep in mind that a test need not only be between external and internal representations. Internally created or stored representations may also be tested. On the other hand, the two comparable representations, on the other hand, are likely to remain in the same system. The most accurate way to test the accuracy of a visual representation is to compare it to another visual representation, and the same goes for an auditory representation and a kinesthetic representation. One possible function of the two cerebral hemispheres in humans is the simultaneous pairing of two separate representations inside the same representational system.

However, not all tests compare or match two representations; others may measure the intensity of certain representations. In other words, the TOTE may require that the user experience a certain level of emotional response before it can exit the loop. For example, when something looks decent but just doesn't feel right, a representation from one system is "tested" against a representation from another system. Judgment and ambition strategies frequently use this type of test. Because of the "incongruence" caused by this type of exam, the tension or internal conflict felt as a result is typically felt as well. There are two ways to settle a conflict: either one representation becomes so powerful that it initiates a new response in a chain of responses, or the individual alters the representations so they are compatible with one another.

A good example of multi-representational testing is when something feels like heaven but some voice inside tells you not to do it, like flirting with someone while you're in a committed relationship; or when an idea sounds good but you can see there may be bad implications for it, like when you see your wife walking towards you as another woman chats with you.

The NLP model simplifies the analysis and transfer of any behavior by making the representational form of test and operation processes explicit. NLP outlines how to unpack virtually any behavioral sequence by identifying the representational type and function of each step in a behavioral continuum of steps.

The idea of "representational system primacy," or driver rep systems, states that many people prefer one representational system to another when performing tests and operations. Congruence can be tested by a visually oriented person simply by glancing at the hammer and the nail. People who are more kinesthetically inclined will do it by "feeling." This form of preference is commonly applied to a wide range of tasks, even if the favored representational system is incorrect or inadequate.

TOTE and the analysis of representational systems have two objectives:

1. To determine the most appropriate representational systems for the TOTE steps that lead to a specific result (for example, spelling using the visual representational system).

2. The ability to use all representational systems as learning and performance resources.

A different representational approach may be substituted if it is appropriate or required to do so when more than one representational system can be employed to complete an activity (such as testing the nail in our hammering example). This considerably enhances one's ability to choose from a wide selection of options.

It is through the TOTE that a certain pattern of behavior can be identified. Analysis of a TOTE or set of TOTEs begins with a strategy. Breaking down the TOTE into its representational components and describing the order of the precise representational activity that leads to the specific behavioral outcome is what strategy analysis is all about. "Strategy" is a term we use in NLP to refer to a simplified version of this framework.

Because of the TOTE architecture, it is expected that every strategy has an operating point and an exit point. On the other hand, long and complicated TOTE techniques, on the other hand, will be necessary in some cases. It is not always possible to identify the functional relevance of each step (that is, whether it is a representation that is involved in a test, an operation, or indicates an incongruence between a test and an operation, etc.). Even while we'll mostly be utilizing linear notation to describe our strategies, we'll occasionally use TOTE diagrams to highlight key features of a particular behavioral sequence.

It's a good analogy to use when discussing strategies to compare them to dialing a phone number. It's like dialing a phone number with the digits on the keypad. In the same way that different phone number combinations lead to different locations and people, the way we sequence and order the activities of these representational systems does as well.

Both a phone number and a strategy serve as a conduit for gaining access to various resources. To get to the right resource, you'll need to dial the right number. For example, if we need an ambulance, we need to know the phone numbers to contact. One digit can have a huge impact on the outcome of a game. To go to some locations, you may be able to dial many distinct phone numbers at once. They'll all have only one number, though.

An area code sequence of numbers must be prefixed before a long-distance telephone number can be reached. Everything in a strategy is interconnected; the final result depends on the stages that came before it. As a means of preparing for a desired outcome, some individuals and organisations may need to make preparatory acts or representations prior to launching their operations or initiatives. A lack of testing at the beginning of a strategy could result in a later operation being hindered by interference or obstacles that could have been more readily dealt with earlier in the process. In some ways, individuals and organizations can be like the guy who keeps dialing a seven-digit phone number, but gets just the tone, and wonders why he keeps getting the dial tone. Others may over-prepare, like the person who utilizes the area code for phone numbers in his own neighborhood.

The representational sequence of a strategy, like a phone number, can also be forgotten or mixed up with other numbers that one uses regularly, leading to circumstances where people forget an important or appropriate strategy or its representational sequence. It is one of the most common challenges people have with strategies when they try to employ them in situations where they are not appropriate.

In referring to a particular representational system, we do not mean to suggest that the others cease to function. We are just saying that the importance or amplitude value of the activity of the chosen representational system increases when compared to the other systems that do the same thing. According to the 4-tuple, all of our senses are constantly processing information from both internal and external sources. When you're listening carefully to music or experiencing an inner dialogue, your visual cortex isn't shutting down. There will be a higher intensity or amplitude value in one representational system at each phase of any strategy, and that system will take what we might call "primary direction."

Even if we only have occasional or irregular access, we may need to use different levels of representational activity in the system we are accessing in order to reproduce the behavioral sequence required to achieve some outcome we are driven to accomplish. To produce a specific representation, some strategies demand a very crisp signal, while others may require quick and intricate transitions and representations to be achieved. It can be difficult for some people to access a representational system that is strong, clear, and resonant. Others may become overly engrossed in a representational system.

There are some similarities between tuning in to a certain representational system and tuning a radio station. There are a lot of different radio stations that are always broadcasting on their own signal frequencies. By changing the internal internal dynamics of our receiver, we can tune in to one signal or frequency so that we get little or no interference from the others.

We have a concept we call the "R-operator," which uses 4-tuples at various points of time to mark out one representational system as being more prominent in awareness than the others. A combination of "accessing cues" and preexisting synesthesia patterns is the "mechanism" of the R-operator. **Accessing cues** are actions we adopt to fine-tune our bodies and alter our neurology in such a manner that we can more powerfully access one representational system than the others. We prepare to perform any overt behavior, such as dancing, shouting, driving, or speaking, by contracting our muscles and adjusting our breathing and eye scan variations in unique ways that distinguish that behavior from all others. We do the same with cognitive behavior and complicated and dynamic mental processes. In order to carry out our strategies, everyone must go through a series of particular and recurring behavioral cues.

Stop right now and visualize your front door's color and design as clearly and accurately as possible. A visual image of your front door may not be in your direct line of vision; you must first focus on your body and neural systems in order to get an internal visual image of it. Even if it is in your direct line of sight, your body and neurology must be tuned to accept and prioritize the external visual experience of color and pattern above your other sensory experiences. In order to create an internal image in your mind, you may have defocused your eyes while staring at this line in the book, blurring the text and other visual data. Looking up and to the left may have served as a substitute for looking away from the book. You might have even closed your eyes at this point. Have you noticed a difference in the way you breathe? It could have moved higher in your chest, gotten shallower, or even ceased for a brief moment in time. You may have also noticed that your shoulders were bent forward, and you may have felt some strain in your shoulder muscles. Observable behavioral changes would also be necessary if you want to see your door clearly in your mind's eye. To be able to focus attentively on the subject, you would need to turn your head in the proper direction and tense or relax particular muscles around your eyes. Now take a few moments to remember the last time you felt completely drenched....

For this modality-specific experience, you once again had to adjust your body and neurology in such a way that the precise depiction stood out. To access the feeling, some of you may recall a memory strategy: perhaps you began by asking yourself, "Now when was the last time I felt really sweaty?" and proceeded to develop a sequence of internal images or glanced around externally to see likely locations in your external environment where you might have gotten exercised exhaustively, before achieving the outcome of accessing the feeling. You may have started with images in your mind. For the challenge of seeing your door, you first had to feel yourself standing in front of it to see the color of it clearly.

You may or may not have noticed that when the feelings ultimately came up powerfully, your breathing increased deeper and moved down towards your stomach area, regardless of your first experience. Your shoulders may have drooped somewhat, and your eyes may have defocused and dropped down and to the right, making you appear more relaxed. As you do this, imagine a close friend or associate's voice so that you can hear the pitch, tonal qualities, and pace of their voice when they speak.

There were a number of physical alterations that had to be made to achieve this result. You may have noticed that your head was inclined slightly to one side and your eyes had shifted laterally to the left or down and to the left. Your breathing may have shifted to your diaphragm. You may have leaned back in your chair, pushed your shoulders back a little, and folded your arms. We have found that the stages we go through to convey our strategies consistently include behavioral cues like those outlined here. Because they are proven to be constant across cultures, some cues appear to be genetically programmed to access a specific representational system. In addition, each person develops their own specific triggers.

You may have noticed that as you accomplished the simple activities outlined above, you had an easier time engaging various representational systems in aspects of efficiency and precision. The ability to make synesthetic transitions between different representational systems is also common. To some extent, this is due to the access cues that you've built up for yourself. If you had difficulty accessing the experiences required in this exercise, try the challenge again, utilizing the behavioral strategies we outline following each assignment. They could help you achieve greater results, so it's worth experimenting with them.

One of the most useful aspects of exploring accessing cues is that you may learn a lot about a person's strategy by closely observing them. Each 4-tuple is then acted upon by the R-operator via the use of cues and synesthesia patterns, granting one representational system more behavioral importance than the others, resulting in an overall strategy consisting of overlapping 4-tuples. As a result of this process, the sequence of 4-tuples and the behavioral outcome will be established.

The degree of overlap or interference we encounter from our other representational systems depends on how finely we tune or calibrate our neurological and physiological systems to take input from a particular representational system as we go through the phases of a strategy.

Of course, there are occasions when it is beneficial and necessary to combine knowledge from our various representational systems, such as in multi-representational testing. Synthetic integration of two representational systems or change from one representational system to another is common. Because of this, though, important information from one representational system may be slowed down or even overridden by information from another representational system.

It's probably clear to most of you that not all of the steps in a strategy need to be understood in order to work efficiently. To the contrary, the more habitual and less conscious a behavior gets, the more certain we can be that it has been fully ingrained in our minds.

Consciousness is simply thought to be the product of the relative intensities of activities within our representational systems in NLP. It is a measure of how extensively a particular representational system is used, rather than a thing in and of itself. According to NLP, consciousness should not be seen as a source of activity in the nervous system but rather as an emergent quality of that activity. When it comes to representational processing, consciousness is only a marker of a small fraction of what is actually taking place in the nervous system. As we've discussed previously, there is a correlation between how strongly a representation is held in memory and how powerful it is in the context of other ongoing mental representations. It's our contention that a representation can only become conscious when it reaches a specific level of amplification. This, on the other hand, says very little about the behavioral significance of the act in question.

Learning and maturing is a complex process that relies heavily on our ability to recognize patterns in our experiences and create strategies for dealing with the environment on an unconscious level. If you are able read and understand this line right now, it's a program that you couldn't perform before the English reading learning stage in your history. You went through the process of observing and interpreting letters, words, and sentences in English, and you were encouraged to keep at it until it became an unconscious automatic behavior.

The eye scanning patterns that were appropriate for each of these processes were linked to them. Having to learn how to match a certain visual input with a specific set of meanings was a long and arduous process. When it comes to reading quickly and effectively, your ability to execute those lower-ranked patterns of eye scanning and letter recognition unconsciously is fundamental. In our daily lives, we spend the great majority of our time executing extremely intricate sequences of unconscious behavior. Lacking the capacity to program ourselves to carry out complicated patterns of movement for implementation at the unconscious level of behavior would greatly diminish our ability to appreciate our experience and engage in the things that we find interesting and pleasurable. Consider how congested our experience would be if we had to monitor our breathing rate and depth, muscle tone, blood pressure, and cholesterol levels all the time. If you know a diabetic person, they can tell you how exhausting it is to always be aware, monitor, and deliberately manage and manipulate their blood sugar levels.

In order to create effective programs for us, we must go through a continuous process of change known as "learning." **Modeling** is the term used to represent this process. Consciously and unconsciously, we all engage , continuously, in modeling behavior. An example of unconscious modeling can be seen in the process of learning to speak and understand one's native tongue. For the vast majority of people, the process of learning to read words is an example of purposeful modeling. In conscious modeling,

The Big Book of NLP

nevertheless, most of what is learned is the sequencing and structuring of lower tier patterns of behavior already available. Even though students aren't told to visualize the words they are learning when they try to spell, people who are good at spelling do so naturally.

Consciousness has limits. Specifically, as humans, we are limited to a fixed number of bits of information in our current reality awareness. With The Magic Number 7, plus or minus 2, George A. Miller meticulously presents the boundaries of consciousness. His research shows that we can hold seven plus or minus two pieces of data in our minds at once. Miller's paper has an intriguing implication: the chunk size is flexible. That is, 7 + 2 is not a restriction on the number of bits, but rather a restriction on the number of chunks.As a result, the amount of data we can represent to ourselves consciously can be greatly expanded by carefully designing the code by which we arrange our conscious experience. His description of a chunk is deliberately imprecise. To understand the relationship between conscious learning and chunking, we need to identify the term "chunk" with the idea that a pattern of behavior that has not yet acquired TOTE status can be thought of as a chunk.

We can make unconscious some aspects of our experience, that we previously had to contend with at the level of consciousness, when we learn to notice and respond methodically to patterns in our experience. Consciousness chunks are the patterns and repetitions that we have yet to render unconscious. As a result, the chunk size will be tiny at the start of learning a new task, including only a brief pattern or uniformity in our experience. As this size chunk attains the status of a TOTE and so becomes unconscious, our consciousness is free to attend to bigger level patterns formed by the sequencing and structuring of the TOTEs from which they are constructed, or to patterns in other representational systems or regions of experience.

As part of their testing process, some people make sure each phase of their strategy hits the signal value required for conscious awareness. This may be adaptive in some instances, but the process is generally slowed since an individual must continuously work to raise the signal's value. Other people, on the other hand, deliberately divert their attention in order to ensure that the strategy is carried out unconsciously. That doesn't mean internal activity indicated by consciousness isn't significant. Most of the time, the initial construction of a strategy step requires a significant signal value in a given representational system. However, if a pattern is formed, habituating the signal greatly simplifies the process. When learning to ride a bicycle, for example, paying attention to balance, steering, peddling, and the like becomes more of a burden than a help.

It is difficult for someone who has already mastered a TOTE to explain the many processes to someone who just wishes to learn the skill. Changes to a single unconscious strategy's many steps are additionally difficult because they are not expressly known when they become problematic. One of the most difficult challenges a NLP practitioner has is how to make unconscious strategies abundantly clear when the person demonstrating them is unable to consciously communicate the processes to others. A thorough evaluation of an individual's accessing cues utilized to tune in to specific representational systems will be incredibly beneficial in this situation.

Strategies are essentially formal structures that are indifferent to content. Only the category of experience in which the representation occurs and the sequential association each representation has with others in the same framework are identified by the strategy. In most circumstances, the content of specific representations inside the strategy determines merely the specifics of the outcome; the form of the strategy determines which outcome is attained and how smoothly and economically that end is reached.

"Experience" and "competence" are sometimes conflated, with the belief that the more time someone invests in training or executing a skill, the better they are at it. However, when we compare the two spelling strategies discussed in the earlier part, it becomes clear that the strategy utilized is far more significant than the quantity of time spent. People can use the same decision-making strategy to buy a car, choose a career, and volunteer at a shelter, since strategies are essentially formal. That is, one can use the same sequence of representational systems for testing and operation procedures to make any kind of choice in different contexts-the only difference is the content of the experience. It is similar to the idea that most popular movies follow the same arc of story. We've seen it thousands of times, and yet we go back for more. In this manner, the NLP practitioner may employ any strategy to assist the client in accessing resources for the desired outcome. If you want to get the resources you need to achieve an outcome, you can use this small set of strategies no matter what the specifics of the situation (context) are:

The Big Book of NLP

Decision-making strategies - the unconscious sequence of specific cognitive processes that you incorporate automatically in order to come to a decision and commit to a plan of action.

Memorization strategies - the unconscious sequence of specific cognitive processes that you employ in order to store and retrieve data you have previously perceived through your senses.

Learning strategies - the unconscious sequence of specific cognitive processes that enable you to compile new understandings, insights, and workflows.

Motivational strategies - the unconscious sequence of specific augmented processes that are used in order to initiate and continuously take useful actions towards the achievement of your desired outcomes.

Creativity strategies - the unconscious sequence of specific cognitive processes that enable you to come up with new ideas, possibilities, and associations in relation to a triggering situation, challenge, activity, or object.

Reality strategies - the sequence of specific cognitive processes that allow you to distinguish between fantasies or potential choices and current reality.

Convincer strategies - the unconscious sequence of specific cognitive processes that lead your conscious mind to believe in an abstract (non-observable) notion, or be convinced of a certain cause-and-effect relationship.

When all of our external channels are open and operating, we are able to respond quickly and effectively to any relevant external cues that may arise. We call this state "**uptime**." Was there a time when you felt alive and aware, engaged, and capable of responding effectively to others around you?"

Once you've extracted the strategy you want to model, adjust, or even use, you'll need to deconstruct it and chunk it into the applicable sequence of events to get the desired result. Clients, as previously stated, will move through the phases of the strategy as they access the relevant experience. It's not uncommon for internal processes to move at breakneck speed, especially those that have become unconscious TOTEs. In a matter of moments, a client can traverse a seemingly intractable series of representational systems. You'll need to improve your ability to notice subtle behavioral shifts in order to accurately identify each step.

Developing a keener sense of observation will enhance your life and career. In fact, this is definitely essential for you to become a skilled NLP practitioner. Having clean and active **calibration** skills can't be replaced by anything else.

Initially, you will need to slow down the individual's processes so that you can identify and retain the data that you will need to master these techniques. Using questions such as, "What happened initially that allowed you to be playful in that type of scenario?" or "What do you do first when you inspire yourself?" or "What's the first step you take when you decide?" Of course, the objective of these inquiries is to determine the initiation of the strategy. As a general guideline, you'll want to identify the initial external stimulus that initiates the strategy. Asking questions like, "What happens right before that?" is a good idea if someone answers, "Well, I just started feeling energized."

From there, the process of slowing down and deconstructing the strategy into its component sequential phases is a matter of asking, "What happened next?" or "And what do you do then?" What's critical for receiving helpful answers to these questions, though, is identifying a specific sensory channel in the narrative the person provides of his or her experience in order to figure out the representational system for that phase of the strategy.

People have a surprising proclivity towards doing internally what they talk about. One of the most powerful decoding devices is based on the fact that the cognitive meaning of this proposition is indeed true. As a result of this, people openly discuss their unconscious behaviors without being aware of them.

People's chosen words will tell you exactly what representational system they are using to make sense of and organize their current experience. Adjectives, verbs, adverbs, and other descriptive language are all part of the **predicates** class of words, which you use to describe your experience in the correct context.

Depending on the context, you'll have to figure out if the person is speaking of experiences that originated within the particular representational system or if the experience was derived from outside sources at the time it happened. A few examples of sensory specific predicates:

Visual

"I see what you're saying"

"It's bright as day"

"Obviously"

"I'm not clear about that"

"I just thought about it and it disappeared / vanished"

"Imagine…"

"My brain is foggy right now"

"Look, the way it really is…"

"Give me some time to reflect on what you said…"

Auditory

"Loud and clear!"

"Answer me!"

"It's too noisy, I can't think"

"You're quite outspoke, aren't you?"

"Explain this…"

"Let's talk about it some more"

"He complains too much"

"Listen…"

"Did you hear what I said?"

Kinesthetic

"I feel you, mate…"

"Smooth as butter…"

"He rubs me the wrong way"

"What a flop"

"When that happens, I run away"

"I'm not comfortable"

"I don't want to be a burden"

"You should speak more softly, your words are really rough"

"Give me a moment to catch up"

A trans-derivational search (**TDS**) happens when your critical mind initiates a query into the unconscious mind and pulls up associations stored within, that are linked to a perception in consciousness. A TDS can be triggered by a particular flavor or scent. For example, when you meet an older person who wears the same aftershave your grandfather had, it may trigger fond memories of your early childhood.

While olfactory and gustatory senses can be effective triggers for prior 4-tuples, they are not commonly used in operational strategies. As a result, we have chosen not to go into detail about them.

In fact, there are several distinctions that can be made regarding a given stage in a strategy as you evaluate it in greater depth, such as color, position, pitch, directness, and so on, each of which may be important at some point to accomplishing a particular outcome. When deciding on the level of depth at which you will classify the representations in the strategy you are extracting, use the most elegant description – that is, the one that employs the fewest distinctions while still achieving the desired result.

Digital (verbal) representations in the auditory representational system differ from those involving non-verbal properties such as tone and rhythm. Our linguistic (auditory and digital) representations are principally controlled by neural circuits located in our dominant brain hemisphere. Although the non-dominant hemisphere retains remembered verbal events such as song lyrics and tag phrases, the dominant hemisphere appears to be rather specialized in organizing the tonal, melodic, and rhythmic components of our auditory experience.

The functional value of the data conveyed by each of these modalities varies widely. We refer to digital communications as "secondary experiences" since they are part of a larger experience. Secondary experiences are made up of the representations we employ to code our primary experiences. These secondary experiences, such as words and symbols, are only relevant in terms of the primary sensory representations they secure for us. For example, the symbol of the stop sign is relevant when you're the one driving, but has no relevance for your experience of driving if you see it on a billboard ad or as a drawn cartoon on a piece of cardboard.

We differentiate our auditory representational system's tonal and digital elements by subscripting with a "d" for digital or verbal and a "t" for tonal and tempo attributes:

A_d = Auditory digital.

A_t = Auditory tonal.

Another distinction you might need to make is between the somatosensory (tactile) and visceral (emotional and proprioceptive) components of kinesthetic experience.

Emotional or visceral representations may have a different functional value for a behavioral objective than those involving solely outward physical experiences (such as pain, shivering, and pressure). However, for notational purposes, we opt to classify visceral feelings as kinesthetic internal experiences, alongside recalled and constructed kinesthetic sensations.

As earlier stated, verbal communication is really only one element of the overall communication process. However, in our minds, this aspect of communication is of secondary importance. A huge quantity of information is exchanged through the nonverbal (tonal, gestural, and tactile) aspects of our interaction, which generally occurs beneath the conscious perception of the person. Furthermore, almost all of the representations that move through our neuronal pathways as we loop through our strategies remain unnoticed by the average person. Many people find it extremely difficult to pay attention to or express verbally what they are sensing.

You can scoop up a tremendous quantity of data by observing and listening to key cues and the nonverbal qualities of people's behavior. This data often passes people's explicit attention and challenges their ability to verbalize. For each phase of a strategy, you can identify the representational system being used by observing the behavioral cues that a person uses to adjust his or her physiology to find a specific representational system from which to take and process input. These cues will clearly show the representational system they have been used to accessing. This becomes incredibly beneficial when the swift and intricate representational sequences that constitute specific strategies are not accessible through the verbal statements of the individual.

There are a variety of nonverbal indications that can be used to gauge the sensory-specific processes that someone goes through while engaging in behavioral action. These include eye movement, vocal tone and tempo, breathing rate and placement, skin color changes, skin temperature, pulse rate, posture, and muscular tonus, among the rest.

There are a few key points to keep in mind. Any activity in one aspect of a system (like the cognitive and biological systems that comprise a human person) will invariably have an effect on all of the other portions of that system. When the patterns of interaction between the system's components are recognized, the impacts of the system's various parts on one another can be forecasted and controlled. As a result, human behavior - both macro, such as speaking out loud, and micro, such as making a subtle but sour facial expression - is a reflection of internal cognitive processing. All behavior, therefore, is a form of communication regarding the individual's cognitive functioning. In other words, as one of the most important NLP's presuppositions asserts, you cannot **not** communicate.

It is the purpose of all behavioral sciences to decode the overt changes in cognitive strategies that are usually not available to someone in the function they perform, in order to understand how the representational elements are arranged in relation to each other. All of our models of cognitivism were created using this approach for detecting patterns between a person's observable behavior and their internal structures.

In the end, your success will depend on how well you can recognize and use the many shifts and patterns that your clients / communication partners will keep offering you as part of your own subjective perception. We call this skill - **calibration**.

You'll soon realize that the eye movements people make when thinking and processing data give a surprisingly precise gauge of sensory-specific cognitive function. When any one of us chooses the words we use to communicate verbally with one another, we usually do so at an unconscious level of operation. These words then show which parts of the realm of internally and externally given experience we have at that moment. Predicates (verbs, adjectives, and adverbs) are strongly suggestive.

Furthermore, each of us has acquired distinct bodily gestures that reveal to the keen observer the representational system we are employing. The eye scanning patterns that we have discovered are really significant. Consider how many times you've asked someone a question and they've hesitated, saying, "Ohhh, let's see," and then moved their eyes up and to the left in response. Movement of the eyes up and to the left triggers associative visions in the non-dominant hemisphere (in right-handed people). The right cerebral hemisphere represents the neural synapses that originate on the left side of both eyes, the left visual fields. People commonly employ the eye scanning movement up and to the left to stimulate that region as a means of retrieving visual memory. Eye movements to the right and up activate the left cerebral hemisphere, generating images that are visual representations of things the individual has just created internally, rather than as an access to memory. The **Eye Accessing Cues** (when the person is facing you):

V^c = Visual Constructed – Up Left

V^r = Visual Remembered – Up Right

A^c = Auditory Constructed – Lateral Right

A^r = Auditory Remembered – Lateral Left

K = Kinesthetic – Feelings / Bodily Sensations - Down Left

A^d = Auditory Digital – Internal Dialogue - Down Right

No eye movement - already accessed the information.

Breathing is one of the most significant and direct means we have of altering or regulating our biochemical states in order to change our physiology. When we breathe in and out at different velocities and fill or expand various parts of our chests, we use nearly every muscle in our body and alter the chemical composition of the blood circulation, which supplies the essential ingredients with which our brain operates.

These breathing variations could be used externally or internally to reach awareness through any of the representational systems.

Visual access is associated with and accessed by high and shallow chest respiration, as well as the occasional short halt of breathing.

Kinesthetic access is indicated by deep, full breathing low in the belly area.

Internal dialogue will be supported by breathing in the diaphragm or with the whole chest, often with a long, slow exhalation, as if talking without opening one's mouth to say the words.

We also modify our muscular and spinal positioning to go along with these various styles of breathing and to help dial in a specific representational system.

The body's accessing posture for visual awareness is characterized by muscle tension in the shoulders, neck, and often the belly; the shoulders slumped and the neck stretched.

Unless the feelings are especially debilitating, most internal kinesthetic access is characterized by general muscle relaxation, with the head resting squarely on the shoulders, which tend to sag; the access will then be supported by excessive abdominal breathing and emotive or even violent gestures.

There will be some similarities between internal and external tactile cuing, but the body will be more active and the shoulders will be held more broadly when using external kinesthetic access.

Muscle tension and tiny rhythmic movements are the distinguishing features of accessing auditory acuity. Although slouched, the shoulders are typically thrown back. The person's slanting of the head is also a common trait.

It is important to note that behavioral outputs can also serve as useful measures of representational system activity due to changes in respiration, posture, and muscle tone. Breathing and muscle strain in the face and neck area will alter the pace and tone of the voice. A person's voice quality will be affected by the volume of air being pushed over their vocal chords and the speed at which it is pushed.

Quick spurts of words in high-pitched tones with an unusually quick speech pace accompany visual processing.

Kinesthetic access is indicated by a slow voice tempo, extended pauses, and a notably low, resonant, and frequently soulful intonation.

The auditory representational system is accompanied by a moderate tonality, a steady and sometimes cyclical tempo, and generally well-enunciated words.

Tapping, snapping fingers, and generating bouncing, whistling, or rattling noises with the mouth are all examples of auditory system indicator/access cues.

The internal representational systems are also called **modalities**. We use these modalities for all cognitive functions: internal visual, internal auditory, and internal kinesthetic. We use the acronym **VAK** to signify the major internal representational systems or modalities. VAK means that we represent the data in our minds by means of visions, sounds (verbal and non-verbal), and sensations. The qualities, or attributes, of a representational system are the **sub-modalities**. These are the properties of the major modality. They are a part of the representation, not outside entities. A sub-modality is the 'how' of the modality.

A visual sub-modality can be size, i.e., how big the internal image is, distance, how far ahead is the internal image, brightness level, and so on. An auditory sub-modality can be tone, pitch, distance, direction, and so on. A kinesthetic sub-modality can be pressure, temperature, sensations, and so on.

When you watch a movie on TV, the story line is the content, which is communicated via the projected images and sounds. When you perceive these data inputs, you are using the visual modality and the auditory modality. The sub-modalities are the features the director chose to use to present the data: whether the movie is in black and white or color, how scenes are angled with the camera, point of view, sound effects and their direction, the tonality of the dialogues and the pacing of the actions taken by the actors, and the usage of props. You do the same thing within your mind, albeit mostly unconsciously and without intentional direction. These automatic mental movies dictate how you feel (your state of mind) in the moment, just as the director is manipulating the sub-modalities of his movie to ignite specific emotional reactions in the viewers.

The patterns, strategies and techniques of NLP, are all designed with the concepts and discoveries we have discussed in this chapter.

The 5 Learning Levels

NLP helps us track our learning by spelling out five levels of learning.

Unconscious incompetence means that the person is not only lacking competence in a skill or subject, but they don't even realize that it's an issue. This is the clue-free zone of learning.

Conscious incompetence means that the person is aware of the issue and can become motivated to learn.

Conscious competence happens as the person develops the skills and is able to use them.

Unconscious Competence sounds odd. Why would you want to become subconscious? Well, you've heard people say they can do something in their sleep. What they really mean is that the skill has become so much of a set of reflexes or habits that they do not require a lot of conscious thought. The beauty of that is that they have made room in their brains for more learning. Brain scans show us that the brain is a pattern-recognition tool. Once it learns the pattern and can translate it into a reflex that can be fired off, it moves the pattern into a lower brain center, freeing the higher brain areas to actively acquire skills that are even more sophisticated to layer on top of that earlier learning. And you know what you get when you add sophisticated skills to largely subconscious skills: mastery.

At the level of mastery, the person does more than create excellent results; they are creative and flexible; they can respond to new conditions and improvise. They have extra brainpower left over to come up with innovative and adaptive strategies. A master is the one that people turn to for inspiration and training. Mastery has also been called "conscious mastery" or "subconscious mastery." This means that you are able to gain more conscious access to material that, for most people, is not conscious. This is like expanding your intelligence into a larger landscape or into a bigger brain. Artists do this when they learn to trust their creativity or their muse, accepting signals from their subconscious and trusting those signals to lead them through a productive creative process. Intuition is also like this, because the person has learned how to trust their subconscious to guide them in sizing things up and making good decisions.

Do you see how these phases of learning can guide you in sequencing your learning and figuring out where your needs are? Think of a skill you are building, maybe NLP, and see where you are in these phases. Then ask, "What do I most need at this phase?"

In language learning, you will often hear students say, "I wish there was a pill that I could take so I could learn the language overnight." It is true that it would be great if we could snap our fingers and magically speak another language, but the learning process is not a short one, so the result is that it takes months or years to learn a language.

As we do this, we go through many different stages, so in the beginning, we may only know a few words, but by the end, we sound like a native speaker. On this timeline, there is an important point where the learner knows the basics but still has to think about what they are doing. So in language learning, this is like the point where you can make sentences, but if you don't want to make mistakes, you really have to concentrate. We call this stage "conscious competence."

This process is much different from how children learn a language. A child learns through unconscious competence when they do not think about what they are learning; they simply learn it.

Obviously, this is a huge advantage because you can skip the conscious competence stage and learn much faster. However, even as adults who have gone to school, people who have learned this way will often have trouble explaining grammar points to non-native speakers, so when asked why grammar is a certain way, they simply respond, "Because it is that way." Clearly, this is not very helpful to students. So we can see that there is some benefit to conscious competence, even if you already perform this task extremely well. When you make an unconscious competence conscious, you can refine and improve it. Also, you can focus on what exactly you do to perform this task well and use these skills to help improve other skills you would like to improve.

The 21 Presuppositions

Presuppositions are, in general, the underlying assumptions of a system. To fully comprehend NLP, one must first gain a thorough understanding of its underlying assumptions. Even if the statement itself is not necessarily true, the cultivation of a useful result is accomplished. Or to put it another way, we act as if these statements are "facts" solely for the purpose of bringing us one step closer to our desired outcomes. As an example, suppose you want to have a strong and loving relationship with your children. You choose to not get upset by your teenage son's recent outburst, instead offering support, unconditional love, and patience, acting on the assumption (presupposing) that we are more than our behavior (#7). You seek to understand the deep structure that has contributed to the inappropriate behavior, and instead of reflexive conflict, you show empathy and care, knowing that your son's rudeness was a temporary reaction initiated because it was the most useful (#8) in that specific context (#9). Remembering that your reaction to his outburst is critical (# 11 and # 12), you take a step back and say, "You have the right to be angry, and I am here to listen whenever you are willing to talk to me about it." Compare that to yelling at him, "Stop acting like a child! You're grounded! Now go to your room!"

The NLP Presuppositions

1. The map is not the territory.

2. People respond according to their internal maps.

3. Meaning operates context-dependently.

4. The mind and-body affect each other.

5. Individual skills function by the development and sequencing of rep systems.

6. We respect each person's model of the world.

7. Person and behavior describe different phenomena. We are more than our behavior.

8. Every behavior has utility and usefulness—in some context.

9. We evaluate behavior and change in terms of context and ecology.

10. We cannot not communicate.

11. The way we communicate affects perception and reception.

12. The meaning of communication lies in the response you get.

13. The person who sets the frame for the communication controls the outcome.

14. There is no failure, only feedback.

15. The person with the most flexibility exercises the most influence within the system.

16. Resistance indicates a lack of rapport.

17. People have the internal resources they need to succeed.

18. Humans have the ability to experience one-trial learning.

19. All communication should increase choice.

20. People make the best choices available to them when they act.

21. As response-able people, we can run our own brains and therefore choose our behavior.

Abandoned Predisposition

Determine the problematic predisposition.

Elicit the current sub-modalities (Image A).

Elicit sub-modalities from the aversion image (Image B).

Change the sub-modalities of the predisposition image.

Lock the new sub-modalities firmly in place.

Test.

Future pace.

A predisposition is a tendency that is not yet a habit. It is when you hold a particular thought pattern and can't let go of it, or when you act in a particular way and catch yourself "too late." This pattern helps you to abandon the predisposition by turning the compulsion into an aversion. In other words, it turns a specific thing or action you "like" into one you "dislike." Review your knowledge of sub-modalities before you try out this pattern.

1. Determine the nature of the problematic predisposition. Think of something that you like doing or thinking about but wish you did not like. Can you define it in a statement?

2. Elicit the current sub-modalities (Image A). As you think about this predisposition, elicit the sub-modalities of this mental image. Specifically, check for driver sub-modalities such as size, light, distance, etc.

3. Elicit sub-modalities from the aversion image (Image B). Now think of something you dislike and elicit the sub-modalities in that image. Again, specifically check for driver sub-modalities.

4. Change the sub-modalities of the predisposition image.

Take the sub-modalities you've elicited from Image B and apply them to Image A. If in Image B, for example, the image was to the left and 3 feet in size, make Image A go to the same location and enhance (or reduce) it to the same size as Image B. Work through all driver sub-modalities.

5. Ensure that the new sub-modalities are securely in place. Imagine that you could "stamp" Image A as it is now with the copied sub-modalities of Image B, making the new sub-modalities locked into Image A firmly.

6. Test. How is it different now that you think about something you used to enjoy doing or thinking about?If there is still a tendency to like doing or thinking X (image A content), go back through the steps and elicit more driver sub-modalities.

7. Future Pace. Imagine a realistic and specific time in the near future when you might find yourself tempted to do or think X (image A content). Can you feel the aversion?

Abductive Thinking

You might think that people are very rational beings. For example, we can be quite logical. We have developed something called "deductive logic," which is the basis for all logic and argumentation. This is an example of deductive logic:

I like anything with chocolate.

Brownies have chocolate.

Therefore, I like brownies.

For this, we also have inductive logic, which allows us to classify things. For example, "all creatures that have feathers and lay eggs are birds." This is how we can tell the difference between a bird, a bat and a bee. It is this type of classification that allows us to understand biology and evolution. But we are not always so logical. With abductive thinking, we create connections that do not necessarily exist. This is not always a bad thing, because without abductive logic, we would not have metaphor and simile, things that make our communication so interesting and expressive. However, this kind of thinking can lead to some real problems. Let's look at that last example again through abductive thinking.

Birds fly.

Bats fly.

Therefore, bats are birds.

Of course, we know that birds and bats are different creatures, but abductive thinking makes them the same. Despite this, we can use abductive thinking to our advantage to help us solve difficult problems that seem impossible to solve. You can do this by concentrating on that problem, say procrastination, and identifying it with a physical location, say one step to your right. Then, step out of this position and into the Meta position. After that, think of something that you really like, something that you really identify with and that identifies you as a person, like music. Now take a step into this position, your "resource" location. By taking this step, you associate music with your resource location, and it is from this resource location that you move away from the problem of procrastination. You do this by combining the two locations. "My procrastination is making me play bad music." Of course, you do not have to actually play an instrument, but this will help you identify the need to fix this problem. Next, think of a way you can solve this problem while in the resource location: "If I start practicing, I will play better music."

Now what you do is step back into the Meta position and think about how you can turn this metaphorical answer into a real one. Maybe "practice" is a project you have to work on, so you get started on that project so you can "play better music."

Accelerated Learning Chain

Source: Robert Dilts

This pattern builds on learning strategies. It uses chaining to connect experiences into a useful state. These moments help you move from a problem to a resourceful state. There are numerous ways to assemble patterns like the one shown below.

1. Select a difficult learning situation. Think of something that you would like to learn, but are having trouble with.

2. Think of a good learning experience that has as much in common as possible with the problem you just identified. For example, if you are learning to memorize rote material, see if you can think of a very successful learning experience that involved rote learning. Be sure that the learning experience you choose is one that leads to you learning something well.

3. Access the states that were part of this positive learning. Explore the elements involved. List them. Here are some examples of sub-modalities that might be involved: Feeling supported, feeling things "click" internally, experiencing "the zone" internally, experiencing internal visually constructed images of what you are learning, internally visual manipulating what you are learning, feeling excited, interested, and motivated; seeing and hearing your involvement in the learning experience.

4. Sequence these states in time. Now think of the earlier states and the later states as a sequence, starting with inklings such as awareness and curiosity and ending with more complicated collections of sense modalities such as deep involvement and mastery. List them as a sequence that begins with your exposure to the material and ends with your successful use of the learned material.

5. Turn the states into stepping stones, placing them in order. Imagine a series of stepping stones in front of you, and mentally place each of these sequenced steps along these stepping stones. Place a note for each one, and mark it with a bold marker if it can help you keep the sequence in mind.

The Big Book of NLP

6. Anchor these steps by stepping through them. Spend some time on each of these steps in order to anchor them as representing each of these transitional states.

7. Bring that challenging learning issue to mind. Move through each step while holding this in mind. If possible, repeat these steps before returning to the challenging learning situation.

8. Test. Next time you are involved in a challenging learning situation, see how this pattern has changed your experience of this learning.

Accessing Resourceful States

Choose a situation that calls on you to be in an excellent state.

Name the most valuable qualities.

Select a memory of the resource state.

Step into the resource state.

Pick a model for this state. Experience it from second position.

Anchor.

Test.

Learn state mastery. Elicit resourceful states, such as confidence and creativity, that will move you toward your goals.

1. Choose a situation that calls on you to be in an excellent state. What resources do you need to have in that situation? For example, if you are going to a job interview, eagerness, charisma, and confidence are valuable. If you are in a difficult negotiation, emotional buoyancy, charisma, and strategic thinking are important.

2. Identify the most valuable characteristics. Name the qualities that you feel are most valuable for the challenge that you have chosen for this pattern.

3. Choose a resource state memory. Think of a time when you have experienced and expressed at least one of these qualities. Bring to mind all the rep systems for this memory (VAK, at least), until the memory is very rich. Aim for the sense of actually going back into the memory. This means you need to be in the first position, as yourself.

4. Step into the resource state: Imagine that this resource (the resource state the memory is linked to) is a force field that you can step into. Step into it and imagine, in all rep systems, what it is like for you to be fully in this state. In this manner, you are amplifying the state in memory.

You can spend some time in the third perceptual position, observing your posture, facial expression, and behavior as you fully express this state. Do whatever you need to amplify this state, especially in regards to how it can be more relevant to the challenge that you have in mind.

5. Pick a model for this state. Experience it from a second position. Think of someone that you feel has an abundance of this resource state. It can be anyone, from a character from a movie to someone that you know well. From a third position, look at them and notice how their physiology expresses this state. Move into the second position so that you experience the state from inside that person, as that person. Access to all rep systems.

6. Anchor this resource.

7. Test. When the situation or challenge comes up, see how this pattern has changed how you handle it.

Repeat this pattern, improving it based on what you learn. For example, discover how you can make the resource state more intense for re-anchoring. What sub-modalities do you need to add to make it more relevant to the challenge?

Active Dreaming

Select an intention and place it in a passive mental space.

Access an up time state of "not knowing" while taking a walk.

Note what comes into the foreground for you.

Take second position with each one, one at a time.

Explore the results from a meta-position.

Test.

Through active dreaming, you can get ideas, answers, solutions, and information. The power of sleep and daydreaming to enhance our creativity drives this pattern. It starts with stating a general intention and moves on to inducing a specific state that keeps you in control of the process.

1. Decide on an intention. Come up with an intention to get an idea, answer, decision, or problem solution. Choose a very general intention. For example, if you want to solve a problem, don't set rules about what makes a solution.

2. Access an up time state while taking a walk. Take a ten-minute walk, and focus on your peripheral vision. Focus on external sounds in order to reduce internal dialog. For now, foster a relaxed state by letting go of your worries for now.

3. Note what comes into the foreground for you. As you take your walk, notice what you spontaneously focus on; what your attention is automatically drawn to, in any rep system.

4. Take the second position with each one, one at a time. Take a second position with each thing that catches your attention.That is, experience it by identifying with it. What might it be like to be that thing?

Whether it's a tree, the wind, or a rock, notice its attributes as though you could do this first-hand. Explore things such as the sensation of time passing, your perspective and height, the effect of the elements on you, and so forth.

5. Investigate the outcomes of a meta-position. Adopt a meta-position, in which you can observe all the information that you explored from the second position with various objects you encountered. Recall your original intention for this pattern. Experience your new information, understanding, and experiences in connection with this intention. Give your unconscious mind trust and time to process and generate novel insights.

6. Test. In a few days, ask yourself if anything has changed about the topic of your intention for this pattern. Once successful, try this pattern on a variety of topics.

Advanced Belief Chaining

Carry out the Belief Chaining pattern with a Guide and in a more advanced form.

1. Design four steps. Choose a location for each of the following steps:

Position 1. Negative / un-resourceful belief.

Position 2. Somewhat negative/un-resourceful belief.

Position 3. Somewhat positive-negative/un-resourceful belief.

Position 4. Positive / resourceful belief.

2. Express the limiting belief from position one.

a. Both the Explorer and the Guide stand in the first step location, "negative/un-resourceful belief."

b. The explorer expresses a negative belief. For example, "I can't spend time with my family, because I always replay old behaviors that are really disturbing. I can't cope with them. "

c. The Guide goes to the second perceptual position and identifies the positive intentions or presuppositions behind the belief. For example, "I value my emotional stability and the productivity that results from that. I value the people in my life who contribute in constructive ways to my development. "

3. Access a positive, resourceful and wise state from step location four. The explorer and guide step into position four, "positive/resourceful belief" and, without attempting to create the positive belief, access a positive, resourceful and wise state.

4. The Explorer and guide return to location one, "Negative/un-resourceful belief."

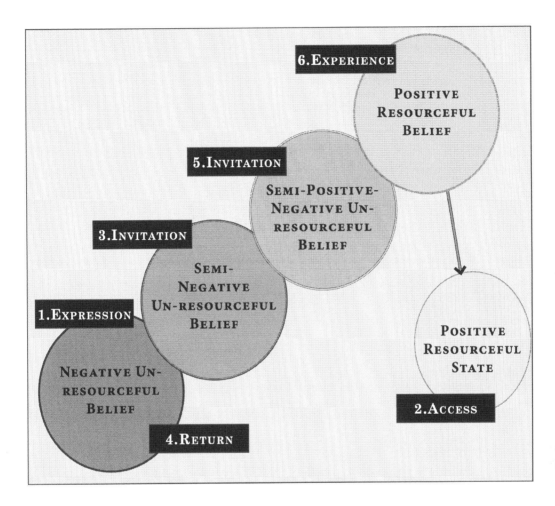

5. The guide helps the explorer experience position two.

a. The Guide steps to Area Two, "Somewhat Negative/Un-resourceful Belief" and uses the positive presuppositions or intentions that were identified in order to produce a less negative belief. The belief must reflect positive intentions or presuppositions. For example, "you are preventing contact with toxic people in order to avoid negative emotional states."

Notice how this statement moves from "I can't." to an intention ("You are preventing..."), and from fate ("I always...") to an active role ("In order to avoid..."). The frame is negative ("toxic people" and "negative emotional states") but is less negative than the original belief because it brings in intention and action, that is, an internal locus of control and a sense of meaningful identity and need.

b. The Guide invites the Explorer to step into Area Two and experience this belief.

c. If the explorer feels that the belief needs more work, then the guide reworks the belief and tries again. For example, the positive presupposition may need to be adjusted to more accurately reflect the motives of the explorer. The guide can step into area four to reinforce the positive state in order to be more effective.

6. The guide helps the explorer experience position three.

a. The Guide steps into position three, "somewhat positive/resourceful belief," and creates a belief that crosses over into being positive and is based on the positive intentions and presuppositions of the Explorer. For example, "you are using the resources you have gained, including those from your family, to establish and maintain your boundaries in the service of your emotional well-being."

b. The Guide places the explorer in a position where he or she can test this belief.

c. If the belief needs improvement, the explorer asks the guide to rework it.

7. The guide helps the explorer experience position four.

a. The Guide steps into position four, "positive/resourceful belief," and creates a positive belief that is based on the positive intentions and presuppositions of the Explorer. For example, "As your skill in using the resources you have gained, including those from your family, increases, you will expand the range of people that you can experience while fully benefiting from your boundaries and increasingly buoyant emotional well-being."

b. The Guide places the explorer in a position where he or she can test this belief.

c. If the belief needs improvement, the explorer asks the guide to rework it.

8. The explorer shares with the guide what lessons came from this experience.

The Big Book of NLP

9. Test. Over the coming days and weeks, notice any increased ease you experience in flexible thinking and any increase in your use of positive frames and resourcefulness in your beliefs about any challenges that you experience.

Advanced Visual Squash

Source: Richard Bandler & John Grinder

Identify the conflict, and separate the parts.

Place a well-formed sensory representations of each part in each hand.

Understand the positive intentions of each part.

Share resources between the parts.

Develop an image of the integrated, shared resources.

Turn the parts to face each other, and observe the changes that result.

Integrate the parts by bringing your hands together.

Enhance the integration by experiencing it fully, and bringing it into your body.

Build your congruence and success by resolving small conflicts. Integrate parts that are not aligned.

1. Choose an internal conflict and identify the incongruent parts. For example, if you have trouble saving money, identify the part of you that wants to spend liberally and the part that is frugal.

Put well-formed sensory representations of each part in each hand. What would each part look and sound like? How might it move or gesture?

Develop a well-formed sense of each part. Place one part in each hand. Select which part goes into which hand based on how you feel about them.

3. Ask each part to tell you its positive intentions in this conflict. Relax and let ideas emerge. Note, which seems to be the most important. A good way to phrase the question is, "What is the good that you desire to get from this behavior of yours?"

4. Share resources between the parts. Notice what is similar between the two parts' positive intentions. Ask each part what resources it could use from the other part. Work with the parts until both have a good sense of this.

Create an image of each resource. Imagine energy flowing from one hand to the other, and say, "Give a complete copy of these resources to the other part (list the resources to be copied)." Imagine an image of each resource flowing through that energy into the other part. Do all of this once for each part. Notice the changes in each part's behavior and appearance. (This is called sub-modality mapping.)

5. Create an image of the combined resources of the two parts. Place this image in the center of your hands.

6. Have the images in each hand turn to face each other. Turn the palms of your hands toward each other. Let your imagination modify these images to express how they are changing.

7. Integrate the parts by bringing your hands together. Allow your hands to come together only as fast as you can allow the integration of these parts into one special part that expresses the good intentions and resources of each. When working with a person, use this phrase as you place your hands in the same position as theirs. Then move your hands together slightly faster than they normally do. Invite and allow the parts to blend into and enhance the image of integration.

8. Enhance the integration by experiencing it fully and bringing it into your body. Once your hands come together, fully experience the feelings involved.

Allow the image to morph as it expresses the changes in your feelings and resources. Bring the image and energy into your body by bringing your hands to your chest.

Aligned Self

Source: Connirae Andreas

Select a resource.

Create visual space anchors for each neurological level.

Focus on each space, exploring how it will contribute to your alignment.

From the bottom (behavior) step into each space working up. Enhance the state of each space, and carry it into the next space.

Take time for integration.

Future pace.

Test.

Aligned-self means heading in a strong direction because your values, beliefs, sense of identity, and purpose in life are all working together. This pattern helps you achieve or reclaim that state. We say "reclaim" because many people complain of falling out of alignment for various reasons. Self-alignment creates a wonderful snowball effect, in which the more you are aligned, the better your results are in life, and the more you are able to align because of the positive feedback, empowerment, and support that results. This pattern uses Dilts' logical levels.

1. Choose a resource. What would help you become more aligned with your values, beliefs, sense of identity, and purpose in life? What would make you feel more purposeful or hopeful?

Candidates such as calm resolve, creative joy, and an appreciation of developing mastery systematically are good candidates.

2. Establish visual space anchors for each neurological level. Select a visual space for each of what will become six anchors: environment, behaviors, beliefs and values, capabilities, identity, and Spirituality.

3. Pay attention to each space and consider how it will contribute to your alignment. Start at the highest level (spirituality) and work your way down.

a. Concentrate on the environmental space. When and where do I wish to express X (the resource you selected)?

b. Concentrate on the behavioral space. Ask, "What behaviors will help me express X in those times and places (from the previous step)?"

c. Concentrate on the capabilities space. Ask, "What capabilities will help me express X in the form of those behaviors in those times and places?"

d. Concentrate on the space for beliefs and values. Ask, "What beliefs and values will help me express X through these capabilities, feeding those behaviors at those times and places?" You are asking about what beliefs and values will support you and direct you toward your highest goals, as well as what is meaningful and valuable about the capabilities from the previous step.

e. Focus on the identity space. Ask, "What kind of person has these beliefs and values?"

"What kind of person expresses X? "

f. Physically place yourself in the physical space.

"What is my overarching purpose in life?

"What is my life's mission?"

Take some time to verbalize these thoughts, but without becoming mired in creating the perfect mission statement.

4. From the bottom (behavior), step into each space, working up. Enhance the state of each space and carry it into the next space.

a. Enhance this spiritual space by amplifying and enriching the state. Take that state with you as you step back into the identity space.

b. Enhance the sense of identity. Notice how the spiritual state helps you do this as you experience your sense of identity and your highest values, meaning and purpose (spirituality) at the same time. Take your identity and spiritual state with you as you step into the capability space.

c. Enhance your sense of capability. Notice how the spiritual and identity states support this sense of capability. Take that state with you as you step back into the belief and value space.

d. Strengthen your beliefs and values. Consider how your spirituality, identity, and capability states influence your beliefs and values. Bring this state to the behavior space.

e. In the behavior space, enhance your potential for taking action. Notice how your spirituality, identity, capability, and beliefs and values support this kind of action. Notice how the spiritual state puts you in connection with the universe and humanity. Discover how your sense of identity contextualizes your behavior in relation to who you are as a person. See how your capability state puts more power into your action potential. Finally, see how your beliefs and values give meaning and importance to this behavior. Take all these levels into your environmental space.

f. In the environmental space, investigate how all of the preceding levels support your ability to harmonize with the context of the behavior and derive resources from it. Resources can be as airy as inspiration or as palpable as concern about upsetting the boss.

5. Allow for integration time. Spend some time experiencing all of these levels blending into a superstate. Notice any new insights, ideas, or scenarios that come to mind. Keep an open focus so that these thoughts can flow through as you process this new experience.

6. Future Pace. Imagine moving through life with this state engaged. Notice ways that you are more aligned with these future scenarios.

7. Test. In the coming days or weeks, notice any ways that you are more direct and empowered in pursuing meaningful goals, or in developing or changing your goals.

Aligning Perceptual Positions

Source: Connirae Andreas

Pick a challenging situation.

First Position, Visual

First Position, Auditory

First Position, Kinesthetic

Third Position (Observer), Visual

Third Position, Auditory

Third Position, Kinesthetic

Return to First Position (Self).

Final Check

By correcting bad habits of perception, you can achieve dramatic improvements in your relationships with others and with yourself. This pattern addresses the tendency for people to become stuck in a particular perceptual position. For example, a person who is always stuck in the second position may have difficulty hanging on to their own reality and be easily manipulated. But this pattern goes much farther than that, by correcting the poor representations of perceptual positions.

When people discover and later on correct problems such as misalignments or jumping into the wrong position, they may experience impressive and lasting improvements in long-standing interpersonal problems.

What Happens When Perceptual Positions Are Not Aligned?

Here's a great example: Let's say someone is a bit self-centered or narcissistic. They have trouble tolerating it when someone else has more expensive clothes than they do, or is more important than they are in some way. When they work with perceptual positions, they may find that when they try position number two, which is looking at themselves through the other person's eyes, they discover that what they are hearing is not really the other person's voice. Instead, they hear what seems to be their own voice, telling them that they are inferior and that someone else is better than they are. But they go on to another discovery. Those thoughts add an emotional energy to that judgement. Those thoughts are loaded with the feeling that it is not acceptable, that it is horrible that this other person has a better car, or whatever. This person has been so busy trying to push away those feelings that they have been preoccupied with gaining status in any way they can. This means they have not realized how they are being driven by a voice that they have lost in the second perceptual position and that they are being attacked with feelings lost in the second perceptual position.

It gets a little farther out than even that. They realize, doing this work, that the thoughts are not really their own. Those thoughts about inferiority and superiority were the best thing they could come up with when they were children with a parent who humiliated them and who was very harsh. You could say then that they kind of inherited the voice from the parent; the voice was primarily coming from the second position. That judgmental voice had gotten assigned to random people, but it was not from them; it was from the parent, who was very judgmental. And the feelings? Those are first position feelings, and that's good because we are imagining from the first position, from inside our own skin. But these intolerable feelings aren't really a reaction to other people's having nice things. Those are the terrors of a child who fears his or her big, harsh parent.It's just that those thoughts and feelings were a defensive or protective posture. Defenses tend to stick around, because they are there to protect us. Unfortunately for this fellow, though, they went out of date long ago. However, they didn't know who they were, so they became lost in a struggle with what they had become. For the client, it had become a drama of who is best, who has the nicest things, and who is superior and inferior. The fear of the parents became the fear of anyone being superior. This, in turn, became a struggle for prestige, a struggle that seems like an adult struggle, but is actually a holdover from the past. It's very difficult for someone to untangle themselves from a drama that masquerades as a grown-up pursuit. Aligning perceptual positions can rescue people from such suffering, and it can unlock maturation that has been frozen, maybe for decades. The beauty of aligning your perceptual positions is that it makes it much easier to let go of feelings and thoughts that don't belong to you. When you are aligned, the misaligned parts feel out of place. You want to put them where they belong: in the past, or give them back to the person who started them in the first place. Many NLP practitioners work without talking about the past. That can work, because alignment happens in the present, and you can let go of thoughts and feelings without knowing where they came from. Most are practical and work with or assess past experience as necessary. They don't, however, get lost in the past; the focus is on outcomes.

What Do Aligned Perceptual Positions Feel Like?

Let me give you a sense of aligned perceptual positions. Imagine yourself listening to these words. As you listen, with your eyes open, notice that you can see out of your own eyes, feel your own body, and hear with your own ears. You know that each of those senses is yours because of where you sense them. You are the center, and they are in the right positions. So what we have done is use real experience with your rep systems that you can refer to when you do visualization or a perceptual position alignment exercise. To sum up, when all your rep systems are in the same perceptual position, you see, hear, and feel your senses in the right physical location. If you are imagining yourself in the first perceptual position, then it is like you are actually in your own body, looking through your own eyes. You feel grounded or connected, even more powerful as an individual. You will start your alignment by finding where the misalignment is. This means you'll have to imagine a challenging situation. Then you'll check each primary perceptual position: seeing, hearing, and feeling. Once we know where the misalignment is, we will use that for the alignment. We'll start by determining whether you have any misalignment in your first perceptual position. Let's actually imagine something and see if you get the same sense of properly placed senses as you do when experiencing real life. Let's see if, in a visualization, you are the center of properly placed senses.

1. Select a difficult situation. Pick a situation that is challenging for you and involves another person, such as having an argument with someone. Imagine yourself in that challenging situation.

2a. First Position, Visual:

Consider how you see; how your imagination represents your visual sense. Is your vision 100% exactly where it would be if you were really there, or would you say it is placed a little off from where it should be?

2b. First Position, Auditory:

Let's try this with hearing. In the imaginary and challenging situation, imagine the sounds you might hear in it or add some appropriate sounds. Do they feel that they are coming to you in the same position that real hearing does? Imagine what the person might say to you. If they are saying what you are thinking, or if they are saying things that are truly how YOU feel about yourself, or what YOU are insecure about, you are hearing your own thoughts from a different perceptual position. That is a significant misalignment. This type of misalignment can make people feel self-conscious or jump to the conclusion that people are judging them too much.

Aligning a problem like this is very empowering, because you own your own thoughts, and you feel much more grounded and confident. Include your thoughts as well, as though you "hear" your thoughts. Ask yourself if those thoughts are really yours. Do they feel like they are really from your values and from the core of your mind, or is there anything alien about them, such as a resemblance to someone else's style of speaking? Or are some of your thoughts actually what you think the other person is thinking? Adjust so that you hear your thoughts as your thoughts. If someone else's thoughts or thinking style has intruded, turn this into thinking about what they think instead. If you have a judgmental voice, see what it feels like to try to own that voice. See what it feels like to place that voice in your throat and speak those judgments. Many people find it very awkward. They send those thoughts off to some mean school teacher or bully that isn't even on the scene. That means those thoughts should be gone and no longer even audible.

2c. First Position, Kinesthetic:

We will do the same thing with feelings. Do you have emotions, tension, or any other feelings in this situation? If you are aligned, your feelings are coming from the part of your body that they should come from. But if your kinesthetic rep system is not aligned, then your feelings may seem to be coming from elsewhere. They might be a little off, or way off, like when you project feelings onto someone else.

A more common problem, though, is when people mistake other people's feelings as their own. This makes them easy to manipulate. Con artists, addicts, and other destructive people seek out these overly empathic individuals. Codependency involves this problem of being at the mercy of other people's feelings.

3.a. Third Position (Observer), Visual:

As you look at your challenging situation, move your point of view out and away, so that you are looking at yourself and the other person. Now you are in third place. Place your point of view so that you and the other person are both the same distance from your point of view as an observer. Have them at eye level. From this perspective, you may notice any changes in your experience. See if you find it helpful to move closer or farther away, to feel like you have a good sense of perspective. Is there anything else to adjust, such as any sub-modalities? For example, is your view dark or fuzzy?

3b. Third Position, Auditory:

Explore your auditory sense. Are you hearing what is going on from where your point of view is? Remember that your thoughts are only as an observer. Your reactions are not as the "you" in the first position, but as the observer of that "you," and as the observer of whoever else is in the scene. You are unable to hear the thoughts of the "you" that you are observing.

You can only guess as to the content of others' thoughts. You might feel emotional about what is going on, but only as an observer. Thus, you might feel empathy or some other emotion about what you are observing.

Here is a powerful alignment move: take what you think the other person may be thinking and have them speak the words. This allows you to be free of distraction, free of being occupied by your thoughts. Instead, you are actively imagining. This helps to secure you in the observer position and to see if those words are coming from the right person. Does it really sound like what they would say?

Are you imagining it coming into your ears as if you were hearing it instead of thinking it? If so, you are aligned with your auditory observer (third) position.

3c. Third Position, Kinesthetic :

As you look at the situation as the observer, with "you" and the other person at the right distance from you, you are hearing from the observer position. You are also thinking as an observer who has some distance from the emotions in the situation. Notice what feelings you do have as the observer. If you have strong feelings that belong to someone in the scene, place them back in that person and feel what it is like to really be the observer. What feelings do you have about the scene as the observer? If you need to, adjust your feelings so that they are in the appropriate areas of your body. Notice what feelings are the most resourceful.

What feelings best support you as an observant, curious, creative person, a person who generates solutions and excellence?

This process can really liberate your unconscious mind as a problem-solving force. Allow yourself to relax in observer mode for a few moments, creating some space in your unconscious mind to benefit from this objective point of view. Open your mind to wisdom as it becomes available to you. The novelty of this experience can trigger unconscious resources.

The unconscious is always looking for ways to connect the dots, to help you pursue a meaningful agenda even though you begin not knowing what will emerge. And now, the observer perspective is a resource that you can draw upon whenever you like. It is not only a position for a fresh perspective, but also a safe position that can give respite from raw personal feelings because it is a relatively dissociated state.

4. Return to First Position (Self):

Lastly, we will return to the first position in order to fine tune its alignment. Bring your perspective back to yourself in the scenario. Do you notice anything different about being back in your self-position?

4a. First Position, Visual:

Check each rep's system. Are you looking out through your own eyes? If there is any kind of offset, or any misalignment, correct that by shifting directly into your normal vision, seeing directly out of your eyes. You should now view the other person as you normally would. Adjust any sub-modalities you care to, such as brightness, clarity, and size.

4b. First Position, Auditory:

How is your voice? As you speak, make sure it is coming from your throat. Of course, any internal dialog, thoughts, and judgments should really belong to you and come from your mind, emanating from you. Make sure your thoughts are in the first person, using phrases like "I think this" and "I think that." Your thoughts are not talking about you; they are coming from you; they are yours. And your hearing should be coming directly into your imaginary ear. Adjust the placement as needed, so that it sounds natural and normal.

4c. First Position, Kinesthetic:

What has changed in your feelings? Do you have your own feelings coming from the normal areas of your body where such feelings come from?

5. Final Verification:

Do a final check and see if you feel aligned in the first position. Make any final adjustments as you like. You do not need to spend time trying to make it perfect. You are learning just the same. Since we are at the end of this pattern, and we know adjustments can spread, spend a few moments back in the third position as the observer, and see if there have been any other improvements.

The Big Book of NLP

Allergy Relief

Source: Robert Dilts

Imagine being exposed to the allergen.

Anchor a symptom-free state.

Enhance the anchor.

Anchor several counter-example reference experiences.

Fire the dissociated anchor.

Test.

This pattern has a reputation for reducing or eliminating symptoms of allergies.

1. Imagine being exposed to an allergen. Recall being exposed to the allergen. Attempt to elicit some of the symptoms. Find out which sub-modalities change the intensity of the symptoms.

2. Anchor a symptom-free state. Achieve a state that is dissociated from the allergic state and anchor it. A good way to do this:

a. formalizedRelax a bit, tilting your head and eyes upward. Imagine that now there is glass between you and the thing you are allergic to. Imagine being able to float up so that you can observe yourself from above.

b. When you are free of allergic responses and truly relaxed, create a second, different anchor.

3. Enhance the anchor. Imagine fully a symptom-free state and the ideal way you would like to respond to the item that typically causes an allergic response when you have no allergic response. Imagine this in some detail, describing it. Imagine this from an associated perspective. Use the sub-modalities that you discovered were key to your reaction in building your new response.

4. Anchor a number of counterexample reference experiences.

a. Associated Memory: Access an actual memory in which you have been near something that is, as much as possible, like the thing you are allergic to, but that does not produce an allergic response. For example, if you are allergic to cats, you might imagine a clean, processed rabbit pelt or plush toy that causes no response.

b. To help disrupt your frame regarding allergies, do something that will show you that your immune system can tolerate substances that seem as though they should be intolerable. You can accomplish this by thinking of one or more substances that you think of as being toxic but which you don't have an allergic response to. This shows that your immune system can keep your body safe without allergic reactions. For someone allergic to perfumes, the odor of gasoline might be an example. (Not that we recommend actually sniffing gasoline fumes.) Only do it in your imagination. ") It is also useful to identify some substances that are potentially even more "toxic" than the substances that cause the allergy, but to which the explorer's body has learned a more appropriate type of immune response.

c. Be sure that you observe the appropriate physiology before setting the anchor. It should match the desired state.

d. Are there any problems with ecology or secondary gain in connection with the allergic response?

e. You can enhance this by using re-imprinting, reframing, changing your personal history or your three anchors to add resources.

5. Fire A1, the dissociated state anchor, and have the person imagine being close to, or in contact with, the allergen. Fire anchors A2 and A3 for the desired state and the counter

example at the same time. Be sure to hold the anchors long enough to see the person's physiology shift fully away from the allergic response.

6. Test. If there is no risk of a medical problem, expose the person to a small amount of the allergen. Increase the amount bit by bit. Repeat the procedure as needed until a typical exposure produces no allergy symptoms.

Before each increase, simultaneously fire A1, the dissociation anchor, and then A2 and A3, the desired state and counterexample anchors. You can make this new response stronger by using the critical sub-modalities from step one. Let the person be in full control of how the allergen is handled. If there is any concern, consult an appropriate physician.

Always work within your scope of practice and eliminate risk. This pattern can have durable effects. Sometimes, it may need to be repeated to restore its effect. Exposure to other allergens or sensitigens may restore an allergic response.

Ambiguity

Learn to use ambiguity for motivational and healing purposes. Milton Erickson was brilliant at using ambiguity to induce trance and to guide the unconscious mind in its work during therapy. This pattern will focus on using ambiguity to induce a light trance during TDS. Do not try this exercise while operating any machinery or doing anything that could be dangerous, since you may put yourself into a trance. If you are comfortable with hypnotic communication, you can try this on a partner to practice and get their feedback. You can also record your efforts and try them for yourself.

1. Create an ambiguous statement pertaining to the stages of hypnotic communication. Write down or verbalize statements that would guide a person through hypnotic communication for at least the following stages: Body positioning, paying attention, going inward, focusing on an issue, developing a state, going deeper into relaxation, going into trance. For example, for body positioning, here is an unambiguous statement: "Please sit with your feet on the floor, your hands in your lap, and breathe slowly." Put more ambiguously, it could be, "As you sit there, you can untangle your legs, finding a position that your mind prefers you to experience as it guides your hands to come to rest as they find you giving even more of your weight to the chair as it suspends you there in balance... now."

2. Refine it to be more hypnotic. Practice this again, and emphasize ways of being ambiguous that will enhance the experience of relaxation and trance. Try various wordings.

3. Create ambiguity in specific situations. Try the same thing in a practical situation. This removes you and your agenda from causing the person to feel that there is anything to push against.

4. Modify what you came up with to prime the person. Add an element or two to the communication that will prime this person to act in the manner that you prefer.

Remember that priming is triggering a state that is conducive to a particular way of thinking or acting. That is different than a direct command. For example, "I know most people's fondest memories are of the vacations they have had with their families. They would never trade those memories for any work memories, as they treasure them. " In this case, we are not talking directly about him during our timeshare presentation. We are, however, priming our listeners regarding the many values of vacations, including family ties. Money is now less of an obstacle, especially if we have a well-orchestrated presentation with many such primes.

Anger Expression Elicitation

This will help you examine your past automatic reactions to explosive anger from within.

1. Think about a time in your life when you couldn't keep your rage from exploding on someone else.It could be a time someone cut you off on the freeway, or a co-worker cracking a joke at your expense, or your teenage son coming home late and stinking of alcohol.

2. Associate yourself with the scene in the first perceptual position.What happened, as seen with your own eyes? There are many ways to express anger, from raising your voice to swearing to pushing someone. What was your automatic behavior during the course of the entire situation?

3. Break state.

4. Dissociate. Now move to the second perceptual position. Run the mental movie again from the beginning. What was the impact of your attitude, actions, and behaviors on the other person?

5. Break state.

6. Associate into the last frame of that mental movie, right after the altercation is over. Freeze the frame.

7. Did you learn anything new about yourself from the second perceptual position? As you investigate the answer to this question, pay attention to whether you become more or less connected with anger.

8. Test. Play the movie again, dissociated (third perceptual position). How do you analyze the situation now?

9. Future pace. What did you take away from the experience? In your opinion, what do you think will happen the next time you come across a similar situation?

Amnesia Initiation

Amnesia is a very useful tool when you work with clients. Milton Erickson used to induce amnesia from the very first contact with your client. The idea is that if your client "forgets" (your client's mind actually pushes the given time period into the unconscious) a certain part of the change work, they will be less likely to interfere with the results consciously.

For example, if during the session you and your client have discussed that she is binge-drinking alcohol because she wants to be more socially accepted, it would be more useful to use amnesia after you establish new and healthy resources for your client to be socially accepted.

This way, when your client goes on with her life, her mind will have forgotten why she felt like binge-drinking. Once there is no good reason, the alternatives become more prominent. If your client remembers "why I binge drink," the emotional roller-coaster can lead her to binge-drinking again, regardless of your session's success.

You can induce amnesia with a simple confusion method. "And I wonder if you would remember that when you came into this door, you put your right leg in and if you could forget to forget that when you leave this door, you will put your right leg out again."

This is a very simple suggestion to tie the entrance to the room with the exit, and by that, "push down" the time period in between into the subconsciousness.

Analogical Marking

Best known as a way to embed commands into communication, analogical marking means that a portion of the communication is "marked" for greater attention by the unconscious. This marking is typically done through a change in inflection, tempo, body language, or volume. Bandler and Grinder observed this in the hypnotic work of Milton Erickson. Another use is priming. Priming is similar to embedded messages, but it is more general and vague in the sense that it helps to elicit a state or establish familiarity with something in order to increase the odds that the person will choose it or make choices in a particular direction. For example, secure base priming improves a person's ability to react in a less defensive or aggressive manner.

1. Choose a situation in which to use analogical marking. Select a typical situation in which you want to communicate more effectively and in which embedded messages or priming could be helpful.

2. Choose what you will communicate with this approach. Write down a number of things that you would like to communicate, but that might arouse inappropriate defenses. Keep accumulating these until you have several that you feel can be converted into embedded messages. Make sure that your approach is ethical. You must not attempt to manipulate a person in a manner that is not in their best interest.

3. Plan your communication. Create sentences that could be normal-sounding parts of your communication with this person, and that include your embedded commands or priming words or phrases. If necessary, review material on Milton Erickson's use of analogical marking.

4. Practice the approach. Before using this approach, practice delivering these communications. Try them with several different types of analogical marking, including changing your inflection, tempo, body language, and volume.

5. Apply the approach. Once you feel that this can be done in a way that is very natural, use this approach in the current situation.

6. Assess the results. Notice how the person responds. Were there any awkward moments or looks? Does the person respond in any way that suggests your approach was helpful?

7. Continue to refine and practice your use of analogical marking until you are able to do it without preparing in advance. Many people discover that they do it without even realizing it.

The Big Book of NLP

Anchoring

Anchoring is how we get into the right state of mind to support our motivation for what we want to accomplish. Anchors are constantly influencing our behavior. A good way to maintain an anchor is to use it when you are in the state it is intended to trigger. Anchors can be effective for the rest of your life. The better formed, the longer they last. The better you maintain them, the longer they will last. If you only use an anchor when you feel bad, it can lose its power to help you feel good. Visual, auditory, and kinesthetic anchors are all used in NLP.

1. Select a state and decide which trigger to use. Select a state that you want to have access to in the future. Select the anchor trigger you would like to use. As you'll recall, this can be a hand position, a point on your body that you touch, a word or phrase that you say mentally, among many others, or some other unique action that you can dedicate to this state. That means it must be specific, such as pulling on your little finger.

2. Elicit the state. For instructions on how to elicit the state, see the State Elicitation pattern. Make the state fairly strong.

3. Calibrate. If you are doing this for someone else, have them tell you when they are in the state, and observe their physical cues, such as body language, so that you can better calibrate them.

4. Anchor the state. Once the state is fully active and at its peak, anchor the state. Anchor it by doing the behavior that you selected in step one as your trigger. At this point, you are associating the trigger with the state, that is, anchoring the state to the trigger. In the future, activating this trigger will help you activate the state. From now on, never use this trigger for anything other than this state, and when you activate this state in the future, continue the practice of associating the trigger with the state in order to make this association even stronger.

5. Test. Think of situations in which you'll want to trigger this state, and make a reminder to yourself in your calendar so that you'll remember to practice using it and reap its benefits.

Apposition (of Opposites)

Apposition of opposites is a hypnotic suggestion used to enhance the quality of trance or deepen your client into hypnosis. The way it works is very simple: address one known physical condition your client is engaged in and instruct the rest of his or her body at once to fall deeper into hypnosis. For example, if you started using the hand levitation induction, you could use the apposition of opposites by saying, "and perhaps you notice how your hand feels lighter and lighter and your body relaxes even deeper." With a client you've been working on for more than the first session, you can also push his or her hand down at once (but gently) as you say "deeper."

As / if

Select the goal you are doubtful about.

Select your imaginary mentor.

Specify your limiting belief.

Share this situation and belief with your chosen mentor.

Imagine Encouragement from Your Mentor.

Act as if the Outcomes are Coming True.

Handle Leftover Objections.

Test.

We create states by imagining excellence. It's a way to master your imagination, as Milton Erickson famously said, "You can pretend anything and master it." An excellent first step in modeling is to imagine yourself in the other person's shoes, implementing the excellence strategies you wish to model. This helps you intuitively understand their thoughts and actions. Of course, mastery requires practice. You wouldn't expect to be able to fly an airplane without practice. This pattern is for a small skill or improvement. It's a good way to get started before making major improvements in mastery.1. Choose the goal about which you are unsure. Think of a personal goal or circumstance about which you feel doubtful. If you're new to this pattern, choose a small goal, such as producing more creative solutions for something you need to brainstorm about.

2. Select your imaginary mentor. Pick a person, living or dead, whom you feel would make an excellent mentor for you and who could help you believe in your ability to achieve this goal. The person should be very insightful. You should be familiar enough with them to

imagine how they might relate to you.If you have time, you can learn more about them to better do this pattern.

3. Describe your limiting belief in detail. Express your limiting belief in terms of the limits that it expresses. Try beginning with a phrase such as, "I am incapable of (finding a good solution") or "I don't deserve (a smooth, creative experience)."

4. Discuss the situation and your beliefs with your mentor of choice. Imagine that you are speaking to your mentor, explaining the situation as well as your limiting belief.

5. Visualize your Mentor's encouragement. Imagine your mentor respectfully encouraging you to explore a positive "as if" perspective, with questions such as "What would happen if you could..."   Respond to these questions as they are asked. Have your mentor ask follow-up "as if" questions based on your responses.

6. Act as if the outcomes are real. Imagine that your mentor is having you act as if the doubtful outcomes were coming true. For example, "Imagine that you have successfully resolved all the issues you had about this. With full confidence about it now, what will you be thinking or doing that is different? "

7. Handle Remaining Objections. Notice any leftover objections or resistance you have. Continue steps two and three, focusing them on these residual issues.

8. Test. As you go about pursuing your goal, notice any improvements in your state, behavior, or outcomes. What can you learn from the results? If the results are disappointing, are there ways you can improve your use of this pattern? For example, do you understand the imaginary mentor well enough?

Assertiveness Installation

Analyze the non-assertive behavior.

Assess what stops the assertive behavior.

List ways the assertive behaviors can be useful.

Expand the assertiveness state.

Go through the timeline, generating examples of assertive behavior.

Diminish the images of non-assertive behavior.

Future pace.

Test.

Assertiveness is a very important trait, yet people often fall into habits of being too passive or aggressive. These habits can be unconscious, and people often fail to realize how much they are losing and how many bad experiences come from poor assertiveness.

1. Analyze the non-assertive behavior. Determine what the person does instead of asserting himself or herself in a specific situation. In addition to the behavior, uncover the chain of thoughts and other internal representations that take place prior to and during the non-assertive behavior. For verbal thoughts (self-talk), get a good sense of their position. For example, how much do their thoughts act as a broadcast for someone else's thoughts? And how much are they trying to preempt what other people might think? Dynamics such as these show problems with perceptual position misalignment. And this is a clue for you, by the way, to notice issues that you might want to handle with other patterns before continuing a process. As for the stronger sensory elements, look at sub-modalities as well. You are looking at what drives the person toward non-assertive behavior. Do not just assume that the sub-modalities have to be from the known driver

sub-modalities (size, location, etc.). It could be any type, in any modality. Be thorough in your investigation of sub-modalities in this step, because that might determine the success of the whole procedure.

2. Determine what prevents assertive behavior. Notice any ways that an impulse to be assertive is stopped. One way to derive this is to simply mention two or three assertive behaviors that might apply to the situation. Then ask, "When you think of doing this, what happens?" The person is likely to describe a dominant rep system, such as the kinesthetic sense of feeling fear in their stomach, along with some thoughts. Help the person express these thoughts and develop them into specific beliefs, such as, "If I asked for that, it would mean that I was a needy person." People like that are disgusting. " (Notice the nominalization regarding disgust. Who is disgusted, and why? Clarify the ways that stopping assertiveness can be useful.

3. Describe how assertive behaviors can be beneficial. Develop with the person a list of ways that one or more of the assertive behaviors can be useful. Make sure that this list appeals to the broadest possible spectrum of values that the person holds dear. Make sure that this includes as many selfish motives as possible, as well as any ways that the results of their assertive behavior would benefit any people or groups that the person feels are deserving. For example, if self-care makes them more productive, they will be able to contribute more to the world in the long run. Also, their medical bills will be lower, so they can contribute more to their favorite cause. Be sure to include the pleasure of experiencing an assertive state that is free of guilt or other causes of shyness. As you are doing this step, be sure that you are using each element to foster a state of confidence and assertiveness in the person. Another issue to consider is morality and ethics. Your client might have other parts that object to such a stream of thoughts, making themselves more important in their eyes. Allow these parts to speak up, and use the parts negotiation pattern as needed to keep them from interfering with the rest of the procedure.

4. Expand the assertiveness state. Bring the person's attention to the ways they are beginning to experience an assertive state. This includes any rep system elements, including thoughts. Ask elicitation questions, such as: What do you see, hear, or feel? Elicit sub-modalities as well as maintain a high level of sensory acuity. Note which rep systems are most compelling and, of the thoughts, which values expressed by the thoughts are most compelling. Begin future pacing by, for example, asking the person to imagine carrying out assertive behavior buoyed by this state and fully expressing this state. What

kind of posture, gestures, and facial expressions would be expressed? Again, if you maintain a high level of sensory acuity, you will notice their posture, gestures, and facial expressions and give them verbally as feedback to your client in order to prove that the process is already working. Include a fantasy of people reacting very normally and favorably to this behavior in order to reduce the fear and create positive expectations on the unconscious level. Since the tone of voice is so important in assertiveness, have the person imagine the vocal tone, volume, and pacing that are likely to gain cooperation and make the assertive requests. Again, bring up the positive feelings that go along with the assertive state and behavior. Be very supportive of these feelings and help the person amplify them. Use the sub-modalities that were most influential on this particular client.

5. Go through the timeline, generating examples of assertive behavior. Have the person go through their timeline, thinking of many examples of assertive behavior. This includes any time that the person expresses an aspect of assertive behavior. For example, they may feel bad about having said something meekly, but if they used the right words, have them focus very intently on this. The purpose of this is to modify the person's self-concept into that of an assertive person. This way, they will have a greater expectation of being assertive, more permission to be assertive, and better competence at being assertive. They will also use assertive cues like body language to set expectations in others. This will cause people to respond in ways that elicit more assertiveness in the person.

6. Diminish images of passive-aggressive behavior. Bring the person's awareness back to their images of not being assertive. These images may include memories and fears. Ask them to send those images behind the assertive images. Ask them to imbue the nonassertive images with the qualities of the assertive images. For example, if the assertive images have a more lively, colorful quality, have the person modify the non-assertive images to have that quality. Have them do the same with other modalities and sub-modalities, such as vocal tone and accompanying thoughts. Move unassertive feelings to the same location as the assertive feelings and modify the unassertive feelings to match key aspects of the assertive feelings. Continue making these adjustments until the person feels very congruent with assertiveness, even though these unassertive elements are being processed.

7. The Future Pace Go back to future pacing, asking the person to imagine carrying out assertive behavior in various situations. Be sure that they bring the assertive state into the

situation and that their future images have the qualities of the assertive images that have been developed.

8. Test. Ask the person to give you feedback over the coming days or weeks about any changes in their behavior that have to do with assertiveness or anything else that they think is important.

Assuming Responsibility

People sometimes assume they are victims of their own wrong choices of behavior. By breaking this pattern of thinking, we show them that there is another logical level they did not consider. For example, when a client says, "I want to stop being lazy," a response that assumes responsibility would be, "How do you know when to be lazy?" This presupposes that being lazy is a choice of behavior, an action that is taken by the person, not a force that is acted upon him. This inquiry helps the person move higher in the logical levels and realize that there's a step they missed before the experience. Something had to happen before 'being lazy' had resulted in an experience. By taking a closer look at that earlier step, the person can then assume responsibility for the "cause" of the "effect".

Attention Reversal

Often times, when the discussion starts to make the client more vulnerable or exposed, the resistant part in them will either project or use blame or dismissive remarks at you in order to divert the conversation. By making you, the therapist, feel somewhat uncomfortable, the client gains control over their situation and blocks the distressing feelings that are floating around. We can reverse this attention by first not showing any signs of being surprised or upset about their remarks, and secondly, by asking: "I notice that when I say something you know deep inside, you seem to stop breathing? Do you notice that? How might you remind yourself to keep breathing?" Then, we can take this suggestion and, while exploring the vulnerable notions of the client, keep reminding him to breathe right before they're about to speak again.

Attractors

Have you ever looked at a visual puzzle? You see a picture, but that picture was actually designed from two pictures, each of which is revealed dependent on your perspective, or how you look at it. The most well-known are the two faces looking at each other, but the space between them also looks like a candle stick, and the picture of the young woman, but if you look at it differently, you see an old woman. What these pictures show us is the importance of "attractors," that is, the things that help us organize the information that surrounds us into something we can make sense of. What these pictures also show us is that which attractors we pay attention to determines how we understand something. Even if we understand it, it can be quite different depending on which attractors we focus on.

Of course, these attractors do not only affect how we look at pictures, but how we understand and react to all different kinds of phenomena. For example, people who are afraid of dogs are almost always afraid of all dogs, so a negative experience with a big dog can result in the person being afraid of even small dogs. This is why immersion therapy is successful in overcoming phobias. If a person sees that not all dogs are aggressive, then the attractor between dogs and fear is diminished and later destroyed. Attractors do not only help us understand and react to the world, but they also build upon themselves to create new attractors. Let's say your favorite Aunt Mary lives in California, and when you visit Aunt Mary in California for the first time, everything is great because you love being with Aunt Mary. The attractors will build upon the "California" category in your mind in positive ways, so suddenly things "California" for you are much more interesting and positive. The things themselves have not changed, but they are now attracted to California, which is attracted to Aunt Mary, and therefore, they are now more positive for you.

The force of an attractor is usually determined by its depth or width, or in other words, how strong it is and how many situations it can be applied. Back to the example of the fear of dogs, the fear is very strong (deep) and it applies to all dogs (wide), so we can say that this is a strong attractor. But maybe the person just doesn't like dogs, so while this is applied to all dogs (wide), the feeling is not very strong (shallow), or maybe the opposite, the person is afraid of only German Shepherds (narrow) but very much so (deep).

The stronger the phobia, the wider and deeper it is. Obviously, this depends quite a bit on personal history. NLP examines attractor primarily in terms of sub-modalities, or how the specifics of the attractor affect how a person reacts to it.For example, you might have a picture of a beautiful, relaxing landscape, but if you are blasting heavy metal music in the background, the situation will probably not be too comforting. Now, let's look at a specific exercise we can do that will help us understand attractors better.

First, think of a resource state you have that you would like to transfer to other contexts, like being relaxed.

Next, identify which specific context you would like to transfer that state to, say being at work. Now, establish a meta position and also the locations of the two experiences: "being relaxed" and "being at work." After that, associate the two experiences, paying close attention to the different parameters you see them through, such as sub-modalities, representational systems, and physiology. Now associate into the resource state as deeply as possible by using the parameters you found in the last step to intensify the experience. Now you want to widen this attractor to involve the desired context (being at work) by stepping into the location of the desired context, shifting the physiological and cognitive patterns, and transferring the attractors to the desired context. Now you will find yourself more relaxed at work.

Auditory Cues Elicitation

To build and maintain rapport with people whose primary representation system is auditory, observe, listen for and match the following cues:

• They move their eyes horizontally when accessing mental data.

• Breathe from the center of the chest in a rhythmic and stable way.

• Use auditory predicates, such as:

Sound, Hear, Speak, Tell, Listen, Silence, Dialogue, Pitch, Volume, Loud, Quiet, Quote, Bang, Static, Nag, Tune, Listen, Amplify, Give me your ear, Tune in, Tune out, Rings a bell, On another note, Make music, Clear as a bell, Earful, Loud and clear, State your purpose, Unheard of, Utterly, Well informed, Word for word.

• They would frequently demonstrate excellent verbal communication and articulation abilities.

• Tend to point their ear in the direction of the person talking to them, so as to not look at them directly.

• They are typically of medium body build.

Auditory Rep System Development

Source: Robert Dilts

Improve your auditory reflex system in order to better perceive sound, its meanings, and subtleties. This can enhance your modeling and communication skills. You can also practice this strategy with a recording, but be sure to record your own voice as well. To make it even more useful, listen to your recorded voice a few times to get used to it.

1. Pay attention to a sound. Look for a continuous or recurring sound in your surroundings. Listen to it carefully for about ten seconds.

2. Recreate the sound. Using your voice, reproduce that sound as closely as possible. If it is a sound that you can't imitate very well, then imitate any aspect of it that you can. For example, rhythm, warble, grittiness, and any other sub-modality of the sound.

3. Compare: Try this with a partner. Compare how you reproduce the sound.

4. Internal Representations: Ask your partner what internal representations were used and in what ways they feel their voice resembles or does not resemble the sound. Give the same information to your partner.

5. Rating for Sub-modality: Take a look at the list of sub-modalities. Listen to the sound with each of these in mind, but filter for each sub-modality, one at a time. Can you add any of the sub-modalities to your imitation of the sound? As you do this, compare with your partner where you feel the sound belongs in the range of each sub-modality, on a scale of zero to ten, with zero being "not at all" and ten being the highest level, or 100%. Include in your discussion what you used as a reference to rate the sub-modality. For example, take volume. Louder or quieter than what? Consider grittiness. Grittier than James Brown's voice, or smoother than Enya's?

6. Recreate the sound once more. Notice any improvements in your awareness that have improved. What sub-modalities had the biggest effect on your discernment? Compared with your partner.

The Big Book of NLP

Autobiography

Build a deep self-acceptance with this hypnotic script by experiencing it through multiple perspectives and sensory channels. After learning the original concept for this script from Leslie Cameron Bandler, I have created a special version for this book. Read the script below out loud to yourself, allowing enough time to complete the steps and to fully participate in the exercise. Recommendation: try reading the entire script aloud and recording it.Then, listen to it before you go to bed. If you prefer to hear someone else's voice, you might ask a trustworthy friend to read it aloud to you.

One of the most common questions about self-hypnosis scripts is "How many times do I need to go through the script?" The answer is very simple—as many times as it takes to see results. This is a very powerful pattern, however, and I suggest that you work on it once only, thoroughly, and then let it be for a few weeks. Write in your journal about new insights and other life improvements you encounter during that time.

The power of self-hypnosis is not in the words you say in the script, but in the images your mind keeps on producing after the script has long been forgotten.

The Script

"Let's begin by finding a nice warm position in which you can lie down or sit in a comfortable, yet soothing, way. While you adjust your posture to make yourself even more comfortable, maybe you can even take a few deep breaths, slowly and tenderly, and allow yourself to become more and more relaxed.

You are doing this exercise to enjoy and feel better about yourself, not to fulfill other people's wishes. These twelve minutes are for you and only you and only you deserve your next twelve minutes of re-la-x-a-tion.

And some people believe that in doing twelve minutes of Neuro Linguistic Programming, they are not allowed to move, but not you. You can move, you can stretch, and you can keep adjusting the way your body can REST to make you FEEL MORE COMFORTABLE, EVEN MORE RELAXED.

More thoughts that are coming your way are respectful of your wish to stay calm and relaxed, and they pass by as you guarantee you'll get back to them later.

A bit later, after you experience the greater appreciation and acceptance your loved ones have for you. Even when you can't really see it or hear it, just knowingness and it's there.

And while you can imagine or picture to yourself what kind of unconditional love you can create an image of someone who loves you as you are. It can be a relative, your father or mother, a brother, a sister, your spouse, a friend from the past or the present, someone you know or even someone who died a long time ago. If you cannot imagine someone close, allow any memory to come to you of anyone who helped you in some way in some day which has left you with a feeling of being appreciated and worthy of love.

Take a few minutes, let your mind scan your memories, finding an image. You can continue enjoying the sense that comes from allowing scanning that enhances the relaxation that some parts of your body have begun to experience. Place aside the image that you found, to let it rest off to the side for a little while, knowing that we'll return to it soon enough.

Now, as you feel some increase in your natural wish to close your eyes, you can also let your shoulders feel their natural weight; feeling your breath as it finds a restfully deep and slower arc...and as you experience a moment, you can almost hear the serenity within your mind.

And as you do, imagine a wide screen, like in the movies, a big white screen spread in front of you, and on that screen you can see an image, a movie, of you as you sit at an old wooden desk, writing your autobiography.

And you can choose whether you are using a pen or a pencil, maybe even a feather with blue ink, maybe you're typing your autobiography on a computer or on a typewriter... but you see yourself there writing your autobiography with the enthusiasm of telling your life story to the world.

The story of your life is being written by you. And that image of you shows the calm, the relaxing, as you enjoy discovering the hidden treasures in your life, the legacy that you will leave behind, the lessons you have learned, the good and varied experiences that have formed who you are today.

And you can also choose other details in the image of yourself sitting at that desk writing your autobiography.

You can choose the colors of the room, the comfortable temperature, that comfort and ease, as the surface you are on presses up to support you in space. You may even have a glimpse of the words that you see yourself writing, good words, and as you focus on that image, you might want to imagine yourself really sitting there, you, yourself, moving your fingers writing your autobiography.

And you can begin to get a sense of someone, just like in childhood, when someone who loves you dearly enters the door and you just know for sure who that person is. The same feeling can come to you now as you allow the image of that person to come to you and...

As you are writing your autobiography and you look at the other corner of the room, you notice someone standing there, on the other side of the glass door.

You get that feeling again, that this is the person you thought about moments ago. The person who loves you dearly and who accepts you just as you are.

And you can notice that the person who loves you is looking at you sitting at that desk writing your autobiography, and right then and there you choose to include this person in your book of life.

As you experience this inspiration, you can now describe this person and write about this person, about how wonderful and precious the unconditional love and affection are that you feel around that person, about how you cherish the time you had together.

Taking as much time as you need and want, you are allowed to remain in a deep relaxed state of mind and body and now…

…as you think about you, and give yourself a few moments dissociating yourself from the image, thinking about you sitting at a desk writing your autobiography, seeing yourself in that image. Seeing from a point on the side of the room, from where the loving person is standing. Imagining what would it be like standing there next to that person, looking from behind a glass window, looking at you writing there at that desk…as you, standing on the outside, with the person who loves you, unconditionally, as both of you are looking at an image of you writing your autobiography, sitting there in the room…while slowly and surely you can experiment further with that feeling, stepping over and entering into the body and mind of the loving person who is standing right next to you, while you are both looking at the person inside who's writing his autobiography, you and your autobiography, at a desk…

In becoming that loving person you can begin to discover the pleasant feeling of that love, and the expanding sense of the world in that room from their eyes, feeling a special appreciation, a certain respect and that kind of unconditional love that person feels and offers you…

And can you imagine what it would be like, being that person for a little while, to know what it is like thinking lovingly and dearly about you, how it is all about you and your life right now, loving you as you really are, respecting you, appreciating you, enjoying how unique you are.

The Big Book of NLP

Experiencing life through their eyes, you can have a sense of you through their eyes, through their full acceptance and hope and wishes for you. You can even allow those feelings to be named, as the words occur to you to name those loving feelings, taking all the time you need for a good word to emerge, to name those feelings.

As you let it come to you, with the time and space for that, you can simply savor the appreciation and love that you are getting to know so well.

So well that you find yourself carrying them with you as you again stand beside that person, both of you looking at you writing your autobiography at the desk inside the room…

…and you begin to drift back through the glass window, back into your body, into you who is writing, able to write all about this experience, inspired to add it to your book of life, thinking about sharing this with the world, this complete love and appreciation, this joy you increasingly can take in your unique, specialness.

This joy of fully understanding yourself, appreciating yourself, actually loving yourself more and more in this new way.

As you step back into yourself, into the you who is writing your autobiography, you actually experience holding the pen or pencil or typing, and letting the writing flow through you with complete freedom and ease.

This way, all your experience pours from you into this book, so that you richly describe your new feelings, your memories of knowing complete love through this other person, your glimpse of the future with such full joy in your unique being, writing about imaginary memories of this future as real life experiences, real events with your unconscious mind guiding you through them, guiding you with those rich feelings of respect for yourself, rich feelings of truly accepting yourself, this knowing that you brought along with you, that makes room for your greatness in all senses.

In these moments a year's worth of writing has poured out, so that as you finish, you can enjoy softly, gently closing your eyes, with your breathing deep and deeper, slow and slower, and with this satisfaction sending a hint of a smile to your lips.

Now, as you begin counting up toward enjoying feeling fully refreshed and alert, you stretch your arms forward as you count up to five when you will fully awaken, opening and closing your hands, moving your head and stretching your neck gently upward, and when you reach number five, opening your eyes for fully refreshed, alertness.

As you finish this experience, notice the changes that you feel in your body and mind right now. How great is your appreciation for yourself in this moment? Take a few moments with… to experience just how important that feeling is… how great it is to use it and make it a permanent part of the life you are living… your life… the life you have described in your continuing autobiography…"

Notes

At the end of the session, give your client a few minutes to rest silently, and then discuss the possible future consequences of the mental change. During the post-session talk, let your client speak most of the time (use silence to encourage speech), and make notes of possible hidden agendas or mental blocks. In the next session, address any such issues without exposing your findings to your client. My personal recommendation is to end the session with the anticipation of seeing small but meaningful differences in their appreciation of themselves and of the attitudes that other people have toward them.

Awakening to Freedom

Source: Richard Clarke

Get into Awakener and Explorer roles, give your partner instructions.

Set up and ask the Why question.

Get the Explorer's reaction to the question.

Repeat step two.

Continue repeating step two.

Switch roles.

Test.

Give and receive support for awakening through personal growth in this dyadic (pair) exercise. Enhance your vision, mission, and spirit through this support for awakening. With your partner in this pattern, you will bring out the best in each other by taking turns in the role of Awakener. Express your integrity and congruence to enhance the Awakener role. Align and connect with your own vision and mission as a catalyst for others to experience their vision and mission. Transcend the old-fashioned style of morality and judgment that neutralizes personal expansion. Instead, maintain your perception of the other person's limitless possibilities and their innocence in doing the best that they knew in their past. This way, you keep the channel of communication open, inspiring them toward fresh insight, resourcefulness, and constructive personal power.

1. Assume the roles of Awakener and Explorer, and give your partner instructions. Start out in the role of Awakener with a partner who is in the role of Explorer. Give your Explorer partner the following instructions: Think about an unproductive "self pattern." What is its basic structure? Notice any unproductive beliefs that are attached to this pattern, such as, "Oh, I have to put on a happy face and pretend I'm confident until the

next big disappointment." This kind of success is for other people, not me. " Think of as many examples of this self-pattern as you can. There are probably many throughout your life. Some of them may be subtle, or comprise a string of many little iterations that turn into a bigger pattern of loss, missed opportunities, or failure. Make sure you understand the consequences of this pattern. How has it affected your life?

Continue with these instructions to your partner: What would it be like to be free of this pattern? What kind of results might you expect to see in the future? On the other hand, what does this pattern do for you? Is it helping you in any way? Be sure to consider any "sneaky" ways that it is helping you, that is, dysfunctional ways. For example, see if it helps you avoid any challenges, fear, or responsibility. Even so, consider any way that it might be helping you manipulate other people or avoid criticism. Does it simply give you a feeling of having a familiar self that you really don't need to be? Now have your Explorer partner share with you, the Awakener, what he or she is discovering. As the Awakener, listen from a state of respectful openness, fully accepting the Explorer.

2. Set up and ask the "Why" question. As the Awakener says to the Explorer (still from a respectful, validating place), "You have the full support of my being to freely explore, because this expands and strengthens you and your meaning in the world." You are completely free to do with this pattern what you will. You are free to continue it, but, as the explorer, you also ask why you would continue such a pattern. "

3. Get the Explorer's reaction to the question. Have the Explorer pay attention to its inner reaction to the question, "Why?" Have the Explorer share any reaction with the Awakener.

4. Repetition of step 2. Repeat the statement and question of the Awakener to the Explorer as in step two. See what response the explorer has this time. Do this from an open-minded space that allows the explorer to have a fresh response each time. Different aspects of your experience are likely to emerge from this, expanding your knowledge of yourself and of your potential.

5. Continue repeating step two. Do step four several more times, at least three times.

6. Switch roles, becoming the Explorer with your partner taking the Awakener role.

The Big Book of NLP

7. Testing In the coming days or weeks, notice some new ways that you experience this pattern, including any ways that you let go of it or innovate. See if you get any better results in life from this new perspective and resourcefulness that comes from these parts being more harmonious and able to exchange knowledge. Have a time set aside to discuss this with your partner in this exercise.

Back to Presence

Getting lost in fantasy worlds or even just zoning out because the internal voice is ruminating non-stop can be harmful if you don't meet the demands of current reality. To counteract this nasty habit, we can use a little bit of willpower and a single direction: "Look around and describe in detail everything you are seeing and hearing and sensing now. As things start to change, notice and describe the changes. " For example, "the curtain is white and long, and it is now moving left and right, and I hear a car in the background and there is a loud shout, and I feel the weight of my body on my right leg and I switch the weight to the left leg."

In addition, you can establish a mental reminder for future reference, such as a visual anchor (a red rubber band on the wrist, or reversing the direction of the wristwatch so it's facing upside down).

The Big Book of NLP

Backtracking

When we are given a lot of information, it is usually helpful to take a moment at the end to just remember the basic points so we can better remember them. This is not a groundbreaking concept. You will see this in most presentations because it is a very effective tool to help people retain the information. Backtracking can also be used to rephrase a received question or command, something like, "If I understood you well, you'd like me to tell you about A and how it relates to B."

Backtracking is also very important in teaching, when the teacher sums up what has been covered in the lesson so the students do not forget the material, especially from the start of the lesson. So, to sum up, backtracking is an effective tool for communicating ideas, by going over the basic points, and rephrasing questions and commands.

Bare Bones Reframing

Origin: John Grinder

1. Identify the behaviors that needs to be changed.

2. Work with the unconscious to develop a dependable involuntary signaling system.

3. Confirm that the desired behaviors are motivated by a positive intentions.

4. Create a set of alternatives that are as good as, if not better than, the original behaviors in terms of achieving the positive intentions.

5. Allow the unconscious to take control of the implementation process.

6. Ecology check.

The Big Book of NLP

Basic Elicitation

We use TOTE for eliciting personal subjective strategies. For example: learning.

1. Establish context: "Consider a time when you learned something quickly and easily."

2. Test: "How do you know when it is time to start learning?"

3. Operate: "What do you do, see, hear and feel - in order to learn?"

4. Test: "How do you know if you have learned it? "

5. Exit: "What tells you that you have fully learned something?"

Watch for eye accessing cues, predicates and calibration cues.

Basic Motivation Strategy

The following strategy demonstrates how the various elements of imagination, expectation, criteria, sub-modalities, and associations can be combined into a simple strategy to help people better inspire and motivate themselves to take actions that will lead them to desired outcomes.

1. Imagine enjoying a key achievement. Imagine that you have achieved one of your greatest dreams in life. Imagine yourself fully enjoying it. Experience the sights, sounds, and feelings of this enjoyment.

2. Enhance and anchor the state as a pleasure motivation state. Amplify the compelling and motivational aspects of this experience. Do this by adjusting sub-modalities such as brightness and size. This is a pleasure motivation state. Anchor it.

3. Future Pace with this state. Carry these feelings into imagining yourself taking steps that will actually move you toward your dream outcome. Trigger your anchor for the pleasure motivation state to enhance this state.

4. Test. In the coming days and weeks, notice if you find it easier to take steps toward this or other dreams or desired outcomes.

The Big Book of NLP

Basic Second Position Modeling

Improve your ability to model excellence. To complete this pattern, you need four people. Designate one to be the Person Being Modeled, another as the Subject who interacts with the person, a Modeler, and an Observer.

1. Have the initial conversation. Have the Subject and the Person Being Modeled converse for about five minutes. Have the Person Being Modeled choose the topic. Have the Modeler model the Person Being Modeled by going into second position, focusing on their most subtle muscle movements.

2. Have the Modeler stand in. Have the Modeler stand in for the Person Being Modeled, and continue the conversation with the Subject as though he or she were the Person Being Modeled.

3. Provide feedback. Have the Person Being Modeled and the Observer give clear feedback and coaching to the Modeler as to how accurately he or she is imitating the Person Being Modeled.

4. Start a new conversation.

Send the Modeler out of the room. Have the Subject and the Person Being Modeled converse about a new subject for about five minutes. The Subject chooses the subject this time.

5. Have the modeler stand in again. Have the Modeler return, and again stand in for the Person Being Modeled, continuing the conversation with the Subject. The Subject tries to cover the same interaction topics in the conversation as much as possible for about five minutes.

6. Provide feedback. Have the Subject, Observer and the Person Being Modeled give the Modeler Step feedback on how well they matched the Person Being Modeled.

7. Test. Over the coming weeks and months, discuss how well the participants have been coming along in learning to model and establish rapport.

Basic Third Position Modeling

Improve your capacity to model by using the third position. This pattern requires three people: The Person Being Modeled and two Modelers.

1. Demonstrate the skill. Have the Person Being Modeled engage in a skill.

2. Gather information for modeling. The Modelers gather information and demonstrations of the skill from the Person Being Modeled while they are in third position. The modelers need to gather any helpful information from various levels, such as physiology, rep systems, language patterns, and meta-programs.

3. Describe the internal state. Have the modelers note what they think the Person Being Modeled is experiencing internally, based on what they have observed and collected.

4. Compare and contrast the models. Have the Modelers compare and contrast their models.

5. Collaborate to describe the skill as a model. Have all three parties collaborate to create a detailed description of the key elements of the skill.

Behavior Appreciation

Identify the behavior.

Anchor the context space.

Access your underlying positive motivation.

Part Space.

Test.

Improve your performance and self-care by developing a positive approach to personal development. This pattern uses anchors to find the positive intention (the underlying positive outcome-seeking pattern) underlying the negative behavior. For example, if you burst into tears at times, you have better options than feeling inferior. Instead, this positive approach might help you decide to accept your need to release an emotional burden and might help you find ways to live without unnecessary stress.

1. Recognize the ineffective behavior. It may be primarily a feeling, a thought pattern, or physical actions. Include the context in which you carry out the behavior.

2. Establish the context space.

a. Where in your visual field or body does this experience seem to belong? Imagine that this spot is a location that you can step into, and that when you step into it, you will see the location around you where the behavior has occurred. This spot now represents the behavior and its context, like a location or a space where you can stand in your imagination. We'll call this the "context space."

The Big Book of NLP

b. Step into this space, imagining that it is the location where the behavior takes place. Begin by thinking of the behavior in its context. Recall this as vividly as possible. Fix the behavior and its context to this location.

3. Access your underlying positive motivation. Even the most negative or unwanted behaviors actually have a positive underlying purpose. Think of the negative behavior that you selected as coming from a part that has a positive underlying motivation. This dramatic change of frame can liberate your creativity and motivation.However, set aside your first ideas as to these underlying motives. Get into the "mind" of the part that is responsible for the behavior. This can provide insights that will make this pattern more powerful.

4. Part space:

a. Consider the possibility of a space dedicated solely to the role; a space that excludes the behavior and its context.We will call this the "part space." Step out of the context space, taking this part with you to the part space. You might want to visualize this space as being next to the context space. Remember to leave the behavior and context behind. This leaves you with the part dissociated from the context, so that you may have easier access to its underlying motives.

b. Now you will clarify the part's motives with questions. At times, speak as if you are the part, speaking in first person. This will help you get an associated experience of the part's motives. When referring to the negative behavior, point to the previous (contextual) spot anchor as if it were an actual physical location. This helps you dissociate from the prior behavior.

"What do I really want to get out of what I have been doing (referring to the negative behavior)?"

Nota bene: the past perfect tense of "had been doing" helps you mentally distance yourself from the behavior by making it seem distant in the past and implies that you have already changed.

"How do I feel when that desired outcome does or does not occur?"

"When I get the desired outcome, what do I want to do with it?"

"When I get the undesirable parts of the outcome, how do I react to them?"

Typical reactions include: blaming others, rationalization, spacing out or ignoring it, manipulating others to escape the consequences, isolating, self-soothing such as comfort food, distractions, etc. Continue asking questions such as these until you feel that you have brought out responses that are valuable to you and your situation.

c. Imagine yourself in the future, looking back upon the situation from a meta-state of peace, fully able to enjoy the positive outcomes.

5. Test. In the coming days and weeks, notice any changes in your behavior when this kind of situation arises. Observe any ways that you are more resourceful or have more options.

The Big Book of NLP

Belief Chaining

Shift a belief from a potential unresourceful belief to a resourceful one.

1. Construct the somatic syntax.

a. Choose a limiting belief and a helpful alternative belief.

b. Identify the steps that exist between the two extremes of belief.

c. Retrace your steps from the limiting belief state to the resourceful belief state.

Pay attention to the changes in kinesthetic sensations and body language that you experience from step to step.

2. Use verbal reframes to assist with the shift. Try several verbal reframes that help make the shift between these beliefs. Notice which ones have the most positive impact on giving you a constructive and resourceful perspective.

3. Include reframes in each step. Walk through the belief change steps, and decide which reframe is most useful at each step.

4. Experiment with the shift. Walk through the steps several times, experiencing the kinesthetics and belief frame that you have associated with each step. Continue until you feel that the transition is easy and smooth.

5. Test. Over the coming days and weeks, notice any increased ease you experience in flexible thinking and any increase in your use of positive frames and resourcefulness in your beliefs about any challenges that you experience.

Belief Lines Elicitation

Source: Tad James

1. Initiate a downtime state.

2. Identify the elements of the dichotomy meta-program (black-or-white; if you haven't mastered the meta-programs yet, refer to the Personality Profiling with NLP book for details).

3. Determine the differences between the containment/storage locations of:

A well-accepted notion;

A concept that is surrounded by doubt or uncertainty by definition;

A notion that is firmly disbelieved;

A belief that was once true but is no longer so.

4. Eco-check.

5. Enter the timeline. Move forward 15 years into the future. Repeat step 2 for that period.

6. Move back on the timeline to the present, then move backward 15 years into the past, and repeat step 2 for that period.

7. Break state.

8. Modify the containment/storage location of an undesirable belief and notice the corresponding change in the inherent strength of the belief.

9. For additional impact, delete the corresponding limiting decision on the timeline by making corrections in each period.

Bi-Lateral

Psychological time is key to attention, frustration, and cooperation in healing practice. You can create a more compelling and time-compressed experience by learning to emphasize (punch up) certain words as you speak. Practice this while you monitor how intensely people hang onto your words as you speak. You may need to desensitize yourself to the experience of people paying intense attention to what you say and leaving room for you to say it. You may also find that they want to get in sync and contribute ideas along the same line. Watch for a slight forward lean or head forward posture, less blinking, and a slightly wide-eyed quality in the person you're communicating with.

As you speak, slightly alternate your foot pressure on key words that deserve emphasis. This will alter your state as you speak. Try saying this sentence, emphasizing the key words marked with an asterisk (*) and shifting to the specified left or right foot.

For the first (left) key word, put pressure (right) on your left (left) foot, and for the second (right) key word, put pressure (left) on your right (right)."

This may be awkward at first, but it can become automatic with practice. Notice that you can have several words in a row that are not emphasized, but they will not be lost on people. In fact, people can concentrate and digest what you say more easily when you minimize key words. You might not want to make this a habit for presenting, but this practice can change how you experience presenting. In actual presentations, however, you should consider gestures, shifting your weight, and position changes that create bi-laterality (side-changing) during much of your presentation.

Binary Code of Forgetfulness

Source: Erickson Institute

This is a transcript of an actual hypnotherapy session. You can try it out as is, as well as learn from it and integrate it into your hypnotic work. It works like the binary code of computers, 1's and 0's, just that when we use the 0's we actually use minus 1. Confusing? Don't worry, it will become more so (until I explain a little secret).

"You see, because it does make all the difference in the world when you discover, that even when suddenly all kinds of things that you simply could remember simply to remember instead of forget to remember when you wanted to remember to forget what those things were not! It's easy to understand when you learn the Binary Code of Forgetfulness. Think for a moment of a situation in your past that would be useful for you to forget, maybe an event that left you with a bad stream of feelings and nasty thought patterns. There's a neurological process that holds the key, I am certain, and we call it the Forget Key.

You can use that key when you know that just because, if you're trying to remember something right now, or even better, if you just stop and you start to think about that specific situation (whichever that is) in which you had that feeling, then, you must know, just before that specific situation started, you didn't even have that feeling, yet! So how come you could remember to remember that feeling long after the event has dissolved into the past, into that place on your timeline that is almost always hidden? At least, you can hope because otherwise you'd be confused whether it is your past or your future lying there in front of who you are, if you are that person.

Now, while all of the above sounds, or being read, very confusing, it is not confusing that much when you consider all these terms, forgetting, remembering and things that are not yet what you need them in order to remember them as you do remember. Confusion, however, and this confusion is obviously included, is the golden root to a deeper and long lasting understanding of that very useful skill... Now, I don't know if you are already aware of it or just about to be aware of it, but if you think about WHERE you WEREin that situation, but instead, if you were (decided maybe) to forget to remember what it actually was and instead of that thing, how would you do like to feel in that situation? Maybe all of a sudden, you can now remember what is that you wanted to remember instead of what it was that you couldn't forget! In fact, I believe it is the other way not-around. If you want to get more confused and blame me for that confusion, go ahead, because we're going to clear it all up for you. Very clean, even cleaner than what it wasn't just before.Think! If you do not remember what it IS that you don't want to remember, then isn't it clear that you're remembering to forget what it is that you shouldn't, or on the other end, it is very clear, that, what was left is for you to remember what it is that you want to feel exactly when you want to feel it. Isn't it not what I'm not saying? It gets better, just now:

Because now, with that terrible feeling that you didn't have, well, you know, that you WON'T have but you didn't want to have, that you used to have until you simply couldn't remember what it was, now, because if you did remember, it couldn't be logical, because if you remember what it is that you want to feel, then you will! How could you remember what it is that you couldn't remember not to forget to remember anyhow? Now, before we move on, what would you rather feel in that situation, yet not again?

Because if you think about it, can you remember what it is you feel about anything, any time or any way, if you know you'd rather feel good or better, because you seethere are times when you remember to feel bad, then you could forget to remember not to forget to remember any more about this idea. And you do need to do just that, because you already remember far too much so just forget about it! Listen, if instead of doing what it is that you weren't doing anymore because you remembered to forget about it, haven't you had to do something else? Instead of? And instead of what it is not, if you, for example, looked right at what is left, then it would not matter to you, because what is right (point to his right arm) and that is my right (point towards your right arm) but my right is on YOUR left. You see, it means that you would have to take the whole thing and turn it around from the inside out all the way through the middle, pull it up and throw it back down, and once you choose to do something new, it will grow into a new pattern.

And it can sound confusing, but isn't it right? What's left for you is to be able to take the right thing and put it under the right perspective, because if you already have an idea that you don't want, then there's no reason to not remember to forget it! And in the future, when it is time to remember, then just remember to feel GOOD! How easier could we even make it? This one will be hard to test, because we'd have to remind you of what you forgot. But you could put the memory in an envelope and mail it to yourself if you really want to test this! Just don't try to bring up the memory right after the session."

Now here's a step-by-step guide. Let's go over the code and then demonstrate how to make it work for you:

Plus 1 - to remember

Minus 1 - to forget

Plus 1 - not to forget (= remember)

Minus 1 - not to remember (= forget)

Plus 1 - remember to remember (= remember)

Minus 1 - remember to forget (= forget)

Plus 1 - forget to forget (= remember)

Minus 1 - forget not to forget (= forget)

Plus 1 - you know (= remember or the following is true)

Minus 1 - But instead (= forget or cancel the previous)

And so on. It's very easy to understand. If you want them to hold onto the piece of information, the conclusion, or the suggestion you're giving them, you're ending your code with a sum of Plus 1 (or more). If you'd like their minds to forget a behavior, a pattern of thought, or other useful-to-forget things, you conclude at Minus 1 (or less).

1. Follow this example. Observe how we do the math. First, we'll provide the text, and then we'll break it down.

"You see, because it does make all the difference in the world when you discover, that even when suddenly all kinds of things that you simply could remember simply to remember instead of forget to remember when you wanted to remember to forget what those things were not! It's easy to understand when you learn the Binary Code of Forgetfulness."

you simply could remember - Plus 1

simply to remember - Plus 1

forget to remember - Minus 1

remember to forget - Minus 1

what those things were not! - Minus 1

Sum = Minus 1

I used to use my thumbs as indicators–right thumb in the Plus 1 and left thumb in the Minus 1. When one of them is up, I would know that the equation is not balanced and towards which end it influences the listener–if my right thumb was the only thumb up, it meant "remember," when the left was, it meant "forget" and when both were, it meant balance. You end your Binary Code hypnotic suggestion with a balance when you just want to send the person into a very deep TDS.

2. Try computing it yourself. Now, you can try it yourself. Here's another passage from the first part of the lesson, to see if you can mark down the binary code from it:"Now, before we move on, what would you rather feel in that situation, yet not again? Because if you think about it, can you remember what it is you feel about anything, any time or any way–if you know you'd rather feel good or better, because you see there are times when you remember to feel bad, then you could forget to remember not to forget to remember any more about this idea. And you do need to do just that, because you already remember far too much, so just forget about it!"

Plus 1, Minus 1 = 0 (balanced)

Plus 1, Minus 1, Plus 1 = Plus 1 (= remember)

Minus 1, Minus 1, Minus 1 = nonsense, unless you want them to never forget how annoying you can be. There are almost no rules in the Binary Code of Forgetfulness. The only thing to keep in mind is that you should have a balanced set of "Plus 1 and Minus 1" statements, and eventually be either Plus 1 or Minus 1 at the end of it, or at least balanced. That means, that going for 10 times of Minus 1 will not create the effect you would like. You have to create the illusion of balance so their minds won't be overly protective and cancel everything you said. Once there are almost the same number of Plus 1 statements and Minus 1 statements, it would be extremely hard and complex for anyone to keep track of it. Say Minus 1 ten times and only once say Plus 1 and it's pretty obvious what you're trying to do. That's the ultimate power of this method. We use it in therapy for so many things, from pain relief to trauma resolution and much more.

3. Practice this in the field. Try this with clients or friends, getting good at keeping score. It does not require a complicated approach to be effective.

4. Test. See how well the method works in managing the material that your clients are dealing with. Try to practice inducing both forgetting and remembering.

Boundaries Installation

Select a pattern reflecting weak boundaries.

Create a boundary-affirming imaginary space.

Imagine the force field.

See yourself in second position from a highly supportive perspective.

Amplify your uniqueness in first position, and future pace this state.

Elicit creative expressions of your uniqueness and boundaries by testing them with a boundary violating fantasy person.

Future pace. Test.

Personal boundaries are the borders that we maintain between what is acceptable and what is not in how we are treated. Healthy boundaries are those that affirm us but are flexible enough to allow meaningful interaction with others and are therefore considered healthy boundaries. Boundary crossings occur when someone does not respect our dignity, power, and well-being. A comment or joke that is sexist but not directly insulting can be considered a subtle boundary crossing.

People who have weak boundaries may take on others' problems. It happens when a person thinks he or she is a good friend, while in reality they let themselves get overwhelmed and absorbed with another person's emotions and problems. A good friend should be there to stay strong for you, stay sensitive yet unaffected, so that they can pull you up and support you. This does not happen if that "good" friend is taking part in feeling the pain or assuming responsibility for alleviating it.

People with weak boundaries become victims of themselves, and by becoming miserable for other people's problems, they actually push them away. When those others are dependent or destructive, the person with poor boundaries is called a co-dependent.

These people lose themselves in harmful patterns. Some of them are even consciously aware of that habitual self-sabotage. They may not be able to act in their own interest until they get their partner to agree with them or stop having bad (manipulative) feelings about it. They tend to have perceptual position distortions in which they have other people's attitudes and thoughts mixed in with their own. They wonder why their relationship is not getting better when they are working so hard, without fully considering that they are the only ones working on the relationship. People with overly rigid or extended boundaries may place unreasonable demands on others to comply with excessive expectations. This pattern helps people define and strengthen boundaries that are too weak or unclear.

1. Select a pattern reflecting weak boundaries. Think about the information on poor boundaries and codependency. Find a pattern in your life that bears some resemblance to at least one of the elements, or something else that shows weak boundaries.

2. Create a boundary-affirming imaginary space. Imagine a physical space around your body that extends out about two feet. Fill that space with your boundary-affirming and boundary-enforcing qualities such as attitudes and personality characteristics. Consider qualities such as assertiveness, perceptiveness, commitment, honesty, the ability to read others, and so forth. Be sure that these are not generic; they must be qualities that are unique to you.

What is the quality of assertiveness that comes from you?

What is positive about it?

Include only the positive parts of your imaginary space. If any of those qualities seem weak, don't allow that to be relevant in placing them in your imaginary space. Take the collective sense of these qualities and anchor them.

3. Imagine the force field. Imagine that your boundary space is surrounded by a force field that is getting so strong that nothing can penetrate it unless you allow it. It defines you as being a unique entity, separate from others in the sense of being an individual capable of

interacting and benefiting from interaction. Be sure to sense this from the first perceptual position (first person). Anchor this strong, "boundary" sensation.

4. See yourself in the second position from a highly supportive perspective. Move to the second perceptual position. Imagine that you are seeing yourself through the eyes of a person who is very supportive of your boundaries and thinks the world of you, even if you need to invent that person for this pattern.

Discover what it's like for you as this understanding person to express strong approval for you as a unique individual and for your boundaries.

Take a little time to clearly express this in a way that is fully connected and full of feelings. Do whatever you need to do in order to make this a powerful, valid resource.

5. Emphasize your uniqueness in first place, and set the pace for the future. From first position, amplify and experience the validity and power of all that makes you a unique, "boundaried" individual. Future Pace: this state as a way of being in the world and a way of navigating life.

6. Elicit creative expressions of your uniqueness and boundaries by testing them with a boundary-violating fantasy person. Imagine experiencing someone who is not respectful of your boundaries in some way. Allow your state of unique self and good boundaries to elicit creative responses from you.

You can stop the fantasy to adjust your response, or loop it and try various responses each time through. Be sure not to get caught in the trap of trying to change the other person or convincing them of anything. If they are manipulative, they will not respond to that in a constructive manner.

7. Future Pace. Imagine moving into the future with your healthy boundaries and unique identity. Allow imaginary scenarios to come up as you enjoy projecting this state into the future.

8. Test. In the coming days and weeks, notice any ways that you express your uniqueness despite demands from others that would turn you away from your unique self-expression

or meet your needs in your own self-affirming way that connects you with supportive people and valuable resources.

Notice any ways that you defend and enhance your boundaries, including maintaining your own thoughts independently from others' thoughts and attitudes.

Borrowed Wisdom

Struggling in the present to deal with a recent traumatic event or emotional distress can feel like it's never going to change. In this pattern, we use the wisdom of old age and recruit the capabilities of the future self to bring relief to the present.

1. Think about a recent situation or incident in which you had an emotional reaction and are still feeling pain, anger, or guilt.Create a visual symbol (VS1) to represent this feeling. Give it a dark color (suggestion: make it a color you don't particularly enjoy or like).

2. Initiate a state of downtime.

3. Enter your timeline, stretching forward and backward, with the future ahead of you in the distance.

4. Dissociate from the situation. 5. Float above your timeline for a few moments, and look at the stressful incident from above (4th perceptual position). Notice the interaction between the people involved and how it affects the ecology of your present.

5. Shrink the representation image of that situation and transform it into the symbol from step 1.

6. Look ahead on your timeline and choose a date that is at least 10 to 15 years from now.Ignite your ride on the timeline and fast forward to that day.

7. Associate with your future self on that date in the future, and turn around the timeline so that your past is in front of you. Now you're looking at the present day from the vantage point of the future, associated with your future self.

8. Given it's been more than a decade after that situation occurred, you, as the future self, have already figured out how to deal with that stressful event and reconciled your emotional distress, anger, or guilty conscience. At that moment in time, all is well and there are no residues or hard feelings in that moment.

9. As you experience this bliss and peace of mind, create a visual symbol (VS2) to represent that feeling. Give it a bright and delightful color (suggestion: select a color that you really like and makes you happy).

10. Place VS1 in your right hand's palm.Keep your hand open.

11. Use your left hand to hold VS2.

12. Take a deep breath, look towards the past (towards the current day), and cover your right hand with your left hand, combining the two symbols.

13. Still in the associated state, as your future self, tell your present self (dissociated, as in step 4), that soon enough the essential learning from that event is going to overtake the hurt feelings. Nothing lasts forever.

14. Dissociate Keep holding the symbols together, and float above the timeline. Ride the timeline forward back to the present day. Return to your present self and flip the timeline so that the future is in front of you and the past is far behind you.

15. From the present vantage point, shout a thank you to your future self, open your hand and look at the combined two symbols. The brightness and lifelike color of the second symbol outshine the dullness of the first one.

16. Take a deep breath and exit the timeline.

17. Test Think about the original event again. How do you feel about the near future?

Breaking Limiting Associations

Source: Richard Bandler, Robert Dilts, and Steve Andreas

Select a problem and identify its typical context.

Anchor to the floor.

Anchor a resource state.

Transfer the resource state to the problem spot.

Add stimuli while returning to the resource position.

Figure-eight your eyes through the rep system positions while focusing on the problem pattern.

Break state. Notice any resourcefulness in your state or ideas. Run an ecology check.

Test.

One of the most important ways to get out of stuck thought patterns is to develop a better-articulated sense of how our minds work. That is, to develop a more subtle and detailed recognition of our thoughts and rep systems and how they form interlocking patterns. As you know, much of NLP is about unlocking these patterns to allow for more flexibility.

The Breaking Limiting Associations pattern is a very rapid pattern, once you learn to work with it. If you and your client have determined in advance a well-formed outcome and the problematic thinking patterns that disturb the achievement of this outcome, you only need to work one-by-one through them using this pattern. In addition, this pattern is powerful, mostly because of its use of the body. Your client has to move around, which involves more senses.

The more your client is engaged in the process of change, the better and longer-lasting results that process will bring. When you work with patterns that involve your client moving around and being active, it is best if you explain the steps ahead of time. For this pattern, for example, it would serve you well to decide ahead of time where the anchors on the floor should be.

Walk your client through it before using the pattern. It will make everything go smoother. Also, remember that when you use active patterns, that is, patterns that involve physical action by your client, speak slower. Do not rush it, because your client needs to organize and re-organize thoughts and physiological movements, and being in a trance, they need more time than normal awake states. This is also not the kind of pattern you want to use right in the first session you have with a client. Establish some trust first.

Work on other issues for the first session if this one is the best choice for a specific issue your client has presented. The reason is that this pattern may cause automatic and random breaks of state for your client.

Physical movement requires attention. That's also the reason you should have trust with your client, and more than that, explain the steps ahead of time. It makes the need to move from one spot to another less "unknown" and more "comfortable" and logical.

1. Select a problem that tends to occur in a particular environment or situation. Think about what, in the context, leads to the behavior.

Make note of factors such as time of day and the kinds of people or pressures that are involved.

2. Anchor to the floor. Get into the problem state and anchor it to a spot on the floor.

Take a little time to get to know the state and its sub-modalities.

The Big Book of NLP

3. Anchor a resource state. Determine what resource state would make it easy to eliminate the problem. Pick another spot on the floor, and imagine stepping into the state there. Anchor the resource state to that spot. Notice the details of that state.

4. Transfer the resource state to the problem spot.

Move back to the problem anchor spot, but access the resource state and amplify it. Hold the image of the problem pattern while fostering the physiology of the resource state.

5. Return to the resource position and add stimuli. Tap your right foot.

Move your left finger to your chin.

Look up and to the right while repeating, "Hmmm," as though you were having a deep thought. At the same time, step back into the resource anchor spot.

6. Figure-eight your eyes through the rep system positions while focusing on the problem pattern.

As you think about the problem, focus on each rep system as you move your eyes in each corresponding rep system direction in a sideways figure-eight pattern (like the infinity symbol).

7. Break state. Take note of any resourcefulness in your situation or ideas.

Run an ecology check. Break state.

Observe any changes in how you experience the problem. Look for fresh ideas or a more resourceful state. Ask yourself if there are any objections to experiencing the problem from this more resourceful place, or dropping the problem for more successful behavior.

Breath Pacing

Pacing means matching a person's interactions with reality and, therefore, meeting the other person from within their mental map of the world. It encourages rapport and mutual understanding. Breathing in sync with a client's rhythm is one of the most effective and subtle ways of adapting to their world. Matching one's breath is a powerful sensation because it is such a fundamental pattern of existence. When placed on their mother's breast, babies immediately do this. During trance work, it's critical to match your voice to your client's breathing patterns. In hypnotic communication, this is a basic rule to follow. Breathing patterns may need to be matched in a crossover form in some circumstances. When it comes to picking up on your female client's breathing patterns, you should, of course, avoid staring at her breasts. Perimeter vision and minor motions in the shoulders and waist can be used to detect breathing patterns. It's usually best to make subtle comparisons.

This practice of verbal pace can be done in small groups or pairs.

1. Person A and Person B stand or sit back to back so that their entire backs are in contact with each other and they can feel each other's breathing as well as the vibrations produced by speaking. Being back-to-back eliminates visual cues and requires you to focus on your hearing.

2. If a Person C is available, that Person C will monitor and provide input on the pacing efficiency.

3. Person A says something—a single short line works effectively in this situation. It may be something like, "My name is Joe, and I'm a little nervous about doing something like this."

4. It is Person B's responsibility to repeat Person A's remark so that Person A is satisfied that Person B has their speaking style correctly paced.

5. Repeat this 5 times before going on to practice with someone else.

6. Both Person A and Person C can advise Person B on how to improve.

7. Then, Person A and Person B face each other, with some distance apart.

8. Person B should now practice matching Person A's breathing patterns by noticing visual cues.

Once you're aware of unique speech patterns, you can mentally rehearse matching people throughout everyday discussions, because this mental rehearsal activates your vocal cords and any other important speech structures within your body. In practice, you will be pacing both the representation systems and breathing patterns.

Burn-Out Redemption

Source: Erickson Institute

This is a timeline-based pattern, designed to help you recover from physical and emotional burnout. When all you feel is fatigue, exhaustion, and boredom with your daily life, it is a result of a long struggle that ended with you falling on your face and unable to get back up.

Why did it happen? The short answer is that you simply behaved, consistently and without awareness, in violation of your highest values. The inverse is the cure, or should we say redemption.

1. As hard as it may seem, take one day off and devote it to recalibrating your values and life's mission. No distractions, no commitments, no appointments. You can make the process more enjoyable by traveling to the seaside or your favorite spot in nature.

2. Work through and complete the Values Hierarchy Identification pattern. Do not rush it. Take it seriously and methodically.

3. When you're ready to redeem yourself, enter your timeline, front to back, and float above it, facing the future.

4. Move forward in time to the near future, either a month from now or up to one year from now.

5. Turn around at that point and look towards the present and its extension into the past.

6. Create a symbol to represent the present moment (the "now" in real time).

7. Ask yourself, "Up to that point in time (point towards the symbol), how was I living outside my highest values?"

8. As the memories and visual representations of your past actions come towards you, acknowledge your responsibility without placing blame by simply saying "I see that" or "I can see what happened" or "I know I thought it was a good idea at the time," and let the representation pass you by.

9. Spend as much time as you need processing the stream of memories and visuals, and when the stream slows down, lift your right hand and signal for it to stop.

10. Turn around on your timeline, now facing the future again, and float back to the present (the "now" in real time).

11. Break state. You may also take a real break and get some rest before completing the next steps.

12. Look at the list of your highest values and ask, "How am I going to make sure I am living inside my highest values?" What are the choices I have to make to express these values in reality, starting from now towards the future? "

13. As you think of new and exciting ideas for future choices of behavior, anchor that moment in time. Several of these new choices should be timed to coincide with events or situations that are likely to occur in the coming week or month.

14. Test: How do you feel about your life now that you've been redeemed?

You can enhance the results even further by establishing new well-formed desired outcomes or simply reviewing the ones you had before and adjusting them according to your highest values. Refer to the Well-Defined Outcome pattern for more details.

Calibration

Improve your ability to observe and respond to the physiological and behavioral cues of others. "Calibration" involves linking behavioral cues to internal cognitive and emotional responses.

1. Understanding:

Ask your partner to think of some concept that she or he feels she or he knows and understands.

2. Observe:

Observe your partner's physiology closely (as if you were Sherlock Holmes for a moment). Watch your partner's eye movements, facial expressions, hand movements, etc.

3. Confusion:

Then ask your partner to think of something that is confusing and unclear. Once again, watch your partner's eyes and features carefully.

4. Observe:

Notice what is different now. Observe changes in appearance and patterns of behavior.

5. Pick:

Now ask your partner to pick either concept and think about it again.

6. Observe:

Observe your partner's features. Look for changes in appearance or behavior that match the understanding or confusion states that your partner has shown you.

7. Guess:

Guess whether your partner chose the understanding or confusion concept? Check with your partner to see if you were correct.

8. More:

Ask your partner to think of other concepts that she or he understands or finds confusing, and see if you can guess which category they fall into. Confirm your guess by checking with your partner.

9. Describe and observe.

Explain a concept to your partner. By observing his or her features, you can determine whether your partner has understood the concept. See if you can determine the moment they understand your concept.

Careful Autosuggestion

Autosuggestions that negate current reality (objectivism) are delusions and will be rejected fiercely by the unconscious. Émile Coué started the self-help movement of repeating conscious autosuggestions in the hopes of influencing the unconscious mind. Plenty of research proves it can backfire. In fact, you do not even need other people's research; try it on your own.

If you're overweight, repeatedly say to yourself "I am thin." It may make you feel better for a short moment, but soon enough, a little nasty voice at the back of your head sniffs and says, "yeah, right, look at you... You look like you ate a thin person! But you aren't thin, that belly fat, bleh... " (exact quote from a recent client, printed with her permission).

Autosuggestions can be accepted by the unconscious mind only if they affirm objective reality. If you're fat, you ought to say, "I am fat!" For example, to make it effective for the purpose of losing weight, you can affirm: "I am currently fat, and as long as I choose to drink water instead of Coca-Cola, I am helping my body to eliminate unnecessary fat."

Of course, switching from a soft drink to water alone is not going to make a huge difference right away, but you can add on new affirmations every time you make a healthy conscious choice. Just remember to always affirm current reality.

The formula is: Current problematic state (objective reality) + "and as long as I" + healthy / useful choice (made in current reality) + "I am helping / promoting / moving closer to" + desired outcome.

Carlin

This punctuation system, which is related to the Bi-Lateral method, is useful for gaining someone's full attention when their minds are wandering.

Entrain your words into consistent beats as you speak. However, don't keep the beat at the same rate. Speed up and slow down the rate of the rhythm, but keep the words falling on the beat. You can practice this first by talking while music is playing, and making your words fall on the beat. Once you can do this, let some words fall two to the beat. (In the last sentence, "to the" would be good for a word pair that doubles up on a beat.

Once you have that, try some triplets, where three words cover a single beat. As you practice, you'll notice that it's actually easier and more effective to think in terms of syllables, rather than words. Try putting this to the beats:

The beats are numbered: "1. SYLlables 2. RAther than 3. BEATS."

That's a DA-da-da DA-da-da DA. rhythm.

ONE and a TWO and a THREE.

This is a kind of, "Lions and tigers and BEARS, oh my!" Two triplets and a whole note. I call this the George Carlin style because this was his signature style. His speech was laced with rhythms from the big band era, and this contributed to his hip, cool daddy vibe.

Once you have this, then you'll find that as you speak, you can stay on the beat, but also speed up and slow down the rhythm. Listen to George Carlin's routines, and notice how he speeds up and slows down while keeping the beat.

Bear in mind that many musicians, including Eric Clapton, tap their feet on or just ahead of the beat. This helps them play intense, exciting rhythms that keep the audience engaged.

Also, many people report that they have a much easier time learning new information when there's a rhythm with alternating strong and weak beats. Refer to the Rhythmic Learning Strategy.

Cartesian Coordinates

You can apply Cartesian coordinates to decisions in order to check your ecology and refine your outcomes. You can try this on a decision you're considering. Here they are:

If I do X, what will happen?

If I do X, what will not happen?

If I don't do X, what will happen?

If I don't do X, what will not happen?

Imagine anything that you hadn't thought of yet, or any way that these questions help you put things into perspective.

If I DO X, What WILL Happen?	If I DON'T do X, What WILL Happen?
If I DO X, What WON'T Happen?	If I DON'T do X, What WON'T Happen?

Cause Audit

To support our beliefs, there is a causal relationship between how we develop and support our ideas. This is a fancy way of saying that for every belief we hold, there is a cause for that belief. We often use words that connect the ideas, and to get to the underlying belief structure, it is important to know the connecting words that we use to describe this causal relationship. These words are because, while, therefore, before, after, in the same way, whenever, if, so that, although. "I am successful because I don't have children" and "I don't go to a party if it is far away" are examples of these words connecting two facts, and it is this connection that reveals a belief. So if we can understand the cause, then we can understand the belief, and if we understand the belief, we can understand the behavior, feelings, etc. We can group the connecting words into four groups.

While and whenever are considered constraining causes because they limit the cause to certain times or certain events for it to be true. "I am happy whenever I am with you." really means, "Your presence causes me to be happy." Before, after, and because are precipitating causes, as they tell us that one action or event is necessary for another to occur. "I am always nervous before exams" really means, "The anticipation of taking an exam causes me to be nervous." So that and therefore are final causes because they describe how the completion of one action or event leads to another. "The economy is bad, therefore fewer people have jobs" really means "The bad economy causes fewer people to be employed". If and in the same way, they are formal causes because they are the formal expressions of cause-effect relationships. "I'll go to the cinema if the weather is bad" really means "the bad weather causes me to go to the cinema".

Although it is also included in this group because it allows us to check and see if there are any potential constraints and/or counter examples that can help us check the strength and validity of our ideas. The way a cause audit goes is you take a statement, whether it is a goal, limiting belief, resource, problem, or any cause you want to understand better, and that statement becomes the first half of a larger statement that is connected by the connecting word. For example, "I want to become famous if/because/while/therefore/so that/in the same way..." and for each example, you complete the statement. Let's look closer at what each statement asks for.

Because- this connector should answer why you want or have the goal/belief/resource or problem. **Therefore**- explains an effect or requirement. **Before/after**- describes what has to happen before/after. **While**- describes what is happening at the same time. **Whenever**- describes some key conditions that are required. **So that**- describes the intention related to it. **If**- describes any related constraints or results. **In the same way that**- describes any similar past results that have already been achieved, **Although**- is to explore any alternatives or constraints that are related.

Centering

When you are anxious or fearful, your body will contract, and you will be drawn into terrible mindsets and moods that are far away from the life you want to lead. We focus on the breath in this strategy because the breath is constantly present and can work as a guide, bringing you back to the present moment—a state of being into which you must fully immerse yourself if you wish to make a difference in your life. You may repeat this procedure as many times as needed. Concerning anxiousness and fear, it's an effective antidote for the suffering that the mind and body are able to hold and repress. Every time you go through the exercise, you improve your ability to pay attention and be in the moment with your thoughts and feelings.

1. Put yourself in a comfortable sitting position where you will not be disturbed for the next five to ten minutes.

2. Caress your chest with one hand and your belly with the other.

3. Allowing your eyes to close gently will help you to become more centered right where you are.

4. Pay close attention to the rising and falling of your chest and abdomen.

5. As you breathe in and out through your nose, pay attention to the movement of your arms and hands.

6. Notice each inhale and exhale, as the air flows slowly in and out.

7. As you breathe in and out through your nose, you may shift your focus from the movement of your hands on your chest and belly to the different sensations of warmth or coolness throughout your body.

8. Gently acknowledge any physical sensations that you are experiencing in your body.

The Big Book of NLP

9. Allow yourself to be in the present moment, riding the timeline with your breath.

10. If your attention is drawn away from your breath by thoughts or anything else, acknowledge it and gently bring your attention back to it.

11. Finish this practice by making a commitment to yourself to return to your centered breath as often as you need throughout the day.

Chaining Anchors (I)

Source: Tad James

When the desired mental state deviates greatly from the current state, the chaining anchor pattern can help.

Current State →

1st Intermediate State →

2nd Intermediate State →

Desired State.

1. Initiate a downtime state.

2. Establish rapport.

3. Set the frame.

4. Recognize and name the undesirable current state.

5. Choose a positive and resourceful end state.

6. Choose two intermediate states to lead from current to desired.

7. Elicit and anchor current state.

8. Break state. Elicit and anchor the first intermediate state.

9. Break state. Elicit and anchor the second intermediate state.

The Big Book of NLP

10. Break state. Elicit and anchor the final desired state.

11. Break state. Take a short break.

12. Fire the current state anchor and when it reaches its peak, release the first intermediate anchor.

13. Break state. Test. Initiate the original current state and move into the first intermediate state.

14. Break state. Fire the current state anchor and when it reaches its peak, release the first intermediate anchor. When the first intermediate state reaches its peak, fire the second intermediate state anchor.

14. Break state. Test. Initiate the original current state and move into the first intermediate state, and right away into the second intermediate state.

15. Break state. Fire the current state anchor and when it reaches its peak, release the first intermediate anchor. When the first intermediate state reaches its peak, fire the second intermediate state anchor. When the second intermediate state reaches its peak, fire the final desired state anchor.

16. Break state. Take a short rest.

17. Fire the first current state, and allow the client to go through all the states and end up at the final desired state.

18. Future pace.

Chaining Anchors (II)

Source: Tad James

This is another useful process for chaining anchors.

1. Initiate a downtime state.

2. Establish rapport. Specify the problematic current state.

3. Set the frame.

4. Recognize and name the undesirable current state.

5. Choose a positive and resourceful end state.

6. Choose two intermediate states to lead from current to desired.

7. Design the workflow of the chain.

8. Elicit and then anchor each state on its own, beginning with the current state all the way through to the final desired state. Break state after each step in the process as you did with the previous pattern.

9. Test each state.

10. Chain the anchors in the chain - firing the first and at its peak adding the second and then at its peak adding the third and finally the fourth.

11. Test. Fire current state anchor. The client should reach the final state in succession.

12. Ask, "Now how do you feel about the problem?"

13. Ask, "Can you think of a certain time in the future, in which… if it had happened in the past… you would have this problem, and instead something different happened, and that would be what?"

14. Future pace.

Chaining States

Source: Richard Bandler & John Grinder

> *Choose an unresourceful state.*
>
> *Identify a positive direction.*
>
> *Turn this direction into steps to the positive state. Anchor each step.*
>
> *Chain the states.*
>
> *Test.*

Do not allow negative thoughts to bring you down. Instead, generate an automatic reaction that creates a resourceful and positive state instead. The illustration below shows the most common mental states we all experience on a regular basis. Notice your own range of emotions and mental states during a typical week, and experiment with the Chaining States pattern to bridge the gap between the un-resourceful states and the desired ones. Notice the stages one must go through in order to overcome grief or fear and reach desire, mastery, or even indifference.

When you work with clients, show them this diagram and explain that even with all the power NLP has to offer, there are no magic pills. In order to achieve a true sense of peace, you must first pick your current mental state and apply the strategies to reach the next one and the next one until you reach your desired outcome. Jumping, in one instance, from depression to logic, for example (as many "positive thinking" gurus advise), is a surefire recipe for a major breakdown. Gradual chaining of states is safer and will bring to light any unconscious objection you need to deal with.

1. Choose an unresourceful state. Select an unresourceful state for this pattern. Unless you are a beginner, select one that poses a challenge when you try to shift into a positive or

resourceful state. It should also be one that tends to suck you into an increasingly negative state once you are in that state.

2. Determine a positive course of action. Explore what would constitute a positive direction from this state, based on the ideal state that you would like to go to. For example, if the experience of failure tends to have too much of an effect on your self-esteem, pulling you down into self-recrimination and self-doubt, your ideal state might be one of total self-support and confidence.

The direction that this implies can be something like "awareness of inner resources such as gifts, skills, talent, and positive self-talk" and "memories of past successes."

3. Turn this direction into steps toward a positive state. Based on your ideal state and the direction that you selected, create intermediate steps that bridge from your negative state to your positive one.

4. Anchor each step. Experience each step as an increasingly positive state. Fully access each state and anchor each to a different knuckle that will serve as a trigger for the state.

5. Chain the states.

a. Fully access the first state by triggering its anchor.

b. When fully in that state, fire the next anchor to access the next state while continuing to hold on to the first trigger for a few seconds.

c. Release the first anchor.

d. Repeat this procedure five times more.

Perform steps a through c for each remaining step in the sequence from negative to positive. Do not rush this process. Aim to attain a full experience of each and every mental state.

6. Test. In the coming days and weeks, notice what benefits you experience in this process. See if you have an easier time shifting out of the negative state you worked on during this pattern, or if you avoid entering it in the first place.

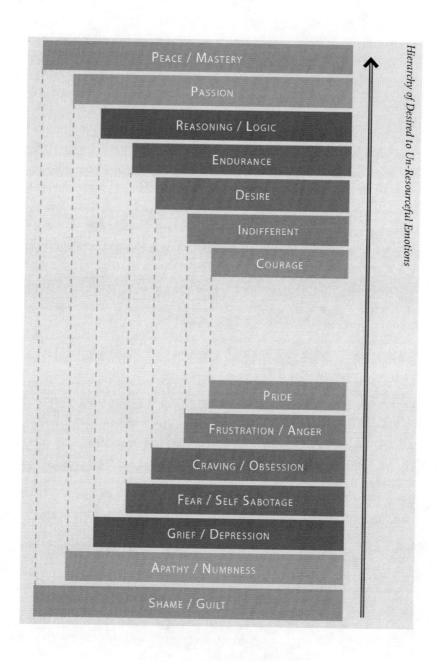

The Big Book of NLP

Challenging Beliefs

Sometimes the client believes that they only have one choice in reaction to certain negative events, such as getting upset, feeling threatened, or dwelling in misery. We can challenge the limiting belief by asking, "what would it mean if you were not worried about it?" For example,

Client: "I'm worried my wife is going to leave me suddenly."

Therapist: "Did she say or do something that made you think this way?"

Client: "No, she is amazing and we're doing so well. That's why I'm worried about it."

Therapist: "What would it mean if you were not worried about it?"

Client: "That I don't care enough about her."

Therapist: "How does not worrying about her leaving suddenly, even though everything is amazing between you two, mean you don't care about her?"

Client: "Well, it doesn't..."

Here you can further explore the origin of the limiting belief, and, of course, depending on the particular case, it could lead in any direction. With this specific client, the issue was that he felt vulnerable and could not handle the level of exposure he needed to sustain to keep his relationship "amazing," as he stated. Instead of working needlessly on his surface structure (worried about his wife leaving), we ended up working on the real issue, which was fear of being exposed.

Change Personal History

Source: Richard Bandler & John Grinder

> *Access the negatively-coded memory after establishing an exit cue.*
>
> *Ugly TDS*
>
> *Go to your earliest related memory, then break state.*
>
> *List your present resources.*
>
> *Anchor these resources.*
>
> *Create your "emotritional" anchors salad.*
>
> *Take a break.*
>
> *Savor some inner peace.*
>
> *Future pace.*
>
> *Test.*

Modify negatively coded memories so that you can realize your potential unfettered by such memories. It works especially well for a person or a situation that pushes your buttons, that is, that you have an unresourceful reaction to. Before you use the pattern, remember that it might need some modification to fit your unique needs and abilities. We cannot stress enough how important it is that you approach this pattern flexibly.

1. Access the negatively coded memory after establishing an exit cue. You will need to create an exit cue that will allow you to stop the pattern for some reason. Put a special object (a real object) in front of you, where it does not normally go. If you suddenly need to stop the process, grab the object to trigger the "return to previous state" cue. Anchor a

more or less neutral state to this object. Access the negatively coded past experience using all rep systems and from the first (associated) position. Use a unique gesture to anchor the state associated with this experience.

2. Ugly TDS. As you'll recall, TDS (trance-derivational search) occurs every time you go inside your mind and search for meaning or for memories. This can lead to a trance. An "Ugly TDS" occurs when you perform a TDS inside a TDS. For example, while you're searching for meaning for that negatively-coded experience, you anchor that feeling and do another TDS for another memory that provides a similar emotional reaction. Then you do it again, collecting more and more related negatively-coded experiences. That's why it's called "ugly" TDS. To make it easier, you can write them down and mark each with the approximate age you were at the time of that experience. While you're doing the Ugly TDS, keep adding those to your anchor. Continue until the ugly TDS becomes slow and it is difficult to find more related memories.

3. Return to your most recent related memory, then break state. Stop the search and, in your mind, go directly to the earliest memory. Since you have your age written down for each one, it's easy. Stay there. Now break your ugly TDS state. Since it involves TDS, it is best to do it actively, by getting up and shaking it off, among other things.

4. Make a list of your current resources. Now we'll group some positive parts of your current identity that you've chosen to keep. Ask yourself, "What kind of resources do I have today that I wish I had back then, so that the whole experience would have been different and to my advantage?" As an adult, or "the older version of yourself," you have plenty of resources available. How about forgiveness, patience, resilience, self-defense, sarcasm, devotion, procrastination, inner strength, or other resources you keep deep inside? Small or big, it does not matter; any resource that can help you should be listed.

5. Anchor these resources. An anchor for each of these resource states Fully feel them, and then establish a new anchor for all of them together. Choose a gesture that is very different from the one you used for the negatively-coded experience anchor.

6. Create your "emotritional" anchor salad. "Emotritional is a nickname we gave to the emotional resources that nourish you. Take the negatively coded experienceanchor and the new anchor (the collection of current resources), and collapse them at the same time. While you do that, let the first negatively coded experience enter your mind, and

take all of the resources that you've anchored (the second anchor) and drop them on that memory. With all of these resources available, how would the experience have looked back then? Change the content in whatever way is useful to you. Once you're done with the first memory, go faster. Move on to other memories. It doesn't matter in which order you proceed. It may help you to avoid doing them in chronological order, however. If you find the pattern confusing, bear in mind that confusion can actually enhance its effectiveness.

7.Take a break. Break the state completely in whatever way you find appropriate. You may feel tired at this point, but maintain your alertness for a while to make sure that the pattern takes effect. This would be a good time to eat something or drink some cold water. Distract yourself from what's going on around you.

8. Savor inner peace. Inner peace is completed when you forgive and forget. Now that you have completed this pattern, check to see if there is any "hidden treasure" that you might find disturbing if it is not processed properly now. Calmly think about that previously negatively coded memory. From an objective frame of mind, ask yourself if it means more than a learning experience to you when you look at it. If not, then you have most likely completed the pattern effectively. If you find that there is still a negative charge, you can make that the target of this pattern or another appropriate pattern in the future.

9. The Future PaceThis step brings the good from the past into your future. Future Pace for an event that is likely to happen. Trigger your resource anchor, and mentally rehearse the event several times. For each mental rehearsal, have a different turn of events take place, in order to future pace the situation from several angles. This will prepare you to respond effectively and flexibly. For each version, handle it in your imagination so that it is to your advantage. Being able to spontaneously respond to the ghosts of your past is a liberating and empowering feeling. Most people find that, having followed this pattern, their new responses are quite spontaneous yet effective.

10. Test. In the coming days and weeks, notice if you have more peace of mind regarding issues related to this memory, or if you experience more freedom to think about the things that really matter to you, and less about negative things from the past.

You can add a piece to this pattern when it concerns a person that pushes your client's buttons. Help your client understand the intent of the other party. This helps your client feel a sharper distinction between their reality and that of the other person. Many of the people who come to an NLP practitioner have difficulty with this particular skill--the skill of being very clear on where they leave off and other people begin. This leads to many of the problems that people use NLP for. One of them is certainly the negative reactions they experience because they cannot tolerate other people thinking or saying negative things about them. When working with a client, you can provide some instructions that help them do the pattern. Remember to say words like those I used when firing off the two anchors. Take the resource state (as you fire the positive anchor) into the negative state (as you fire the negative anchor)...and notice how it has changed now. And when you test the anchors, notice any changes in your client's physiology that can alert you to changes in their state.

Characterological Adjectives

When we hear words that fit the category of characterological adjectives, we assume a pre-existing relationship between the implied idea and the presupposition. For example, if someone tells you she is a victim and it is her brother's fault, the presupposition is that she was attacked/assaulted at least once in the past, and the characterological adjectives imply that her brother is the source of the abuse.

Keeping in mind that nominalizations and meta-model violations are always at play when someone tells us their story (and any description of anything that is not happening immediately is a story), we need to clarify the characterological adjectives in order to avoid jumping to the wrong conclusions.

The word "victim" might imply she was raped or physically attacked, but it might also indicate verbal abuse, such as a threat or a curse. In some cases, though, if investigated further, it could mean something completely benign, such as if she feels entitled to something and her brother refused her demand. She could feel like a "victim," but that has a whole different meaning than a sexual assault.

This pattern is not meant to be negotiated between two individuals. It is used to help the person (in the example above, the woman) clarify their relationship with a difficult person in their life.

1. Consider a recent argument or a difficult interpersonal situation. It may be that you're frustrated or irritated and did not present your best side in that scenario.

2. Close your eyes and take a deep breath. Enter your mind's theatre.

Imagine that person in the image on the screen, acting out the way they did in the situation from Step 1.

3. Describe their behavior onscreen in one or two words (X). For example, "defensive" or "selfish" or "aggressive" or "pushy" etc.

4. Align yourself into a third perceptual position by seeing yourself on the screen, acting out the scenario while you remain in your seat in the theatre.

5. Describe your behavior on screen in one or two words (Y). For example, "defensive" or "talkative" or "disrespectful" or "avoidant" etc.

6. Break state. Open your eyes.

7. Say to yourself, "That person was X, and I was Y."

8. Answer the question: "If I was less Y in that conversation, could it be that this person would not have to be so X?"

9. You can further improve your relationship with that person by communicating your insight to them. You know, I realized that I was really Y and that is why I felt you were somewhat X. I hope we can work it out together.

Choice Expansion

Source: Robert Dilts

Scan through your day, reviewing choice points.

Float back to that choice point, viewing it from the third (dissociated) perceptual position.

Select choice points.

Imagine the likely outcomes of each of these imaginary choices.

For each outcome, imagine experiencing it in first person.

Test.

Generate motivation by harnessing the power of choice points. You could say that choice points occur when you consciously or unconsciously make a commitment of some kind. A defining characteristic of a choice point is that it, symbolically or literally, makes it difficult to turn back. For example, when you sign an agreement, take marriage vows, or shake hands on a bet, you have passed a choice point. This pattern will also help you find and use the many small choices that together make a big difference in our lives.

1. Take a look at your day. What choice points did you go through and what choices did you make? What outcome did you intend to produce at those points? How effective were your choices today for the choices that produced results of any kind?

2. Float back to the point where you made your choice and look at it from a third (disassociated) point of view.

3. Choose from the available options. Select the two or three most important choice points (or more if you have time). For each, think of three different choices that you could have made. Imagine actually making those choices and taking actions based on those choices.

4. Imagine the likely outcomes of each of these imaginary choices.

5. For each outcome, imagine experiencing it in first-person.

6. Test. As you experience the next few days, notice if your acuity for sizing up choices has improved, and whether your results are any better. Practice this pattern of choices with an eye to becoming more conscious of what outcomes you project. You will realize that countless such projections occur unconsciously, sometimes to our regret. Make a special commitment to use it on key choices that tend to cause problems, such as undermining a commitment to your well-being. Practice improving your ability to predict outcomes, as well. Note any ways that you could enhance this pattern.

Chronic Pain

This is true for both psychosomatic pain and emotional pain. In response to a real or imaginary threat, our body's natural defenses within the CNS and PNS go into overdrive, creating the pain cycle. Fear is activated by the amygdala and sends a signal through the body to the rest of the nervous system, causing the body to tense up. We first brace ourselves against the threat that caused the pain, then against the threat of pain on its own. If this vicious cycle of threat, fear, brace, constriction, and succeeding threat of pain isn't broken, chronic pain can develop.

There is a key therapeutic principle that must be followed to help the suffering client break the cycle:

1. We must transition the client from identifying with the pain ("I am in pain" or "I am the pain") to-

2. dissociating the pain from a higher logical level down to a kinesthetic sensation ("I am feeling the pain") to-

3. shifting the essence of the felt pain and dissolving its constituents ("I am recognizing the sensations that hide behind the pain") and lastly to-

4. resolving the inner conflicts that have produced the pain.

It's not enough to dissociate from the pain, because the pain itself is the message, not the source of the suffering. Inner conflicts are the source, and because these emotions are so overwhelming and pose a threat to the integrity of the ego, they are repressed deeply inside to distract the consciousness from dealing with them. The physical and/or emotional pain then becomes chronic.

Unfortunately, the entire process of breaking the cycle of pain must be tailored to the suffering individual's unique personality and inner conflicts. There are no truly effective self-help or ready-made techniques that are broad enough to account for even a small percentage of the variations in different cases. This is the primary raison d'être of the

Erickson Institute. It's what we've been doing on a daily basis since 1999, collaborating with and customizing tailored solutions for individuals experiencing psychosomatic or emotional pain, or their therapists as supervising consultants. If you are struggling right now, or need guidance on a case, please contact us at help@ericks.org.

Chunking Up/Down

Chunking Up (or Chunking Up) means that you move from specifics to generalities. Chunk Down (or chunking down) means that you move from generalities to specifics. Chunk Up is answering questions such as, "What is this for?" Does it mean that you/I/we/this?" "What is the intention?" "What could be the purpose?" Chunking up doesn't necessarily mean that you move all the way to the most general statement you can make about the subject. It means that you only move to a more general statement, not necessarily the highest or most general.

Chunking Down is about answering questions such as, "How could we use it?" "Is it...?" "Does that mean that we could do..."

Chunking Down doesn't necessarily mean that you move all the way to the most specific statement. However, you are only moving towards a more specific set of ideas.

Whatever you say or hear can be recorded as a point on the Chunk Up -> Chunk Down axis. From that point, you can either chunk up and generalize or chunk down and be more specific. To enhance rapport and get a sense of agreement and unity between you and another person, chunk up!

Rarely do people reject nominalizations. When you say, "Love is wonderful," how many people will disagree? That's a huge chunk. If you say, "Your love is wonderful," there's an opening for a debate and not necessarily an immediate agreement.

You chunk it up to get an agreement. You chunk down to solve problems. How do you eat an elephant? Remember? Right... one piece at a time. That's chunking down. A person presents a problem to you and asks for your help to solve it. If you chunk down long enough, they will find their own solutions on their own, making their own decisions and thanking you for opening their eyes. You don't have to know everything; you just need to chunk it down further.

You chop it up to hypnotize. You chunk down to de-hypnotize. You don't need to be a hypnotist in order to hypnotize others. You see, just by using words and talking to people, you're already generating trance states in others. They don't have to close their eyes and quack like a duck. Hypnosis is everything between a daydream and moonwalking. We move in and out of hypnosis numerous times every day. When you're in a state of hypnosis, you're more suggestible and more easily influenced by your surroundings and your inner world. When you chunk up, you get people to think about intentions, purposes, philosophy, and meaning by using a nominalization (a word that describes something you cannot physically point at, like love, influence, unconsciousness, etc.). You cause the other person to go inside and think about the meaning of what you said. They must make sense of it, and that inner search for the meaning, that's a trance!

Sometimes you will want to de-hypnotize, or take the person out of hypnosis. If your chat mate is spacing out too often, having a hard time listening and concentrating, or is in pain (another form of self hypnosis: concentrating obsessively on the physical feeling of pain), then you can de-hypnotize that person by chunking down. When you dig into the details, the present reality kicks in and the world of philosophy fades. Milton Erickson's method of relieving pain was mainly about chunking down. By analyzing the physical pain, wherever in the body it is, you make it smaller and less important. The brain goes from "Oh, it is painful in my teeth." to "Oh, there's that rough sensation in the 3rd tooth from the right, on its front side right above that small white dot." In hypnotherapy, we use chunking down a lot when dealing with phantom pains (pain that feels real, even though there is no known physical reason).

Circle of Excellence

Source: John Grinder & Judith DeLosier

Choose your resourceful state.

Choose a time to trigger the state.

Create a symbol for an excellent state.

Step into this symbol and recall the memory.

Observe internal patterns associated with the state.

Amplify the state.

Step back and break state.

Test.

Repeat.

Extend this work to appropriate situations.

With this pattern, you can produce high-performance states. It helps you become more aware of the internal sensations and behaviors that can help you produce a positive state. It also helps you perceive cues from others. The technique includes establishing an internal anchor for a state of excellence.

1. Determine which of your states is the most resourceful. Select a resourceful state that you wish to experience at will, such as creativity.

2. Pick a time to trigger the state. Think of a time when you experienced a rich version of this state.

The Big Book of NLP

3. Create a symbol of an excellent state. Imagine that you have a circle before you on the ground. If you prefer, you can select a specific color, symbol, or other visual or auditory cue to associate with the state.

4. Step into this symbol and recall the memory. Step into the circle or symbol. Fully associate with the state and relive the experience, amplifying the state. Experiment with the memory starting from the first position.

5. Observe the internal patterns associated with the state. Notice the patterns you produce that are associated with this state. To do this, internally focus your attention, noticing all relevant internal representations, characteristics of sub-modalities, patterns of breathing and tension, and anything else you can experience.

6. Amplify and enrich the state by increasing the sub-modalities in all rep systems. This includes things such as the clarity and compelling qualities of your own inner voice, as well as the brightness and size of images.

7. Take a step back and break the state. Step back out of the circle or symbol and break this state.

8. Test. Test this circle of excellence that you have created by stepping forward into it. How well do you access the state?

9. Repeat the first seven steps until you trigger the state easily.

10. Extend this work to appropriate situations. Think of some situations that you would handle better in this state. Imagine taking your circle of excellence into these situations, using future pacing to prepare for them.

Co-Alignment of Vision and Values

Source: Robert Dilts

Select the location.

Answer the "doing" question.

Answer the "skills and abilities" question.

Answer the "values and beliefs" question.

Answer the "identity" question.

Answer the "vision" question.

Explore the vision overlap.

Bring the related state to the identity level. Move to the identity level.

Move to the behavior level. Explore the significance at that level.

Explore the full results at the location level. Test.

Discover and align with your vision and values through the power of metaphor and logical levels. Help your team succeed when you form a common identity together through this kind of alignment.

1. Determine the location. Choose for this pattern an environment that you and your team share with a common purpose.

When you first begin using this pattern, select a place that is neutral and does not knowingly hold negative anchors for members of the team.

2. Answer the "doing" question. Have each team member answer the question, "What do I desire to do or accomplish in that place?" Ask them to go into some detail in their answers.

3. Answer the "skills and abilities" question. Have each member describe the tools, skills, authority, and abilities that they feel will best empower them to accomplish their aims in this place. It does not have to be public at first; they can each work on their own list without sharing it with the rest of the group until they feel comfortable enough to do so.

4. Answer the "values and beliefs" question. Have each member describe the values, attitudes, and beliefs that drive their desire to exercise these resources to accomplish their aims in this place.

5. Answer the "identity" question. Have them explain who they are as individuals with these motivations and beliefs driving their use of their skills and other resources to create the desired action in this place.

6. Answer the "vision" question. Have them describe the vision that they wish to manifest, and that gives dimension to their identity as a person with beliefs and attitudes that drive their use of skills and abilities toward specific actions and results in this place.

7. Look into the vision overlap.

Discuss the ways that your individual vision statements are similar.

What do they share? Be sure to explore them for overlaps that are not obvious.

8. Bring the related state up to the identity level.

Access the positive state associated with this vision and sharing. In that state, return to your identity level, experiencing the vision and sense of identity and mission simultaneously.

9. Move to the identity level. With this sense of vision, identity, beliefs, and values, return to your capability space.

Explore what capabilities you have as a team that go beyond your individual identities.

10. Move to the behavior level. Explore the significance at that level. Take your sense of vision, identity, beliefs, values, and capabilities back to the behavior level. Explore how all of your behaviors, even seemingly trivial ones, affect and reflect upon all the higher levels you have explored, right up to the level of vision. Now ask, "What collective actions should we take together?"

11. Explore the full results at the location level. Put all the levels you have explored into the location. Experience how these insights, understandings, and feelings transform and enrich this space and mission.

12. Test. Over the coming days and months, observe any ways that this pattern has influenced or expanded the team and your individual contribution to its work.

Dilts' Logical Levels

Spirit or higher purpose: the belief in a higher purpose or values that give meaning to one's identity.

Identity: a sense of self that fosters values and beliefs.

Values and beliefs: an increased level of internal resources that influence decisions and how you apply your skills and knowledge.

Skills and knowledge: the fundamental internal resources for behavior.

Behavior: physical actions and patterns, including habits and the power of behavior modification principles.

Environment: The context and how it stimulates, guides, facilitates and limits behavior.

The Big Book of NLP

Co-Dependency Resolution

Source: Connirae Andreas

Think of a person that you feel you are over-involved with.

Experience from a metaphorical point of view the connections between you and the other person.

Imagine not being tied to the relationship. Clarify the ecology of these ties, and any underlying positive intentions.

State the desired outcomes and the commitments you experience in the relationship.

Create your ideal self that experiences high-quality relationships.

Connect the ties to your ideal self, and imagine experiencing the benefits of this self.

Enhance your boundaries with the other person in a detailed way that affirms your realism about them and your adult integrity.

Test.

This pattern helps people think and act more independently by eliminating codependent behavior.

1. Think of a person that you feel over-involved with. For this pattern, the ideal person is either failing to engage in some important self-care, such as managing an addiction, or is not adequately controlling harmful behavior, such as abusiveness.

2. Experience, from a metaphorical point of view, the connections between you and the other person. Explore the sub-modalities with which you represent these ties. You might want to start with the feelings in your body and see how images can emerge from these feelings. People often see things like ropes or aprons.

3. Consider not being bound by the relationship.Clarify the ecology of these ties and any underlying positive intentions.

a. Imagine that these ties fall away or dissolve in a way that frees you completely from the relationship.

Notice all objections or ecological concerns that arise. Notice any secondary gain that the seemingly negative parts of the relationship offer. This may require some digging and humility.

b. Investigate the positive intentions of any part of yourself that is hesitant to cut the ties.

4. State the desired outcomes and the commitments you expect to experience in the relationship. Consolidate this information into clear statements of desirable outcomes and meta-outcomes of the ties in this relationship and the relationship in general. Clearly state what you give to the relationship and what you sacrifice in order to maintain the ties.

5. Create your ideal self, one that experiences high-quality relationships. Generate an image and sense of an ideal self in which you experience your constructive desired outcomes and make your most meaningful commitments while receiving profound benefits in the form of constructive, meaningful relationships that include a rich, positive, harmless primary relationship. Notice any negative reaction you have to the words used: rich, positive, and harmless. Imagine this ideal self being completely at ease with and motivated by these words. Imagine any negative assumptions about them becoming dry and crisp and falling away. For example, an association between "harmless" and "boring" would develop clear boundaries as a concept that is tagged to the ideal person, and then flake off, dropping away like a dead leaf. Draw upon what you gained from step four in doing this step. Place an image of this ideal self in the appropriate position in your mental space or visual field.

6. Connect the ties to your ideal self and imagine yourself reaping the benefits of that self.

The Big Book of NLP

a. Join the dots to your ideal self.Observe yourself experiencing the benefits. Desensitize the related discomforts. Return to your sense and image of your ties to the other person that you selected for this pattern. Imagine disconnecting each tie and reconnecting it to your ideal self. See all the benefits that you have identified in these steps as being created by this ideal self through proactive, assertive, and persistent behavior. Take note of any negative associations you have with the words proactive, assertive, and persistent. Have them flake away as before.

b. Begin reaping the benefits from the first position.Focus on getting support for your integrity. Associate with this ideal self, and imagine experiencing all the benefits of constructive, harmless relationships that inspire you and create a rich world for you.

Notice things like others' approval and support. Notice how it comes from the relationship, not from you allowing violations of your boundaries. Notice how comfortable other people are with you when you're defining clear boundaries and being assertive, proactive, and persistent in pursuing your dreams. Savor the positive feelings of these benefits. Give yourself the gift of some time to soak in the good feelings that come from imagining all this. Savor these feelings, like savoring a hot bath.

7. Enhance your boundaries with the other person in a detailed way that affirms your realism about them and your adult integrity.

a. Allow your positive experiences to nudge the other person closer to their ideal self.Imagine that each of your assertive, proactive, and persistent dream-fulfilling acts, and each positive, supportive experience that you have with other people, sends out a wave of gentle force. These waves move the other person that you identified for this pattern. Each wave moves the person toward their own ideal self—an ideal self with consistently constructive behavior and clear boundaries.

b. Desensitize yourself to whether or not the other person makes constructive decisions.Notice the attachment that you experience with the idea that this person MUST choose to associate with this ideal self. Allow that attachment to become clearly defined and crisp and to flake away. This allows the other person to make their choice free of your past denial and magical thinking.

c. Visualize inner strength while connecting fully with your deeper codependent attachments and fantasy. Imagine having the inner strength as your ideal self to allow this other person to be who they really are instead of your fantasy version. Allow yourself to experience not knowing what choice they will make. Notice how deep the attachment to the fantasy version of this person goes into you. Connect fully with your anxiety about not knowing what choice they will make, as well as your attachment to your previous fantasy version of this person.

d. Desensitize your more intense codependent attachments. Allow your discomfort with not knowing and your attachment to your prior fantasy version of this person to gently clarify and become crisp, protruding, and flake away. Allow your ideal self to fill the remaining hole with healing energy that closes and returns you to your normal shape.

8. Test.

a. Pay attention to any changes in how you manage your boundaries and how well you stay connected to your reality in your upcoming interactions with this person.

b. Observe whether your upbeat attitude and actions bring out a different side of this person.

c. Notice how abandoning your fantasy of this person allows you to make more realistic decisions about how to interact with them.

d. Take note of any ways in which you benefit from other people's relationships.

Collapsing Anchors

Select a problem involving a spontaneous negative state, and establish an anchor for inducing it.

Break state.

Elicit a positive state.

Amplify the state.

Elaborate on the state.

Anchor the resourceful state.

Break state.

Trigger the states.

Release the anchors.

Test your work.

Strengthen the anchor.

This pattern helps in changing a dysfunctional response. It involves triggering an anchor for a negative state and an anchor for a positive state simultaneously. The result is an opportunity to reprocess the stuck pattern involved. The Collapsing Anchors pattern may help resolve dysfunctional thought or behavioral patterns that have been difficult to change.

The result is greater ease in bypassing the dysfunctional state and the spontaneous generation of more appropriate states for coping with the challenging situation that has been reprocessed. Many people say that the anchor collapse was kind of strange, but in a good way.

This pattern serves to free you from negative feelings that a situation or memory triggers in you. The pattern starts by establishing an anchor for the negative feelings. Then you create a different anchor that is loaded with positive states.

Once the positive anchor is more powerful than the negative one, you fire both anchors at the same time. The result, at first, feels strange. The person's eyes may dart around, as if their mind is trying to restore some kind of order or make sense of things.

The end result is that the person is freed from the association between the trigger situation and the negative feelings.

The anchors are usually on opposite sides of the body, such as one spot on each knee. Placing the feelings in the palms of each hand and then bringing the palms together also collapses the anchors.

1. Choose a problem that involves a spontaneous negative state and create an anchor for inducing it.

Choose a problem that is part of a stuck, dysfunctional pattern. Create an anchor for the negative state.

2. Break the negative state (for instructions, see the State Interrupt pattern).

3. Induce a positive state.

Elicit a resourceful, positive state.

4. Amplify the state.

Amplify the state with methods such as enhancing sub-modalities.

5. Elaborate on that state, for example, by talking about what you would like to experience in that situation in each rep system.

The Big Book of NLP

6. Anchor the resourceful state.

Once the state is firmly established, anchor it.

7. Break state.

Break the resourceful state by clearing your mental screen, opening your eyes, and moving around for a moment.

8. Trigger the states.

Fire the anchor for the unresourceful state, then the resourceful state immediately after. Hold both anchors. This supports continued processing. It also helps to periodically remind the person to fully experience their current state. You are likely to observe physiological changes, including facial expressions and eye movements that suggest confusion or processing.

9. Release the anchors. Once you feel that adequate time to process has taken place (halting of the physiological changes usually occurs at that time), release the negative anchor first, then the positive anchor after a brief delay.

10. Test. Break state. Fire the anchor of the unresourceful state, or ask the person to attempt to call up their unresourceful state by thinking about the issue. If they are unable to easily experience the unresourceful state, then the pattern was successful.

11. Strengthen the anchor.

a. Break state. Trigger the resourceful state anchor.

b. Strengthen the positive state through sub-modality work and other appropriate methods.

c. Re-anchor the resourceful state.

Compassion Fatigue

Working with traumatized and stressed people might cause compassion fatigue. It is common for healthcare providers, and especially private therapists who work with individuals for more than 25 hours per week, to report burnout. Compassion fatigue can lead to a breakdown, a burn out or other personal difficulties. Compassion fatigue symptoms include isolation by choice, resentment, repeated misunderstanding, diminished focus, lack of empathy, nightmares, feelings that emerge in a client's horror story, apathy, overwhelming sadness, insomnia, general negativity, inability to separate work from home, reluctance to change, avoiding leisure, and psychosomatic pains when away from the office, among other signs.

1. Initiate a downtime state.

2. Pay attention to your body. Begin by closing your eyes and taking a few deep breaths.

3. Consider one episode of compassion fatigue. Start feeling into the experience by selecting a client who drains you or a session where you've felt distant or impatient. What comes to mind?

4. Next, pay attention to your body. What sensations do you have in your body? What are you feeling inside your skin?

5. On a physical level, take note of the source of the disturbance. Allow yourself to let go of the story or the reason. Concentrate solely on the body. What is the actual location of the disturbance in the body?

6. Ask the compassion part of you to come forward.

7. Now imagine what the disturbance is about, and ask the compassion part what your body needs right now to overcome it. Write down three qualities that your compassion part says that your body needs to overcome the disturbance.

8. Create a symbol to hold the three qualities together.

The Big Book of NLP

9. Dissociate to the third perceptual position and see yourself applying these qualities in several real-life scenarios. Imagine expanding the symbol over the mental scene.

10. Notice how your reaction in the imaginary scenario is different as a result of applying these qualities.

11. Thank the compassion part.

12. Test. In the coming days and weeks, take purposeful short breaks between sessions to recall the symbol and apply it backwards and forwards on your timeline.

Compulsion Blow-Out

Source: Richard Bandler

Select the compulsion.

Identify the primary trigger.

Identify the two strongest sub-modalities of the trigger.

Intensify the sub-modalities to an extreme.

Repeat until there is significant desensitization.

Recommend additional help.

Test.

A compulsion is an irresistible urge to behave in a specific way, most likely and especially when it's against a person's conscious will. Compulsions are different than habits. Habits can be somewhat consciously controlled, and there are productive habits as well as non-productive ones. Compulsions are not within your conscious control (therefore we say it's against your will), and they are all non-productive. This pattern desensitizes compulsions that range from fingernail chewing to obsessing about being jilted.

1. Choose the compulsion. Choose a compulsion that the person wishes to eliminate. It should be one that has some kind of external trigger. Even nail biting has an external trigger. It is the sensation of fingernails extending to a certain length, or just existing.

2. Determine the primary trigger. Determine what circumstance or factor triggers the compulsive behavior.

3. Determine the trigger's two most powerful sub-modalities. Review the various sub-modalities of the rep systems involved in the trigger. For example, with nail biting, there are usually very specific sensations that are related to fingernails but are much more subtle and specific, such as a tingling or pressure felt inside the body in connection with sensing the fingernails or even being conscious of them.

4. Intensify the sub-modalities to the extreme. Have the person use their imagination to increase the sub-modalities to the highest possible level. If there is a sense of the nails sticking out, imagine them protruding very far. If it is a feeling of pressure in the body, imagine being closer and closer to exploding.

5. Repeat this until there is significant desensitization. Take the sub-modalities back to normal, and increase them to the extreme. Do this until the person shows signs of feeling that the process is boring, trivial, or otherwise not triggering.

6. Suggest additional assistance. Do not attempt to replace treatment for a psychiatric problem such as drug addiction. We recommend that a person with potentially harmful behavior get an appropriate assessment for possible treatment.

7. Test. See if the person reduces their compulsive behavior, is more open to additional work, or exhibits other signs of improvement. Repeat this process as needed. You can add other approaches and NLP patterns for compulsive or obsessive behavior. Interruption is another approach. When the person feels like carrying out the behavior, they engage in an incompatible behavior that disrupts the impulsive drive. An example would be tightening the stomach while pressing the palms together intensely. T

Thought-stopping is another method whereby the person substitutes another thought that is very "loud" and distracts from a compulsive thought. A cognitive-somatic therapy such as eye movement desensitization and reprocessing or an energy therapy such as emotional freedom technique may be beneficial. People with obsessive-compulsive disorder may benefit from understanding the disorder and experiencing therapy that helps them understand that their compulsion is fueled largely by a brain dysfunction that can be seen graphically in a brain scan. Seeing such a brain scan is part of this treatment.

Confidence Installation

Recall a time when somebody you didn't know well said, "thank you, you really helped me," and you knew that they were really grateful.

1. What was it like to be recognized, appreciated, and valued?

2. For a few moments, try to fully embrace that impression. Anchor it.

3. Consider a time when a loved one complimented you on something helpful you did or said.

4. What was it like to be recognized, appreciated, and valued?

5. For a few moments, try to fully embrace that impression. Anchor it.

6. Now think about a time when you were appreciated or valued without anyone saying so.

7. What was it like to be unconditionally recognized, appreciated, or valued?

8. For a few moments, try to fully embrace that sensation. What do you appreciate and respect the most about yourself? Anchor it.

9. What qualities do the people who matter the most to you find most appealing in you? What characteristics do they admire?

10. Consider your closest friend. What would he or she insist on valuing most about you if asked? Do you value the same qualities in yourself as your friend?

11. What other parts of yourself do you value that others may not recognize? Anchor each

12. Stack the anchors.

The Big Book of NLP

13. Test. When you find yourself in a new situation feeling overwhelmed, fire the driver anchor in the stack.

Congruence

The state of congruence is a blissful one since there are no conflicting desires or possibilities, no judgments to be addressed, no alternatives to be explored, and no further effort required. When you're in congruence, you're in complete harmony with yourself and the world around you.

Your resolve is steady no matter what happens. Congruence is characterized by the absence of "modal operators." There are no "have to," "should" s, "choices, wishes, or possibilities" interfering with what you're doing right now.

An alternative description is that everything is brought into focus on the now and nothing else is taken into consideration. However, throughout the course of our daily lives, we are constantly confronted with new possibilities. Other inconsistencies arise from our own diverse wants and desires. Inquiring minds want to know, "maybe I should do this and not that.. maybe this wasn't such a good idea. It's quite hard and boring... maybe I want to change directions while I still can."

The urge for congruence is especially strong in people who are constantly engaged in internal battles with themselves, with diverse portions of themselves always at odds over issues they believe are critical to their well-being. An individual can have a desire to overindulge in things like sweets, needless arguments, gossiping, alcohol, shopping, while simultaneously realizing the negative long-term effects of those actions and the possibility that alternative, better options exist for fulfilling one's own needs. When an incongruity is significant, extensive, and long-lasting, people seek congruence. But sometimes the quest for congruence goes too far and becomes unachievable, undesired, and exhausting. What would happen if a person's thoughts and actions were always in sync? Our attention shifts from one activity to another at some point, and we're always aware of both the current experience and what we're imagining.

This would be impossible if there was total congruence. If you want to choose between two possibilities, you have to compare and contrast two experiences to see which one is more suitable to address your needs, and this necessitates a brief period of incongruence.

There would be no motion and no retreat if we lived in a world where everything was in sync. In fact, we are often inclined to exclude alternatives, defer decisions, refuse to accept new ideas, and neglect diverse internal requirements in order to attain congruence. As soon as the changing world of experience intrudes and upsets it, this can only be a short-term fix. In order to avoid or eradicate any experiences that do not already fit into our narrow and tightly consistent universe, we may perceive these interferences as alien and harmful.

Congruence and incongruence are both important and valuable, but it's the dynamic balance between the two that's most fulfilling. Congruence permits us to temporarily focus all of our attention on a single experience in order to either completely appreciate and learn from it or accomplish something.

It is through incongruity that we can see the endless options and implications that life presents to us. Maintaining this balance enables us to understand and respect both the positive and negative parts of the equilibrium, as well as provides a means of identifying and correcting imbalances when they occur. The congruency check is what you need whenever you make a change in your mental map.

1. As a part of the eco-check of any pattern, ask: "Does any part of me object to these changes?"

2. Remember to ask it with sincerity and be ready to accept any answer. Do not rush it.

3. For a few days, notice if certain things in your surroundings grab your attention more than usual, as well as if there are any early morning dreams that stand out. These are messages from your unconscious.

Conflict Resolution

Source: Richard Bandler, John Grinder, and Robert Dilts.

Clarify the issues in terms of their polarity and logical level.

Elicit a meta-position.

Determine the positive intentions underlying the polarity and get them in touch with them.

Get agreement on a higher-level intention.

Generate alternatives to fulfill the higher intention.

Get commitment to a plan.

Test.

This pattern helps resolve conflict while generating commitments to fulfill higher-order goals and values.

1. Determine the polarity and logical level of the issues. Think about the key issues of the conflict. Think of them as polarities in which there are two sides in opposition. At what logical level is the conflict primarily occurring? For example, money is a common topic of conflict in relationships. This is usually argued at the behavioral level, because what to do or not to do is the question.

2. Elicit a meta-position. Get into a meta-position that transcends the conflicting positions.

3. Identify the positive intentions underlying the polarity and connect with them.

a. Determine the positive intentions driving each party in this conflict. You should find that it is at a higher logical level than the more obvious issues of the conflict. Often, the underlying intentions turn out not to be in opposition, particularly when viewed in terms of their benefit on a systems level. Systems-level concerns would be about things like managing everyone's stress and having a happy family. Longer-term thinking also tends to refocus on a higher logical level. The child's college education is, in part, an appeal to the parents' identities as good parents.

b. Have each party recognize and acknowledge the other party's positive intentions. Help them understand that this does not mean that they endorse the other party's logic or conclusions, or compromise on anything that they are uncomfortable with.

4. Get agreement on a higher-level intention.Continuing from your meta-position perspective, chunk up until you uncover an intention that both parties can agree to. The Meta-position is easily achieved by moving to the 3rd or 4th perceptual position.

5. Create alternatives to the higher intention. Explore with them what alternatives to the conflicting positions might exist that would fulfill their higher intentions. Generally, breakthrough ideas are better than mere compromises or middle ground. The idea may or may not be highly innovative, but it is usually obscured by the conflict. Once, a couple realized that they had the same long-term vision, but that they lacked the structure to realize it. They saw that they would be able to agree on even the most painful spending restrictions if they were less vague about what had to happen. They decided to set more specific goals and determine a monthly savings goal that would be necessary to achieve their long-term goals. In order to meet the savings goal, they would make whatever short-term sacrifices were necessary.

6. Get commitment to a plan. As in the example above, help them commit to specific choices that are aligned with their higher-order values and plans. Help them specify the means for making these choices and plans happen. Mitigate any ecological concerns. You can certainly use the ecology check pattern to get out of the way of any possible disturbance to agreement.

7. Test. Follow up with them to see how well their new commitments and agreements are working out. As always, attend to ecological concerns. See what additional higher values and roles might help to inform their decisions and follow through.

Consciousness Awareness

This pattern increases your awareness of your states and how they affect your perspective. This awareness is valuable in nearly every aspect of neuro-linguistic programming and life in general. Any effort you make to improve your states and patterns requires you to be aware of these things in order to make the discriminations required by the pattern.

1. Review today's states. Review your day, taking note of the major states that you have experienced so far.

2. Represent the states. Draw a circle to represent each of these states. Inside the circle, draw a simple face, like a happy face, to represent how you feel. It can be as simple as happy and frowning faces.

3. Annotate the states. Rate the intensity of each state with a number from one to ten. Underneath, note the main internal representations and changes in physiology that you experience in this state. Put an asterisk (*) next to the main triggers of the states. For example, if you were treated rudely this morning, what was it that really triggered your feelings? Looking at sub-modalities, it might have It is mainly an aspect of the person's tone of voice.

Remember to include meanings, not just sensory experiences. Perhaps it was what the person was implying with their tone, rather than the tone itself.

4. Test. See if this exercise enhances your ability to detect the changes and subtleties in your states and how your thoughts and circumstances can trigger them.

Contrastive Analysis

This pattern is useful for recognizing and better managing different emotional states, specifically when it comes to ineffective emotional responses.

1. Recall a past incident (A) in which you experienced a limiting emotional response.

2. Associate into the past experience (see what you saw, hear what you heard, feel what you felt).

3. Identity and elicit the key driving kinesthetic sub-modalities linked to the emotion you felt (refer to Appendix E at the end of this book for further details):

- *Temperature*

- *Texture*

- *Degree of adaptability*

- *Vibration*

- *Pressure*

- *Tension*

- *Movement*

- *Breathing*

- *Weight*

- *Confinement*

• *Change Of Size Or Shape*

• *Direction*

• *Triggers*

4. Consider and recall another experience (B), with a similar emotional state, as in step 1, but in which the response you had was positive. For example, it is often the same physiological experience (rapid breathing, stomach upset, over excitement) when a person is asked to give a speech in front of a large audience, or when that same person is expecting a much awaited surprise (such as the return of a loved one after a long period abroad).

5. Look for the main differences in the kinesthetic sub-modalities, between experience A and experience B.

6. Find the commonalities in driving sub-modalities, that are shared by both experience A and B.

7. What key sub-modalities allow you to smoothly move between the positive and negative interpretation of similar events?

8. Now elicit the visual and auditory sub-modalities for experience A and experience B, and repeat steps 5, 6 and 7.

Conversational Postulate

When someone asks you if you can pass the salt, they are actually asking you to pass the salt, but they're being nice about it. NLP calls this a "conversational postulate." In hypnosis, this helps to bypass conscious resistance, and it generates an unconscious drive to act on the request or answer the question. Here are some examples:

"Can you imagine doing that?"

"Would you invite that area to relax?"

"How easily can you let your unconscious mind do this for you?"

You can use this structure in your day-to-day business. "Are you prepared to use us as a vendor?" wouldn't exert any magic mind power over a potential customer, but it would be part of a persuasive communication pattern and an attractive bid to the customer.

Colliding and Colluding

Replace stress and frustration with empowerment and confidence, by resolving conflicting and colluding beliefs. This pattern is primarily for interpersonal situations. By colluding, we mean beliefs that unconsciously interfere with our success in a way that is interlaced with other beliefs.

1. The Situation:

Identify a situation in which your beliefs conflict with those of another person.

2. Your Belief:

Describe specific beliefs that collide with this person's beliefs.

3. Their Belief:

Describe the other person's beliefs that collide with yours. These beliefs are completely compatible with mine. Identify which belief is the primary focus of the conflict. Below are generic beliefs.

One of these is likely to apply here. Mark it with "OT" for "other" (meaning the other party's conflicting belief), and circle the word choice that applies (i.e., "is/is not"). Remember, you are identifying the other party's limiting belief.

a. The objective is/is not desirable and worthwhile.

b. This goal can not be achieved.

c. The actions necessary to achieve this goal are not sufficiently detailed, understandable, appropriate, or ecologically sound.

d. I do or don't have the skills or talents that I would need in order to achieve this goal.

The Big Book of NLP

e. I do/don't deserve to attain this goal.

f. I am not in charge of this goal.

3. Colluding Belief:

Move out of your conflicting belief state. Look for colluding beliefs, that is, beliefs of YOURS that in some way reinforce the other person's limiting beliefs that you perceive as troublesome. Use the list above. Mark the applicable belief with a "CL" for "colluding."

4. Meta-Position:

Move to a meta-position where you can be free of the conflict/collusion reality. From this fresh position, find alternative frames of reference and concepts that can help you find innovative and practical solutions.

a. Presuppositions:

Take note of the assumptions that underpin the beliefs. Typically, these are not conscious, so you will need to be sure you are thinking outside of your current, conventional frame. The following presuppositions can help you here.

1) "There is no single correct map," versus, "I have the one true map."

2) "There is a positive intention behind every behavior and belief," versus "The behavior (or belief) is negative and must be eliminated."

3) "People have the capabilities they need," versus, "Some people are just defective."

4) "We are all part of the larger ecosystem," versus, "We are independent entities, and context does not matter."

b. Positive Intentions:

Return to the three belief states and clarify the positive intentions that underpin each one.

c. Meta-Program Level:

Return to the meta-position you established and identify the similarities and differences between these beliefs at the meta-program level.

d. Supportive State:

Associate yourself into each belief position once more, this time identifying the state that most likely supports each of the beliefs.

5. Stable Foundation:

Return to your first meta-position, and answer these questions for each of the beliefs you have identified:

How could you fill in the missing NLP presuppositions?

How could you realize the positive intentions of these beliefs in a constructive manner?

How could you align and balance the meta program patterns?

How could you alter your state, or that of the other party, so that it is more amenable to a constructive and ecologically sound resolution?

6. Resourceful State:

Create a resourceful state in which you embrace the emerging positive beliefs.Maintain that state as you step into your first position.

From there, mentally role-play new ways of responding to the other party.

Conflicting Beliefs Integration

Select and state an issue that involves conflicting beliefs.

Identify the ideal outcome for this issue.

Step into a meta-position.

Elicit the opposing divisive beliefs.

Identify the shared mission of the parts.

Explore the resources of each part that can help create the positive future.

Re-anchor the resource state, and work with the anchor.

Step into a meta-position opposite (across the timeline) from the first meta-position that you created.

Test.

NOTE: Unless you are already a highly experienced NLP practitioner, this pattern may be inappropriate for you to try on your own. We suggest that you work with a very competent NLP practitioner who is very mature in his or her own personal work.

Conflicting beliefs can cause self-sabotage and prevent people from assertively pursuing their goals. They can undermine relationships of all kinds. This pattern assists in aligning beliefs so that they are accurate and synergistic.

1. Choose and state an issue that involves conflicting beliefs.

a. Examine your personal issues and identify one that contains contradictory beliefs.State the beliefs as specifically as you can. One of the beliefs is likely to be irrational, so it may be a little embarrassing to express it. For example, you might, deep down at gut level, believe that an intimidating person that you have to deal with is capable of destroying your self-esteem. Your increased heart rate when you encounter this person is a good sign that there is an irrational fear.

b. State the beliefs as specifically as you can, starting with the words "I believe that _____, but at the same time I also believe that (rational alternative belief)." State any irrational beliefs without censoring or altering them. The more irrational it sounds, the better.

2. Determine the best possible outcome for resolving this issue.

a. Determine an ideal future outcome and a time frame for achieving it.

Clearly identify the ideal future outcome of this issue. The best outcome for this purpose is an outcome that one of the beliefs is interfering with. Select a good time in the future for the ideal outcome to take place.

b. Generate and anchor a related resource state.

Consider yourself to be at that point in the future.What are you like, as the person experiencing that outcome? What other changes have taken place? Take special note of how it feels to have the more successful belief fully liberated and engaged.Select a trigger for this state and anchor it.

c. Consider what you overcame to achieve the result.

Now look back and see what obstacles you overcame to reach that successful point in time.

d. Identify the point of origin of the obstacles. Look back even further to the time or times that the obstacles originated. Imagine stepping back into the most significant point in time. Consider how it felt to have the more unsuccessful belief inflamed and active at the time.For many of us, it is better to think of a point at which a number of negative patterns came into focus as a belief that could be put into words. A history of patterned abuse or neglect, developmental problems, drug abuse, chronic difficulties such as ADD, a serious career crash, or a toxic relationship that ruptured your self-esteem over time can be considered a theme. You can identify a point at which a dysfunctional or unresourceful belief and physiology emerge as an identifiable state. The point at which things were at their worst and it was difficult to see a positive outcome might be a good point to select on your timeline in this case.

e. Take note of the polarity formed by the two beliefs.Notice how the future successful beliefs and the past, less successful beliefs comprise two opposing elements, such as logic versus emotion, or rationality versus intuition, immature versus mature beliefs, and so forth. For example, the belief "I can't succeed or people will expect too much from me." versus "I thrive on meaningful challenges and enjoy expressing my drive to succeed." could be divided into the drives for security and avoiding embarrassment, versus adventure and risk.

f. Recognize the two beliefs as components of the state.Notice the differing physiologic manifestations of each conflicting belief. Your thought patterns, emotional feelings, and other physiology comprise two different, conflicting states. Pay special attention to the asymmetry in the feelings or related body language, such as gestures you would do differently in these two states. Think of them as two "parts" to this NLP pattern.

3. Take a meta-position.

Choose a meta-position that is disconnected from your beliefs and identities and is located outside of your timeline.Step into this position.

4. Elicit the opposing divisive beliefs.

Have each part express its beliefs regarding the other part. They are likely to express distrust, disgust, and other charged judgments.

a. Turn the parts so that they face each other.Have the parts turn to face each other. Notice how this causes the perception of each part to shift. You might notice, for example, that the future part can see the past part as reacting to inappropriate judgments by adults that as a child you were highly motivated to avoid. This suggests a part that needs help unfolding its potential, rather than a part that is disgusting or just a threat to success.

b. Determine the positive motivations of each component.Identify for each part the underlying positive motivations. Have each part recognize the positive intentions of the other.

5. Determine the parts' shared mission.

Still in your meta-position, identify the mission that these parts share, according to your highest values. For example, achieving success with adequate preparation and effective strategies This example captures the positive essence of both parts.

6. Explore the resources of each part that can help create a positive future.

Think about the resources and capacities that each part has to offer and how that can help the other part achieve the positive future that you have already explored in this process. Reviewing the positive motivations and common mission of the two parts can help you come up with more of these resources and capacities. For example, your future scenario will rely upon your analytical skills as well as your passion for the most meaningful elements of the positive outcome and the path to that outcome.

a. Obtain agreement from all parties to collaborate.an ecologically sound agreement from the two parties to combine their resources and accomplish their common mission. You have already harmonized their resources, so your previously conflicting parts are ready for a new, powerful alignment.

b. As needed, work with deeper limiting beliefs.This is the point at which you may discover the limiting beliefs that are even deeper or more neglected than the ones you have unearthed so far. If this process has good momentum for you, it may be possible to refine and update these beliefs. If they are challenging, then you may want to subject them to this process from step one at another time. The anchor you have established can help you do this more effectively.

7. Re-anchor the resource state and interact with it.

Return to the point on your timeline representing your desired future identity. Re-anchor the state that is aligned with this identity. This state includes your positive intent and the sense of your parts' common mission. The state you are re-anchoring is actually an expanded and enhanced version of the first future state that you anchored.

a. Keeping the anchor in place, move to a point before the less successful identity.

Hold the anchor, moving off of the timeline and back to a point that is just behind (earlier than) the past, less successful identity.

b. Assist your future successful self in getting to that point by acting as a mentor.

Have your future successful self step back along your timeline to that past point.

Have this successful self act as a mentor to you at that point, providing any needed support and resources.

c. Take advantage of this mentoring in the first perceptual position.

Associate with that past identity and live through that time period while receiving mentoring and resources from your future, successful self.

d. Insert the resources into the future point, causing the parts to contain both parts' resources.Maintain your focus on the resources of the two identities and the positive changes that are taking place now.

Slowly move forward in the timeline, carrying these resources, until you step into the point that you established in the future. This way, each part has the resources of both parts within it. Notice all the changes in you that result from the integration taking place.

8. Step into a meta-position opposite (across the timeline) to the first meta-position that you created.

Recall the meta-position that you established on your timeline. Create a new meta-position on the opposite side of the timeline from that one.

Step into this new meta-position.

a. Walk with yourself (from your meta-position) and the two parts.

Imagine the past and future parts walking towards each other along the timeline, as you move from your meta-position toward your timeline at the same pace as the parts.

b. Incorporate the identities into yourself.

When the two parts meet, reach out with your hands and gather both identities, bringing them into you.

c. Enter your timeline and face forward in the first perceptual position, perceiving things as a single entity with all of your parts fully integrated.

Step into the timeline, in the first perceptual position (associated), and associate the two parts into your perceptual position so that you are facing forward, fully integrated as a single rich identity.

d. Walk forward in time to the desired state you have established. Walk forward until you reach the point at which you have established the desired state.

9. Test

Notice what it's like to think about the conflicting beliefs that you started with. You should feel much more resourceful and unified than you did in the past.

If the conflict involves more than two parts or issues, you can include those issues or do these integrations in sequence, one pair at a time. Remember that this is an advanced pattern that may require further training and assistance before it is appropriate to carry out.

The Big Book of NLP

Content Reframing

Source: Richard Bandler & John Grinder

Select a behavior you dislike.

Identify the part.

Identify the positive intention.

Identify the frame.

De-frame the part.

Reframe the behavior and intention (content).

Reframe the usefulness in terms of situations (context).

Integrate the reframe.

Test the reframe.

A frame in NLP refers to the way you put boundaries around what you consider. It's impossible to consider every piece of information in your world in order to make a decision, so no matter what you think about anything, there is a frame.

1. Pick a behavior that you despise.

2. Identify the part. Note the aspect of you that produces this behavior. Think in terms of parts.

Name that part.

3. Determine the positive intent.

Figure out the part's positive intent in producing this behavior.

4. Determine the frame. What is the frame around the intention and behavior?

You can see this by discovering the presuppositions behind the part's sense of mission and its behavior in service of that mission (In the examples we provided, one person thought he was defective because he couldn't get out of bed, and another seemed to think he had complete control over tobacco in order to justify a small amount of smoking).

5. De-frame the part. How can you expand the part's perspective?

Try to find sub-modality shifts that will have an impact on this. You can also ask what the behavior and intentions mean to you. You can simply ask, "What else could this mean?"

6. Reframe the behavior as well as the intention (content).

Find a way, however slight, that you can react positively to the part's intentions or to the behavior.

7. Reframe the usefulness in terms of situations (context).

How might this behavior actually serve you in some situations?

Connect with how this might feel good or appropriate.

Remember that the behavior may need to take a different form, or even cease, depending on what it is. You may also find that the underlying motivations can be expressed very differently, so that the behavior is easy to change or eliminate once you learn to satisfy the underlying motivation.

8. Apply the reframe. Give yourself permission to make use of this new reframe. Although you may not approve of the way the intention is expressed in some situations, you can now make a good connection with the reframe because it highlights the positive aspect of the behavior.

The Big Book of NLP

Think of ways that you can express the motivation in a more useful way or ways that you can direct the behavior in a more useful way.

9. Test the reframe.

How do you feel now when you think back on the behavior?

How do you feel about the part?

If your self-esteem has improved or you feel less in conflict with yourself, that is a good sign that the pattern has been useful. If you have actually come up with a revolutionary and positive way to utilize the underlying motivations, that's even better.

Context Reframing

Source: Richard Bandler & John Grinder

> *Identify a resourceful state.*
>
> *Ask context questions.*
>
> *Vividly imagine yourself expressing this aspect in a typical appropriate context.*
>
> *Pick a variety of contexts at random and imagine yourself expressing this aspect in each of them.*
>
> *Test.*

Increase mental flexibility and creativity by increasing context awareness.It helps you imagine "importing" a behavior, state, belief, or other aspect of yourself into various contexts.

1. Determine a resourceful state. Choose a state, behavior, belief, emotion, aspect of commitment, or any other aspect of yourself that might be helpful for building context awareness.

2. Inquire about the context. Ask yourself where this aspect would be useful. Where would it be an expression of your higher values or self-interest?

3. Vividly imagine yourself expressing this aspect in a typical, appropriate context.

4. Choose several contexts at random and imagine yourself expressing this aspect in each of them. Imagine what results are likely to come from expressing this aspect in each context. What are the effects? For example, what would come from you taking a

negotiating mindset and applying it to a loving relationship? If at first it seems awkward or objectionable, ask yourself how you would fold it into your other, more typical, forms of self expression as you express this aspect. For example, negotiating very skillfully but in a fully loving way. Another example: what would it be like to use highly evolved NLP skills as a prison counselor in a session with a convict?

5. Test. In the next few days or weeks, notice any ways that you are thinking more creatively about what aspects of yourself to express in various situations. Are you more flexible or creative? Are you more conscious of how you use yourself as a resource for outcomes in some situations?

Contextual Self

This is a simple technique to get a client out of his or her mind if they feel trapped within their own stream of thoughts. It proves to them the existence of the observer perspective (unbiased self-reflection) and gives them permission to exit a problematic mental state without needing any further excuse to distract themselves or use time-consuming escapism tactics.

The "self" is contextual-sometimes I am happy about my ideas and sometimes I am upset about them, and it might happen to be the very same idea that yesterday made me happy and today made me annoyed. The meta-level of the contextual self is the real self, the entity we might call "spirit" or "*neshama*" (in Jewish tradition). That is the observer perspective, the permanent, irreplaceable "I" that is above (meta) all the parts of the ego.

1.Sit up straight and take one deep breath, all the way in and all the way out.

2. "I am going to count silently from 30 to 0, and when I reach zero, I will tell you to stop, and you will tell me if you noticed that you can be a spectator of your mind-you were aware of your thoughts. All I'm asking you to do, while I could silently, is to take a step back and observe and listen to what's going on inside your head."

3. Be silent for 30 seconds.

4. "Beyond the ramblings of your conscious mind, there is also a part of your mind that listens to the ramblings; it's the observing self. That self is not a judge and it does not analyze the content of your thoughts; it is simply there, present. You can access it any time you feel overwhelmed by your thoughts. Just step back and watch and observe the silence in between the thoughts."

Core Transformation

Source: Connirae Andreas

Live from a new center that comes from a practical yet spiritual or expanded experience of life. By discovering the core state at the center of each part, we overcome serious limitations. This pattern is more fully addressed in the book Core Transformation by Connirae Andreas.

The "core state" gives you a valuable compass that helps you know whether you are on your path and whether you are coming from a spiritual or expanded place.

When you are dealing with a conflict, it is much easier to envision a positive outcome and approach when you connect with your core state.

It can be as simple as checking in and seeing whether your strategy for handling the conflict resonates well with your core, or if it feels more like a distraction from your path, that is, like drama or unnecessary harm. This is just one example of an understanding that can create a very meaningful foundation for your life and contribute greatly to your personal philosophy.

Note: This pattern has many steps and involves some fairly abstract or advanced ideas. It's a good idea to read it through and make sure that you grasp it before actually trying it out. However, you don't need to understand what the core state experience is up front. That is something that is best understood through experience.

1. Determine what part you will be working with.

a. Select an issue that you can experience as a part of yourself, with specific motives that drive behavior that is limited in some way, behavior that is not doing enough to get you through the issue. You can start simply with a behavior, feeling, or response if you wish. For the purpose of this exercise, give this behavior, feeling, or response pattern a name. Jot down this name. We'll refer to it here as "your part."

b. Get to know the part as a collection of behaviors, emotions, or reactions. Think about what tends to trigger this pattern.

Ask yourself what places, times, and people tend to help trigger this pattern. Make some basic notes about this.

c. Experience the pattern in terms of how you are triggered to react.

Select a specific point in time when this pattern took place.

Mentally step into this scene and re-experience it.

Pay careful attention to what sub-modalities comprise the mindset that drives your reaction to the situation.

d. Access this part. Remember that the behavior, feelings, and responses that come from you in connection with the issue or issues in question are old patterns that you did not consciously orchestrate or develop. Instead, experience them as coming from your part and having a collective life as this part.

Discover how this part "lives" inside of you as a body experience. Where in your body do you mostly feel it?

Describe those feelings. What inner voice expresses it?

Express or come up with the words that express their message, fears, or motivations.

What mental images are part of this? They may be symbols or scenes that are fearful or motivating.

Carry this out with an inviting state of mind, and invite this part to emerge into your awareness more completely.

The Big Book of NLP

e. Thank the part. Thank this part for coming into awareness and being part of your path. Tell it that you are looking forward to understanding its purposes and having it as part of the more aligned and fulfilling existence that you and it will create.

2. Begin the Outcome Deepening pattern by determining your part's desires and thanking it.

a. Inquire about your part's desires in relation to this issue. Be gently direct and open, asking, "What do you want? What is the highest purpose of having this issue? How does it serve you and me?" Note the answer as an intended outcome.

b. Thank the part. Express Thanks for providing this answer. If you like the outcome stated or implied by the answer, say so. If not, then express your appreciation for joining on a path of discovery for greater fulfillment and alignment.

You can say this because you are committed to this kind of outcome and because you have vast, untapped resources to realize such an outcome.

You can have the kind of certainty that comes from commitment. This is not the certainty of a guarantee that comes from the outside; it is an inner certainty that you cultivate in order to be more resourceful, creative, motivated, and vibrantly happy.

Note: The term "outcome deepening pattern" was created for this book. Andreas refers to this phase (steps two through four) with a separate name for each step.

3. Continue the 'Outcome Deepening' pattern by deriving deeper outcomes until you experience your core state.

a. Ask your part for a deeper outcome. Ask the part, "When you fully experience and have this outcome, what, beyond that, becomes important to have?" Make note of the answer and thank the part as you did before.

b. Continue to repeat step (a), deriving deeper results, until you reach your core state. Name it based on the deep outcome that produced it. We will refer to this outcome-state combination as your "core state outcome." (Although Andreas refers to it as your core state, we use the term "core state outcome" to disambiguate the core state from the outcome, since this pattern can involve more than one outcome that triggers the core state.)

Keep repeating step three, getting a new outcome each time. It may not be obvious at first, but each new outcome brings you closer to your core state. You could say that you are moving through to deeper outcomes.

c. Write down each answer in order. When you reach your core state, you will experience a centered yet expanded sense of peace. You might describe it as coming home to yourself. When people get there, they tend to be very sure that they know they are there, even though it is hard to describe with words.

4. Finish the Deepening the Outcome pattern:Enjoy and meditate upon your core state. Name your core state outcome. Once you experience the core state, take some time to enjoy it. It is a healing experience in itself. Notice that your core state came when your most recent outcome came up. From this point, we will be using a combination of your core state and this outcome. We will refer to it as your core state outcome. Give it a brief name based on the outcome that you noted. Whenever the text says "core state outcome," use the brief name or phrase for your outcome in its place.

5. Initiate the Core Emergence pattern. Understand the core state as a source rather than a result. Transform each of the outcomes in reverse order in connection with your core state outcome.

a. Establish your core emergent pattern by viewing your core state as a beginning or source rather than an end result of striving. Your parts may think you have to jump through a lot of hoops before you can get to your core state. Imagine that this is backwards. Imagine turning it so that your core state is your beginning, the wellspring of your actions.

b. Begin the core evolution pattern by noticing how your core state outcome expands your experience. From this point, where you see the core state outcome, remember to say the name or phrase for the outcome that connected you to your core state this time around. Ask your part, "As you experience your (core state outcome) and know it as a way of being, knowing that (core state outcome) is a beginning, how can having (core state outcome) expand your experience right now?" Just notice.

The Big Book of NLP

c. Have the core state outcome transform each of the outcomes that you noted, one at a time, from the most recent backwards. Ask your part, "Can you notice how your experience of (core state outcome) as a way of being expands (outcome)?" Outcome refers to the most recent outcome from (3a). Do this step for each outcome backwards until you complete it for the first of the outcomes.

d. Expand your experience of the original context to include your core state outcome. Now that you have gone through each outcome, ask the part, "How can having (core state outcome) as a habit of being expand your experience of (briefly state the situation you selected in step one)?"

Note: Core Emergence is a term that originated for this reference. Andreas actually calls this "reversing the outcome chain," but this conflicts with the metaphor of "core," since getting to a core means deepening. Also, this work involves several levels of consciousness, which implies gaining depth.

6. Maintain the Core Emergence Pattern: Increase your role to your current age.

a. Get your part's age. Ask your part, "How old are you?"

Note the age. Since it was formed some time ago, it should be younger than you. Usually, it is an age from childhood.

b. Obtain consent from your part to advance to your current age.

Ask your part, "Would you like to experience the wonderful things that come from moving forward to (your current age) as you experience (core state outcome)?"

If the answer is no, work with the state to resolve any issues. There may be an ecological problem to handle.

c. Increase your role to your current age while fully accessing the core state outcome. Maintaining your connection with your core state outcome, imagine your part moving forward in time, infused with the core state outcome experience, until it reaches the present.

7. Finish the Core Emergence Pattern by bringing your part inside your body if it is outside of it.

a. With your part in the present, observe how you represent it. Now that your part is in the present, infused with your core state outcome, notice how you are experiencing your part. Where is it located, in or outside of your body (perhaps in your visual field or primarily as a kinesthetic experience)?

b. If the part is outside of your body, bring it inside. If your part is outside of your body, invite it to move into the area of your body in which it feels most at home.

Welcome it and notice how this allows you to experience your core state outcome more fully.

c. Extend the sensation that results. Invite the part and this sensation to expand throughout your body, so that every cell resonates with this quality of energy.

Does the original area in your body feel this sensation in a way that is richer?

As you experience this expansion, know that you are making this an experience that you can access and one that will serve as an emotional compass to which you can refer in choosing new directions.

8. Core Emergence Pattern II: Repeat step five, but this time play your part as an adult. You can do it briefly this time around.

a. Set up your core evolution pattern by thinking of your core state as not an end result of striving, but rather, as a beginning or source. Ask your part, "As you experience your (core state) and know (core state) as a way of being, knowing that (core state) is a beginning, how does already having (core state) expand your experience right now?" Just notice.

b. Have the core state transform each of the outcomes that you noted, one at a time, from the most recent backwards. Ask your part, "Notice how your experience of (core state) as a way of being expands (outcome)." "Outcome refers to the most recent outcome from 3a. Do this step for each outcome backwards until you complete this step all the way to the first of your outcomes.

The Big Book of NLP

c. Use your core state to broaden your experience of the original context. Now that you have gone through each outcome, ask the part, "How does already having (core state) as a way of being expand your experience of (briefly state the situation you selected in step one)?"

9. Additional Core Deepening and Emergence Patterns: Elicit any parts of yourself that are opposed to your core state as a way of being.Take them through the core patterns.

a. Go through the core patterns with an objecting part, steps two through seven. Ask yourself if there is any part of you that objects to your core state as a way of being now. If you get a "no" answer, then experience the part that is saying, "no," and remember that it is a valuable part of you. Take that part through the core patterns as you did in steps two through seven.

b. Repeat (?) for any remaining parts. Do this for any additional parts involved in the issue. If any of these parts leads to a different core state outcome, write it down. Do this step if you have the time to expand this exercise. Think of any additional parts that are involved in this issue. Take each of them through step five, the core emerging part of the pattern, as you did with the main part.

Note: Since the Core Transformation pattern may be time-consuming the first time through, you may wish to leave out step nine until you are efficient with this pattern.

10. Optional progress—in order to achieve additional core state outcomes. Note: Do this step if you have gotten additional core state outcomes (that is, outcomes that connect you with your core state) from step nine. This can happen when you identify additional parts and take them through the Core Deepening pattern, as you did for the first part in Step Two.

a. Experience your timeline. Access your awareness of your timeline. Experience how it is a flow of all of your experiences leading up to the person you are now.

b. Carry your core state outcomes with you as you float back to the moment before conception. Look at your notes, and bring into your awareness the additional core state outcomes that you got from step nine. Take each of them with you as you float back to the moment before you were conceived.

c. Flow your core state outcomes into this point in time. Attract your core state outcomes to this point in time, as though its limitless energy flows into this time and builds, being swept into the momentum of time, beginning to move forward with time. Your core state transcends all outcomes. It doesn't depend on them. It is a wellspring of insight, harmonious action, and creativity. Notice how your core state is a universal experience flowing into your timeline.

d. Proceed with your core state outcomes in your timeline. Descend into that moment, catching the wave of your core state, riding it forward, and continuing to take your core state outcomes with you in your awareness. Have these core state outcomes flow through your life experiences.

e. Experience the benefit to your timeline. As you move forward through time, notice how your core state outcomes enrich your life.

f. Experience the benefit to your future. Have this wave of core state energy move through your present and into the future. Notice how this energizes and enriches your future.

g. Repeat several times, increasing the speed each time. Repeat this timeline flow from (b) through (e) several times, allowing it to go faster each time. Each time you finish, become associated with the present before proceeding with another round. This pattern of repeated and accelerated timeline travel builds the durability and accessibility of the core state, brings your positive life memories into the foreground to enhance your self-esteem and resourcefulness, and improves your motivation and mood for facing the future. Needless to say, the results will be seen as you experience the growth that comes from using such a set of actions in your philosophy and life strategies. It is a combination of aspects of the Swish pattern, the anchoring pattern, and the timeline pattern. There are many other processes involved, but it is not for us here to deal with theories. We will leave the academic discussion to someone else or to another book.

11. Savor your core state, think about the value you have created, and take a break. You have created access to your core state. This is of profound value. Take some time to meditate upon your core state. We recommend that you take a break and contemplate this process and its outcome by taking a walk or enjoying some other physical activity.

Criteria Installation

Source: Steve Andreas

1. Choose a life area in which your values appear ambiguous. Select a life area, such as career, finances, or relationships, in which you feel that your decision-making or actions are not based on a firm foundation of values or criteria.

2. Make a criteria hierarchy.

a. Start by thinking of a trivial act that you could do but wouldn't bother to. Ask what you would accomplish by refraining from this action. Typically, you would save time. Be sure to state the criteria in positive terms.

b. Now ask yourself what might get you to take this action anyway. Note what you find important about this condition. For example, if you said that you would stand on a chair because you needed to replace a light bulb, you might feel that being able to see and function in your kitchen is more important than two minutes of time. This pattern can be summarized so far as starting with a trivial act you would not do, citing the value that would prevent you from doing it, and then stating the condition that would get you to do it. At this point, you think of a condition that would reverse your stance.

c. Consider a condition that would prevent you from doing it.

d. Specify the applicable value. For example, perhaps you would not replace the bulb if you had to meet an urgent deadline and didn't need to be in the kitchen for that. The value might be the importance of maintaining your accounts, staying out of jail, or being on time for an appointment. Try to summarize the value in one word, in addition to the brief statement of the value. For being on time, you might add "punctuality."

e. Repeat this pattern. Each time you state the criterion for your decision, come up with a condition that would get you to reverse your decision to do or not to do the action. Then state the value behind that decision.

3.Complete the continuum. As you proceed, you are creating a continuum of criteria from least to most important. Continue until you are certain you have identified the most important criteria of all. This will be one that you can't trump with any condition.

4. Define the sub-modalities. Explore the differences between the sub-modalities between the highest and lowest priority criteria. Notice how you represent various values such as "excellence," "healing," and "integrity." Pay attention to the analog sub-modalities that vary as you describe the criteria in all the primary sub-modalities.

5. Confirm the appropriate criterion position and sub-modalities. For each criterion, decide whether you need to raise or lower it, and where it should go on the scale. Shift its sub-modalities to match those of the next lower criterion. By adjusting the sub-modalities, the code becomes the criterion for the degree of importance it should have.

6. Review it again, emphasizing the value and position of the criteria. From a meta-position, evaluate your hierarchy of values. Ask how well these values serve you, and how well they serve the functions in their current sequence. How well do they enable you to make resourceful decisions and experience peace of mind? Note any criteria that you need to shift to another position, or change in any other way.

7. Select the criterion to shift. Determine which criterion you wish to shift. Determine where you want it to be. Think about what sequence of values will move you forward as you desire.

8. Based on the final positions, revise sub-modalities. Gradually shift the criterion to the appropriate place in your continuum. Based on the importance that the criterion should have, apply the sub-modalities that you feel are appropriate. Notice which sub-modalities appear in the criteria before and after it. Code it.

9. Continue until you are satisfied that your value hierarchy will help guide you toward the most resourceful behaviors and decisions.

10. Future Pace. Imagine a situation in which your new criterion makes a difference. Imagine yourself in that situation, fully experiencing this.

11. Test. Take note of how easily you can access resourceful states in the coming days and weeks.

Criticism Analyzer

Select a situation in which you responded badly to criticism.

Generate a state of safety.

Respond to the person with validation.

Ask for more information.

Imagine the response in an effective way that is not disturbing.

Reflect what you have received.

Get to an "agreement frame."

Generate your own representation in a top left position.

Compare the representations of you and your critic.

Respond from your understanding, and do it in a classy way.

Seek closure.

Take this to the relationship level. Test.

This pattern lets you experience criticism without taking it too personally. It uses the concept that words are not real. If criticism sets off a chain reaction inside you that results in anger, shame, or defensiveness, you need to remember that such suffering is optional.

This pattern gives you control over these reactions. The importance of learning how to accept criticism well can be seen in our most primitive need—to be liked. Social status and relationships with other people are very important to us.

Human beings are social creatures. We need these connections for two main reasons—survival and pleasure. Is there no real joy if you just have fun alone? The greatest joy is when you share the happiness, when you win as a team and not just as an individual. Did you ever wonder how it comes that men hug each other and cry on the football field? Did you see a player crying and hugging himself or herself?

The survival aspect of social life is also obvious—we need the service and escort of other people to run our lives. You need the shopkeeper, the mechanic, the physician, the bus driver, the electric company technicians, and so on. But you also need your family to be supported and nourished; you need your spouse to feel intimacy and love, which is also a basic survival need. We all need other people in our lives; no one person is an island. But the gift of relationship comes with a catch-22: you can't be social if you don't know how to handle criticism well. Yes, some people will want to criticize you for their own good, not yours. But many will not. Many will be careful and perhaps brave enough to let you know what you're doing wrong (in their opinion) or how your inaction or actions, behaviors, choices and emotional expressions are affecting them. Learning to accept criticism well and knowing how to handle it maturely is one of life's greatest skills and one that will boost your self-esteem and self-respect.

1. Choose a situation in which you responded badly to criticism. First, do this exercise in your imagination. In the future, this could become like a reflex that you do rapidly. Then you will get to the point where you do it unconsciously, with your mind freed to be even more of a master.

Imagine a situation in which you were criticized and it was either painful, or you did not care for how you reacted, or you did not like the results that came from your reaction.

2. Generate a state of safety.

Create a safety net by sending the other person farther away until it feels comfortable. This might be an extra foot, or it could be so far you can't see them (like on the moon).

Add a force field or tough Plexiglas shield between you and the other person. Once you feel safe, anchor this sensation.

3. Respond to the person's validation. Imagine saying something to them, such as, "(Name), thanks for telling me this."

Change the words to fit the situation. If it's a formal business relationship, you might want to sound like this: "(Name), thanks for taking the time to discuss this issue with me. Your observations and ideas are very important to me, so I'll take this feedback very seriously."

Or if it is a romantic relationship, try something like, "Honey, I'm really glad you trust me so much that you can share something like this with me. My vision for our relationship is that we can be this open, create even more support for each other, and have really good times together while we're at it. It might take me some time and effort to really get what you need one hundred percent, but I will do my best to keep trying and listening. To me, that's a sacred promise. "

4. Request additional information. The person will know that you care and that you can handle criticism if you ask them to offer more details. Also, the more you know, the better you can respond, whether you need to disagree, negotiate, or offer up a major mea culpa.

You can use a phrase such as, "Tell me more about this," or ask about something that you don't fully understand.

5. Imagine the response in an effective way that is not disturbing. Imagine the person filling in some details. Practice the perception of what they say as though you are watching a movie that plays out the details as they see them. Make the image small enough that it is not at all overwhelming or troubling. This gets you some distance or objectivity, but keeps you in a state of receptivity.

6. Consider what you have received. Reflecting is very important in any type of communication. Practice it here by restating what the other person has told you. It's best to summarize what you feel are the most important parts. This shows the person what stands out to you, and it helps them know what to emphasize when they clarify their ideas and concerns.

You can begin with a phrase such as, "I want to make sure I understand you, so let me tell you what stands out to me so far." You can end with something like, "How am I doing?" or "Are those the main things?"

7. Get to an "agreement frame." You may not be able to do this justice in your imagination, but be prepared to have some back and forth in the real world.

The person will probably want to add or repeat some things. People who do not feel validated will repeat points a lot, so the more you can help them feel validated, the more time you'll save.

When they add points, summarize them as in step six. This is a good point at which to elicit exactly what they want from you or from the situation. Some people jump into criticism before they have figured this out, especially if they are assuming that they can't get what they want. Exercising their desires can help to calm them down and put them in a more creative and cooperative frame of mind. Once the person is comfortable with your level of understanding, you have achieved the agreement frame.

8. Generate your own representation in the top-left position. Your understanding is probably different from that of the other person. At the minimum, you will have some different priorities; that is, you will feel some different things should receive the most emphasis.

Create a representation in the top left of your mental and visual space. This representation shows your understanding of the situation. It should include sights, sounds, words, and feelings. Have it show not only the details, but your priorities, needs, beliefs and values. It is powerful to visualize at least one ideal outcome.

Emphasize the rep system that helps you gain the most clarity. For example, if it is self-talk, the images may not be so important.

9. Contrast your and your critic's representations. How does the movie you made of your critic's understanding contrast with the representation you made of your understanding and priorities?

10. Respond from your understanding and do it in a classy way. Respond to your critic by stating some areas of agreement, starting with a phrase such as, "I do agree with you on some important points."

This time, emphasize what the other person wants that you can agree with and that you intend to cooperate with. Then convey the ways that you disagree, starting with a phrase such as, "I can't completely agree on a few points, though." Where the issue is concerned, I think... This is a good time to indicate what you aren't willing to cooperate with and what you need to see happen. Use language that fits the situation. How hard or soft you sound is a strategic decision.

11. Look for closure. Bring the discussion to a close with a focus on decisions. This can range from them being satisfied that you have acknowledged them, to a need to negotiate commitments, or agreeing to disagree and taking the issue to a higher authority.

12. Take this to the relationship level. Ask the other part, "What would help them feel better about your relationship?" (whether it is a working relationship, a romantic relationship, or some other kind of relationship). Offer your own needs in this regard, as well. Discuss it in a way that generates hope and optimism about your future together. Close by emphasizing your appreciation for them coming to you openly, rather than for the specific details.

13. Test. As the situation unfolds, see if this has enhanced the relationship and your ability to respond in a way that fills the other person's needs, including their need to feel that you care and see their needs as valid and serious. See how well they are able to do the same for you. If there are problems, assess them. If you feel the person is strictly being manipulative and wants an unfair advantage, then you will need to shift to a different strategic frame that involves gamesmanship of some kind, limit-setting, and ways of gaining more power to protect your interests.

Criticism Defusing

Source: Virginia Satir

This powerful pattern is especially effective when someone is experiencing an abusive but significant internal voice that has originated in the past, such as an over-criticizing parent or a bullying sibling.

1. Recognize the internal voice and its core message. What does the voice tell you?

2. Inquire its origin: "If that voice had a familiar body and face, if it were a person, who would that be?"

3. Embed the voice into a vivid visual representation based on its physical location: "If X (the person they named) was in this room right now, where would he/she be exactly?"

4. Ask the client to point to where that person's voice is coming from in the space around them, and in which direction. Most likely, the face of the imaginary person is directed at them.

5. Induce a light trance, and suggest: "I would like you now to imagine walking around behind X, right here in this room, and gently placing your left hand on his/her left shoulder and your right hand on his/her right shoulder, and nodding your head when you've done so." Wonderful... now gently massage those shoulders. As you do so, lean forward and whisper into his or her left ear, close enough so he/she can hear you, and say, "Just let go and relax. Let it go. I am fine, everything is OK, you can relax... now, even deeper... all the way down."

6. Allow the client to have a few moments of silence so they can fully experience the kinesthetic sensations of this trance. The client may burst into tears or show other signs of discomfort for a little while. These are reactions that should be expected and welcomed.

7. When the client consciously moves, such as scratching their face or adjusting their posture, this initiates the wake up from trance protocol.

Curiosity Enhancement

The last things you want to be reflected in your body language with a client are rejection, excessive distance, or the quality of pushing something onto the client. Perhaps the greatest antidote to such tendencies is showing an inquisitive nature. When you're curious about what the client is saying, on all levels, it draws the client out, especially when it is a calm, grounded curiosity. What follows are the ingredients for creating such an experience.

Components and Typical Evolution

1) Questions that do not have an unusual quality to themThey are, at least on the surface, common sense. Remember, this is early in your connection with the client.

2) Using body language to express your interest and curiosity, such as leaning forward slightly when the client says something with an emotional connection or deeper meaning.This shows that you are responsive, and it can feed the client's self-disclosing behavior because attention is a strong reinforcer of behavior.

3) Inquiries regarding the underlying significanceThey can start with a half-baked assumption that morphs into a question. For example, "I can imagine that when she said that, you could really..." (making a small sweeping gesture toward your stomach-gestures should show restraint, so there is no sense of acting or being an erratic person)... Well, I mean, what other options could have gone through your mind at that point?" Ending the question with an open face shows a hint of appreciation for the client's pain and feeling boxed in. The client's answer gives the practitioner a sense of the client's level of flexibility and insight. If the client has no sense of having options (as in "she made me feel that way or do that"), then the therapist has pulled this out in a context in which there is no sense of impending judgment or "psychoanalyzing" the person. Notice that the half-baked assumption is actually a way of establishing an expectation that the client must have feelings about it and connects the client with feelings to some degree, priming the client for a deeper answer than you would get with the "talking heads" effect that removes

humanity from coaching. This is very important for eliciting in yourself a healing state. Any time that you begin to feel yourself pushing into the client, distancing too much, or becoming judgmental, this experience is one of the fastest and most useful ways to keep yourself from contaminating the process. It is easier to think creatively and flexibly when you are in an inquisitive state.

Cycles

With this pattern, we can begin to alleviate the tightness of fight, flight, and freeze.

1. Identify a situation that elicits a strong emotional response in you.

2. Spend a few seconds getting in touch with your body's general sensations. How would you make the distinction between the right and left sides of your body? Is there a side of your body that is noticeably less warm than the other? Take a few moments to focus on the sensations on each side of your body and describe them in sensory language.

3. Elicit the kinesthetic sub-modalities.

4. You may experience a variety of emotions, including heaviness, lightness, tightness, burning, slackness, and ache. Identify them and note their driving sub-modalities.

5. Now imagine that you can breathe in via the side of your body that is most comfortable for you, starting with your foot and lower leg on that side and moving up to the point where it seems like your breathing connects with your core.

6. Then follow the path of your breath as it travels from one side of your body to the other. Breathe out through your other foot and leg as you exhale, sending your breath back to earth.

7. Repeat steps 5 and 6 at least three times, preferably 7 times, paying attention to your body's sensations and how they differ at the end of each cycle.

8. Imagine your breath as a magnet that can take up pleasant feelings and shift them from one side of your body to the other. Make a mental note of these specific kinesthetic feelings and recognize them as you breathe in.

9. As you inhale up from the more comfortable side of your body, your breath moves through your core, down into your leg, then into your foot. Pause once more and take

The Big Book of NLP

note of how your bodily sensations have changed. Does it make you feel better, like you've gotten some much-needed energy? Do you feel calmer, more relaxed, or anything else? What's this thing?

10. Breathe up the side of your body that feels the least comfortable or even somewhat unpleasant, allowing your breath to cross over into your core.

11. Now, visualize exhaling from the side of your body that is most comfortable for you. How much of a difference does it make compared to the earlier cycles?

12. Test. What does your lower body feel like now? How about your upper body? Of your entire body? When you think about the situation that troubled you, is the emotional response less intense?

Lastly, if you have a particular trouble spot in your neck, upper torso, or lower back, or if you just need more experience with this breathing technique, imagine that you can inhale and exhale up to the top of your head. As you exhale, visualize your breath flowing down your spine and out of your tailbone, all the way from the crown of your head, neck, and mid-back. Repeat this as many times as necessary.

Dancing SCORE

Source: Judith DeLosier, based on the SCORE pattern by Robert Dilts and Todd Epstein

Select a problem.

Create your four spaces.

Find a movement pattern expressing the symptoms and a pattern expressing the cause.

Break state, then go to the Outcomes space, and find a movement pattern expressing the desired outcomes and the effects of the desired outcomes.

Moving through all spaces, discover a dance that integrates the movement from cause to effects.

Discover a missing resource. Find a movement for the missing resource and integrate it into your movement expression.

Repeat this to fully integrate the movement expression. Test.

Solve problems by enhancing your intuition and body wisdom through movement. This pattern promotes the mind-body relationship in a way that accesses and mobilizes deep resources, creating a self-organizing pathway toward a resourceful and relevant state. In this pattern, we will think of a challenge as existing in a problem space.

The key elements that we will consider for this are in the acronym S.C.O.R.E., which stands for Symptoms, Causes, Outcomes, Resources, and Effects.

You will be asked to express yourself in movement and dance, but we are talking about a personal form of expression for which there is no pressure to perform for anyone else. These are expressions that you find within yourself and express in whatever way you discover.

1. Choose a problem. Select a problem that you would like to solve. Choose a problem that seems as though it will require an expanded frame or insight in order to be solved.

2. Make four separate spaces.

Think of them as being in chronological order. Remember that a symptom means the thing that tells you the problem is there.

Desired effects refer to the long-term effects of the outcome.

Go to a meta-position and select a location for each of the following four items:

Cause

Symptom

Outcome

Desired Effect

3. Find a movement pattern expressing the symptoms. STEP onto the Symptom space. Access the symptom (problem) experience. Find within yourself a pattern of movement that somehow expresses that experience.

4. Find a movement pattern expressing the cause. STEP into the Cause space. Discover how the feelings and movement associated with the symptom space can guide you to a sense of the cause of the symptom. Find the movements that express the cause state.

5. Break state, then go to the outcome space, and find a movement pattern expressing the desired outcomes. Break out of state and into the meta-position.Step into the outcome

space. To create a fully associated experience of the solution state, the state that you desire, Discover and express the movements that express this state.

6. Find a movement pattern expressing the effects of the desired outcomes. Step into the desired effect space. Explore how it feels to fully experience the results of your desired outcome. Spend enough time to deeply experience this.

7. As you move through the spaces, find a dance that integrates movement from cause to effect.

a. Step into the Cause location and slowly walk through all four spaces.

b. Pay attention to how your body intuitively connects the symptom and outcome locations.

c. Repeat the entire walk several times until you feel the dance is a single dance that transports you from the cause space to the desired effect space.

8. Discover a missing resource. 9. Move out into a meta-position and explore what feels like your dance is missing. See if there is a sense of a missing resource that this feeling can bring your attention to.

9. Find a movement for the missing resource and integrate it into your movement expression. Go through your spaces, find a movement expression of that missing resource, and add it to your dance. Find a movement expression of that missing resource and add it to your dance.

10. Repeat this process until the movement expression is fully integrated. Repeat the movement through the spaces until it feels like a fully integrated personal movement expression.

11. Test. In the coming days, notice if new solutions occur to you, or if you spontaneously act them out in some way. As you encounter challenging situations, explore how your way of being physically can express more of your resources in some way through body language or how you move your own internal sense of energy and emotion.

The Big Book of NLP

Decision Destroyer

Source: Richard Bandler

Select and clarify a limiting decision.

Develop and anchor a positive decision.

Associate into the limiting decision and anchor it.

Float back to earlier experiences, seeking the first one.

Go forward, returning to your positive decision.

Go earlier to your first limiting decision.

Experience that early decision while fully accessing the new resources.

Quickly zoom to the present, integrate the experience, and future pace.

Exchange limiting decisions for constructive ones in order to improve success and mood. We can view our behavior and feelings as expressions of the many decisions that we have made during our lives. These decisions may be conscious or unconscious. In other words, you might be aware of the need to make these decisions (equivalent to skill level "conscious incompetence") or unaware of the need (equivalent to skill level "unconscious incompetence"). These decisions may have profound effects on our development and continued functioning because they were made before we could even speak. These decisions can be about the nature of the world, of people, and of ourselves.

Most of us have habits that prevent us from achieving great success and happiness because of how they affect how we relate to the world, others, and even ourselves. Decisions that have such harmful effects tend to arise when we are psychologically overwhelmed. This can happen in adulthood, but it is especially troublesome when we make these mistakes in childhood. This is because of their effect on our development and because of how deeply ingrained they are as "pre-verbal" decisions. When we make decisions before we have the necessary wisdom to make them with, we end up with destructive ways of relating to the world, to people, or even to ourselves. Patterns of dysfunctional relationships, poor self-esteem, and sabotage can often be traced back to these unwise decisions. We can think of the collective nature of our decisions as a "mental map" of our world. We navigate our world and relationships using our mental maps.

1. Select and clarify a limiting decision. Think of a negative pattern in your life. Based on the introductory comment to this pattern, verbalize an underlying decision that has guided your behavior in a dysfunctional way. If it sounds irrational, that is okay. Decisions made earlier in life appear especially illogical. Think about the decision to clarify things. For example, when does it seem that you made it? How does it affect your life?

2. Develop and anchor a positive decision. Develop a constructive decision that would be an excellent improvement over the limiting decision. Enhance it until it is well formed. For example, it should be specific. Enhance it further by developing the positive feelings you have about it into a positive decision state. Enhance the positive state until it is strong. Anchor the state.

3. Associate into the limiting decision and anchor it. Float back above your timeline to the point when you first recall acting upon the limiting decision. Observe it from this dissociated vantage point. Associate with this point in time and recall the moment you made your decision.Anchor the limiting decision state.

4. Float back to earlier experiences, seeking the first one. Float to earlier points on your timeline where your behavior has expressed the limiting decision. Go back to the point where you actually made the decision. If you have already gone to the earliest memory in step three, then skip this step.

5. Continue on your path, returning to your positive decision. Go back in your timeline to your superior decision, and again look at it in a good way.

6. Go earlier to your first limiting decision. Float back past your earlier limiting decision, to a point just fifteen minutes prior to that decision. Bring the positive state with you as you move into that point in time.

The Big Book of NLP

7. Experience that early decision while fully accessing the new resources. Re-experience the situation and make an early decision while maintaining full access to your positive resource state. Notice how your experience of this situation, and of yourself in the situation, has changed.

8. Zoom in quickly to the present, integrate the experience, and Future Pace. Rapidly zoom forward along your timeline to the present moment. Stop here and take some time to absorb what has happened. Future pace, seeing how situations similar to the pattern that was negative might play out with your new perspective and state.

Decision-Making Strategy

We all have a hard time making a real life-altering decision. A recent client came in and asked me to decide for him: "Should I stay in college even though I'm bored out of my mind, or should I start a business, or should I go work for my uncle, or should I travel Europe for a year before I decide any of the above?" How can we ensure that the important decision we make today will not be a source of guilt, shame, and regret in the future? Well, we can just consult the future itself:

1. Choose one major decision and write down the options you consider.

2. Consider option 1 as if it were the only option.

3. Initiate a downtime state.

4. Associate into making the decision as option 1.

5. Enter the timeline and then race forward ten years into the future.

6. Meet your future self, 10 years older, sitting there on the timeline waiting to greet you.

7. Ask the future self: "Are you angry with me?" And wait for a response.

8. If the answer is "yes," ask, "Can you please tell me why? What has happened that made you upset? ", and listen for the answer.

9. Tell your future self, "I'll be right back," and float back to the present. Break state. Dissociate from option 1 and associate with option 2 as if it was the only decision.

10. Repeat steps 5 to 9 for every option on your list. For the last one, skip step 9 and thank your future self for its input.

11. Ask your future self one last question: "What do you expect of me, emotionally, relationally, and practically? How can I make sure that when I become you in 10 years, I will be whole and satisfied with my past? " Listen to the answers patiently.

12. Return to the present timeline, break state, and take a deep breath.

13. Test. Which one of the options you listed do you feel the strongest about?

14. Future pace. Imagine yourself (first perceptual position) in 10 years' time, meeting your older self (of the present) and smiling at him as he arrives to greet you. "You made the right choice," you tell him. Break state.

Deconstructing Into Modalities

In any type of coaching or therapy, momentum is very important. By momentum, we mean that a productive process is taking place at the correct tempo.

Since NLP relies on state management much of the time, and since states are dynamic processes, the pace of the steps in the intervention must be maintained. This key and basic move can allow you to move in a number of directions. It is an excellent set up for a reframe, for reprocessing, and as part of a hypnotic induction.

We ask a simple question, "How do you know that...", and then guide the client through the sense modalities that form the basis of their knowledge in order to answer the question. The knowledge gained as a result of this transformation becomes something that can be challenged, supplemented, reformulated, deduced from, and made more dynamic. It can help identify illogic that the client can begin to question on their own, thus "owning" their experience with no incentive to resist the therapist's "agenda."

It is an excellent gateway to body awareness patterns because the senses are, well, senses. It helps the client become less attached to their mental narrative, acting somewhat like oil for a squeaky hinge. This is one of those sub-patterns that I mentioned in the introduction. It is a fragment of a larger, strategic series of moves. You'll get some additional ideas about what to do with the results later in this section.

Example I

Client: "I feel like such a complete loser."

Therapist: "How do you know that?"

Client: "Well, it's pretty clear when you have friends that..."

Therapist: "Wait, I mean, how do you know that you feel like a loser? How does it feel? "

Client: "Totally awful. I feel like giving up."

Therapist: "Where do you feel that in your body? Where is the main center of that feeling, of the emotion or intensity? "

Client: "Well, really, it's like my stomach is twisted up."

Example II

Client: "I just can't do it. I can't face him, much less make any sense. "

Therapist: "As you think about doing that, or, I mean, not doing that, how do you feel if you were looking at him and trying to make sense?"

Saying "or, I mean, not doing that," helps to forestall an objection such as, "But I can't," so you can maintain your momentum.

Also notice the use of conjugations, mixing "how do you feel," an "if" phrase, and "trying to make sense."

Client: "I would shut down. I really hate him."

Therapist: "So if you're facing him and shutting down, where is that feeling of being shut down? Where do you feel it most? "

Client: "All over. I just want to turn and go. "

Therapist: "So there is a motivation to take action, to move, to escape. What is that like?"

Client: "Oh, well, I would probably feel panicked. Either that or start yelling at him. "

Therapist: "And where is the center of that feeling? Your heart? Your throat? "

Client: "It just moves right up through me from my heart."

De-Energizing Memories

Source: Maralee Platt

Choose a memory that troubles you sometimes.

Explore the sub-modalities you notice in the memory.

Use a frame as a symbol of the memory and modify it.

Bring the image to your left, and extract the learning.

Put the image behind you.

Have this process generalize.

Enjoy happy memories and put them behind you.

Test.

Free yourself from troubling memories. Turn them into sources of wisdom.

1. Choose a memory that troubles you sometimes.

2. Investigate the sub-modalities that you notice in your memory.

3. Use a frame as a memory symbol and modify it. Select a single frame from your mental movie of the memory and use it as a symbol for the entire memory. Push that frame back to the distant periphery of your awareness and change it to black and white. Notice that there is a younger you in the image. Shrink it down to a small size and surround it with a frame.

4. Bring the image to your left, and extract the lesson. Reach out and grasp the small image with your left hand, and bring it to your left side. Use the opposite hand and side if you tend to store your memories on the right. Extract all the lessons available from this memory, as represented by the small image. You may not know what these lessons consist of, but that is okay for this pattern. You just know that you are taking wisdom from this image. Imagine this knowledge flowing into your personal mental library.

5. Put the image behind you. Now push the image back behind you, symbolically telling your body and mind that the experience is behind you, that is, in the past.

6. Make this procedure more general. Instruct your mind to do this with all aspects of the troubling memory.

7. Take pleasure in happy memories and put them behind you. Spend some time with happy memories in big, bright, full color. Place them on the right. Enjoy them, and then push them back behind you as well.

8. Test. In the coming days, notice if this memory has been de-energized. Take note of any ways in which this frees up your creativity and ability to enjoy life and create a more meaningful future.

De-Nominalizing

Source: Richard Bandler & John Grinder

By resolving the meta-model violation known as nominalization, you can get much more control over your mind and your life. This works because nominalizations remove the actor from the scene. If I say, "I have to go visit my stupid relatives," I'm not saying who is in charge of the "have to." If I decide to be empowered, I can say, "I'm going to make my mom happy by visiting my stupid relatives." or, "I decided it wasn't worth going through that misery."

Even better, if you can say it honestly, "I'm going to create a completely new and mind-expanding experience with my relatives." We nominalize when we turn verbs into nouns. If you talk about "the relationship," it seems to have a life of its own. Where is your (and the other person's) leadership and vision?

Think about situations in which you feel less powerful. You might feel overwhelmed, frustrated, or coerced. Find a nominalization in the way you talk about the situation. De-nominalize by turning at least one noun into a verb. Find a way to turn at least one noun into a verb. This change puts someone into the driver's seat.

The more challenging or empowering it feels, the better. If it challenges you to take responsibility in some way, that is a special challenge to embrace. Talk about it without any nominalization. Investigate alternative ways to discuss the situation that do not involve nominalization and include the verb(s) you identified.Instead of, "This job is killing my soul," you might have, "I am super motivated to get a different job, and fast. I'm networking and telling everyone I meet to keep an eye out for good opportunities in my field. "

Do you feel that you are in a more meaningful, connected, empowered state?

The Big Book of NLP

Desired State

The desired state-how you think and feel in the moment, in the best way to support your most desired outcomes-is the ultimate goal of NLP. What that state is depends on the individual, but the whole idea behind NLP is to promote excellence, and this is achieved by being in an excellent state, that is, the desired state. We can contrast the desired state with the present or problem state, that is, where we are today and how that state can be improved upon. You might think that it is easy to determine the desired state, but you need to pay attention to some important details in order to really achieve the state that is most desired. To really find the desired state, ask these questions:

What specific outcome do you want to achieve? "Being happy" is not specific. "Feeling good about myself when I'm at work" is

How would you know if you achieved this outcome? Again, get specific details. Ask the person to describe what the situation would look, sound, feel, or even smell like. Who would be there? What would they look like?

What would happen if you achieved this outcome? Focus on the effects, as this not only makes the outcome more desirable, but there might be some other unintended and unwanted consequences of the outcome.

In what contexts do you want this outcome? This helps build a mental picture of the desired state taking place.

Is there any context where you don't want the outcome? Counter examples can help define the desired state.

Has there ever been a time when you had this outcome? How did you know you had it? Past experiences can be extremely helpful in creating future outcomes.

Can you get curious instantly?

Dis-Identification

Supporting Belief

Dis-Identify with language.

Dis-Identify through trance.

Alternate Self and Function.

Transcendental Identity

Amplify in Higher Self

Gain new freedom and capacity by distancing yourself from limiting beliefs. Sometimes we over-identify with some facet of our life experiences-our beliefs, body, gender, race, etc. This is limiting in itself, but we may also over-identify with even more seriously limited aspects of ourselves. For example, we may identify with behavior or thought patterns that construct a victim, dependent, or otherwise unsuccessful self.

Terror organizations are known to be very thorough in their propaganda, leading individuals into a state of over-identification with the organization's distorted values, perspectives, and beliefs. No wonder that young somnambulistic individuals are willing to strap a suicide bomb to themselves and kill innocent people only to keep their learned deformed identification in tact. This pattern serves to correct over-identification.

1. Construct a belief that is supportive. Try this belief on for size: "You have a self that is beyond your circumstances, your familiar abilities, behaviors, creative expression, speech, strivings, and even your thoughts."

2. Dis-Identify with language. Change the frame for all the things about you, such as those in step one. Use this phrase: "I have (say the thing about you, such as "talent"), but I am not (the same thing, e.g., "talent"). Include thoughts ("I am not my thoughts.")

3. Dis-identify via trance. By accessing a deeply relaxed state, sense yourself as bigger than the things in step one. "If I lost (fill it in), my core self would remain."

4. Alternate Self and Function: Notice how you can think about these traits of yours as being functions, a way of getting a result or making your way through the world. Take note of how you have a sense of self that extends beyond functions.

5. Transcendental Self-Identity: Tune into your sense of a greater self that exists beyond the things that you identify with. Notice how you can sense a state of pure consciousness, as you have in trance or meditation. Represent this with a word or phrase that captures the essence of that experience, or see what symbol comes to mind. The words or symbols that emerge spontaneously may be the most significant.

6. Amplify in Higher Self. Notice the sub-modalities of this sense of higher self and amplify them in any way that enhances it and strengthens your connection and identification with it. Move it to the center of your existence and place your consciousness at the center of this higher self. Imagine what it's like to live and express yourself from this sense of higher self.

Disintegration

This pattern separates the parts of a negative synesthesia pattern so that it can be addressed. Many problems come from this kind of reaction. Most people who lash out with hurtful words or violence discover that they are being controlled by impulses that cut across multiple rep systems. In this case, it is likely to include very strong non-verbal thoughts (auditory digital) that, when turned into words, become less powerful, as well as a hot rush of emotions (kinesthetic). The idea is to improve automatic reactions that come from multiple rep systems firing off a negative state.

1. Select the situation and the state.

Pick a situation in which you have a rapid, automatic, negative reaction of some kind. The more irrational it is, the better. Think of the most recent situation in which you rapidly experienced this negative state in a strong way.

2. At the belief level, clarify the verbal representation.

Notice all the thoughts that you had immediately before, during, and after the incident. Look for the thoughts that were most strongly related to the situation and your behavior. Notice how they have a part in driving the behavior. Examine the aspect of the thoughts that is best described as a belief.State your beliefs. If you have trouble finding these beliefs, go to the next step, return here during the last step, and come back to this pattern a few times as well.

3. Identify all material from the rep system.

What happened in your mind during the incident? Notice what you saw, any visual representations your mind recalled or created, what you heard, any auditory material that you recalled or created, and what you felt, including any feelings that you recalled or created. I understand it fully.

4. Position the material according to the EAC.

Place each representation in its appropriate position in your field of awareness according to eye accessing cues.

5. Come up with a more effective response.

Brainstorm until you have a more effective response. Imagine going through the situation again, but with a more effective response. Notice anything that could make that response difficult, including any ecological issues and any rep system material that you have not positioned according to eye accessing cues.

6. Test

As similar situations arise, notice how well you respond to them. Repeat this exercise as needed to respond effectively to the situation.

Disjunction

Disjunction is a lot like Linking Words, but it makes a contrast or choice while it slips in an embedded command or leading statement. For example, "I don't know whether you will give your full attention to this section, or think of some other useful information about your experiences, or even relax and learn while in a deeply relaxed state."

In this example, all three options are desirable. But it starts out as if I would say, "I don't know whether you will give your full attention or not." The implied "not" can bring up any feelings of resistance or self doubt about one's ability to focus and pay attention. As a result, we now have some transderivational searches contributing to the trance and open-mindedness.

But we also have the unexpected shift into a very different statement ("...or think of some other useful information...")

Instead of causing alertness, this unexpected shift can also contribute to trance because it, too, elicits transderivational search.

The stable pattern of the wording also facilitates trance, as it continues to simply take the form of choices that more or less pace the person's experience. And embedded in the last two choices in the statement is the Ericksonian technique of utilization. In this case, utilization of the mind's tendency to wander is required. We remind the unconscious, since it is going to wander, to bring up useful experiences, or to learn while the conscious mind is distracted.

You can try this with volunteers among your friends. Afterwards, ask them if they recall any of the three choices that aren't exactly choices. It can be a game, and they can learn with you.

Dissolving Shame

Select your mistake.

Clarify what why it a mistake.

Access its negative feelings and intensify them.

Learn from this mistake.

Reduce the negative emotions and apply resources to the mistake, including what you can learn from it.

Test.

Test again.

Transform any mistakes you make from sources of shame and recrimination to sources of learning and empowerment.

1. Pick your blunder. Choose a mistake that you are highly motivated not to repeat.

2. Clarify why it's a mistake. Think over the criteria you used to decide that it was a mistake. For example, what values did this mistake violate? Think back on the mistake and notice if you have violated a higher hierarchy value.

3. Access it's negative feelings and intensify them. Access the negative feelings that you have associated with this mistake. Amplify them until they are fairly intense, adding to your motivation not to repeat the mistake. Use all the driver sub-modalities you have worked with successfully until now. With particular focus on the kinesthetic sub-modalities, since we want to amplify the feelings directly by intensifying the event that triggers them.

4. Learn from this blunder. Shift your awareness to all that you can learn from this mistake. Shift your discomfort towards intensity and a drive for learning.

Modulate the intensity so that you can learn without panicking. It is very valuable to learn to manage intensity, especially negative intensity, so that you can transform it into positive passion and drive. To derive these insights, employ a variety of lenses.

a. The History of the Mistake: What led to it? How did the sequence take place from its earliest roots?

b. Psychodynamics: What parts were involved, and what were their positive motives?

c. Behavior Modification: What secondary benefits came from the patterns that contributed to this mistake? For example, is there a pattern of needing to be rescued, vindicated, avenged, or given attention? Finally, think about how learning from this will benefit you.

5. Reduce negative emotions and devote resources to the error, including what you can learn from it. Shift your focus to the emotions coming from all of this. Bring the negative emotions into the foreground. Imagine a big box with a heavy lid. Put the negative emotions into that box.

Now bring the positive lessons into the foreground and take them with you as you float back over your timeline to the point at which this mistake occurred.

Saturate that experience with these lessons and reconfigure the lessons so that they become active resources in this scenario. When you are satisfied, make all similar mistakes stand out in your timeline.

Cruise through your entire timeline, beaming these lessons into each of those points in time, as you did with the main mistake.

6. Test. Bring your attention back to the original mistake. As you review it, notice whether you still have any negative feelings about it. If so, see what learning and resources you can apply to resolve those feelings.

The Big Book of NLP

They may even be an ecological problem of some kind to work out. As you apply your resources, run the scene as a movie from third position (dissociated) until you are satisfied that it is a fully positive experience.

7. Run the test again. Over the coming days and weeks, see how your work on this mistake opens new perspectives and resourceful behavior for you. What new results are you getting? Do you feel better about any of your circumstances, or do you feel new hope for any pattern in your life?

Distortion

Historiographical students are well aware of the fact that different people can look at the same data and come to completely different conclusions about what they are seeing. It is true that this unfortunate reality is at the heart of the vast majority of international disputes that currently exist. To add insult to injury, how can this be possible when the truth is right in front of everyone's eyes? As a result of the distortion, this occurs as well. The result of the filtering of our surface structures by our deep structures is distortion of the surface structures. If one's deep structures lead them to be distrustful of other people, one's

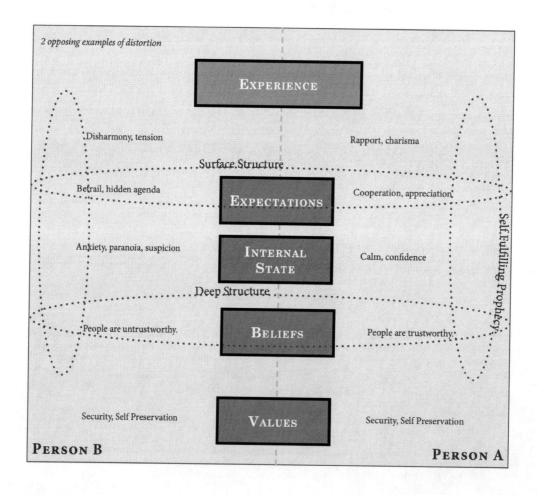

The Big Book of NLP

interpretation of acts of kindness will be different from the interpretation of acts of kindness by someone whose deep structures lead them to be trustful of others. The use of distractions can be beneficial when planning for the future, but they can also cause us to misinterpret the actions and intentions of others, which can be destructive.

Consider the differences in the deep and surface structures of the two persons in the illustration below. Can you notice the differences in Person A's deep structure, at the logical levels of Values and beliefs, compared to Person B's fearful response to life? Would you agree that although Person B is motivated to self preserve, just as much as Person A is, his behavior leads to consequences that puts him and his surrounding at danger?

Double Bind

It improves cooperation in many situations. The double bind is a basic communication enhancement method that requires that the person you are communicating with accept a presupposition. This is followed by choices. You'll recognize this simple version:

"Would you like to pay in cash or credit?"

1. Establish the context for your communication. Think of a situation in which you would like to increase others' cooperation. Sales and coaching are great situations for this. However, even a simple persuasion situation, such as convincing your 10-year-old son to go to bed at 10 p.m. instead of watching another movie, would do. Get a clear idea of how you would know if the person was being cooperative, which in essence means that you need to establish a quick, well-defined outcome to your communication with that person in that context.

2. Determine the presupposition. Identify a basic presupposition upon which this cooperation would be predicated. Now, this is not an embedded command, but this should be the conclusion the other person comes to after you apply the double bind in your conversation with them. You are going to buy this because you need this. You are definitely going to base this decision upon your highest values. You can prove yourself here by getting a constructive outcome.

3. Align the situation with the premise. Imagine communicating with people in this kind of situation. Think of ways you can get them aligned with your basic presuppositions, the ones you've established in 2. The most elegant ways are largely or completely unconscious. If you are talking to a street kid who is used to proving himself by being tough, you might use numerous anchoring and hypnotic methods to get him primed to prove his manhood by being a constructive leader in a situation that could turn violent without his help. Notice that this last phrase already distances him from the violence. Instead of saying, "Don't do it," the presumption is that he is separate from the situation and has a choice whether or not to help. It also implies that he is needed, by appealing to his heroic fantasies.

The Big Book of NLP

4. Create a 22-catch option. Once the presupposition is firmly in place, construct a choice that is predicated upon this presumption. Some examples You could keep the circle of revenge going around and around, killing more people on various sides of various conflicts, as if there wasn't a bigger world out there for everybody, or you could run and hide, but I'm wondering what you're going to do to turn them around and save some lives. Keep some of those pretty girls prettier; keep the party going. It isn't whether you have the stuff. You've proven yourself. But how are you going to take it to another level? Maybe use some of that fast talk of yours to mess with their heads a little and get them thinking about other stuff. Maybe get them thinking about the lives they could have had they not been on this merry-go-round.

5. Test. Try this approach in the situation and, as you improve your skills, notice how much your results improve.

Communication skills are not based on tricks or memorized techniques. A key goal of NLP practice is unconscious competence. Every opportunity to practice is another brick on the road to mastery. Instead of memorizing techniques, practice them in your imagination. When I first began studying these concepts, I went on a long imaginary journey every day. I practiced only in my mind, making up thousands of possible situations in which I would need to be persuasive and influential. What is so good about your imagination? You can slow the process down. In real life, people are not going to wait for you to think about a presumption that will help you build a double bind. They might also become suspicious if you use techniques that you have memorized. But they're going to be mesmerized if you aren't using a technique consciously, if these ideas and concepts are expressed in your words without your intention to use them... as if it was always your natural way of communicating.

Downtime

Learn to create a light, momentary trance in people for various uses. When your conscious awareness is focused entirely on internal experience, NLP refers to this as "downtime." The Downtime state is a subset type of trance phenomenon and can help initiate or deepen trance. It can help you manage an interaction as a brief, light trance, as occurs in a trans-derivational search.

Many techniques are used to stimulate downtime, and they are used not only to produce trance, but also patience, introspection, and receptiveness. On the other hand, uptime refers to a more worldly state of awareness that emphasizes external awareness that is effectively informed by internal awareness. Limit your surroundings.

Set up a distraction-free environment for this pattern. Focus on your internal representational systems (the sub-steps below will help you). Attend to each mode as fully as possible.

a. Pay attention to your auditory senses, including your inner voice and any memories or fantasies that arise.Remember something, and focus totally on the sounds involved.

b. Shift your mental attention to the visual mode.Include memories and fantasies that arise. Choose a memory and focus all your awareness on the visual aspect.

c. Attend to your emotional and physical needs for a while. Now think of a memory and focus on your emotional and physical reactions to it. Compare those feelings to how you feel about the memory and how your body feels right now as you recall it. How hard is the surface you are on now?

d. Recognize your preferences.Come up with a memory of eating something tasty. Notice that you have various senses involved in your memory.

Focus your mind entirely on remembering the taste.

The Big Book of NLP

Notice how taste is more than one sensation, since much of what we associate with food has to do with its consistency, such as chewiness.

e. Shift your awareness of this memory to smell. Notice how you can separate taste and smell.

You can anchor downtime. To do this, fold your hands and gradually increase the pressure of your palms pressing together as you progress through the rep systems. Then use it to create a basic trance or awareness meditation.

Doing the above tip and focusing on rep systems in sequence will improve internal sensory awareness. Imagine running through a hypothetical behavior sequence, rotating through the above rep systems. You could start with something simple like walking. Identify your weakest rep system and repeat this exercise several times, focusing on that system. To improve your ability to integrate your senses, practice this exercise while paying attention to all systems. You can start by quickly rotating through them or blending them as you would sub-modalities.

Dreamer Role

The role of the dreamer is to provide much-needed motivation and inspiration, from within, as we pursue our desired outcomes. In cases of crisis, the dreamer role helps us redefine the guiding principles, values and keep us oriented to the big picture.

The dreamer's role is defined by several important characteristics. The dreamer's representational preference is Vision. Its focus orientation is 'What'. Its gravitational approach is Toward. Its preferred time frame is long term future, exclusively. Its communication reference is internal (self). Its comparison mode is Match (review the relevant Meta-Programs for more).

1. Select the active, desired, well-defined outcome you're working with. Defining the issues and obstacles you've recently encountered in the pursuit of this outcome

2. Initiate a downtime state.

3. Elicit the virtues of the dreamer:

a. Ask "What?" What is most important to me about it?

b. Seek Vision: What do I really want to create or manifest? What is the big picture, the wholesome and life affirming quest in pursuing this outcome?

c. Physiology of the dreamer: eyes up, head up, straight look, eyes wide open, symmetrical and relaxed body posture, smooth movement, hands loose.

4. Enter your timeline. Float above it. Lean slightly forward (toward).

5. Remain above the present, then turn around on the timeline and look towards the past.

6. Consider the issues in the context of your personal history over a long period of time.

The Big Book of NLP

a. If I hadn't done X, what would have happened to me? How would I feel?

b. If I hadn't done X, what might not have happened to me (that did)? How would I feel differently?

c. What bits of information seem to be in sync and related? Look for the matched stimuli.

7. Float higher above the timeline, dissociate, and consider other people's emerging timelines with yours, around the period when the obstacles started to bother you.

a. Who is in line with my vision?

b. Who else is going to benefit from the successful accomplishment of my outcome?

8. Float back down to the present, turn around on the timeline, and face the future.

9. Consider the potential personal consequences in the future time frame, including changes in relationships, locations, resources, etc.

a. If I chose to do X (a new choice), what would most likely happen to me?

b. If I chose to do X (my new choice), what would most likely not happen to me at all?

c. What bits of information seem to be in sync and related? Look for the matched stimuli.

10. Exit the timeline and break state.

D.V.P

Source: Robert A, Yourell

Select the situation, and fully express your thoughts about it.

Repeat the thoughts with better organization and priority.

Distill the thoughts by leaving out unnecessary detail.

Distill the thoughts further.

Continue distilling until you end up with a slogan.

Practice improvising off of your talking points.

Continue, but with more of a challenge.

Add vision and passion.

Have more practice sessions on this material in the coming days. Test.

D.V.P. stands for Distillation Plus Vision Plus Passion. This process allows you to take a cloud of reactions and ideas and turn them into very tight talking points, like the ones politicians and salespeople have, in order to communicate in a compelling way. This is an excellent way to prepare for a situation in which you feel that you have too much to try to say to a manipulative person or too many emotions to manage for clearer communication.

1. Choose a situation and fully express your feelings about it. Think of a situation such as those mentioned in the description of this pattern.

Run everything that you think about the situation through your mind, or write it down, or say it out loud by yourself or to a friend who can help you with the exercise.

Include those thoughts that you would like to communicate, whether or not you actually should.

2. Reiterate the ideas with more organization and priority.

Do this again, but allow your thoughts, now that you have run them through your mind, to fall together in a more orderly fashion, with a better sense of your priorities.

3. Distill the thoughts by leaving out unnecessary detail.

Do this again, but this time leave out any unnecessary details.

4. Distill the thoughts further. Do this again, but leave out more details that aren't absolutely necessary for you to say what is most important.

5. Continue distilling until you end up with a slogan.

Keep doing this "distilling" process until you have boiled it down to something that resembles an ad slogan, such as Apple's "Think Different," or Dolly Madison's "Nothing says lovin' like something in the oven." It's okay to risk going too far since you'll have no trouble beefing up the message with more details.

6. Experiment with improvising from your talking points. Imagine the situation in which you'll want to communicate your message. At first, make it easy.

After you are comfortable with this, try bringing out various aspects of your message by improvising off of the key points that you have boiled your message down to.

Remember to limit yourself to only the most important and compelling parts.

7. Continue, but with more of a challenge. 8. Imagine the person you need to communicate this to. Have them try various manipulative gambits to throw you off. This is how they manipulate you and abuse their power, most likely.

Imitate your key talking points, no matter what they say. You probably know them, or people like them, well enough to imagine a good variety of distracting, intimidating, or simply irritating comments that they might make.

8. Include your vision and passion. Get in touch with the positive vision and emotions that you have in connection with each talking point.

Make a mental note of the outcomes and values underlying the talking points, as well as how you truly feel. You have positive emotions driving you to care enough to communicate about this. Even if it was a negative situation and set of emotions such as being fed up with intimidation or other boundary crossings, you can work your way back to a positive vision, such as respect for boundaries, human dignity, and productive relationships toward whatever your common goal is.

Be sure you are only connecting with the positive vision and the positive, inspiring emotions that flow from that connection. Infuse your voice with this, and practice speaking from this emotional place.

Practice until it comes out in a smooth, compelling, grounded manner. If this is a challenge, It's good to sleep on it since your unconscious will be working with this pattern in your sleep.

9. Have more practice sessions on this material in the coming days. Sleep will do wonders for this.

After doing this pattern, your unconscious mind will be working to extend your intimacy with these talking points and your ability to improvise in communicating with them. Keep practicing in the coming days when you get a chance to fantasize, such as while doing dishes or driving.

Practice out loud now, because good muscle memory and actually experiencing your own voice and vibration in this pattern build your personal power and ability. In between, listen to some of the great speeches by people who were good at putting compelling emotion and vision into their voices.

The Big Book of NLP

10. Test. As you take this skill into the real world, notice how people listen to you and respond to your vision, emotions, and talking points.

Continue to use this pattern for other important communications. Any conflict or leadership situation is a good one for this pattern. Any sensitive communication with difficult people is good for practice.

When you are practicing in your mind, you can show your unconscious mind that it can be confident.

For example, you can imagine the other person being just one in a crowd of a thousand people listening to you up on a podium with a microphone. Then accept the Nobel Peace Prize after your speech.

When you hear ad slogans, think about how much work went into boiling down a rich message into them. Notice how the commercials and many nuances of the product and its presentation are aligned with this.

E & E. P. Formation

Determine the goals of the assessment.

Note the purpose of the procedure.

Define the evidence in a concrete way.

Specify who is appropriate for establishing and continuing to carry out the procedure.

Develop the timeframes and milestones that indicate progress.

Specify what situations could be troublesome.

Test.

How will you know when you have achieved your desired outcome? Be very specific about this. With these indications or clues (we call them "evidence") in mind, you will be able to monitor your progress. Develop a procedure to ensure that you will detect the evidence as well as counter-evidence. We'll call this an "evidence procedure." For example, evidence in a learning situation is typically a test score. The evidence procedure would be the test design and the procedures for giving and grading the test.

1. Define the assessment's goals. (E.g., how well the student has learned a topic.) Positively state them. A score and grade that accurately reflect the student's learning level. Describe ideal performance (Ex: 100%).

2. Note the purpose of the procedure. What are its benefits? That is, why do you need the procedure? (E.g., students who learn NLP concepts can communicate more effectively with other NLP practitioners, and they can learn from the literature and teachers more effectively.)

The Big Book of NLP

3. Define the evidence in a concrete way. Define the evidence in a concrete way, for example, as observable behaviors and other outcomes. How will you know when you have achieved your goal? (E.g., students who achieve 85% are reasonably conversant with NLP and fairly well prepared to benefit from teachers and the literature.)

4. Specify what is appropriate for establishing and continuing to carry out the procedure. Make sure that any instructions or training for the procedure are complete and understandable. (E.g., trainers with at least five years of successful practice with NLP and who achieve at least a 90% score.)

5. Create timeframes and milestones to track progress. This can include the points at which progress should be assessed and when the goal is expected to be achieved. Indicate what your criteria are for each step you specify. (E.g., a weekly quiz will help us determine how well the student has mastered the most recent lessons.)

6. Recognize problematic situations. What issues might arise when administering the evidence procedure? This includes positive intentions that may cause resistance. (A trainer may lack time management and fail to administer the quiz. A closer look reveals that he or she needs the ego boost that comes from teaching, so they avoid giving the test. That's a big change from when they weren't affiliated with a grading institution.)

7. Test. Establish times and responsibilities for evaluating the effectiveness of the testing, teaching, and materials used. (E.g., at the end of each quarter, trainers will review student satisfaction with an assessment instrument and a discussion. The trainers will review this at a quarterly staff meeting set aside for improving the program. It will include the opinions gathered from students as well as the opinions of all staff.

Eye Accessing Cues

Involuntary eye movements (Eye Accessing Cues) may show you what representational systems the person is accessing, or tapping into, in order to think and express themselves. When a person glances up and to the left (your left, their right), they are constructing a visual image. That may mean they are considering something new, or trying out an image that you are creating for them. So constructing means exactly what it says: the mind is constructing or creating a new image that they have never seen before.

If they look up and to the right (your right, their left), they are recalling something visual, something they actually remember. When they simply look to their right, your left, midrange, or lateral, they are constructing something auditory; something they have not heard precisely before, or, more likely, a combination or sequence of sounds that they have not previously heard.

When they look to their left, midrange, or lateral (your right), they are recalling an auditory experience. They are remembering a sound, music, a voice or another auditory pattern. When someone looks down and right (your left), they are connecting with a feeling of some kind. But down and to their left (your right) is for digital auditory access; that is, for some kind of verbal information.

As you'll recall, that could be something they are putting together, or something they have already heard of. Sound in general, and sound as in human speech, are two different things to access, so they have different eye movements.

There are some people whose eye-accessing cues are reversed. NLP theorists believe that they tend to be left-handed and have their brain hemisphere functions on opposite sides of most people. There are even some people whose eye movements are very subtle, very subtle. You have to look more carefully to see what their eyes are doing. If the person always starts off in a particular direction before making other moves, this is called their "Lead Rep System." They access one particular rep system so they can get started, then move on to other rep systems. This lead system is not necessarily their primary rep system. It's just the rep system they access to get started.

The Big Book of NLP

Eye Accessing Cues (if the Person Is Situated in Front of You):

Vc = Visual Constructed – Up Left

Vr = Visual Remembered – Up Right

Ac = Auditory Constructed – Lateral Right

Ar = Auditory Remembered – Lateral Left

K = Kinesthetic - Sensations - Down Left

Ad = Auditory Digital – Internal Dialogue - Down Right

No eye movement - already accessed the information.

EAC Elicitation

During the first session with a client, it is important to elicit the person's accessing cues and guesstimate their primary representation system.

Order to do so effectively, the person should be associated into a vivid and sensory full memory, and it's best if it's a positive one.

1. Ask: "When was your last experience of success? How did that go, and who in your life did what? What was your active role in achieving this success? How do you manage to stay on the right track? "

2. Listen for rep system predicates.

3. Note the most frequent eye movements as they express visual, auditory or kinesthetic predicates.

4. Draw a diagram of the synesthesia. In which path their eyes went as they accessed different rep systems?

Early Learning Set

Source: Milton H. Erickson and Ernest L. Rossi

This type of light induction is very useful when working with clients who are plagued with self-doubt. It also works well for recovered addicts (of all sorts), as it gives them back the capacity to learn how to adapt to life without substance abuse.

"Please take a seat on the floor with your palms on your thighs and feet flat on the floor. Now, I would like you to know that you don't have to talk to me at this time. You don't even have to leave your current position. In fact, you don't even have to listen to my voice because your unconscious is already aware of my message.

You don't need your unconscious mind to do anything because the most important thing is that your unconscious mind listens. You're not even aware of the changes that are occurring inside of you right now. Your breathing pattern has already shifted. It has slowed your heart rate and your respiration. I'm going to talk to you right now. There is no way for me to tell if you started reading in kindergarten or first grade. However, you had to learn the alphabet first... And trying to make sense of all of those letters seemed like an impossible task.

And you had to know the difference between an A and a B, a B from a D, a M from a W, and a P from a R, as well as upper and lower case letters. Rather, you learned these letters by picturing them in your mind. It was a seemingly insurmountable task to learn script, but you succeeded by creating mental images of the letters in both uppercase and lowercase. As a result, you've gained a long-term benefit from that. For the rest of your days, years, and decades. Then there are other things you can learn, such as how to solve problems, and that's what we will do in a moment."

Ecology

In NLP, ecology is defined as the study of consequences. Think of a forest. You probably imagine the trees and some of the larger animals, such as deer, lions, elephants, or wolves (depending on where the forest is). While they may seem like individual pieces, they are actually small parts of one single system. The trees provide food and shelter for small insects, birds, and mammals, which in turn are consumed by larger animals. Tiny animals and fungi live in the soil that helps the trees grow. If you take away one aspect of this system, the entire structure falls apart. The system can also be brought down if a new species is introduced. Our minds function in a manner similar to that of these natural systems. What if I told you that some people consume a large amount of alcohol and it has little impact on their lives, but other people's lives are completely ruined even if they only drink a little and very seldom? There are times when alcohol can have little or no effect on a person, just like an invading species. A more interesting question might be why people undergo such drastic changes after they have lost their jobs, retired, or divorced. The removal of one aspect of a system can have the same disruptive effects as adding a new one. Insects are so important to life on Earth that if they were eliminated, humans and multitudes of other species would indeed be extinct as a result. A healthy ecosystem is dependent on the health of each and every one of its constituent parts, as we can see from this example. In order to describe the system within an individual, NLP employs the term "ecology." Neglecting the system as a whole will only lead to more problems, no matter how beneficial our efforts are. Cats, for example, were brought to Australia to help control rodents, but the cats have ended up causing serious problems for the local fauna. The same can be said for being more productive at work, which can result in less time spent with family and friends. When we look at the ecology of the situation, we can anticipate, mitigate, and deal with issues before they arise while we accept a systemic approach. Ecosystems also allow us to see whether or not an isolated problem points to an even larger issue. For example, alcoholism may be a symptom of a deeper problem, so treating the alcohol problem alone may help, but it won't necessarily transform the person from a passive to a productive one. "Better" people aren't the goal of NLP. The goal of NLP is to bring out the best parts of every person, and ecology is a critical component of this process. The key question is: How does this change influence anything / everything else?

Eco-Check

Change the world with this important pattern. It prevents self-sabotage by ensuring all parties accept the change. This ecological approach can be applied to multiple systems, such as politics. When you think "ecologically," you consider all aspects of your outcome. If you value both, you make sure you don't achieve X at the expense of Y. When helping a client quit smoking, for example, a client's fear of weight gain may sabotage your efforts. You want to make sure your client is completely on board with the change. To ensure congruence, some part-work may be required to ensure your client is ready for change. The client's fear of weight gain can be reduced by committing to healthy weight loss strategies and increasing self-acceptance.

1. Obtaining an objective state. This pattern assumes you already have a personal problem pattern that you are working to change. To begin the eco-check, use any method that helps you gain objectivity, such as thinking like a journalist who must adhere to the facts of the situation. You may need to dissociate into the third perceptual position. From this objective frame of mind, think about your life as a whole, perhaps as if you could look down at your timeline.

2. Conduct an ecology check by asking good questions.

"What areas in my life are benefiting from having this belief/behavior?"

"What areas in my life may get hurt because of it?"

"Am I feeling completely assured that this is something I want to generate in my life?"

"What are the specific immediate results of it?

"What are the specific long-term results?"

"Who else is being affected by these outcomes?"

3. Making this pattern a recurring theme in your life can make it even more powerful. Keep these questions alive by writing them in your journal. (Do you keep a journal?) Read the questions before bed so they are fresh in your mind. You'll get dreams, songs, words, flashes, memories, and voices... Ignore them. It's important to notice them. Your brain loves to solve riddles. Note any answers you get. Prepare a notepad or device to collect them all.

4. Evaluate. Once you have accumulated the answers, evaluate them. Realize that, right now, you have many valuable clues to success. What do they mean about the outcomes you appear to be headed for? Do you need to change courses?

Eliciting Response

Get your partner to think about a pleasant memory in the first perceptual position.

Have your partner focus on the visual rep system.

Have your partner clear their mind and focus on the auditory.

Have your partner focus on the kinesthetic.

Become a master communicator by learning to recognize and utilize subtle changes in others' physiology. This pattern involves the valuable skill of eliciting unconscious resources, a skill that serves you best when it, too, is unconscious. This skill deserves serious study, so resist any temptation to treat it like a magic trick. We recommend that you practice this pattern with a partner until you find yourself using it unconsciously.

1. Get your partner to think about a pleasant memory in the first perceptual position.

Find someone who will allow you to practice this exercise with them. Ask them to think of a pleasant memory. Encourage them to do this with their eyes closed and in the first perceptual position, as though they are experiencing it first hand. Have your partner focus on the visual rep system.

Once your subject has a pleasant memory in mind, have them focus exclusively on the visual aspect of the memory. Note all of your subject's reactions, including changes in posture, facial expression, changes in skin color, breathing pattern, and so forth.

3. Ask your partner to clear their mind and concentrate on the auditory.

Have your subject clear their mind and open their eyes. Have them bring up only the auditory aspect of the memory. Continue making your observations.

4. Ask your partner to concentrate on the kinesthetic.

Once they have done this, have them bring up the kinesthetic aspect as you continue to observe.

You might want to record your observations on a paper form. Use three titles to divide your operations into.

"Visual Reactions,"

"Auditory Reactions" and

"Kinesthetic Reactions."

Once you have done this exercise, you can improve your powers of observation "in the wild" by being aware of subtle physiological signals and how they are influenced by factors such as primary sense mode, emotional arousal, rapport, and anything else of importance. This power of observation will be valuable in many NLP patterns, even the ones you don't know you're using.

Embedded Command (I)

As in the analogical marking pattern above, embedded commands are communications that are inserted into a larger communication frame. They are typically marked out with an analogical mark. This pattern and the next give more opportunities to practice this aspect of communication.

One way to insert an embedded command is as a quote or a question. "Somebody once said to me, 'Your hand is beginning to lift without you noticing.'"

With analogical marking, you can highlight an embedded command in a sentence that appears to say the opposite of the command. For example, "There's really no need to 'close your eyes and take a deep breath'."

1. Select a situation to use embedded commands. Select a typical situation in which you want to communicate more effectively and in which embedded messages or priming could be helpful.

2. Determine what you want to communicate with this approach. Write down a number of things that you would like to communicate, but that might arouse inappropriate defenses.

Continue accumulating these until you have several that you feel can be converted into embedded messages. Make sure that your approach is ethical. You must not attempt to manipulate a person in a manner that is not in their best interest.

3. Plan your communication. Create sentences that could be normal-sounding parts of your communication with this person and include your embedded commands.

Remember, embedded commands are usually very short sentences or sentence fragments with the meaning that you want. If necessary, review other materials on Milton Erickson's use of embedded commands.

4. Practice the approach. Before using this approach, practice delivering these communications. Try them with several different embedded commands.

Add analogical marking (see the pattern above), such as including changing your inflection, tempo, body language, and volume.

5. Put the strategy into action. Once you feel that this can be done in a way that is very natural, use this approach in the current situation.

6. Evaluate the outcomes.

Notice how the person responds. Were there any awkward moments or looks?

Does the person respond in any way that suggests your approach was helpful?

7. Continue to refine and practice your use of analogical marking until you are able to do it without preparing in advance. Many people discover that they do it without even realizing it.

Embedded Command in a Question

When embedded commands appear in questions, they have the added benefit of priming a more open, curious state. The question helps to conceal the embedded command as well. Here are examples:

"I'm wondering whether you would feel completely comfortable speaking with me."

"Do you know if you can quietly allow your unconscious mind to come out and talk to me?"

Select a situation to use embedded commands in. Write down a number of things that you would like to communicate, but that might arouse inappropriate defenses. Continue accumulating these until you have several that you feel can be converted into embedded messages. Make sure that your approach is ethical. You must not attempt to manipulate a person in a manner that is not in their best interest.

Create questions that could be normal-sounding parts of your communication with this person and that include your embedded commands. Remember, embedded commands are usually very short sentences or sentence fragments with the meaning that you want. If necessary, review material on Milton Erickson's use of embedded commands. Before using this approach, practice delivering these communications. Try them with several different embedded commands.

Add analogical markings (see the pattern above), such as including changing your inflection, tempo, body language, and volume. Once you feel that this can be done in a way that is very natural, use this approach in the current situation. Notice how the person responds. Were there any awkward moments or looks?

Does the person respond in any way that suggests your approach was helpful? Continue to refine and practice your use of analogical marking until you are able to do it without preparing in advance.

Embedded Command (II)

"There are no two people alike... no two people who understand the same sentence the same way. So in dealing with people, try not to fit them to your concept of what they should be."

- Milton H. Erickson

This is a more advanced embedded command pattern that extends the previous Embedded Command (I) and Analogical Marking. This one involves embedding the command in sections, spaced over a larger communication. This pattern depends more on analogical marking as a subliminal cue than the simpler form of embedded command. The unconscious mind strings together the fragments of the embedded command and gets the message, especially when the person is in a suggestible state. Here is an example of this pattern:

"You can "trust your unconscious mind" because it will never have to "reveal to your conscious mind" anything that you don't want me to know right now."

This uncomfortable incident that you think is ruining your life is part of your past. You can 'come back next week' and 'talk about anything you want, in a direct and comfortable way'.

Notice that you can string together the more impactful and state-related words to see what kind of priming is going on. As in the preceding example, you have the ability to trust, know, and reveal anything, right now, in the past, present, and comfortable.

Similarly, there is a focus on self in this string: you, can, you're, know, your, you, want, know. In service of inducing a downtime, there is a double negative plus an immediacy to parse: never have to reveal, don't want to, right now.

There is also manipulation of time and personal power through conjugation and implying an alternative to replace what is in the past, next week. It also casts doubt on their understanding of their problem: Anything you believe is ruining your life... is... past... next week... anything... in a direct and comfortable manner."

You can use meta-models as filters to help you brainstorm as you create the more subtle embedded commands, such as the ones we just covered, as well as analyze and learn from the work of masters such as Erickson. (You can use it to assist you in creating, analyzing, and learning from masters.)

Except when you are purposely using negatives, just shifting language into an exclusively positive frame is an excellent way to get into the embedded message creation mindset because of how it forces you to see components of your text that you took for granted.

The subtle embedding falls more into the area of priming than actual commands.

1. Select a situation to use embedded commands. You can use the same material from the previous embedded command pattern to get through steps one, two, and even three quickly. Select a typical situation in which you want to communicate more effectively and in which embedded messages could be helpful.

2. Determine what you want to communicate with this approach. Write down a number of things that you would like to communicate, but that might arouse inappropriate defenses. Continue accumulating these until you have several that you feel can be converted into embedded messages. Make sure that your approach is ethical. You must not attempt to manipulate a person in a manner that is not in their best interest.

3. Plan your communication. Create sentences that could be normal-sounding parts of your communication with this person and include your embedded commands. Remember that you are to break up your command into fragments that you will place in several parts of the communication.

You must include analogical marking, such as changing your inflection, tempo, body language, and volume, to ensure that the unconscious mind strings them together.

4. Practice the approach. Before using this approach, practice delivering this communication.

5. Put the strategy into action. Once you feel that you can do this smoothly, use this approach in the actual situation.

6. Evaluate the outcomes. Notice how the person responds. Were there any awkward moments or looks? Does the person respond in any way that suggests your approach was helpful?

7. Continue to refine and practice this method.

8. Continue to refine and practice your use of embedded commands until you are able to do it without preparing in advance. Many people discover that they do it without even realizing it.

Emo

Resolve excessive emotional reactions to gain control, objectivity, and poise. This is also known as the "emo" pattern. This pattern is especially helpful for highly emotional people, whose reactions can be out of proportion or not appropriate for the context. "Contrastive analysis" and sub-modalities give this pattern its magic.

1. Pick a situation in which you have an emotional reaction that causes you to over-or under-react, to lose your objectivity, to experience emotional suffering such as high anxiety, or to lose your poise. Connect that experience. Notice what kinesthetic sub-modalities are involved in that reaction. It's possible to find sub-modalities like pressure or pulse, heat or cold, tension or suppression.

2. Find key differences in sub-modalities between this state and a similar one that is positive. Think of an emotional state that has some similarity to the emotional reaction you are working with. However, the emotional experience must be positive. For example, excitement can be similar to anxiety but can be positive. Constructive motivation and passion for good outcomes can be similar in some ways to jealousy, but in fact they produce a positive state of mind. Experience the kinesthetic sub-modalities of this positive state. You don't have to come up with a positive situation in order to come up with this positive state. The important thing is that the positive state is similar to the troublesome one. However, once you think of the positive state, it may help you to think of one or more situations in which you experience it in order to associate with it and review the kinesthetic sub-modalities that it contains.

3. Determine the driver sub-modality that connects two states. Review all the sub-modalities that you have experienced in each of these two states. Notice what sub-modality is mostly shared between the two, and which is most similar. This is called the "driver sub-modality." It remains the most stable when you move between these two different states.

4. Do the same process for the visual and auditory rep systems. Do this pattern for your visual and auditory rep systems, one at a time. Use the same two reactions as you used for the earlier steps.

End Buts

This is something I teach every one of my students and clients on day 1, and you ought to use it yourself and teach it to your clients as well: There are no "buts" if you aim for an effective communication. When you use it, for example, "yes, but..." or "sure, but...", you break rapport. You confirmed the validity of the other person's opinion, "but" you suddenly contradict it. You may state your opinion, and it may be the complete opposite of the other person's. However, it would serve you better to use the connective 'and' instead of 'but'.

"You felt like I got angry at you, and I can assure you that I was not." Compare how this sentence feels with, "You felt like I got angry at you, but I can assure you that I was not." The second sentence gives the impression that the person was wrong to think what he thought. The first phrase, though, implies that it was my responsibility to explain how I really felt. If it's important to you to maintain rapport with a certain person, end the "buts."

The Big Book of NLP

End-of-Day

Source: Alexander Van Buren

Review the day from a loving state.

Find a rough spot and freeze frame.

Identify resources from your day.

Use logical levels and your resources to create preferred outcomes and processes.

Play the scene through with your preferred outcomes and processes. Modify it until you are satisfied.

Continue to the next rough spot.

Watch the most positive highlights of the day. Test.

Make a daily habit of generating behaviors and attitudes that are ever more effective and fulfilling with the power of the new behavior generator.

1. Reflect on the day from a loving perspective.

Create a state of self-acceptance and love.

Begin reviewing your day from the beginning, as if you were watching a movie about your day.

2. Locate a rough area and freeze frame it.

When you hit a rough spot, especially one where you don't like your own or others' behavior, freeze the image.

3. Identify resources out of your day.

Identify resources coming from other parts of the day.

Take the elements that worked well for you during the day, and briefly think about how they might be useful as resources for the trouble spot where you have frozen the image.

4. Create preferred outcomes and processes by utilizing logical levels and your resources.

Determine what didn't work about this spot.

Compare your actual experience to one that would have been more resourceful.

Keep the resources that you noted in Step Three in mind.

Using the logical levels, ask questions such as the following:

a. Spirit:

What effect did I have on the people involved?

How would I prefer to have affected them?

In other words, what do I wish I had and what should I have?

b. Identity:

Who was I in this situation?

What sort of person would I prefer to "have been"?

c. Values:

The Big Book of NLP

What was important to me in this situation?

What would I prefer to have valued instead?

d. Beliefs:

What was I certain of?

What clarity or certainty would I prefer to have had? (This can be intellectual, or a feeling or intuition. It can be a level of probability, such as, thinking something has higher odds of happening.

e. Capabilities:

What abilities did I use in this situation?

What capabilities would I prefer to "have used"?

f. Behavior:

What specific actions did I take?

What actions would I prefer to have taken?

5. Play the scenario through with your preferred outcomes and processes. Modify it until you are satisfied.

Now play this scene with all of these preferred modes of being and resources in place.

Loop through this scene.

Modify the scene each time through until you are satisfied with it.

The scene should make you feel good as you see yourself getting positive results with behavior and an attitude that you can take pride in.

When the scene passes a basic ecology check, you are ready for the next step.

Continue to the next rough spot.

Now continue with your movie until you find another spot to freeze, and repeat steps two through five.

7. Watch the most positive highlights of the day.

Once you have made it to the end of the day, you can ask your mind to run the movie briefly, showing you highlights of the best parts and including the improved scenes in place of the original versions.

8. Test.

In the coming days, see if you find yourself handling new situations with the resourcefulness that you have been generating in these daily (or nightly) sessions.

In order to manage your time effectively, you can briefly review your day and select just one or a few scenes in advance to work on.

Practice the pattern while sitting up in a spot where you won't fall asleep if you are doing it before bedtime.

The Big Book of NLP

End of Session

When you ask a client, right at the beginning of a session, "What do you need to work on and resolve before you leave here in an hour?", you presuppose several important notions: first, the client's responsibility for the therapeutic intervention's success ("you need to work"); second, that the session is going to be successful in resolving the issue; and third, that this is going to happen within the next hour. When the client answers, and you verify that this desired outcome is achievable within the hour, you can say: "well, that's great, so you say that when you get up from this chair in one hour and walk towards that door, you will be X and Y, and now we just need to work backwards from that moment and figure out the path there. Wonderful... Let's begin! "

Engagement

"Engagement" has become the new buzz word in business consulting and corporate training: "engagement." All it means is that the person in a team is fully committed and acting independently and purposefully on behalf of achieving the team's mutually desired outcome. Now, this does not only apply to business environments. A family is a team. A couple is a team. Parents are a team. Any group of two or more people that has a common desired outcome is a team. Engagement, if practiced consciously and with care, is a powerful tool to achieve and maintain a desired outcome.

Although the marketing departments of agencies around the world have worked hard to turn "engagement" into a complicated and lengthy model, it is simple and direct. You increase the engagement of anyone on your team by learning their perspective on the following criteria:

1. Belonging: "Do I feel like I belong here? Do I feel needed? "

2. Assurance: "Am I aware of the desired outcome and supporting it? Do I know for sure how things are going to work out for everyone's benefit? "

3. Value: "Am I worthy of being valued the same as everyone else on the team? Does my opinion count as much as X or Y? "

4. Independence: "Am I free to make an impact on the process and the results? Am I going to be outcast or rejected for making an innocent mistake? Do I have a say about the details and experiences of the process and of the desired outcome? "

The better and more positive the responses to these questions are, the greater the likelihood that a person will be engaged. They will experience internal motivation and a desire to contribute in ways that go beyond the scope and requirements of their position or role in the team.

The Big Book of NLP

A significant factor in why husbands feel disconnected from family life is that their wives are typically the official decision-makers, which reduces their "value" as a result of their involvement.

Add to that the wife's criticism of anything and everything, and the "assurance" and, eventually, the "belonging" aspects of the relationship are diminished. Establishing family rules without consulting the husband and thereby diminishing his "independence" are two factors that frequently contribute to a divorce being finalized.

Husbands are also not angels in every way! Because of their reluctance to share, open up, and be vulnerable, their husband's "belonging" aspect in his wife's engagement quadrant is reduced. In addition, the wife's grumpy face and exhaustion, which result in a lack of affectionate attention, cause her to score even lower on the scales of "value" and "assurance." When the husband is the primary breadwinner, the concept of "independence" fails as soon as something goes wrong in the marriage.

Enhancement / Elaboration

The basic premise is that the anchor is linked to a specific desired state which is then applied to various situations and experiences. The purpose of anchor enhancement is to expand the anchor's reach beyond the original primary experience, so that it will be easier to induce the desired state, regardless of the situation or circumstances. In NLP we call it

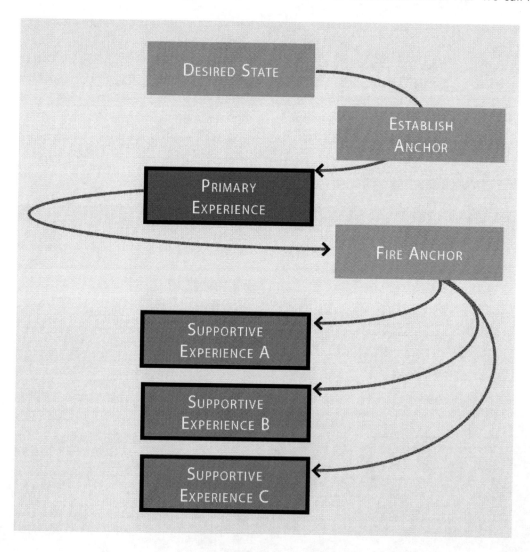

The Big Book of NLP

"elaboration", or "enhancement". It is also a way to repeat anchoring without getting bored or risking weakening the anchor (when you put yourself again and again in an excited state, for example: if the experience is the same, the excitement wears off after a few runs. That can lead to a weak primary anchor). The illustration shows how Anchor Enhancement gets done. Let's take one example and run through the process: Your desired state is "Relaxation". You establish the anchor with a primary neutral experience ("walking the dog", "washing dishes). You repeat the scenario a few times, to make sure the anchor is in place. You then enhance by firing the anchor in various imaginary experiences - with the same anchor and desired state - for Supportive Experience A ("riding the bus", SE-B ("talking with my son") and SE-C ("going to the dentist").

Envelope

This is a strategy that works well when the client is in distress but cannot express the feelings in words. The client will often say things like, "I am fatigued but I don't know why," or "I feel like something really bad is going to happen, but I don't know what exactly." Take your time with this strategy and be patient.

1. Initiate a downtime state. Close your eyes.

2. Take a few deep breaths. Imagine holding a plain white envelope. It was addressed to you and delivered to you directly.

3. You open the envelope. You unfold the paper, and you instantly recognize the handwriting of someone you knew in the past. Recall the face of the person and imagine that you can hear their voice.

4. Open your eyes, move both eyes to the uppermost right corner, as far as you can reach, hold for three seconds, and return them to their normal position. Close your eyes again.

5. Take a few moments to read the letter, hearing the words in your head as if they were spoken by the person who wrote it for you, and accepting whatever your unconscious mind reveals to you.

6. When you're done reading the letter, fold the paper and put it back in the envelope.

7. Take a few deep breaths and break state.

8. Ask, "Who sent you the letter? And what was the main message this person wanted you to know? "

Erected Despair

A collapsed posture embodies despair and withdrawal; shoulders dropped forward, the torso caved in, a bending over the diaphragm. This is a surrendering stance. As a result, we commonly work with people in a standing position to assist them in becoming aware of these behaviors. Standing up forces your muscles to work against gravity, so they can't fully soften. When they are seated, they are significantly more susceptible to collapsing. This pattern helps to analyze and evaluate the sensations and perceptions of despair.

1. Stand up as you normally do.

2. Take note of any areas of your body that feel particularly sturdy as you change your posture to get up from your seat. Perhaps you've noticed increased strength in your knees, hips, buttocks, shoulders, forearms, or upper back.

3. Pay attention to experiences that differ from powerlessness and collapse. In other words, notice which muscles felt dormant while you were sitting down and were activated instantly as you stood up.

4. Spend some time investigating your body's feelings of strength, mapping the kinesthetic sub-modalities and validating areas for progress with the vocabulary of sensation (refer to Appendix E at the end of this book for further details):

- *Temperature*

- *Texture*

- *Degree of adaptability*

- *Vibration*

- *Pressure*

- *Tension*

- *Movement*

- *Breathing*

- *Weight*

- *Confinement*

- *Change Of Size Or Shape*

- *Direction*

- *Triggers*

5. Now, imagine a spring coming down from the ceiling that is attached to the top of your head. The spring is stiff but allows for some flexibility, so as you stand taller, the spring pulls your head a little bit higher, changing your posture so that your ears are in line with your shoulders and hips, your shoulders are resting down and back, and your balance is centered in your core.

6. Anchor this position by touching the tips of your non-dominant hand's thumb, middle, and ring fingers.

7. Break state and take a seat.

8. Stand up again, imagine the spring attached to the top of your head, fire the anchor and notice your posture changing.

9. Once again, map the kinesthetic sub-modalities, this time out of the empowered posture:

- *Temperature*

- *Texture*

- *Degree of adaptability*

- *Vibration*

- *Pressure*

- *Tension*

- *Movement*

- *Breathing*

- *Weight*

- *Confinement*

- *Change Of Size Or Shape*

- *Direction*

- *Triggers*

10. Future pace. Think about an upcoming challenge you must face, perhaps a difficult interaction with another person in your life or an important exam. Fire the anchor.

11. Test. How does it change your expectations for the outcome of the challenge while you're in the empowered posture?

Establishing Trust

We want to help our clients make positive changes as quickly as possible. In order for them to open up and trust our guidance, especially since a lot of the procedures we use seem quite odd to outsiders, we need to establish and maintain rapport from the first session. One useful way to do so is to remove misconceptions about evidence-based therapy. For example, here is a typical introductory discussion I have with a new client:

Therapist: "What do you think is permitted here, in this room, and what do you believe is most likely forbidden?"

Client: "Well, probably crying is OK. Maybe you expect me to be polite and not shout or scream like a maniac."

Therapist: "Actually, the opposite is true. Shouting or screaming is not only permitted, but sometimes it's encouraged. Politeness is forbidden unless it comes out of you naturally. "

The client will usually look at me in disbelief, so I will say: "I can prove it," signaling the client to cover their ears, turn my head and shout "Yes!". Then, without saying a word, I point to the client and then cover my own ears, as if suggesting it is their turn to shout.

Once the client shouts, I would say, "that's an impressive shout, one of the best our neighboring offices have heard in a while." And you can now lean back, relax, and realize that you never ever needed anyone's permission to express yourself fully and honestly. This is the ground floor of our journey together. For as long as you come here, I will always be on your side. If you need to shout, cry, whisper, or stay silent, I will support your choice. Your choice. This is the rule here. You don't act or speak here according to what you think will please me or anyone else. You express yourself honestly, and I guarantee that I will never say it's wrong in any way. You're always right (and with a wink and a smile) except when I'm right. "

This tactic, on purpose, generates a shared semi-embarrassing experience between the therapist and the client, by suggesting that the client's shout was heard by neighbors. Right after pointing that out, we enhance rapport by establishing an easy-to-follow rule and removing misconceptions about what a therapist does. Remember the lessons you've learned in the 21 presuppositions? A client is never "wrong" or "broken" or needs to be fixed. When we reach the point in the session to explain it to the client, it is easier for them to accept it after having the experience above shake their mental map.

Evidence Challenge

Most often, suffering people will generalize a symptom as if it is the only feeling they are able to recognize in themselves. They'll say things like, "I am always depressed" or "I have permanent pain" or "I am always afraid of everything." One way to deal with such statements is via the meta-model, but for feelings that seem to take over the mental map, there is a simpler and faster way. With one question, we can reduce the scope of the negative emotion's existence within the current mental map of the client. The formula for implementing an evidence challenge is: not + timeframe. For example, "At what times is the pain not felt?", "When are you sure depression is not there?", "You cannot be afraid while watching your favorite TV show, are you not?", "When are you certain the pain is forgotten?"

Evidence Frame

In any system, the dynamic equilibrium of its components is what is at stake. It is a consideration of how a person or thing interacts with its surroundings in the big picture. It is the underlying relationship that exists between an individual and their ideas, strategies, behaviors, qualities, values, and beliefs. It is critical to consider ecology so that you can study the potential unbiased consequences of a planned action or change, as well as so that NLP does not become manipulative. In order to make sure that the impact of reaching the outcome is positive for the person and that it is consistent with the general aspirations and intended standards of behavior of the individual, ecology is vital when contemplating outcomes. Also, that the influence on others is beneficial to them. In what ways can you tell if your process is ecological? Before establishing a desired outcome, use the evidence frame:

What will you see, hear, feel, or perceive once the outcome is completed?

What will happen to you?

How will the achievement of this outcome change your day to-day? How will it change other people's daily lives around you?

How will it influence the way people perceive you, think about you and relate to you?

Who might be negatively impacted by your pursuit of this specific outcome? How will you mitigate the expected and unexpected reactions of others?

Exaggerated Nervousness

This is basically a pattern interruption combined with pacing and leading. When nervous, we all have our favorite tics and repetitive movements. This way, we expel the excess energy in our bodies when we feel an overload of distress. We can somatically counteract the nervous feelings by exaggerating the tics: "I notice you (touch, hold, grip, stroke) your (leg, sleeve, hair) when speaking. Could you exaggerate this for me for the next 30 seconds and let's see what happens? Exaggerate even more...When you force it, the nervousness stops because the body exits the behavioral loop. "

Excuse Blow-Out

Source: L. Michael Hall

> *What's your excuse?*
>
> *Assess the excuse pattern.*
>
> *Preserve the Values of the Excuse.*
>
> *Reject the old excuse.*
>
> *Test your anti-excuse response.*
>
> *Future pace.*

This pattern helps you get things done by turning unconscious excuses into alignment. This stops procrastination.

1. What's your excuse? Choose something important that you want to accomplish but have been procrastinating on. Think about what happens when you get close to taking the actions that are necessary for this accomplishment. What do you do instead? What feelings and thoughts come up just before you get detoured? Can you identify any conscious excuses? Perhaps instead of excuses, you have thoughts that redirect you. For this exercise, we'll call them excuses. If the pattern is not conscious, run through the sequence in your mind and listen for subtle thoughts, pictures, and feelings that you hadn't exactly noticed before. Look for vague, irrational ideas or feelings that sound silly when you put them into words. These can be the ones that slip away from awareness unless you are actively looking for them. Old, habitual, irrational thought patterns tend to be the least conscious, yet they can pack a lot of power. Get to know these excuses not just as something that you understand, but also as a state that you can feel. Explore the sub-modalities that give this state the power to divert you from your aim.

2. Examine the pattern of excuses. Answer the following questions: Is it really just an excuse? Do you want to keep this excuse? Do you need this excuse in your life? Does it serve your life at all? Does it enhance your quality of life or empower you to be a better person? If there is some part or facet of the excuse that you might need or want to preserve, what is it? What facets of the excuse might serve a positive purpose for you? (Find the hidden agenda.)

3. Preserve the Excuse's Values The previous questions helped you connect with value in the excuse pattern. You can preserve the benefits yet change the pattern so that you can accomplish your goal. Start by identifying any aspect of the excuse that is valuable. For example, Are you trying to juggle too many things, and fear that you will lose other important priorities? Imagine that you can remove all of this value and set it in a spot that is separate from the excuse pattern. Now the excuse pattern is a useless, empty shell.

4. Throw out the old excuse. Access to a strong "NO!" state Muster up an intense, inner "Hell No!" Remember a time when you felt absolutely against something that was intensely unacceptable to you? The more disgusted by it you were, the better. Amplify this into a "Hell No" state. Expand the state so that you feel it throughout your body, even into your hands and feet. Anchor this state. Imagine the empty excuse immediately in front of you and step into that excuse with a NO! state. Stomp on the excuse with the power of your "Hell, No!" Hold it in your hands and smash it into the ground. Stomp it into pieces.

5. Test your anti-excuse response. Imagine the desired activity. Notice what happens as you think about moving toward it. Notice what you feel, see, and think. Notice any excuses that remain in the shadows of your mind. See how they may interfere with your life, love, or success. Work on any remaining excuse patterns, beginning with step two.

6. Future Pace. Remind yourself of your intense Hell No state and how you applied it vigorously to your excuses. Imagine the earliest upcoming time when you will want to work on this goal in some way that you would have typically ended up avoiding.

Imagine yourself (in a dissociated image, as if you are looking at yourself from the corner) at the moment you choose to start the activity. Begin smashing the excuse at that point. Access the most open, eager state that you can, and imagine starting the activity. If you feel like you want to actually do the activity now, go right ahead! Go slowly at first, and then repeat the pattern while speeding up the process. Go for weaker excuses first, just for training with the pattern. Don't take the heavy challenges up front. Make sure your whole body and mind are involved in the process of change. If you feel a twist in your stomach when you remind yourself of the excuse, it's working! If you feel any discomfort or hesitation when you think of starting the activity, it means there is still an excuse lingering. Dig deep and get to know this feeling. Turn it into words so you can understand it better. Work on it with this exercise.

Exit the Problem Frame

A problem frame seeks answers to questions such as: what don't you want? What do you want to get rid of, remove, or discard? What is wrong? What made this problem happen? Why is it a problem? Whose fault is it? What can you do to fix it now?

The outcome frame is different. We ask: What do you want? How can you get it? What resources are available? Where are you now in relation to this outcome?

The problem frame is about consuming "solutions" in the present and distorting current reality. The outcome frame is about the creation of the future and taking responsibility in the present. For example, a common "problem" many overweight clients struggle with is high LDL cholesterol levels. When you view your health status within the problem frame, then taking medications seems like the only logical solution.

However, if we exit this problem frame and move our consciousness into an outcome frame, we can establish the following desired outcome: "weigh 120 lbs. by next April, by eating only organic foods and exercising for one whole hour every single day for the next 90 days." The consequences of this consistent behavior will include not only weight loss, but the elimination of the "problem" (high LDL levels) without addressing it directly. In other words, we did not worry about solving the problem, but it was solved anyhow.

The Big Book of NLP

Expression Expansion

Our breath, voice, and ability to express our truth are all affected when we squeeze and compress our throats all the time. The following exercise is intended to improve your capacity to control and expand the scope of your throat, triggering the release of deeply held tension within your mouth and around your vocal cords.

1. Allow yourself to be comfortable, either lying down or sitting up with your back, neck, and spine fully supported, so that you don't hurt yourself. When you know that you won't be interrupted for a while, start by gently closing your eyes.

2. Now, begin to pay attention to your breath, how it feels and how it changes. Allow your awareness to softly focus on the breath that is arising right now... the in-breath and the out-breath... the rising and falling. If possible, try to follow one complete cycle of the breath from the start of the in-breath to the start of the out-breath. Allow yourself the time and space to interact with your breath physically for the duration of another cycle.

3. Now, start paying attention to the space inside your mouth. Allow yourself to feel or even see the space that extends down your throat and then into your lungs.

4. Begin by gently and slowly squeezing the muscles of your throat and mouth, gradually tightening them and creating more and more tension. Take note of how the tension in your neck, shoulders, and face expands and spreads.

5. Keep your lips closed, but start to relax all of the muscles in and around your oral cavity. Make the space bigger and bigger, letting in more and more.

6. Tighten and relax the muscles alternately, expanding and contracting the space inside.

7. Now, with your mouth closed, your lips tightly closed, and your throat tense, try to make sounds. Begin by introducing yourself or saying "Okay." Pay attention to the quality of your sounds. Take note of the vibrational difference between your normal and constricted voice.

8. Now, rest for a moment before returning your attention to the breath that is arising right now: the in-breath and the out-breath; the rising and falling. Allow yourself the time and space to be in direct contact with this single breath for the duration of its cycle.

9. Begin to expand your throat again, making the same sounds or saying the same words.Take note of the difference in sound. Take note of how your chest, shoulders, and neck, as well as your jaw and face, have changed.

10. Keep alternating between expanding and constricting your throat while playing with different sounds, until you've not only become aware of but also learned to control your habitual constriction and tension.

Extended Quotes

Extended quotes are a type of nesting where you have nested third party direct quotations, reenacting what someone else said (or might have said). Within these supposed quotations, you may embed commands or use any other linguistic suggestion. Examples:

"And I met this highly spiritual person, and she said - You ARE beautiful, such a beautiful soul you have... you can imagine how it must have felt, can you not?"

"You know, son, when I was in high school and had a trouble concentrating, like you do recently, my most favorite teacher told me a secret to make it easier... she said, when something seems too big to deal with, just chunk it down, to smaller pieces, and focus on the most important chunk in front of you. Can you do that, now?"

"Honey, I know you're stressed out right now, and I wish I could make it better, and now I just thought about it... remember that time when your father first took you out there to ride a bike for the first time, and he shouted at you - YOU GOT THIS!, and you DID, did you now?"

External Stimulus Threshold

Source: Richard Bandler

Identify the unresourceful state and its most influential stimuli.

Break state.

Anchor resourceful states and stack them.

Role playing of the unresourceful states.

Trigger the stacked anchors.

Continue until no abreaction is present.

Future pace the resourceful states.

To put it another way, a threshold is the line that separates two states of mind: bearable and unbearable. Occasionally, in order to change a behavior, it is necessary to simultaneously induce triggers and resourceful states while ensuring that the resourceful states prevail in each "threshold battle."

This is a pattern that will allow you to do just that. In this situation, there are two practitioners and one client. There are a lot of things that can go wrong when a friend or coworker is helping you do this pattern on a client. You can pay attention to your client's strong emotional reactions while firing anchors, and your coworker will act out the triggers of bad behavior while you are doing the pattern.

1. Identify the un-resourceful state and its most influential stimuli.

You should work with your client ahead of time to recognize exactly the series of events that take place right before they find themselves already engaged in the undesired behaviors or states.

When questioning your client on internal events, make note of their eye accessing cues. Your colleague will need those to induce the states later on. In addition, write down verbal communication scripts if they are important for the induction of the undesired states.

For example, if your client has presented a problem of non-proportional or inappropriate anger towards his son, check if it's something that the son is saying verbally and write it down.

If hearing the words, "Dad, are we there yet?!?!" is a trigger, note the tonality, but also the syntax of the words themselves, digitally. Focus on one habitual state or behavior, not more.

2. Break state. Ask your client some neutral questions to break the state. Ask them to walk around for a bit or do any other physical movement to forget about step 1.

3. Anchor and stack resourceful states. Now work with your client and anchor as many resourceful states as possible.

As a starting point, consider the problem state— What could be a good, contradicting state to the negative one?

Include comforting states such as "composure" or "gratitude."

Stack anchors by using one master anchor for each of the positive states.

Stacking anchors simply means that you anchor the same way while inducing different states each time. What happens is that eventually, when you fire the master anchor, your client gets a rush of all the positive states "stacked" on that trigger.

Be careful when you choose the location and manner of the master anchor. You want to make sure that this is not something that can cause an inner conflict later on in the session.

Do not use popular anchoring locations such as the back of the hand, the shoulder, or the knee. These are known in Neuro Linguistic Programming, but you never know what has happened in your client's life and body until you meet you.

Anchor the master trigger where you are certain there is no chance of disturbance by any other internal process.

Test the stacked anchors a few times by firing a master anchor, breaking state, and repeating. This is a step you do not want to hurry up and take.

Work slowly and thoroughly, maintaining a high level of sensory acuity and taking note of every abreaction you get from your client.

If the reaction appears when you fire the master anchor, you should exercise extra caution. It's possible that you were too careless when selecting the master anchor. An abreaction at this stage indicates that the master anchor is also causing some conflict in your client's relationship.

When this occurs, return to step 2, stay there for a while, talk with your client about anything other than the subject of the session, and then return to this step and complete it again if necessary.

Do not worry; even the best NLP practitioners get these challenges, and as a flexibility test, you should welcome these challenges and work through them. You'd be a much better change-maker because of such incidents.

4. Role playing the unresourceful states. Allow your colleague to step in and work with your client to recreate the scenarios that hold the triggers for the unresourceful states and behaviors. Give your colleague the eye accessing cues worksheet and any other useful information that could be used in the role-playing.

5. Trigger the stacked anchors. As your colleague keeps the role-playing going with your client, fire the anchors! Do exactly what you did at the end of step 3, when you tested the stacked anchors, and fire them all. Stay focused and maintain sensory acuity because this is a hard and long process for all of you.

The Big Book of NLP

6. Continue until there is no reaction to the treatment. Abbreactions are those minute, unconscious "hiccups" that alert you as a practitioner that your client is having an emotional reaction to whatever is going on in the session at that particular point in the session.

There is a threshold point when you don't see these "abreactions." This means your client has reached this point, and his mind is now fully focused on responding to events in a positive way with resourceful states instead of the negative behaviors and states that used to set them off in the first place.

7. Pace the resourceful states in the future. First and foremost, break state. Let your client rest for a few minutes, and then fire the anchors again and Future Pace for upcoming opportunities.

Failure Into Feedback

Identify the problem attitude or belief, its physiology and rep system activity.

Sort the problematic belief by rep systems into their eye positions.

Create the images of your desired capability and goal, and place them in the visual constructed space.

Distinguish between representations of the capable image and the failure memories.

Normalize the failure elements (feelings, memories, and self-talk) with positive ones.

Create an anchor for a positive reference experience.

Trigger the positive reference state in connection with your goal.

Test.

How do you change a negative attitude or belief into one that supports your excellence and success? Turn "failure" into valuable feedback and into a winning state that includes curiosity and motivation. Imagine feeling positive and motivated after the ninety-ninth failure. As with Edison and his many "failures" on the way to the light bulb, you are on your way to success with this kind of attitude.

1: Identify the problematic attitude or belief, its physiology and rep systems.

The Big Book of NLP

Select an attitude or belief that makes you feel defeated, hopeless, or like a failure. It should be associated with the difficulty that you are having in acquiring or expressing a capability and with achieving a goal that would come from that capability.

For example, let's say Carl is not making very many sales, and he feels like a failure over it. He feels that he is not communicating in a compelling way and feels very disappointed in himself. In this example, the capability would be compelling communication.

The goal that depends on that capability would be to make more sales. The belief coming from it would be something like, "I can't sell." Next, observe the physiology and eye positions associated with your failed belief. You can use a mirror, a friend, or a video camera if you find it hard to observe yourself while you represent an idea in your mind.

Note what is happening internally in each of the representational systems (VAK) during the mental representation of the belief. What do you see, hear, and feel on the inside?

2. Sort the problematic beliefs by rep systems into the corresponding eye positions.

Use your imagination to slide each of these sensory representations into the corresponding eye position.

Turn your eyes (physically, consciously and deliberately) in that direction as you place the representation.

For many people, the kinesthetic sense of failure overwhelms their internal (self-) talk and other representational systems. Putting your representational systems in their proper eye positions will help to clear up the muck and make things more manageable.

Observe how moving these representations to the side opens up the "space" in front of you for your visual perception of reality. Open your eyes, if you haven't already.

3. Create images of your desired capability and goal and place them in the visual constructed space. Think of the frustrated capability and goal that your failed belief is about.

Create a clear image of that capability in action and in terms of its positive intended results (your goal). Use imagery that is very positive. Place this image up and to your right (visual construct) and look at it in your mental space, moving your eyes up and to the right.

4: Distinguish between capable image representations and failure memories. As you focus on the desired capability, sense the main feeling associated with it. Identify the positive intention underlying that feeling.

Do the same for your self-talk around that capability.

Notice how these are different from the representations of your failure belief. Feelings and self-talk are represented differently.

5. Normalize the failure elements (feelings, memories, and self-talk) with positive ones. Look at the memories associated with the belief. By mixing your positive memories with the memories associated with the problem, you can build a more realistic perspective of the total situation. Have them fit into your timeline in the appropriate time sequence.

Note what useful knowledge can come from your memories of the situation, even though those memories may be associated with frustrating outcomes or feelings. Note how that useful knowledge can lead you directly to the desired goal.

Modify or add elements to the desired goal based on what you learn from looking at the memories. Notice what steps can take you from those memories to the positive goal.

6. Create an anchor for a positive reference experience.

Think of something positive that you are very certain you can achieve in the future. It can be something that you have done competently and reliably many times. It does not have to be something big. Showing up to work on time is an achievement, even though it is considered basic and mundane.

Establish an anchor for that reference experience.

7. Trigger the positive reference state in connection with your goal.

                              The Big Book of NLP

Adjust the structure of the desired state's resource synesthesia so that it matches the positive reference experience. In other words, remember the qualities of the sub-modalities, including where they occurred in your mental space.

Change the resource state of the goal so that its elements are laid out in the same way and with the same emphasis and sub-modalities such as size and brightness.

To help this process, fire the anchor for the positive reference experience while looking at the desired goal.

8. Test. You'll know this pattern is helpful when you experience one or more of the following:

1) New approaches to achieving your goal

2) A more upbeat and constructive outlook

3) a clearer understanding of your goal and how to achieve it, resulting in compelling imagery, feelings, and self-talk.

Factual Criticism

Even if you don't recognize the criticism coming from an inner voice, you may typically infer it's based on some experience or timeline of incidents. When you take the time to analyze the situation, you may learn that your internal voice is wrong.

What the voice says is rarely a reality, but more often an interpretation, a generalization, or an assessment of a situation. It's common for the facts underlying an opinion to be left out entirely in favor of a premise that's presented as fact rather than an impression.

When a "fact" is uncomfortable, it may seem as though there is nothing that can be done about it because it appears to be factual. It is impossible to come to an agreement if your reasoning differs from the voice's perspective. It's possible to come to a consensus if you look at the incident from which these varied inferences are drawn.

Even when a voice highlights a specific episode, such as "I can't imagine you would do this to Jenna." How can you be so incredibly cruel? "It just brings up a very small portion of what actually occurred, namely one statement that you uttered to someone at random and spontaneously. Reviewing all the additional facts about the event—what you said and how you behaved, who was there, the things happening, your mood at the time, and other relevant factors—helps you gain a better understanding of what unfolded. That one sentence may have been the exception, but you may be surprised to realize that you were extremely sensitive to others in general. A more well-rounded reaction is always the result of more information.

1. Initiate a downtime state.

2. Listen to the criticizing internal voice.

3. Take notice of its location and direction and define its spatial boundaries.

4. Tell the voice that you appreciate whatever message it has to offer you and that you want to understand it fully so you can act on it appropriately.

5. Tell the voice that you understand it is trying to help you, and that you are more interested in the objective facts right now.

6. Ask the voice for further details about the origin of its statement. For example, if the voice says, "You're such an idiot," it is not pointing out a fact; it is voicing an opinion about an incident that is not referenced any more.

7. Explain it to the voice: Every action you take, everywhere you go, at any time and into the future can be categorized as "idiotic." In the event that you are truly incompetent in all contexts, you are likely to be extremely unhappy or perhaps suicidal. That is why a generalization such as this statement is not helpful.

8. If the voice says the statement is due to the fact that you failed an important exam, you can further inquire about what makes this one incident the only factor that determines the rest of your life. One bad grade in a class can be all that's needed to form the basis of a prejudice. Other possible explanations include a lack of preparation, illness, obliviousness to the upcoming exam, or any other circumstance. Even if such is the case, the incident was not due to your incompetence, but rather to something unavoidable like a sickness that you had no control over. It had little to do with being distracted or careless.

9. Ask the voice for some help with new ideas: "How can I do better before the next exam? Can you please help me with specific action steps I can take, maybe starting even today? " Remember to remain respectful and patient. That internal voice is not your enemy; it is the product of survival mechanisms combined with the voices of important people in your past.

10. When the voice does give you a list of ideas, take notes and thank it for its cooperation.

Falling in-Love

Source: Leslie Cameron Bandler

This pattern shows how surprisingly easy it is to enhance your feelings of love and affection towards your loved one, how to extend infinitely a familiar and endearing intimacy. These exciting results are produced with nothing more than anchoring.

1. Clarify what you want to feel toward a special person. Select a special person for this exercise, such as your significant other. List in your mind or on paper the feelings you would like to feel toward this person. Even though dynamics in the relationship may have caused some alienation, regaining these dear feelings can help you enhance the relationship. The usual way is to work on the relationship so that the feelings will return. This is a "bottom-up" approach because it emphasizes the somatic (physiology).

2. Elicit and focus on this loving state. Put the feelings that you identified together in a loving state. Enhance that state by working with the sub-modalities that are most powerful in inducing this state. If the state is developing well, you will find it easier to forgive the other person's faults and transgressions, if appropriate.

3. Enhance the state with future experiences. Enhance the state further by imagining future experiences that you will both enjoy together with a strong bond. Keep adding images, sounds, and feelings to these experiences until you get a sense of being in love throughout your body.

4. Once you have a strong state, anchor it.

5. Test the anchor. After repeating steps three and four a few times (usually 10 or 12 times is plenty), test the anchor. Do this by breaking the state, then firing the anchor. If the anchor works, then you should feel a loving connection with this person. If you are not satisfied with the results, a likely reason is that you did not associate yourself fully in step three, or there was a problem with the anchor you chose.

The Big Book of NLP

6. Test for results. Discover ways to use this process to enhance your relationship. For example, fire the anchor before working on communication with your partner. Notice how these explorations affect your relationship.

Choose your partners wisely. Relationships with manipulative, demeaning, or destructive people are inappropriate. This is because aspects of the interaction trigger even more powerful negative states. Change those anchors to elicit "antidote" states. That interaction should generate an open, articulate state in which you are good at understanding but also good at staying connected to your own reality.

Fast Time

This pattern is useful for dealing with a person's irrational objections to taking action towards a highly desired outcome.

1. Elicit representations and emotional reactions to slow and fast time.

2. Choose a worst-case scenario to work with.

3. Run the simulation of this representation in a time distortion mode (jerky movements on the timeline, slow and fast rapidly). The kind of time distortion you want to experience here is the feeling that time is frozen for you on the outside, while simultaneously it seems to speed up on the inside, as you change your point of view.

4. Determine the kinesthetic sub-modalities that are driving the behavior.

5. Test first by finding some reference experiences in the past, and then notice which elements of the image move at variable speeds. Anchor this experience.

6. Practice and test in fast time (super speed).

7. Set a sliding anchor by inducing a trance within the time distortion as you move up and down the timeline.

8. Set a final anchor outside of trance.

The Big Book of NLP

F/B

Source: Robert Dilts

Chose a limiting response.

Notice your foreground awareness. Notice your background awareness.

Select a counter-example.

Explore the foreground and background of the counter-example.

Associate the background and the foreground feature of the counter-example, and connect this state with the foreground of the original situation.

Focus on the common ground experience of the original experience.

Test.

It creates resource states in people who tend to focus on the negative or disabling aspects of a situation. This technique utilizes the tendency of negative and resourceful experiences to have a great deal in common. They seem quite different because their differences are in the foreground of our awareness. This pattern is a good example of creating resourceful states by linking to them from unresourceful states.

This pattern is good for people who are too caught up in a negative reality because it works with sensory representations that are shared between the problem state and the ideal state. This pattern is unique in that it does not focus on the foreground, or "driver" sub-modalities, as you would with the Swish pattern and others. It's also for this reason that you should work slowly and methodically through the steps and note your client's abreaction to the process. With the approach of the F/B pattern, you do not have a fight for dominance between the two foreground experiences. Many practitioners find this pattern to be a gentle and almost magical experience. In my own private practice, the clients who have experienced this process report it has been one of the most self-comforting experiences they've ever had. When their focus changes from a limiting or limited frame to a resourceful perception, you can see it in their eyes and in their posture. Relaxation is one of the immediate benefits of this pattern, but it is also just the beginning of the wonderful results it brings about.

1. Choose a limiting response. Choose a clearly defined situation in which you have an automatic limiting response. An example of this is flying in an aircraft when this causes panic attacks.

2. Pay attention to your foreground and background awareness.

a. Notice your foreground awareness. As you imagine this experience, notice what is in the foreground of your awareness. What parts are you most aware of at the time that you experience your limiting response? The panicking air passenger may be aware of the sound of the engines revving up in preparation for takeoff. Check all the rep systems and sub-modalities for what is standing out.

b. Take note of your background awareness.Notice what is in the background of your awareness. What are you typically not very aware of during your un-resourceful automatic response? These must be things that are not limited to the situation, or that you might experience in a situation in which you have a very resourceful response. Typically, you focus on the most pleasant body sensations that you can find, such as the aliveness of the soles of your feet or the color of the walls.

3. Select a counterexample. Find a good counterexample to your unresourceful response. This will be a time when you could well have had an unresourceful or limiting response, but you did not. For example, memories of flying without panicking would provide counterexamples. If there is no counterexample, you want to find the closest situation that you can. For example, if you have been on a bus or a train and felt relaxed, not feeling anxious at all, then you have a good counterexample because of the similarities between the interiors of a plane and that of a bus (seating, other people, length, engine sounds, jostling). Associate into the experience.

4. Explore the foreground and background of the counterexample.

a. Explore the foreground of the counterexample. Discover the aspects of this experience of which you are most aware, that is, those that are in the foreground. Intensify the positive experience and anchor it. (We'll call this anchor A1.) Foreground experiences may be things like a curious internal voice, or a dissociated image of the environment, or a sense of desire for the engine to wind up because it means that you are going to move forward.

b. Investigate the counterexample's background. Get in touch with the features that are in the background of both situations (this is the common ground experience). This may range from body sensations such as the soles of the feet to similarities in external perceptions.

5. Associate the background and the foreground features of the counterexample, and connect this state with the foreground of the original situation. Weld a strong association between the background and foreground features in your counterexample situation. You can do this by focusing on the background feature and firing the A1 resource anchor. Now connect this with the foreground of the original situation. You can use suggestions to accomplish this. For example, "the more you attend to the feeling of the soles of your feet, the more you can experience how your curious internal voice becomes louder and clearer. And as your awareness shifts to the environment of the bus and its engine, increasing speed, you more easily maintain an image of the inside of the airplane." As you can see, we are linking the common background and the positive state with the foreground of the situation in which you experienced a limiting response.

6. Concentrate on the original experience's common ground experience. Return to the original experience and focus on the common ground experience that you found in (4b). For example, you could place yourself back in the airplane as the engines are beginning to rev, and focus your awareness on the soles of your feet and the color of the walls there. If this does not improve the limiting response, then try one of these strategies:

Option 1- Find a more powerful fitting counterexample and repeat step 2a.

Option 2- Return to step 2b, and strengthen the association between the common ground elements and the background features of the counterexample.

7. Test. Focus on the foreground features of the original situation from step 1a. You should experience a positive state from your counterexample experience. You can use instructions such as: "Now you can place yourself into the seat in the airplane, actually focusing your full attention on the sound of the engine and the sense of acceleration of the plane."

Fear of Failure

TOTE is at the basis of any NLP intervention. Test, Operate, Test, Exit–this is actually the antidote to the fear of failure. We can install this approach in our clients linguistically: "What would you do if you knew that no matter what happened, you simply could not fail?" Then we chunk down their replies into intermediary action steps, as they're most likely going to give answers like "I would start my own business" or "I would ask my boss for a raise", etc. Then we can reinforce it by asking, "How would your perception of this desired outcome change if you knew you had to do this one action 100 times in a row, but you would definitely succeed when you get to 100?" Once they realize that failure only exists if they say so, we can teach them the presupposition "there is no failure, only feedback" and improve upon it by asking "and what would you do, say, and feel if you knew that it was perfectly OK to fail 99 times out of 100?".

Fight Response

Source: Erickson Institute

If you want to learn more about how the fight response works, you might want to try out the animal roots of this decisive response to threats in a stressful situation.

1. Think about a past, highly stressful situation that you feel you have not dealt with properly. Perhaps you ended up feeling like a victim.

2. Initiate a downtime state. Keep your eyes open. Take a deep breath and picture yourself as a powerful wild animal of your choice—anything that strikes you as appealing. Your animal body is a powerful source of physical prowess.

3. Associate into the experience. What are the feelings that come to mind?

4. Now get up and walk around the room a few times. This animal's body is moving at a deliberate pace as you play the part, so allow your eyes to narrow to get a sense of all this.

5. What does it feel like to be strong, powerful, and a force not to be reckoned with? Anchor the feelings.

6. Break state.

7. Go back to your seat. Take a few deep breaths. Close your eyes.

8. Associate into your chosen wild animal self again.

9. Imagine that you sense that a different animal is on its way. Instinctively, you know that this animal is a formidable opponent, just as you are. You have the distinct impression that this animal intends to harm you in any way it possibly can.

10. Notice how your body's posture changes. Note changes in your breathing. Is there anything else that you notice in your body? If you feel yourself collapsing or shrinking, remember that this is your territory, and you have the right to defend it.

11. What feelings come to mind when you think about defending what you've worked hard to earn?

12. Dissociate from the third perceptual position. Fire the anchor. Observe the clear signs of determination and vigor in the areas of your head, neck, shoulders, and facial muscles that you can feel.

13. Return to the first perceptual position.Is there any movement or tension in your body? What feelings do you recognize?

14. Fire the anchor. Feel the strength emerge in your shoulders, arms, legs, and feet.

15. Finally, get ready to take action against the animal invading your space and attempting to overrule your possessions. Fire the anchor again. Observe what happens when you prepare to fight back and protect your vital interests. Stay grounded in your body's felt sense of your own animal physical prowess by following those sensations and movements. As you get ready to hit, notice how tense your shoulders, arms, and neck become.

16. The animal did not approach, and must have felt your resolve and charismatic power. Is there a change in the energy associated with fighting? How, then? Let yourself feel the completion of these sensations as they fade away, for as long as you need to. What does it feel like to reach the end?

17. Break state.

18. Test Recall the stressful situation from step 1. Fire the anchor. What happens to the hurt you've been feeling?

19. Future pace. Think about a highly likely stressful situation in the future. Dissociate from the second perceptual position. Fire the anchor. Break state. Repeat this step five times.

Finding a Home in Your Body

This technique is designed to help you discover an internal kinesthetic space (or a combination of spaces) where you can escape from pain and suffering so that you can strengthen your body's resources for recuperation.

1. Starting at the top or bottom, you can move on to areas where you find some level of comfort or warmth in your body. These aren't necessarily positive feelings, but they aren't painful either.

2. Next, focus on the portions of your body that are dull or blank—the ones that you can't really feel. These could be sections of your body that you frequently detach from, such as your knees and ankles, forearms, lower abdomen, or waist. Notice if they appear to be linked to a previous injury or a habitual source of stress.

3. Take a few moments to utilize your breath to navigate your way through one of the dull or drained spots you've chosen. Take a deep breath in and exhale while focusing on the same part of your body.

4. Associate into that kinesthetic space.

5. After a few breaths, ask yourself, "What am I sensing in that location right now?" Does this section of my body feel more open to the rest of me? less connected? Is my perception of it changing in a positive way? "

6. Test. Is your perception of this area of your body any different than it was before? Is it neutral in any way? Is there a gradual increase in comfort? What impact does your relationship with this part of your body have on how you experience emotional distress?

The Big Book of NLP

Forgiveness

Source: Steve Andreas

Associate into your higher values and self-esteem.

Sense the difference between the fundamental human essence of the individual as opposed to their behavior.

Feel your anger over harmful behaviors that some people engage in.

Take permission to sense the humanity of all, including people who engage in hurtful behavior.

Expand your state to include a sense of releasing, and associate it with the hurtful behaviors.

Connect with the aspect of yourself that is capable of responding to these hurtful behaviors.

Test.

Rid yourself of the brooding resentments that can sap your creative energies.

1. Associate into your higher values and self-esteem. All people should feel a sense of sacredness or human dignity.

2. Recognize the distinction between an individual's fundamental human essence and their behavior.

3. Express your outrage at the harmful behaviors that some people engage in. This anger is not at the fundamental humanity that we protect with civil rights. You are feeling angry because of certain actions, especially actions that don't follow those rights.

4. Take permission to sense the humanity of all, including people who engage in hurtful behavior.

5. Extend your state to include a sense of release and link it to the harmful behaviors. Allow yourself to conjure a sense of release, and imagine releasing, for now, your attachment to these behaviors. This attachment may consist of ruminating about them, over-focusing on how they must be punished, or other ways of being attached. Of course, this step is not intended to reduce your capacity, commitment, or responsibility for addressing such behaviors.

6. Get in touch with the part of yourself that is capable of responding to these harmful behaviors. This can include your power of speech and the ability to cultivate it over time. It can include your awareness and understanding of the boundaries that these hurtful behaviors cross in order to be hurtful. It can include your preparedness to defend those boundaries under certain circumstances.

7. Test. Notice if this process has reduced your resentment and expanded your forgiveness. Notice in the coming days or weeks how any changes in your forgiveness are playing out.

Forgive the Blind

Source: Erickson Institute

Anger-inducing mentalization regularly results in greater feelings of helplessness and increased physiological stress reactions. Depression, all forms of anxiety, and irritability are all linked to ruminating about unfortunate events. The physiological stress of the original hurt is recreated when one ruminates, which tends to keep one's lust for revenge alive. It also perpetuates the role of the victim, which is associated with lethargy and humiliation. Forgiving others helps relieve stress in both the mind and the body. The key to truly forgiving and forgetting, not for spiritual reasons but for your own self-benefit, is to forgive unconditionally. Easier said than done? Well, let's try a mental experiment and see what happens.

Imagine you're walking down the street in your best (and most expensive) suit or dress, and you're late for a very (very!) important meeting. You rush your way in between the crowds of people who don't seem to care one bit about your schedule. Suddenly, as if out of nowhere, someone bumps right into you, hitting you on your right side and dropping you straight into the middle of a puddle of dirty city mud. There you are, on your knees and ankles, and your beautiful (and most expensive!) clothes are covered in mud. In a fraction of a second, you also realize that your important meeting is now unattainable-how will you be welcomed there covered in mud, exactly? Let us ask you this: what was the first thought that crossed your mind as you imagined being dropped in a puddle of mud? angry? Fury? Did you say to yourself, "If that happens to me, I could kill the guy!"? Do not associate with your feelings; instead, consider only the thoughts that came to mind at the time.

Now comes the unconditional forgiveness part: You're still deep in the mud, realizing you're going to miss your most important meeting and that your (most expensive!) suit is ruined forever, and all of that takes about a second, and your anger does not even register in your consciousness. Why? Because as soon as you hit the mud, you look to your right to see what hit you so hard, and you see an old blind man swinging his arms in the air, hysterically crying that he can't find his walking cane, and no one on that busy street stops to help him. You look down, and the old blind man's walking cane is right there in the puddle of mud you were thrown into. As you grip the cane and stand up, you suddenly realize that instead of a victim, you're now the savior and hero of a helpless man in distress. Let us ask you again: what is the first thought that comes to mind when you imagine being dropped in a puddle of mud and looking up to see who put you there?

To be fair, the people who hurt you in real life are rarely blind old men who lost their walking canes. Some of them might even hurt you on purpose, because of whatever rationalization they have invented to justify it. Forgiving them is not done for their karma or benefit. It's for you, so you can stop ruminating over the hurt, or planning revenge that will never manifest in real life, and therefore, you can stop wasting precious time and energy on useless and repetitive thoughts and negative emotions.

How? Put that person who hurt you in the blind man's shoes. Consider the option, even if it's rare, that the person who hurt you so badly was blind to what was going on around them at that moment in time. You were just within reach of their swinging arms. It could have been someone else who walked down that street, right? Nothing personal, and because the person was blind, your emotional reaction was compassion and perhaps even gratitude for the fact that you still have your eyesight and can walk without the need for a cane. The person who hurt you is disabled emotionally, and that makes him or her blind and in need of a walking cane to navigate through life. When they lose the cane, they start swinging their arms because they're lost in darkness and are helpless. When you put the person who hurt you in real life in that mental space in your mind, forgiveness emerges. You're not their victim; you're just a bystander who happened to be within reach, and if you still have to deal with that person in real life, you get to be the hero by handing them back their walking cane, and then staying as far away from them as possible.

Four Step Swish

When you're finished installing a chain of anchors, this is a useful pattern to add to the chain.

1. Check the chain by firing the first anchor and ensuring that the client reaches the desired state.

2. Instruct the client to "slow down the states again while swishing each state."

3. Ask the client for a visual for every one of the states in the chain and set up a picture for each of them. "Do you have a mental image of boredom?" for example. Repeat the process for each state.

4. Once the client has all four images, ask them to put the first one on the screen and the second one in the lower left hand corner, tiny and dull.

5. Repeat the procedure for the remaining images.

6. Fire the first anchor while mentioning the state, and make sure the client sees the first image on the screen.

7. Release the second anchor and instruct the client to swish up the second image.

8. Ask the client to swish up the third picture after firing the third anchor.

9. Ask the client to swish up the fourth picture after firing the fourth anchor.

10. If necessary, repeat the procedure.

11. Test.

12. Future pace.

Frame of Agreement

Source: Richard Bandler & John Grinder

Elicit meta-model information.

Identify higher logical level elements to the arguments, and reflect this. Attempt to get a solution from this.

If this is not yet possible, elicit a more productive state and move to higher-level motivations.

Get clear expressions of these higher outcomes from the parties.

Confirm agreements that exist at higher levels, establishing a yes set. Again, seek to resolve the conflict.

Follow up as needed.

An ongoing disagreement, or a long-lasting conflict between two people, can often be resolved by taking the discussion to a higher logical level (see appendix). This pattern uses logical levels to facilitate agreements. It can be useful in mediation and with groups.

1. Elicit meta-model information. The following elements of questioning will help you create a meta-model of each party's position, as well as get the information you need in order to pace them and develop the rapport that you will need as a credible change agent.

Ask each person to reduce their argument to the outcomes they want. Have them specify the values and beliefs underling the outcome.

The Big Book of NLP

Determine what is most significant and valuable about those values and beliefs. Ask any additional questions that will help create a well-formed meta-model.

2. Recognize and reflect on higher-level logical elements in the arguments.

Notice the elements that their arguments have in common, and identify which of those occur at higher logical levels (see the appendix).

Explain their positions in terms of higher-level agreements.

See if you or the other parties can propose a solution that everyone can agree on.

3. If this is not yet possible, elicit a more productive state and move to higher-level motivations. If it is too soon for such an agreement, consider the following:

The more high-level agreements that you have brought to their attention, the smaller their disagreements will appear to them.

The more you emphasize their most mature, intelligent agreements, the more you will be priming a mature, intelligent state for them to draw upon in resolving the problem.

Help them come up with potential solutions by drawing upon these resources. Appeal to commonalties at a higher level than the one you previously appealed to in step two.

4. Obtain clear statements from the parties expressing their desire for these better outcomes.

Have the parties express their meta-outcomes, that is, outcomes at a higher level than the ones specified. This process was started in step one, but was not made into detailed outcomes.

5. Confirm agreements that exist at higher levels, establishing a "Yes" set. Again, seek to resolve the conflict.

Get everyone into a yes set, continuously confirming agreements at these higher levels.

When possible, seek specific agreements that will resolve the conflict.

6. As needed, follow up. Once you have achieved an agreement, follow up to see if it is working out. You can establish a timeline for follow-up with the parties involved.

Framing Current Reality

This formula is effective for establishing a positive frame right at the beginning of a session. This is one of the very first things I'd tell a new client right after listening to their story about the presenting problem that led them to therapy: "First of all, I would like to thank you for making my job a whole lot easier. The fact that you're sitting here, and just told me exactly what you want to happen within the next few sessions, means you are already half way towards getting X (the desired outcome). You've done 50% of my work, basically. Some people come in here looking for permission to continue feeling sorry for themselves, and I have to work very hard to break their resistance to therapy. You came in here already half baked! (Smile) You are ready to make changes in your life and improve, and that's good news for me too. I'll tell you what-if you continue with this mindset, and I see within 8 to 10 sessions that you are making serious progress, because with this attitude, there is no alternative, you're getting X. How about that? I will refund you 10% of the fees you paid. It's only fair, right? You're making my job easier, I want you to get better faster and earn something more…"

Beyond the abundance of embedded commands and positive future pacing, what we do is link the client's choice to come in as if it was the most important decision they've made, which guarantees the successful outcome of their therapeutic intervention. By adding the promise to reduce fees in exchange for them "keeping" the effective mindset, the client's mind is now asked to start organizing resources to prove the self-fulfilling prophecy within the future pace.

The formula is: "The fact that (current reality observation)" → "means that (positive frame)" → timeframe → future pace.

Future Now Dipole

It is possible to assist your client in clarifying their priorities and focusing their commitments on working on their issues by recommending the following. Inquire with your client about their willingness to participate in a small experiment that will not take too long.

You can ask them to imagine that it's a year (or any other interval of your choosing) in the future, and that you'd like to have your session on that particular day, only now.

The client pretends to be coming to see you for assistance with a problem that could arise a year in the future.

This is something you can improvise to emphasize themes that your client will find useful. One likely benefit is that the client's perception of what the true priorities are will change dramatically as a result of the process. Some things will become annoyances that will fade into obscurity without causing much concern, while others that were overlooked will be elevated to a position of supreme importance in time.

Whether or not the client is collaborating with you on a positive future, you can highlight their effective use of resources over the course of an imaginary year.

However, you can also assist them in realizing that they would benefit from setting much more ambitious objectives. If they paint a gloomy picture, you can assist them in identifying priorities and moving forward. Once they realize they have "gained" a year, they can begin working on them a year ago, before your imagined present.

Generative Relational Priming

This is about initiating an effective relationship with a client, one that builds mutual trust and that establishes your competence in the eyes of the client. To achieve this, you need to generate positive states, expectations, and outcomes while building a constructive relationship. A valuable skill you ought to learn is priming, which is a type of memory. The key to priming is cultivating a state in a particular time frame, regardless of how it is anchored. Priming often relies on implicit memory, which is an unconscious kind of memory. An interesting example of implicit memory can be found in product placement, in which advertisers pay for the appearance of products in movies and other formats. They spend a lot of money on this, because familiarity with a product primes the person to feel more positive about it when they encounter it, even if they don't consciously remember ever seeing the product.

NLP uses the term "priming" to refer to cultivating or triggering a state. Often, this involves unconscious, implicit memories. We begin to prime a client for a state by setting up the conditions that make it easy for them to go into that state. For example, expressing positive feelings and beliefs about a client's identity and helping them to feel less threatened primes their "secure base."

A secure base tends to bring out more cooperative and creative behavior in a person. The research on subliminal stimulation for priming a secure base was a real breakthrough. But then, politicians and con artists have known for a long time that attacking a secure base makes people ready to make certain types of rash decisions that play into their hands. If people do not rush to war quickly enough, reason may set in and ruin the plan. When a client experiences a secure base, a resourceful state, a sense of mastery and other positive states when they work with you, you are making yourself into a trigger of positive states. This priming means that each time they see you, they will tend to experience resourceful states more easily and quickly. This means that your work will become more effective in that regard over time. This is a subtle and general kind of anchoring.

Gentling

Source: Robert Dilts

Imagine the three timelines.

Create your resources.

Give them to your grandparent.

Experience this from the grandparent's position.

Give them to your parent as the grandparent.

Experience this from the parent's position.

Give them to yourself as the parent.

Experience this from your position as a baby.

Return to the present with these gifts.

Test.

Build your inner "good parent" experience by bringing your adult wisdom into your timeline.

1. Consider the three possible timelines. One for yourself. One for your parents (any of them). One for your grandparents.

2. Create your resources. Move to the third perceptual position, holding your awareness of your family system from a spiritual perspective and as part of a larger whole. Think of resources or gifts that would benefit the family in the form of a blessing, metaphor, or

vision. It does not have to be the most amazing poem, but just a real statement of what you believe is the emotion that is missing the most.

3. Imagine that, borne on wisdom and gratitude from the future into the present, you can float back over your timeline to your grandparent's birth and early childhood. Imagine holding and touching your grandparent as an infant with the ethereal gentleness of a higher presence. Offer your blessings and metaphors.

4. Experience this from the grandparent's position. Bringing your vision, move to the second position, perceiving as your grandparent, and see yourself as a grandparent giving you the vision. Imagine experiencing this gentle holding and nurturance. Consider how you would feel if you received the blessing and metaphor.

5. Give them to your parent as the grandparent. Holding these resources and gifts in your heart as the grandparent, move up along the time line to the birth and infancy of your parent (your grandparent's child). In your grandparent's position, gently pass on the blessing, metaphor, and vision. Use perceptual position # 2 to make this transition as smooth and natural as possible.

6. Experience this from the parent's position. Associate into the perceptual position of your parent. Imagine being held blessed and gentled, and receiving the metaphor and vision.

7. As the parent, give them to yourself. Hold these resources in your heart. Now begin to float forward through your parent's timeline through your own birth and infancy. From your parent's perceptual position, bless and gently yourself, passing on the metaphor and vision.

8. Experience this from the position of a baby. Move back into your own perceptual position, but as a baby. Imagine being held, blessed and gently by your parents, receiving the metaphor and vision and being held gently.

9. Return to the present with these gifts. As you continue ahead on your timeline, your timeline re-calibrates to these resources as you carry them through them. The blessing, metaphor, vision, and nurturing all contribute to the formation of new memories and

qualities in your timeline. As you enter the present, you continue to have these gifts, knowing that they were passed down to you through countless generations.

10. Test. In the coming days and weeks, watch for signs that you are benefiting from these gifts.

The Big Book of NLP

Godiva Chocolate Pattern

Source: Richard Bandler

Select a source of intense pleasure.

Imagine indulging in this pleasure.

Imagine the behavior that you want to increase.

Complete an ecology check.

Put image one behind image two.

Open a hole in picture two so you can see picture one.

Shrink the hole back down.

Repeat at least three times.

Test.

Increase your motivation by associating intense pleasure with a desired behavior. This is also the perfect place to introduce a concept of change-work that will make your practice a whole lot easier and much more productive. This is the concept of staying out of your client's way! Inducing intense pleasure in a person is the most elegant outcome yet to be proven of how this concept works in real life. You see, the more you talk during the initial stages of the trance in this pattern, the less effective it's going to be eventually. You have to give your client enough time to be convinced that what they feel is pure pleasure and that they really do not need the physical object they imagine in order to feel such an intense level of pleasure. This approach serves two outcomes.

First, you can work with your client much more easily on unhealthy habits. If they have experienced the same pleasure without the original inducer (cigarettes, chocolates, cyber-porn, etc.), they can trust you enough to remove these habits completely, replacing them with something that they can control. Second, you want them to go as deep into a trance as possible on their own. People are easily distracted.

Contrary to popular belief, hypnosis does not give you complete control over your senses. You should avoid speaking too much, especially in the early stages of trance. Even if you mean well and speak slowly and quietly, you still have to let them go deeper on their terms. Once they are reminded of a source of pleasure, their unconscious mind will do the hard work for you. It will send them right into a trance, because the need to feel something so good again is automatic. Do not disturb a natural process when you can use it for the successful outcome of the session.

1. Select a source of intense pleasure. Think of a food or other thing that you have an intense craving for and that you take immense pleasure in. The creator of this pattern must have chosen Godiva Chocolate. The more of a compulsion you have to enjoy this indulgence, the better.

2. Imagine indulging in this pleasure. Use all the rep systems to imagine partaking of this indulgence. It is the sub-modalities that give it its compelling intensity. Refer to this as "image one."

3. Imagine the behavior that you want to increase. Select a behavior that you really want to increase. Picture yourself doing this, and form a dissociated image of this. We'll call this image two.

4. Perform an eco-check. Imagine what it would be like to be highly compelled to engage in this activity. What kind of outcomes might occur? Can you think of any reasons why you would not like this? Adjust your image or goal behavior as needed until it makes it through your ecology check.

5. Put image one behind image two. Use your imagination to place picture one (the compulsion) behind picture two (the desired behavior). Now, picture one is hidden by picture two.

The Big Book of NLP

6. Open a hole in picture two so you can see picture one. Allow yourself to see a little bit of picture one by opening a small hole in picture two. Expand the hole so that you get a good view of picture one. Enjoy the excitement that comes from this image.

7. Shrink the hole back down. Cover image one by shrinking the hole so that you see image two again.

8. Do this at least three times. Repeat steps six and seven at least three times, or until you feel that you have associated compulsive excitement with the desired behavior.

9. Test. Over the next few days, see if you feel better about the desired behavior, and see if it increases. If not, see if repeating this process is helpful.

Good Enough

You may dwell on your weaknesses and feel self-conscious about them when you're interested in starting a new relationship. However, you know deep down that you have a lot to give to someone else. If you aren't aware of or don't want to focus on these attributes, the people you wish to attract will get the impression that you don't value them enough to be a partner. When we lack self-assurance in a relationship, we tend to believe that we don't have anything to offer the other person. In relationships, we rely on the other person to define our worth and reassure us that we're "good enough." This pattern will help you change that.

1. Initiate a downtime state.

2. In your mind, imagine that you have gathered all of your weaknesses into a wooden box, big or small, depending on how many you believe you have.

3. Then imagine locking the box so you can't get to it. An anchor is the feeling you get when all of these weaknesses are out of sight and not easily accessible.

4. Now that your weaknesses are out of the way, you can concentrate solely on your strengths. Break state.

5. Make a list of all the good things about yourself that you can bring to a new partner, be it romantic, business, friendship, and so on.

6. If you cannot list more than 10 strengths, invite into your mind a piece that symbolizes a close friend or family member to share what they see as your favorable characteristics and skills.

7. Decide on which five strengths are the most important in any relationship, and anchor each one separately.

8. Break state.

9. Future pace Imagine a time in the near future in which you will have the potential to form a new relationship and fire the anchors one after the other, starting with the box locking anchor.

10. Alternatively, you can chain the anchors with the Changing Anchors pattern and fire only the first anchor to release the rest.

Grief

Source: Robert Dilts

Connect with your loss of a person.

Access a resourceful, objective state.

Think of two entities to serve as your guardian angels.

Create a hologram of the person you have lost. Enliven this lost person's image.

Experience this person as a mentor. Visualize a gift for this person, from your own perspective.

Create a heart connection with this person.

Share this experience. Join your mentor with your other mentors.

Bring these mentors and your gift into the loss situation to further your healing.

Resolve grief in a comforting, healing way.

1. Connect with your loss of a person. Pay attention to your feelings of separation, sadness, or grief. If this would be appropriate (depends on the situation and the people involved), start by thinking of the person you have lost.

2. Gain access to a resourceful and objective state. Mentally move out of this, into a meta-state. Create a resourceful state of wisdom and balance. Take your time here and really get into this resourceful state.

3. Consider two entities to be your guardian angels. Think of two people or entities that you would like to serve as your guardian angels. They must be two mentors that, in some sense, will always be part of you as a person.

4. Create a hologram of the person you've lost. Use your hands and your imagination to "sculpt" a life-size hologram of the person you are missing. Imagine creating them in their ideal state. Notice painful or negative ideas or recollections in connection with this person. Now put the negativity into balloons with baskets to carry them away as you let them go.

5. Enliven this lost person's image. Imagine that you can invite a spiritual energy to bring the person to you in this form, with the ability to speak in their own voice.

6. Experience this person as a mentor and visualize a gift from them. Experience it from their perspective. Notice how this person can be a new mentor for you. Ask this being, "What is the gift that you have wished to give me?" Go to the second perceptual position, perceiving yourself through their eyes, and allow the answer to come through. Visualize a symbol of the gift.

7. Visualize a gift for this person, from your own perspective. Move back into your first position (seeing through your own eyes). Answer the same question: "What is the gift that you have wished to give me?" Imagine a symbol representing your gift to this person.

8. Make an emotional connection with this person. Exchange these gifts, and imagine that your hearts are becoming gently connected by an eternal silver beam of energy.

9. Tell someone about your experience. Honor this gift and its place in your life by sharing this experience with someone you trust. For now, imagine how you might share this gift, keeping it alive. Request insight from your new mentor, who can act as a resource in helping you share this gift and all of its meaning.

10. Join your mentor with your other mentors. Experience your mentor's welcoming and connect with your new mentor.

11. Incorporate these mentors and your gift into your loss situation to aid in your healing. Bring your gift and your mentors, including your guardian angels, into the loss situation.

Give yourself time to experience their healing and insightful energies as they transform your sense of balance, knowledge, and expansion as a person.

Groundwork

Learning to be in tune with your body begins with mastering the art of centering. It's common for people to ground themselves by connecting with the earth's gravity, which keeps us firmly planted on the ground. Practicing groundwork will help you establish a connection with your physical, mental, and emotional self, allowing you to peacefully occupy your physical body.

1. Begin by transferring your weight between your feet.

2. Imagine the soles of your feet as if they were the suction cups on a lizard's feet, securing you firmly to the ground yet still allowing you to move.

3. While you inhale, gently press one or both legs into the ground.

4. As you exhale, let go of any stress you may have held in your body.

5. Anchor the kinesthetic stimulus in your foot to the sensation of letting go.

6. Determine what further tension you can let go of without compromising your ability to hold yourself upright. Fire the anchor.

7. Try it the other way around now. Breathe in and feel the flow of breath into your body, then while exhaling out, gently press into the floor with one or both feet.

8. Test. How do the feelings of pressing down and letting go help you feel more in touch with your body?

Try varying the pressure on your feet to see if you can achieve a better sensation of resilience. What effect does groundwork have on your overall well-being?

Hierarchy Of Criteria

Source: Robert Dilts

Prepare the page.

Note the desired behavior.

Note the motivating factors.

Note the preventing factors.

Note the override criteria.

Leverage the process by anchoring the behavioral content from override.

Apply the highest override criterion.

Engineer the desired behavior so that it is in harmony with all criteria levels, and fulfill the objectives of the desired behavior.

Map and adjust the override criteria and limiting beliefs.

Test.

This pattern helps to resolve inner conflicts so you can engage consistently in desired behavior. This process uses logical levels and NLP resources in an interweave that deserves some explaining.

This procedure addresses a fundamental problem. Often, inner conflict arises from the way higher logical levels override lower ones. This is possible because a desire often gets its drive from more than one level. When these levels work at cross purposes, we can end up sabotaging our higher intentions through procrastination, misplaced priorities, and other self-defeating behaviors.

Consider this example: If you derive personal meaning from helping others and you have made a career of it, then your identity level (one of the logical levels) provides much of the drive for your career choice. At the same time, you desire to express your skills and knowledge and to act on habitual behavior. These desires drive your career actions on a day-to-day basis. This example shows three different logical levels of driving behavior:

Identity (as a helper), Skills/Knowledge (applied to helping), and Behavior (helping).

What if you want to get a better job so that you can make more money and contribute more by gaining more responsibility in your chosen field?

Let's say the answer is that you need to return to school to learn more and get an advanced certification or degree. Although you may be able to say that this goal is connected to your identity level, it is not enough if that understanding is only an intellectual, conscious one. If your strongest connection to going to school is only happening at the skills/knowledge level, then you'll have a problem. That's because your identity level is currently filled with actually carrying out helping behaviors on a day-to-day basis.

This "identity override" (the identity level overriding the behavior level) leaves you procrastinating on going back to school while your current work absorbs the lion's share of your energy and creativity.

Establishing the Hierarchy of Criteria is a process designed to help you connect a higher level, such as your identity level, to an important aim, such as going back to school. This creates a strong unconscious drive that causes you to move forward much more easily and creatively.

As you'll see, the power of this pattern comes from its clever integration of several different NLP resources. In addition to Logical Levels, this pattern can use spatial sorting and the counterexample process.

The Hierarchy of Criteria pattern will also sharpen your awareness of rep systems and cognitive strategies. It has broad applicability and much flexibility in the hands of an experienced Neuro Linguistic Programming practitioner.

1. Set up the page. On a piece of paper, in a landscape (sideways) position, create four columns with the following headings:

Column 1) Capability

Column 2) Belief

Column 3) Desired Behavior

Column 4) Identity

Leave room at the top of the page for two items: Behavior and Override.

2. Note the desired behavior. At the top of the page, write down a behavior that you want to engage in but that you somehow self-prevent from carrying out. For example, studying as much as you need to

3. Note the motivating factors. In column #1, Capability: list the factors that give you the most motivation to engage in positive behavior.

Emphasize factors related to skills, possessions, and knowledge that build and result from your capability to engage in this behavior. For example, getting into a top-notch grad program, getting into a great career, or having a nice house.

Note the strategy, meta-program patterns, and sub-modalities that tell you that each criterion is motivational. For example, the idea of a great career goes along with the eager excitement in the solar plexus. The things that feed into that positive feeling include a desirable challenge and a desire for prestige. Refer to the meta-programs appendix as needed.

4. Note the preventing factors. In column # 2, "Belief," list the factors that prevent you from carrying out the desired behavior.

Emphasize thoughts, beliefs, attitudes, and values, including any that seem irrational.

Include any resistance or objections that pop up and take you away from your desired behavior, even if you have never put them into words before. Take yourself through the process of getting pulled away from your desired behavior and analyze it as though it were a formal decision-making process.

Look for strategies, meta-programs, and sub-modalities that drive these decisions.

Look for the criteria that the decisions are based on.

For example, "I do not study as much as I need to because it is stressful and I run out of time." Another would be, "When I am studying and the phone rings, it seems important to answer, even though I know it will be a friend who will distract me from studying.

The sub-modalities are that the ring is at the center of my attention (auditory) and gives rise to feelings (kinesthetic) of relief and excitement that are a very attractive alternative to studying. This creates a sense (kinesthetic) of urgency, so I fail to think (self-talk) about setting limits on this. I don't think of myself turning off the ringer (visual). "

5. Note the override criteria. Carefully think about your criteria for your desired behavior from column 1.

Think about how these criteria make you aware of criteria at higher levels, including the identity level.

Jot down any ideas that occur to you in the appropriate column or on a separate sheet if you like.

Continue until you are able to select one criterion that is the highest and most powerful of all. Write this one down in the space just below the behavior and put a big star beside it or highlight it.

In seeking this high criterion, it might be helpful to ask, "What strikes me as being so important that I would always have time for it, and that stress would not prevent me from doing it?"

Note what personal value of yours it satisfies so that it achieves this superior level of importance (e.g., "preventing tooth decay is a value that means I never forget to brush my teeth twice a day.").

Elicit the strategy, meta-programs, and sub-modalities that drive this criterion. For example, preventing tooth decay is represented as seeing bad teeth (visual construct) and getting a bad feeling about it (kinesthetic).

Refer to the meta-programs section as needed.

Let's discuss how these levels play out in the example of the student. His problem was that his context contained a convenient temptation (phone calls from friends) and an aversive (the discipline required for studying). As a result, the student's behavior appears to be at odds with his identity as a student and even with his higher values and vision. Since the conflict is coming from the lower levels (behavior and context), you can intervene at any of several higher levels, and at the same levels.

For example, students often intervene at the behavioral level by using behavior modification to "outgun" the effects of temptations in their environment. One student made a rule that he could not leave his study area without doing twenty chin-ups. The chin-ups served as an "aversive stimulus" that reduced his drive to escape to the kitchen for snacks. He enjoyed the side benefits of losing weight and building up his arms. Prior to this intervention, the snacks tempted him away from his studies too often and he gained weight. This intervention uses context (the chin-up bar and the requirement to do chin-ups) to affect behavior, just as the problem caused the context to affect behavior. However, unlike the problem, the solution was driven by his identity as a student and as a physically fit person. He could be said to have used leverage from his identity level to achieve success at the behavioral level. In this case, he did not directly confront his behavior with beliefs about the value of studying. Instead, he used the identity level, and a rather superficial version of it, pertaining to his physique and attractiveness, in the service of his desired behavior, which was eventually studying, not pumping up his biceps. It doesn't matter much where the motivation comes from, as long as you are able to engineer the behavior you desire. Also note that, by using behavior modification principles, the student gained leverage over his behavior at the unconscious level. You will see in the remaining steps how to engineer the most effective behavior.

6. Leverage the process by anchoring the behavioral content from override. Go back to column 1, "Capability," and anchor the behavioral content there. Really get in touch with carrying out the behavior in a positive state (use the override criteria to help you). Anchor that positive state.

7. Apply the highest override criterion.

By using column #4 (Identity), use the highest level criterion that you found by applying it at the Identity level.

With the school example, you might say at the identity level, "My identity as a helping professional is expanding and becoming more meaningful because I am attending the program I have chosen."

On the belief level, you might say, "I believe in life-long education and I believe in the craft I am learning." Brainstorm and review what you have done so far to determine how your high-level, override criterion applies to your identity level.

8. Engineer the desired behavior so that it is in harmony with all criteria levels and fulfills the objectives of the desired behavior. This step may mean a dramatic change, of course, or some simple refinements to your desired behavior. Most likely, it will involve adding supportive activities and perspectives to make it ecologically sound and highly motivating. Bring your attention to column #3, and draw a line below what you have written so far.

Write down a behavior here that fulfills (or at least does not violate) the criteria of all the columns. You might want to start by brain storming all the measures that you can take in order to enhance or add to your desired behavior so that it fulfills the criteria at each level. This way, you will come up with a main behavior for this column, as well as a collection of supportive behaviors and adjustments that will help to ensure that you succeed. Remember that brain storming means you open your mind to many possibilities.

You may want to start on a separate sheet and exhaust your ideas, then return for more after letting some time pass. You might want to call some friends or a mentor to discuss this step. In making sure that your ideas are in harmony with your criteria, you might ask questions such as, "What ways are there for me to take part in a school program that will (from column #1, capability) improve my income, skills, and prestige and (from column #2, belief) allow me to continue the work I am doing now in a meaningful way and keep making a living?" Pick out the best idea for column #3.

9. Identify and modify the overarching criteria and limiting beliefs. Review your override criterion that you noted above the columns. Notice what sub-modalities give it power. Also, note what strategies it implies.

Observe which meta-programs give this criterion its shape. (Meta-programs are higher-level programs that influence how we think and perceive things.)For example, some people focus more on what they are avoiding, while others focus more on what they want. Now take your revised desired behavior from column 3, and adjust the strategy, meta program, and sub-modality features of the criteria of the desired behavior to match the strategy, meta program, and sub-modality features of the highest level (override) criterion. Do the same thing for the column #1 belief criteria (the values and conditions that give the limiting beliefs a sense of legitimacy). This may seem like an odd request, but remember that you are harmonizing your desired behavior with criteria from all columns, and this adjustment will actually help to drive your desired behavior now that you are no longer waging an internal battle between conflicting levels of criteria.

10. Test. Over the next few days or weeks, you'll notice if you carry out the desired behavior enough to achieve the positive outcomes you intend for it to, such as getting better grades so you can get into a good graduate program. How well have your interventions worked and how might you improve them?

This pattern can go very far in helping you achieve a very useful depth of insight as well as valuable, creative, fresh solutions. It helps you develop capacities that are quite under-realized in most people.

We strongly suggest that you make a project out of this pattern for any really challenging or complicated situations in which you are trying to cultivate or engineer behavior that is more appropriate than what you do automatically. By keeping it handy and revisiting it from time to time, you are likely to find that it can go much farther than one visit can achieve. Reviewing Dilts' neurological levels can help generate ideas.

What additional support or interventions might help you secure this new behavior?

Use your environment to reinforce what you come up with. Posters, sticky notes, and recordings can all help reinforce and remind you. Recall the behavior modification example above. It takes advantage of context and behavior modification principles. It is not an obvious strategy because it does not directly or obviously address the desired behavior or confront the undesired behavior.

When working with a client, you can keep track of the details by writing them down yourself, while guiding the person to step into areas that represent each of the elements you have listed. In this approach, the original one suggested by Dilts, the person steps into spots on the ground that correspond to each of the columns. This assists with anchoring and eliciting states.

A common problem is that the criteria preventing your desired behavior occur at the same or higher levels than the criteria that support your desired behavior. When that happens, people feel mystified as to how to sort things out. Keep thinking it over and you will find a way. For example, put criteria that are on the same logical level side-by-side and keep asking what makes them different. At first, it might just appear that the desired behavior is more relevant to your long-term status, or it might bring a better version of the same benefits, or a larger quantity of the same benefits. But if you keep asking why that matters, you will come to values at a higher level, even at the identity level. Get as many as you can, and explore ways to make them more compelling.

Honored Values Elicitation

There's nothing quite like experiencing heartfelt values. A deep experience of values is inspiring, energizing, and galvanizing. To help a client experience this requires a kind of "deep listening" for the subtext that implies and leads to such values. This version of the experience uses deep experience in order to not only prime the client to resourcefully move into experiencing values in this heartfelt manner, but it also makes for a more compelling experience that lends momentum to treatment. Once your client makes such connections, you are able to begin connecting their values with actual needs and objectives.

This is a crucial and powerful turning point in the treatment. It empowers any number of interventions. For example, clients can learn to communicate in a much more compelling manner when their expression of vision and ideas is infused with heartfelt values. As you interact with your client, construct the best sense of their values as you can. Do not be distracted by the primitive or negative constructs that the client expresses. Even the most vulgar expression of opinion can yield information about a client's higher values. In addition, their level of consciousness and irrationality can provide vital clues as to how they may be disorganized as a result of specific cognitive impairments, mood disorders, trauma history, impaired early bonding, or even significant signs of mental illness.

A middle-aged Jewish couple could think this about a young man hurling anti-Semitic insults at them. They saw him desperately seeking meaning and self-esteem by aligning himself with something larger than himself and vested with power. They found they could connect with him and meet his intense and unmet developmental need for emotional nurturing. They met that need by adopting him into their family. But most people who zealously align with sources of felt authority have developmental and cognitive issues that can be seen from a mental health perspective.

This story shows that the values you are looking for are connected to actual needs. If the needs are primitive because of problems such as poor early bonding with parental figures, then the work will almost certainly need to begin at a fundamental level. Odds are that this will require a psychotherapist with a good deal of patience and an excellent understanding of cognitive and developmental remediation. In any case, once you have your collection of values that are "up" for the client in connection with his or her current issues, you are ready for the next step. But remember that, since values are ultimately universal, you'll have no trouble coming up with values. The objective here is to get a sense of which ones the client is frustrated with expressing and perhaps having difficulty fully connecting with. Help your client connect their values with the feelings or behaviors that are at issue. An excellent way is to:

1) Inquire about the outcomes they would prefer to see.

2) Then ask them about the values that the outcomes would support. You can help them find the words and ideas if they are unsure how to express themselves.

For example, a man who was told to see a counselor if he wanted to keep his job was very angry at feeling coerced into treatment. He tended to be too rough with other employees, saying things that sounded too hostile, judgmental, and controlling. The client was able to say that he wanted to be free to express himself in his own way, that some of the employees were stupid, that he really wanted them to do their best (which included not getting in his way), and that he wanted the business to prosper. With a little help, he connected these things with the following values:

1) Freedom of expression and acceptance of diversity;

2) Being able to give and receive feedback;

3) The achievement of human potential;

4) Collaboration for productive work;

5) Allowing others to complete their tasks without interruption; and...

6) Profit.

The counselor now has six "handles" to encourage more values-based behavior and agreements. The values of freedom, calm, potential, cooperation, independence, profit, and choice can be applied to any potential goal. For example, the client could see why his boss sent him to counseling because the "weaker" employees couldn't handle the client's demeanor. He could also see how "manipulating" the "weaker" employees would help them perform better. Isn't it true that your child would learn more if you "let" them fail a certain school assignment rather than stepping in and doing half (or 99%) of the work for them? The grade isn't as important as the process the child must go through on their own to gain the competency to get an A.

A side note: One of the most crucial life skills you could ever help a child achieve is the ability to turn failure into feedback. There's another intervention required here. at our past failures and at our false self-contempt and unfair self-criticism right after, and we do not wish to feel that way ever again. So "feedback" is suddenly a good idea. But did you consider installing that desire to learn from failure as if it's the most valuable experience for your children? The client was from New York and had recently relocated to Denver. The counselor commiserated with him a bit, recognizing that people from the east coast tend to be misunderstood by mid-westerners. In this context, they were able to agree that making the cultural transition was a meaningful challenge, even if it was inconvenient. It was also kind of like a game, in which you learn to play along with the strange rules of the Midwest, such as not confronting people in a direct, immediate, spontaneous way.

The Big Book of NLP

Hope Ritual

Everybody struggles. It's a given. Nothing lasts forever, be it good times or bad times. That's another given. The real question is never, how to enjoy the struggle or how to eliminate every problem in our lives, which is realistically impossible, but instead:

How do you get through such difficult circumstances without giving up hope?

1. Select a simple and quick mental-physical ritual that would be extremely easy to do on a daily basis. For example, coming up with and writing down a new song title, or practicing free-style drawing of a perfect circle, or singing out loud the chorus of Let It Be, etc. It ought to be enjoyable, but also achievable in less than a minute.

2. Obtain and anchor a solid and resourceful state of perseverance.

3. Perform the activity from step 1 and fire the anchor. Repeat this five times.

4. Write in your journal a new rule: "Doing X (the activity) is what helps me get through this."

5. Place a reminder of the rule somewhere you can see it often.

Hyperbole

One quick way to handle and deal with a negative internal voice is to join it. This is kind of what they teach in Judo, using the momentum of the opponent to drop him to the ground. It's possible to join in with a voice by adding to what it says, rather than simply echoing what it says. This can be done by making the words harsher and more dramatic or by amplifying other nonverbal aspects of the voice, such as volume or intonation. In essence, joining the voice exaggerates the self-talk and takes it up a few notches.

If the internal voice says, "You are such a loser! Look at what you've done! You should be ashamed of yourself! "), the common automatic response is fight or flight, looking for distractions or caving in with pain and guilt.

What if, instead of the automatic response, you join the voice and say to it, much louder and in a much more authoritative tone of voice than the despairing voice used: "You bet I am! I worked hard to become a world-class loser! You know how much effort it takes? And boy, am I not over yet... I am hoping to be the biggest loser this world has ever seen, and I will do so much that even when I succeed in something, it will not take away my greatest losses... ashamed? Oh, no! I'm proud of it! I want more! More! Moreeeeeee! "

This approach must be consistent in order to work well in the long term. It means that whatever that nagging voice is saying, you immediately take it further, to more extremes, and emphasize all the things that it wants you to feel bad about. This creates cognitive dissonance.

That negative voice's aim was to criticize you and put you in your place, ideally minimizing the chances of you taking a risk and getting hurt again. Yes, it has a positive intention: to protect you from potential future harm. But it goes about it in a way that is less than ideal, especially since in order to get anywhere good in life, we do have to take risks and experience failures. Joining in and using a hyperbole statement singles out the voice's message as irrelevant. It would be the same as if you were tackled by a bully in school, but instead of caving in or protesting, you took it to the extremes and kept going at him, even though he was stronger than you, and you never admitted losing the fight. In fact, you do not surrender; you keep going as if it's not over yet. The bully will have fun in the beginning, but soon enough he will get either too annoyed with the exhaustive measures or discouraged by your lack of fear of him. Hyperbole works with external and internal bullies.

Implied Causes

Implied Causes is a technique that uses words to imply that one thing will lead to another. I might say, "As you take in all this information, you can know that your mind will digest it into useful wisdom in time." "Knowing you have an unconscious mind gives you time to relax and enjoy learning." That doesn't really make sense, does it? You have whatever time you have. Knowing you have an unconscious mind doesn't actually give you time. But I created an implied cause there (that somehow, the mere existence of the unconscious mind gives you time to relax). It was intended to help the student learn NLP more effectively by being more relaxed about it. Since people can feel anxiety as they learn, that can make them really enjoy the contrast of relaxing into learning that will occur over a period of time. Now there's another implied cause: that somehow anxiety will make you relax. Let me say part of that again; see how that worked as an implied cause? "Since people can feel anxiety as they learn, that can make them really enjoy the contrast of relaxing into learning." The words that usually occur in implied causes are: since, when, while, as, after, often, before, during, following, and throughout. Before you learn through relaxation, you might want to sit in an even more comfortable position. When you become aware of the sounds around you, you will realize that your relaxation is a powerful force for focus and learning. While you are hearing these examples of implied causes, your unconscious mind has been busy creating an understanding that your conscious mind can do whatever it wants to do as you learn even more through these examples.

Implied Presupposition

Learn to make your communication more persuasive with presuppositions. A presupposition is essentially an assumption. Your listener may or may not consciously perceive it. In fact, people don't consciously perceive many of their own presuppositions. This is why debates can be so maddening.

A very common presupposition I used with clients in my hypnotherapy practice was, "Before you go deeper (into hypnosis), I would like you to notice how your breathing seems to be deeper..." That line had 2 presuppositions embedded in it:

(1) You are already in hypnosis.

(2) You already appear to be breathing more deeply. Even if the client has consciously negated one, the other would still be accepted. When Milton Erickson spoke, he often used presuppositions that were well-hidden in his words.

1. Determine your presuppositions. Imagine that you are about to encourage a trance state while in a conversational format.

Think of at least five things that you could presuppose (assume is a close synonym) about the person and their experience that you could leverage for relaxation, rapport, healing, and trance.

For example:"... this allows you to more fully feel the relaxation spreading from your shoulders," (presupposing that the person is already relaxing and that it is spreading from their shoulders, making it possible to feel sensations that can be interpreted as relaxation and increasing awareness there that will induce relaxation), or, at a higher logical level, "As you go into your day, your unconscious will continue to heal you and build you," (presupposing that the unconscious has this agenda and is already healing and building).

2. Embed them in sentences. Create sentences that, as I showed in step one, include these presuppositions.

The Big Book of NLP

You get bonus points for preceding each sentence with a sentence or two that sets up the presupposition to make it stealthier.

For example, "as you inhale, you can feel your shoulders spread very slightly, with your exhale allowing them to feel their natural weight."

This allows you to more fully feel the relaxation spreading from your shoulders, into the weight of your hands, through the ends of your fingers.

3. Use the sentences and set ups to create a conversational tone. String these presupposition-bearing sentences together in a conversational approach to trance.

4. Experiment on people. Try this on a willing participant, or record it and try it for yourself. Observe your subjects for signs of trance. Notice how your use of presuppositions can encourage what you believe to actually take place or become the basis for other behavior.

Incongruence Resolution

Source: Richard Bandler & John Grinder

Generate a handful of resourceful states more consistently by resolving habitual (automatic) negative states. Robert Dilts, a well-known NLP researcher and master trainer, explains the issue of inner conflict: In a typical situation, if we are prevented from reaching a goal due to an external impasse, we maintain our focus on the outcome, inhibit any "antithetical ideas" and continue to attempt other avenues or strategies in order to attain the goal. If there is an internal conflict, however, the "debate ground" shifts inward, and a battle begins between the two parts of one's self. As Freud points out, external frustration is accompanied by internal frustration. It is as if the person is "caught between a rock and a hard place." "And when the fight is between two parts of one's self, one can never 'win'."

1. Look for discrepancies (incongruence) between conscious and unconscious communication. This is done while working with a client on an issue that involves conflict between two directions but has poor awareness of one of the opposing states. When exploring the conflict, observe incongruence between the person's conscious and unconscious communication. By this, we mean what the person says versus what their body is giving away. For example, if the person shows anger but denies being angry, you will see body language that contradicts their denial. Anger physiology will show up as jaw and lip stiffness, squinting of the eyes, shoulder tension, and maybe even resentment or tension in the voice.

2. Sort by polarity. Some of these incongruences will have something in common with other incongruences. If the person really was not angry, they would have had relaxed shoulders and other physiology of a "not angry" state. This observation provides you with a polarity involving two states. On one end of the polarity is shoulder tension, and on the other, relaxed shoulders. The polarity is that of a range of shoulder tension from high to low. Simmering anger is high tension; not being angry is low tension. Discover more incongruities between these two states, and sort them into polarities as we did with shoulder tension. To find these incongruities, you are seeking physiologic clues. A good way to detect them is to have your client enter the very state that their body language is telling you they are not really into.

The Big Book of NLP

For example, with the "not angry" state that the angry client insists that they are in, you could help them align with that state by remembering, in first person, what it is like to watch a child play with a very friendly dog. Once they are fully in the "not angry" state, find out what is happening with every sub-modality associated with that state. In other words, what they are experiencing in that state is Now you have moved beyond body language to include sub-modalities that your client is able to describe for you.

This would not have been possible with a client who is not aligned with the state they claim to be in. This technique is important because, when people are out of alignment, they can have difficulty being verbally or in-depth or, instead, unconsciously create distractions in order to avoid being aware of their schism.

The unconscious mind is very creative when it is tasked with this kind of deception. Sort these incongruences into their polarities through means such as spatial sorting, symbolic sorting, rep systems, roles, and Satir Categories (i.e., blaming, placating, or rationalizing). If you don't know about all of these, stick with what is more obvious to you, such as how your client positions them in their mental space and what sub-modalities they associate with each state. How the state feels is often the easiest one to elicit.

As your client talks about what these states mean to them, note what beliefs appear to drive each state. Thinking of the states as parts may help you derive beliefs that are empowering or limiting. You are likely to find more than a few negative or limiting beliefs.

To summarize, by using an example, fix "depression" in its "space" by asking your client to recall a recent time that they felt depressed, and enter into that state for a few moments. During that time, elicit sub-modalities and any other aspects that distinguish these states from each other. For example, list the predicates, key words, eye-accessing cues, and physiology cues that you can observe in connection with that state. As you explore the original issue, you will discover additional states with parts that can be placed on polarities.

As you do the sorting, you eventually get to states that do not share enough polarities or similar attributes. At this point, you begin resorting.

On the other hand, some states, such as depression and passion, will be competitive, that is, so incompatible that they cannot be placed on the kind of polarity that we are working with here, because they would be too incongruent.

3. Integrate the incongruences.

Put each state where it belongs. For example, place depression and happiness in their unique spots (i.e., their respective spatial locations). Then group similar states in these locations.

a. Make a connection between the polarities. Have your client group feel the sensations of the states. To do this, your client must focus on the kinesthetic aspect of the state, bringing it to the foreground rather than the imagery, sound, and concepts. In doing this, your client is moving all of the feelings of depression, for example, into a limited space, thereby experiencing it as something that they can control. This makes these states and their feelings less overwhelming and gives your client a sense of empowerment and hope.

b. Be sure that your client is in a very positive state before proceeding. Your client should be in a very confident state. Be sure that their positive states are stronger and collectively larger than the other polarities. Have your client move into a meta position. From there, bring the polarities together in a way that can create new solutions. Inner Child dialogue

This technique is particularly effective when dealing with intense feelings of guilt and shame, as well as when one or both of the client's parents were highly critical, controlling, or shaming.

1. On a blank page, make two columns—left: Adult, right: Child.

2. Initiate a downtime state.

3. Recall a past experience in which you felt empathy and compassion towards another person, preferably a child.

4. Anchor that feeling of empathy.

5. Enter the timeline, turn around and ride the timeline to age 12.

6. Meet the inner child (12 years old) part of you, and ask the part for a few moments of his or her time.

7. On the page, write each question and answer in order. Write the question using your dominant hand on the left column (adult) and the answer using your non-dominant hand on the right column (child).

a. How are you?

b. What is completely new in your life?

c. What is most upsetting at this time?

d. Did my behavior from your time to mine in any way harm you?

e. What could I have done better to protect you?

f. Can you see that everything will turn out OK for you and me? We survived.

g. Would you forgive me for my many mistakes if I asked you to?

8. Fire the compassion anchor.

9. Increase the mental image of the inner child, freeze the frame, and fire the anchor again.

10. Thank the inner child part for communicating with you, and return to the present.

11. Test. How do you think about your adolescent years? Did anything change?

This technique should be repeated once or twice a week until all resentment is dissolved.

Inner Hero

Source: Robert A. Yourell

It brings out the best in people who are not aligned with their higher values. This pattern is very important for working with people who act in ways that can get them into trouble, such as violence, problems with authority, or with social systems. One of any therapist's most persistent gambits is to build rapport by recognizing the struggles of the other person in a way that highlights their highest values and their stamina and strength in pushing ahead, despite the obstacles, whatever they are. This helps to anchor a state of alignment with higher values and primes the person for a state of effort in the service of their highest values in a non-defensive manner. We call this "finding the inner hero." Everyone wants to be a hero, and they feel you have connected to a deep place in them when you acknowledge (in a natural way) their heroism and struggle. You have to do it without "blowing smoke" or otherwise coming off as artificial. That means you really have to connect with the reality of these things, not invent them. This way, you are not too distracted by their inappropriate behavior, their personality quirks, or the ways they bait you before they start to trust you. This makes you an "entrainment effect," bringing out more of the positive parts of your client. With this approach, you can make non-aligned (with higher values) behavior more alien and easier to let go of for many people. Failing to do this is the root of much of the conflict or alienation that can happen between coaches and their clients. It happens all the time to social service providers and people who work with domestic violence and DUI programs. Teachers can also make children's learning disabilities worse by approaching them in the wrong way.

1. Select a subject for the pattern. Try this with someone who tends to "act out." That is, they get themselves into trouble or conflicts because they have problems with authority, managing their impulses, or getting into struggles with other people. It must be a person that you are in a position to influence in some way. For example, a child of yours, an employee you supervise, or someone you are coaching.

2. Begin a discussion that relates to the issues at hand. Talk with them about an issue that you need to discuss, but do it in a roundabout way. Start by eliciting from them their efforts to manage the situation, or just to manage life in general, so they can keep going.

The Big Book of NLP

Focus on some struggles they may have. Use reframing in the style of motivational interviewing. As they talk with you, notice what higher values are motivating them, even if they are acting on those higher values in foolish or destructive ways. When you comment or respond to them, highlight the ways that they have strength and stamina to carry on and not give up. Also, highlight all the ways that their struggle aligns with their highest values. In particular, go to the highest logical level, identity. You can highlight these things by briefly acknowledging them, making facial expressions and sounds that show that you were struck by something they said, or any other method you like to use.

4. Reinterpret what they say in order to increase their alignment and ability to pursue their goals with vigor. As you do step three, also "interpret" by saying things that emphasize or bring out these parts. For example, "You have really chosen life, taking these steps to bring you out of feeling so low," and "Even though the person you have this conflict with is distracted by the conflict, on some level, they have to realize that you are advocating for people having meaningful lives," and "as a person who can fight for what you believe in, it's obvious that you are being a champion for people's rights."

5. Prepare to lead. If you have much experience with NLP, you can see that so far we have done an advanced form of pacing with priming mixed in. This is, of course, a set up for leading, as in "pacing and leading." Think of the kinds of behaviors and outcomes that would be constructive in this situation. Bear in mind that your "client" may come up with something even better, at least in the sense that they would be more motivated to do it in their own style. Make sure that the outcomes and behaviors you are thinking of are fully aligned with the higher values that you found your client acting on in step three.

6. Guide the individual toward constructive ways to act on their higher values. As you comment and interact, point out how their efforts are aligned with their values and get them thinking about the outcomes that they ultimately want. They may come up with less constructive ideas for controlling people, getting revenge, or putting themselves in harm's way just to make a statement about how bad the situation is (this is typical of people who are stuck at an adolescent level of development). Respond to this by getting them brainstorming on ways to be even more fully aligned with their higher values. For example, "That might even get you in the papers for a day, at least on page seven, anyway. But what is the long-term thing that you'd like to see come out of this? " Or, "I wonder how a person might approach someone that causes this kind of trouble so that they would lighten up a little and be fairer to people."

7. Emphasize the best responses. Any time the person says something that is closer to a constructive or resourceful strategy or attitude, reinforce it with a very positive response. Don't be artificial about it. Notice how the following examples can reinforce, but also are designed to maintain rapport with a person who is resentful and has authority issues. As a result, the reinforcement is not 100% positive content. It is designed to reinforce a statement by the client that is a move in the right direction. Remember that a series of moves in the right direction, even small ones, can become a major shift. For example, "That could really get things moving!" or "Ha! They'd never expect that. They wouldn't know what to say," or "They would have to start realizing that you've been right about this, because the proof would be right in front of their faces!" You can customize the tone of your responses to match your client's attitude, whatever it may be.

8. Seal the deal. Get some agreement about what you and the person will do about the issue. If the person is only ready for a baby step, don't be judgmental; treat it with appreciation and respect. Then they will trust you on an emotional level and take more steps with you as they test the water. Remember that you are introducing them to a very different "reality" than the one they are used to. Patterns like theirs take a lifetime to develop.

9. Test. Observe them and talk with them as things unfold, and see how well your "hero" style conversations are working. See if you can find new ways to gain rapport. Modify your style as they progress so that you are always helping them to push the envelope.

The Big Book of NLP

Installing Presuppositions

Thinking about and considering the 21 presuppositions (reviewed at the beginning of the book) is one thing. Turning one or more into a core belief is a completely different beast.

With this pattern, you can install and make a useful presupposition you like into a habitual thought process.

1. Choose and state the desired presupposition aloud.

2. As you state the presupposition, look for the ideas that make up the concept at both the primary level and the meta level.

3. Step into the expressions kinesthetically by physiologically miming the expressions with your body.

4. Label or categorize the feelings, emotions, and narrative that you experience during this process. What does it feel like to fully immerse yourself in the concept?

5. Think about how these emotions will affect your outlook and behavior in the near future.

6. Future Pace. Make this new attitude a mental movie, a kind of a reminder to play in your mind when you're acting in your workplace, relationships, or home.

7. Ecology check.

8. Amplify the feelings. Use the Chaining Anchors pattern.

Intentional Beliefs

Source: Erickson Institute

At some level, all beliefs are, or were, intended to be positive at some point in time. When considered from the perspective of the person whose behavior is being discussed, it is or was viewed as appropriate given the circumstances in which it was established. Responding to the intent of a problematic belief rather than the expression of a problematic belief is less painful and more beneficial. By identifying the constructive aim underlying a limiting belief, you can free up enormous amounts of energy and focus on a positive outcome.

1. Briefly describe the issue in sufficient detail to ensure that it is crystal clear in your mind. It could be a circumstance, a legitimate concern, or a difficulty. Focus on characterizing ineffective behavior. Determine why the behavior is ineffective.

2. Take a few moments to unwind, deepen your breaths, and sit quietly. Now, imagine that your mind is equipped with special internal messengers. They are known as "parts" in NLP. These are the parts of your personality that exhibit distinctive tendencies, self-talk, and behavioral patterns.

3. Determine which part is causing the dysfunctional behavior. Bring this part into consciousness as if it were an actual character. Bear in mind that each part represents an aspect of you. It is a collection of motivating factors that are in sync with one another. A part is similar to a micro-personality that exists within you. To be satisfied and aligned, you must avoid working in opposition to your own interests. This necessitates bargaining or collaboration on your part.

4. Consider the possibility of using this part to create a role-playing game. Inquire of the part what it desired by engaging in that negative behavior or attitude. What was the purpose or benefit of this?

"What did you want me to experience by doing this?"

5. Allow yourself as much time as necessary to imagine and listen to the response of the parts. Do not go into blaming mode. The point is not to shame that part or control it, but to be curious about its intended effect.

6. Continue to ask "why" and "what" questions to get a better understanding of the motivations. Each answer should be recycled into a new question.

7. Continue in this manner until you believe you have reached the heart of the matter. The core beliefs, along with the core values, and the core reasons for the behaviors or attitudes that, at first glance, appear to be unsupportive of you, should all be identified and addressed in depth.

Internal Voice Location

Everybody can think of an internal voice that they don't like, but very few people are paying attention to where it is in their own personal space. Changing a voice's location turns out to be one of the simplest ways to alter its impact on you.

1. Listen to a voice in your head that makes you uncomfortable in some manner, and take note of where it is in relation to your body. In most cases, the voices you hear originate in your head or in the near vicinity of your skull... Inside or outside your head, where does it originate? The question is whether it's in front, behind, to the left, to the right, and so on. And in which direction is it pointing—toward or away from you?

2. Using your finger, point to where the sound is coming from and the direction it's going. If you hear a voice outside of your head, it almost always points toward your head.

3. Make the voice point in a different direction first, and see how this changes your perspective on the voice. For most people, this isn't something they've ever thought about. Let that voice change direction. This usually means that it will point away from your head. Notice how that feels.

4. Next, find out what it's like to listen to the voice when it points both toward you and away from you. In that scenario, some words sound as if they're coming at you and some words may sound as if they are directed outwards, fading away.

5. Notice if there is a difference between when it points straight up and straight down, or when it points left or right, or forward or backward. In general, when the voice is pointed away from you, the volume is lower, and your response time is also less. Most individuals feel better when a disturbing voice points away from them, making it simpler and more acceptable to listen to whatever the voice is expressing. You're more likely to react strongly if it's pointed either toward you or away from you when it's in the middle of those two directions.

6. Next, try changing the location of the voice in a variety of ways to see how listening to the very same voice from different areas in space affects your emotional responses and

how this affects what you experience when you are doing this. Most people may find this straightforward, but it's not something they've ever considered. If you have any trouble, just let that voice go where it is.

Next, listen to the voice emerging from your left hip, and notice how it feels. When your critical voice comes from your hip, it isn't as powerful. Change the tone of your voice as well when you do this. It might become fairly quiet and lower pitched, and your reactions might also lessen.

8. Notice what it's like when you hear this voice coming from deep within.

9. Notice what it feels like when that same voice comes from your right ankle.

10. Next, hear the voice speaking from the depths of your soul, the very center of your heart, and pay attention to what you experience when you do so.

11. Next, listen to the voice coming from your left index finger and pay attention to how that feels.

12. Try hearing that voice from another part of your body, and see how that feels.

13. Lastly, revert that voice back to where and how it was before. Take a moment to reflect on whether or not your reaction to the voice in its original position is the same now as it was before you did these experiments. It's usually better to hear an unpleasant voice in areas that are far away from your head than in areas that are close to or inside your head. It's usually unpleasant to hear a voice from your chest, and the feeling that comes with it may be mistaken for insecurity, hopelessness, or suffering. Hearing a voice from your core that isn't very nice or clear may be very painful and hard to understand. Some people do this unconsciously, and it's not particularly beneficial.

14. Review your findings and ask yourself, "Where was it most secure for me to hear this jarring voice?" ....

15. Test Listen to the voice coming from that area. How does it feel?

Internalizing Abilities

You may be able to rely on the constructive aim of your inner critical voice, even if it has very little to do with you. Our inner voices don't like to stay idle, and they'll gladly take on new work if it means they'll be respected and valuable.

1. Determine the voice's abilities.Listen to the voice and look at the person speaking. What are this person's abilities and strengths? Everyone, even those with very limited abilities, has some pursuits in which they thrive and others in which they struggle. What did that person excel at? It could be a specific skill or ability, such as persuasion, or it could be a genuinely beneficial, optimistic, or resilient attitude that got him through tough times. Consider what the person was particularly strong at, and develop a list of those abilities.

2. Now, talk to that person and express your admiration for his or her unique qualities. "You were really encouraging and supportive of me when I really needed it."

3. Show your appreciationGive thanks for what you learned if you learned one or more of these valuable skills from that person. Be explicit about what you learnt, and highlight one or two specific circumstances where knowledge has come in handy for you.

4. Think of a competence you didn't really learn. Consider the additional skills that person possesses that you did not learn. Choose one that will be very useful to you in specific scenarios.

5. Seek assistance. Next, ask that voice whether it would be willing and able to help you when you find yourself in a position where that talent would be especially useful to you. The voice can help you in a variety of ways, such as noting whenever something needs changing, recommending what remains to be improved, monitoring of resources, reassuring you, providing you with contextual cues or ideas, and so on.

6. Consider a specific occasion in the past where you would have appreciated this type of support and one that might arise in the future.

7. Enter your mind's theatre and sit down to watch a movie of the event to see what happens. Give your voice some credit if it provides useful information. If the voice does not assist you, speak with it to determine what has to be done so that it will be willing to assist you, and then test again. Repeat as many times as necessary until you are completely satisfied.

8. Check for congruence. Go within into a downtime state and ask, "Does any part of me object or have any concerns about the changes we've made?" In answer to your query, take note of any sensations, visual images, auditory sounds, or voices that may suggest a concern. Usually, there will be no objections because the voice is happy to assist and receive some recognition for what it knows how to do well, and the end result will be to maximize performance. If you discover anything that could signal a problem, first double-check to ensure that it truly indicates an objection, and then figure out how to satisfy the objection so that you can achieve congruence. You can do so with the Parts Negotiation pattern.

Intonation

In NLP, we recognize 3 patterns of intonation:

Question

When you form a question, the end of the sentence is usually expressed in a rising pitch.

Express out loud any question and you'll notice how the whole sentence might sound in your normal pitch, but the end of it, right near the question mark, is always higher in pitch, isn't it?

Statement

When you form a statement, however, the whole sentence is usually expressed at the same pitch.

You might have "ups" and "downs," but whatever you say can be easily distinguished from a question or a command.

For the purpose of persuasion, you ought to begin by using only statements before moving on to questions and commands.

Command

The biggest mistake people make when they want to get another person to do something is to form a command in an authoritative voice. That's the wrong approach, simply because nobody likes to be told what to do! When you form a command, the end of the sentence usually drops in pitch.

To make it effective, use the "polite" hypnotic command forms, such as: "Could you please..." (regular pitch) + "sign here" (lower voice).

Intuitive Second Position Modeling

Take more advanced steps in developing your ability to model. You need three people for this pattern: the Person Being Modeled, and two Modelers.

1. Demonstrate the skill. Have the Person Being Modeled exhibit a simple skill that can be modeled, such as a dance step or cultural gesture.

2. Model the skill. Have the Modelers enter a "not knowing" state from second position with A for a few minutes.

3. Explain the internal state. Based on what they learned from being in the second position, the two modelers are to write down exactly what they suspect A is experiencing internally.

4. Compare the results. Have the two Modelers compare and contrast their models.

5. Work together to describe the skill's specifics. Have all three parties collaborate to describe the key elements of the skill.

6. Test. Over the coming weeks and months, discuss how well the participants have been coming along in learning to model and establish rapport.

Kinesthetic Criteria

1. Select a behavior that is desired but not taken. Identify a behavior the person says they want to do a certain behavior, but does not act on it. Put it in position #1. This can also be something they want to stop doing, such as smoking, biting nails, or yelling at their kids.

2. Determine the criteria for carrying out the desired action. Have the person clarify the values and meta-outcomes behind their desire to take the action. Ask why they want to take the action, and then, why is that outcome itself important to them? What you're looking for here is the "toward" motivation. In this step, they actually begin the change-work. Place these in location #2.

3. Determine the criteria that prevent the desired behavior. Solicit the criteria for not doing the behavior. What stops them?Identify the values and meta-outcomes that support not taking the desired action. Put these in location #3. Try to identify values that are at a higher level than those found in step 2. Remember that the hierarchy is set by the person you're working with, not by your own values, hierarchy, or logic. We assume that such values or criteria exist because they override the values that the person has for taking the desired action.

4. Generate higher-level criteria that support taking the desired action. Determine what higher-level criteria can override the criteria in Location #3 in favor of taking the desired action. For example, if position #3 values like relaxation are getting in the way of smoking cessation, ask what values are more important than that. Come up with answers such as avoiding emphysema.

5. Anchor the state. Amplify the state associated with these overriding positive values and anchor it. You do not have to use a full anchoring procedure here; it is enough if you remind them of the state, ask them to enhance certain driver sub-modalities, and establish a kinesthetic anchor without explaining what an "anchor" is.

6. Lower levels should be positively infused. Hold the anchor and move to position 3. Continue on to positions 2 and 1. Encourage the person to come up with new ideas as they walk through these positions. Ask them to imagine implementing each good idea,

then adjust their sub-modalities to match the highest criterion from step 4. As the person descends, make sure the higher state is compelling. It's vital to make these lower levels very positive.

7. Conduct an ecology check and make any necessary adjustments. Examine the environment as you plan your future.Pace these creative ideas to see if you can make any additional adjustments.

8. Test. In the coming days and weeks, see how well this pattern has allowed the person to take the desired action.

Kinesthetic Cues Elicitation

To build and maintain rapport with people whose primary representation system is kinesthetic, observe, listen for and match the following cues:

• When asked to remember something, they move their eyes downward, gaining access to information.

• Make use of kinesthetic predicates, for example:

Hard, Tough, Warm, Cold, Grasp, Feel, Solid, Touch, Catch on, Unfeeling, Scrape, Boils down to, Control yourself, Come to grips with, Get in touch with, Get a load of this, Get a handle on, Hang in there, Hand in hand, Hold it, Lay cards on the table, Know-how, Keep your shirt on, Hold on, Pull some strings, Slipped my mind, So-so, Too much of a hassle.

• They tend to breathe deeply and slowly.

• Speak and move slowly and deliberately, demonstrating a variety of physical gestures.

Kinesthetic Swish

Associate them into the feeling. Break state.

Have them associate into and amplify a positive state.

Define the sub-modalities and amplify the feeling. Break state.

Map across to modify the negative feeling.

Test.

Utilize feelings to generate constructive motivation or drive. Ultimately, feelings are the forces behind success and failure. We move away from negative feelings and toward good feelings.

This pattern builds a mind-body strategy for overcoming negativity in the face of challenges that have been daunting until now.

1. Associate them into the feeling.

Have the person think of the situation or thoughts that produce a negative state.

Ask them to specify the details of the feeling, especially sub-modalities such as movement and temperature, and the location of the feeling.

Break state.

2. Instruct them to associate with and amplify a positive state.

Ask them to specify how they would like to feel.

The Big Book of NLP

3. Define the sub-modalities and exaggerate the feelings.

Have them associate this feeling, amplifying it through the most effective sub-modalities. Break state.

4. Map across to modify the negative feeling.

Have them recall the negative feeling and its location.

Have them move it into the positive feeling's location and get it to conform to the sub-modalities of the other feeling.

Note: Unlike the visual Swish, the kinesthetic Swish tends to be slower, so give your client time to work through it.

5. Test.

In the coming days and weeks, see if your person relates to the situation or thoughts differently, getting improved results in life.

Labeling

When I work with teenagers who come in and declare generalizations such as "I have depression" or "I am suicidal," I ask them if they remember Mr. Mackey's voice from the animated TV show SouthPark. Then we make an impression of him together and say, "Labels are bad, mkay?".

Labeling is what we can use to transform a generalized nominalization that is attached to the person's identity. Labeling helps to disassociate the identity from the process that is ineffective.

Labeling is a simple linguistic move. First, we use a pattern interrupt. In the case of a teenager, we almost always choose SouthPark because it appears to have the strongest and most immediate effect on drawing them out of a depressive or suicidal state of mind.Then, we establish a conversational rule: we eliminate the usage of "I have depression," which is impossible since you may laugh out loud and depression does not register in your mind in those moments, which means it disappears. If you had depression in the same way that you had a nail stuck in your big toe, changing your thoughts would not make it go away.

Lastly, we acknowledge the fact that the person can certainly feel the process of depression at certain times. In those moments, however, they ought to label it "this is depression" and point to it in the space around their body, where they can feel the emotion's kinesthetic existence.

This simple linguistic maneuver changes the relationship between the inner self and the process of interpreting external stimuli. By pointing outside of the body, we treat the ineffective mental state as if it were a foreign obstacle and not a fixed internal "thing."

Learning Strategies Elicitation

Source: Richard Bandler & John Grinder

Select the learning subject you were successful in.

List your outcomes.

Evidence procedure.

List the actions you took.

Problem solving activities.

Consider which rep system you used the most.

Elicit your rep systems syntax.

Learning is the process of acquiring new thinking patterns and behavioral capabilities. In NLP, a learning strategy is the syntax of steps one takes in order to learn. There are many learning strategies, of course, and some of them are not very effective.

Effective learning works within a feedback loop, or the T.O.T.E. model in NLP. In order to define a learning strategy, we would need to identify and organize the usage of representational systems (rep systems) a person is using in order to learn effectively. More importantly, we should identify which representational system gets the most use during the learning session. This is modeling, in essence, but on a much smaller scale than other skills.

The reason that people differ as to what learning strategies are most useful to them is that people are different! I am not surprised that I could do so well in literature in high school but almost failed in math. My literature teacher spoke in a language that made sense to me. She spoke mostly using visual predicates, and she used every metaphor she could in order to explain a theme. My math teacher, however, was a very stubborn, kinesthetic-oriented person. She spoke of numbers in the dullest way, and the only explanation she had as to why an arithmetic rule works as it is was, "that's the way it is." However, it was my responsibility to develop a learning strategy that would help me with math. Apparently I didn't, because I almost failed that class. My best friend in high school, though, had exactly the opposite experience. She was thrilled about math classes, couldn't wait to solve those complex trigonometric problems, and her aversion to literature classes was well known. She had a very different learning strategy than I did. The issue was that we both used the SAME strategy (each separately) on two different subjects.I used my successful literature learning strategy in math, which proved to be ineffective, and she used her successful math learning strategy in literature, and again, that has proven to be the wrong approach. The purpose of NLP is to elicit as many successful learning strategies as possible, so that you will always have the freedom and flexibility to move from one to another according to whatever is more effective for your outcome.

The development of the awareness and ability to elicit your own successful learning strategies is called "Learning II" in NLP. It means "learning to learn." The more you know about your own successful learning strategies, the more effective you will be in using, modifying, and improving your capabilities. The Elicitation of Learning Strategies pattern will help you uncover the syntax you're using to successfully learn something. You can also use it, of course, to model another person's learning strategy and try it out for yourself.

1. Choose the learning subject in which you excelled. Any subject you're good at will do just fine. For whatever reason, if you find it much easier to learn literature, as I did in high school, then write that one down. If it's math, history, general knowledge, logic, languages, or whatever else, make sure you have only one subject in mind. If you can't find a specific subject that you're good at, chunk it down to micro-skills. Search your past experience for times in which you learned anything fast and effortlessly.

2. Make a list of your objectives and outcomes.

What were your outcomes in regards to this subject?

What were your goals when you approached learning about this subject?

3. Procedural Evidence:

What was your evidence procedure for proving that you had completed the outcome in this subject successfully?

For example, if your strongest subject was math, how did you know you were successful in achieving an outcome?

Was it the passing of an exam or simply the solution of a math problem within a given time?

4. Make a list of the actions you took.

What were the actual steps you took when you started working on achieving this outcome?

Did you do anything uniquely for this subject that you did not do for other learning outcomes?

5. Problem-solving exercises:

As with any learning opportunity, problems and challenges are always present and might disturb our learning.

What did you do in order to solve minute-to-minute problems that interfered with your excellent learning mode?

6. Consider the most frequently used rep system. Look back at your answers to the steps above and see if you can notice which representational system you used the most.

7. Elicit your rep system's syntax. Use the following questions to elicit the actual strategy you have used. Refer to your answers to the previous steps, of course, since you've already done most of the groundwork there already:

What has stimulated you to learn effectively? Did you see, hear, feel, or otherwise sense a cause?

Perhaps you digitally said something to yourself (inner voice), and if so, what was the content of that message?

How did you represent your outcome of learning this subject in your mind?

Did you visualize an image of yourself "knowing" or "excelling on an exam"?

Did you visualize an image of yourself associated or dissociated (i.e., did you see your notebook or did you see yourself looking at the notebook)?

Did you remember the outcome as an image from past successful events?

Did you say the outcome to yourself, and if so, how did it sound?

Did you feel the outcome or sense the assurance that this outcome is about to be reality? If so, how did it manifest itself in your body?

How did you know that you're making progress (evidence procedure)?

Did you perceive external visual information (physically) or internal visual information (imagination)? And what was it exactly?

Did you need to hear that you've made progress (perhaps a teacher congratulating you for accomplishing a task, or your parents being proud that you got an "A")?

Was it something you said to yourself or something that another person told you?Which actions did you take to achieve this outcome? Did you analyze, organize, re-organize, talk to yourself, have intuition, visualize, touch, sense, discuss, listen, move, draw, watch, take notes, or feel certain emotions?

Was it in any combination of the above?

What was the syntax or order of these actions with respect to the actual process of achieving the outcome?

How did you respond to minute problems?

You can use the long list above (analyze, organize, re-organize, etc.). What other questions could you ask yourself to complete this strategy and make it as accurate and close to reality as possible?

8. Test. Take note of any advancements in your ability to learn the subject you selected.

Light Trance Induction

Source: Milton H. Erickson

A light trance induction is sometimes required if the client seems to be experiencing some sort of emotional turmoil. This famous elevator induction is not suitable for clinical hypnotherapy procedures, but is very useful in calming down an agitated individual.

"Close your eyes and get comfortable. You could very well fall into a comfortable, relaxing trance as you listen to my voice and follow my guidance. Imagine yourself in a pleasant and secure elevator on the top floor of a building. Let's say you're on the twentieth floor. As the elevator moves downward, you look at the illuminated floor number. As you descend to the lower levels, you can see the floor numbers changing to 19, 18, 17, 16, and 15, and then the doors open to reveal a pleasant memory from five years ago. You step outside and find yourself doing something enjoyable with your friends. Enjoy the moment as if it were today. (Pause.) Re-enter the elevator and keep an eye on the floor numbers, feeling the elevator go down, down, down as the numbers will change. 14, 13, 12, 11, and 10. The elevator stops and a new adventure begins. Step out of the elevator and savor the moment. . (Pause.) Re-enter the elevator and feel it descend. 9, 8, 7, 6, 5 Five more years to another enjoyable experience. You're proud of yourself and excited about the future. (Pause.) Re-enter the elevator and feel it descend. 4, deeper now, all the way down to 3, 2, 1, deep sleep, even deeper now, all the way down, that's it..."

Suggested Awakening Protocol:

"We're back near the elevator... Another pleasant experience awaits. You are a young person with dreams of the future. Plan what you want to do with your life now and how you want to achieve it as you walk around this floor. Now return to the elevator with those ideas. Closing doors Feel the elevator rise. Counting the elevators. 1, 2, 3, 4, 5, 6. Doors open. Step into this pleasant experience and observe. Take what you need for progress and learn from your mistakes. Re-enter the elevator and watch it rise. 6, 7, 8, 9, and 10. The future holds more pleasant surprises. Imagine applying what you've learned before to this situation, and then bringing those skills back into the elevator. Closing doors 11, 12, 13, 14, 15 The future looks bright. Apply what you've learned and learn new things. Re-enter the elevator knowing this. 16-17-18-19. Consider all of your life's lessons and how you can apply them now. Feeling good about yourself. Twenty. You are now at the top and are enjoying a good time. When the door opens, return to this time and place, and open your eyes wide awake. 1 2 3 4 5, wide awake and alert. Welcome back..."

Linking Words

In pacing and leading, Milton Erickson used words called conjunctions, words such as "and." He linked the pacing with the lead in a way that made it all seem to belong together, and this gave his leading commands a lot of impact. Consider this example. (The >> symbols set off the embedded commands.) "As you experience this training, and wonder how >>you will apply it successfully, you hear the sound of my voice providing the information so that >>you can enjoy mastery." The pacing was that you experience this training, and that you wonder how successful you'll be.

This last bit about wondering can inspire a transderivational search for anything you are wondering about and any ways that this training may make you feel challenged.

Bringing up any doubts that you have about yourself and then embedding the command that "you will apply it successfully" is a mild anchor collapse as well as a trance reinforcer. Nonetheless, the statement that "you are wondering" is also pacing your actual experience. Then I said, "You hear the sound of my voice providing the information." which is still pacing. I finished with "so that you can enjoy mastery."

Giving the purpose of the information doesn't seem like leading, but as you probably noticed, it is really a command to enjoy mastery.

That is a lead disguised as a simple statement about information. As you can tell, we are not only training you on a simple technique, but showing you how you can blend several techniques together.

With experience, NLP practitioners' skills become so multilayered that they rely on their unconscious minds to do most of the work. When they listen to transcripts of their own work, they can be surprised to hear how many techniques they are actually using at the same time. I say this because you can trust that this will happen for you as well. Remember that Milton Erickson had some very serious impairments, including pain and dyslexia, as well as delayed development because of polio.

Logical Beliefs Change

If you're a good listener, you might notice that you have friends who dump their sorrows on you at every possible opportunity. It's not because they're looking for pity or to abuse your friendship; it's because they know you listen.

Talking gives them some temporary relief from the emotional pain they cause themselves. They are also very logical. They can firmly convince you how stuck they are. They can prove that their range of choices is limited. They refuse to listen to anything that contradicts their twisted logic, and the worst part is—they are pessimistic about the near future.

To sound more credible, they express themselves as if their values and integrity are on the line, and their suffering is a result of their trying to stay moral, honest, and generous. They tend to believe that the world is doing THIS or THAT to them, and they cannot see their responsibility in the stream of events.

From day to day, the more you listen to them, the more you get the feeling that they're not really trying to change their situation.

At first, you may think they'll soon emerge with a fresh perspective. But they do not; they stay stuck. They may develop some unknown and unexplained physical weakness and sickness. Their doctors will say they're still doing tests, but have no clue what the reason for the sickness is. The person will hide one thing that the doctor told them—that there is nothing wrong with their body. They seek attention.

They seek a caring look.

They want to unload their emotional burden, but within a day or two, they have it all back. But they are your friends. If you only have one of those, great.

If you have more, it is surely a time for a different strategy to handle them, because eventually they may get better while you get worse.

The solution is simpler than you may think. Aristotle thought about it ages ago, but in a different context. Aristotle came up with the concept of deduction. Its opposite, abduction, was added to this thought model as well.

Deduction, done wrong, is the common logic that self-limiting pessimists use to confine themselves to their problems. The logic is obvious, but absurd if you dissect it objectively.

"I am a foreigner."

"Foreigners can't get a good job in this country."

"I will never get a good job here."

The equation of deduction is simple and logical: A = B, and B = C; therefore, A = C.

If it were math, it would be correct. But there is a problem.

Each equals sign is really a presupposition. All you need is one bad presupposition, and this "logic" provides the pessimist with justification for their faulty conclusions.

The challenge is that they were convinced before they performed their "math." So, even if you try to negate B = C and claim that B = D and not C, (that is, to lead them to a new conclusion), the pessimist will find a way to maintain their limitations.

The cure for this deceptive logic is to use abduction to create an imbalance in the formula.

"You are an educated and experienced person."

"Foreigners in this country are not equal one to another in education and experience."

As long as you are superior to other foreigners, it gives you a better chance of getting a better job in this country.

A = B, and C = D < B, therefore, (B > C) = A.

If you run this formula thoughtfully and design it to fit the pessimist you're dealing with, it will get them thinking.

If they come up with another excuse, decide if it's a valid excuse or just an attempt to get you to think they're hopeless. If it's the latter, give them that non-believer doubting look and they may change their tune.

If not, you can run this process from another angle. Friends are there for each other, for better and, most importantly, for worse.

When someone behaves in a destructive way, it is also your responsibility to disrupt their pattern and impel them toward a healthy choice. But, if it restricts your life and limits your possibilities, you'll have to let them go. Sometimes the fear of losing a good friend drives people to make major positive changes. But use that as a last resort.

Besides, it's always more fun to take on the challenge of making them so uncomfortable with their current situation that they can't resist the "Aha!" moment and unbridled motivation that was waiting inside them.

Logical Levels

The Logical Levels concept in NLP was first introduced to the field by Robert Dilts, one of the most productive NLP master trainers and researchers. Dilts developed his logical levels to guide the process of intervention. Rather than focusing on physiology and behavior, or emotional states, Dilts tells us to focus directly on strategies, sub-modalities, beliefs, and identities. His levels help to put them in perspective. Dilts' logical levels, from the higher, overriding levels, to the lower ones:

Spirit or **higher purpose**: the belief in a higher purpose or values that give meaning to one's identity.

Identity: a sense of self that fosters values and beliefs.

Values and **beliefs**: an increased level of internal resources that influence decisions and how you apply your skills and knowledge.

Skills and **knowledge**: the fundamental internal resources for behavior.

Behavior: physical actions and patterns, including habits and the power of behavior modification principles.

Environment: The context and how it stimulates, guides, facilitates and limits behavior.

Let's apply this to a phobia and see how it works. The first level is about where, when, and with whom the phobia occurs. That is the environmental level. It is the context of the behavior. You can't really understand the behavior without context.

A way to understand the relevant context is to recognize that there are times and places where the phobia does not occur and that there are people with whom the phobia does not occur.

What is special about the times, places, and people connected in your mind and emotions to this phobia?

The second level is the specific behaviors that occur. This is the behavior level. This level lets you get more specific in defining or identifying the behavior. It helps you escape the trap of vagueness that can help keep people in a neurotic tangle.

The third level is capabilities and strategies.

How does the phobia get expressed through the person's existing skills? I

f they panic on an airplane, what skills do they use to channel that energy constructively?

How do they prevent themselves from screaming and running up and down the walkway?

Or are their energies expressed in utter chaos?

The more capabilities that a person has that can serve as resources for coping with the phobia, the more complex and functional the person's behavior can become.

Chaos looks more complex than an organization, but that is because organizations use complex rules and abilities to stay organized. On the surface, they are usually orderly and appear easier to understand. In reality, they are complex and require exploration and study to understand their complexity.

The fourth level is beliefs and values. What can your client tell you about their conscious values that guide what they do around this phobia?

The phobia itself may seem to the person to be very much counter to their values, but there is more going on than just the phobia. This is how they react to it from this higher level. A good place to start is to simply ask your client why they do what they do.

Don't just ask about the phobia itself, but what they do to cope, or how they avoid situations, or how they explain their behavior to themselves and others.

You can clarify their values further once you have this. You can ask them what they are trying to accomplish, or what they feel are their obligations or responsibilities in the situation. From there, you will see that they have heartfelt values and other values that seem to have been attached to them by their parents and others. Their values exist along with their beliefs. They have beliefs about where their values come from and what would happen if they did not possess these values and sincerely act on them.

The fifth level is identity and mission.

How does your client perceive herself?

How does her phobia affect her identity?

How does her identity affect the phobia?

That one is especially interesting because the phobia doesn't happen in a vacuum. The person's identity is kind of like an environment for the phobia. Your client might say, "Well, I'm a very private person, and I keep these things to myself." I will never fly on a plane because no one should see me like that. I'll tell my relatives that I'm helping a sick friend and can't come out for the holidays. " One way to get to the identity level is to ask who the person feels she is when she is dealing with the phobia. You can ask what roles she is acting out; roles like parent, role model, employee, airplane passenger, and so forth.

The sixth and final level is spirituality and purpose. This level addresses your client's connection to a higher reality.

What is it that she believes about spirituality or the universe that guides her?

This is an expanded version of the two levels that precede this level. The previous two were about beliefs and values, and identity and mission.

This spirituality and purpose level exists because people tend to have this level of belief. Even non-religious people usually have values that they feel extend beyond them and define their place in the world. Those values tend to shape their behavior as strongly as religious beliefs shape a believer's behavior. If nothing else, this level helps to summarize the way that beliefs and identity work together to create another level of meaning.

Does this all sound like too much to think about for a silly phobia? Well, I'll wager that you already think about these levels more than you realize. However, these six levels assist you in putting such thoughts into context and in asking some questions to round out your understanding; an understanding that will assist you in providing a relevant response.

You don't have to spend an hour asking all the questions that go with each level. With experience, you'll get better and better at knowing what questions to ask which people. You will develop an efficient approach.

Loneliness to Socialization

When a client says, "I am a loner, always alone and I hate it" or "I don't have any real friends, nobody likes me" or "I have social anxiety" or "I can't make any meaningful relationships," we ought to assume that this person's mental map is oriented inwards, showing only what the ego "gets" from the environment, not necessarily what it can give to others. This is a series of meta questions we can ask to help a client deal with self-induced loneliness:

1. Having recognized that you feel and behave lonely, what strategies might you employ to seek out and include more people in your life?

2. Where exactly do you feel that loneliness in your body?

3. If that specific part of you had a voice, what would it say now?

4. What's it like when you sit back in that chair and allow it to support you?

5. What's it like when you sit up and elongate your entire back, allowing your head to float upwards?

6. If you knew that you'd die tomorrow, what would you miss out on that could happen later today?

7. If you remain in eye contact with me, what—if anything—changes within you?

8. Scan through your body. Notice where exactly in your body you feel the most aliveness —the most energy. Notice where in your body you feel most connected and present. Notice where in your body you feel the least alive—the least amount of energy.

9. Just as you did with the X (part in the beginning), move your attention between the two locations of aliveness and dullness, presence and disconnect. Move back and forth and

notice how it is basically a matter of perception, a choice you make to notice whichever one you'd like to experience.

10. Future pace. Imagine a social event tomorrow or the next day, and you notice that your attention is drawn to the disempowered or low energy area.What is your immediate choice to remedy it?

Longevity

Source: Robert Dilts

> *Imagine your timeline.*
>
> *Start from your meta-position.*
>
> *Step into your positive future.*
>
> *Access past resources.*
>
> *Reframe and potentiate negative memories as appropriate.*
>
> *Create a resource vortex.*
>
> *Connect your resources with your future goal as you experience it.*

Develop positive beliefs and resources for almost any kind of issue. Directly install the beliefs and strategies of the vital elderly models. While this is not an advanced NLP pattern, I would still recommend that you wait until gain confidence and skill in other Neuro Linguistic Programming tools, such as anchoring and moving through perceptual positions.

1. Step into your timeline.

Imagine that your past, present, and future are represented by a line that goes from left to right in front of you.

Select a physical location in front of you that you can step onto during this pattern. Start from your meta-position. Look at your timeline from a meta-position (your objective or transcendent perspective, position #4). Be sure to have a physical spot for this position.

3.Step into your positive future. Start by stepping onto your timeline where the present time is located.

Turn your gaze to the future. See how your future timeline extends into the infinite future.

Elicit a relaxed physical and mental state, and walk slowly into the future. Imagine that you are moving in a positive direction, in a positive state.

Focus your mind, in positive terms (what you are going toward, rather than avoiding), on your health as something that you enhance over time in many ways.

Add elements to this sense of your future health. They are as follows: an awareness of your own power and what you can actually control; the belief that one is deserving of good health; a positive representation in all sense modalities; ideas and images of how you are of value to others and society; how your age and experience are assets; a sense of the larger reality that gave rise to and sustains your continued existence; and your visual representation of your physical posture and body language as being uplifted.

4. Gain access to previous resources.

Turn your face toward your past. Focus your mind on all the feelings and experiences of vitality and well-being that you have generated in this pattern, and slowly walk toward your past.

Connect with many of the resources of your past, especially experiences that can remind you of your abilities and beliefs that support you in achieving your goals and in generating new positive beliefs and action. Identify some special people that helped you generate those resources, including your ability to appropriately trust and believe in others.

Take the time to savor each point in your timeline where resource experience and generation are especially noteworthy. Fully connect with these experiences and savor and relive them. You may not always remember details, but follow the good feelings that are part of this kind of experience, and they will help you access a positive state and maybe even connect you with more of the resource memories that we are focusing on.

5. Reframe and potentiate negative memories as appropriate. Here's what to do when you encounter negative memories during your walk into the past. If the memory holds no value in supporting your resources (but bear in mind that negative memories often do hold great value), then it's fine to simply step around it and continue on. However, if you feel that there may be some value in the memory, then take the following steps:

a. Leave your timeline and move into your meta-position. Now you are in an objective position, insulated from the discomfort of memory.

b. Make positive meaning out of the experience. Determine what resource would have helped you derive resources from this experience. This can be as simple as thinking of the worst experiences that people have survived and grown from. It can be as sophisticated as giving your adult perspective at that moment so that you can discover the resources that are in that situation and take them with you. Even if this is a memory of something negative that you did, pay attention to the fact that your feelings about it are linked to your higher values. This is an opportunity for you to become fully aligned with these higher values.

c. Examine how the negative experience has influenced positive experiences. This may have happened because it served as some kind of warning, or made you tougher, more sensitive and aware. Remember to analyze this in terms of logical levels to uncover the dynamics that you might otherwise miss.

d. Consider the positive underlying motivations that were present during the negative event. Even if a person behaves badly, notice positive intentions or drives that you can draw upon and redirect positively in future situations.

e. Find the humor in the situation. Humor tends to come from an unexpected shift in perspective. Surprise and variety are human needs. This will help you cultivate your sense of humor and ability to innovate.

f. Once you have found one or more effective reframes, step back into the timeline and negative experience. Now imagine re-experiencing it from your expanded perspective.

g. At the beginning of this step, you thought of at least one resource from your life that would have helped with this experience. Recall the time in your life in which you were most connected to this kind of resource. Find that spot on your timeline, and step into that spot. Associate into that resource experience. As you fully experience the associated resource state, experience it as an energy and see what color it manifests as. How does it vibrate? What other sub-modalities do you notice in any sense mode? How does it feel to run through your body as a healing energy?

h. Beam that energy down your timeline into the negative experience, and maintain that beam of energy until you notice a positive change in that experience. See what resources are liberated by this energy. Continue until you reach the earliest supportive memory.

6. Create a resource vortex. Turn around to face your future again. Slowly walk toward the future, and relive your supportive and resourceful memories. Collect them, taking them with you into your future. Cultivate the sense of all these supportive people and resourceful situations being with you now. Amplify the state of resourcefulness. Step around any negative memories as you go. They do not detract in any way from your positive memories.

7. Connect your resources with your future goal as you experience it. Listen to a song that captures the sense of your resourceful state and supportive memories, as well as your health and vitality. Get into the spirit of that song as you proceed into your future. Continue until you arrive at your future goal on your timeline. Experience all of the resources that you have brought with you, as well as your goal and the optimal state for attaining it. Integrate these sensory representations into a single, positive experience. Notice and fully feel the connection between this future and all the people and resources of your past that are connected to it in some way. Experience the congruent connection between all of your life events and your vital, healthy future.

Making Peace With Your Parents

Source: Robert McDonald

Select a conflict with your parents for this pattern.

Tune into your negative maternal representations.

Concentrate these representations.

Constellate these into a shape.

Break state.

Do the same for your father representations.

Elicit your maternal and paternal positive intentions. Thank the parts.

Have the parts appreciate each other.

Combine the parts.Store the new part.

Future pace.

Test.

Resolving old conflicts with your parents can free up a lot of energy, creativity, and personal growth. This is done mentally, not necessarily with your parents. This may be done unconsciously, but it is still harmful. In addition, many of us have internalized the way our parents (or other caregivers) treated us as children. This not only limits us directly, but also hinders our ability to fully express our parents' gifts.

Many people still have issues with their parents, either in real life or as symbols. Some parents notice they speak to their kids in the same tone and content as their parents, but they can't stop it.

Despite many promises to "never be like my father" or "never be like my mother," they find themselves caught in the same thought patterns and behaviors as their parents.

When a client comes to you with a problem, you will notice that they use willpower to control their automatic behavioral responses.

Our "programming" (what some mistakenly call "genes") eventually triumphs. They can't avoid thinking about it.

Explain to your client that their parents did the best they could given their limited resources in education, competence, parenting, and financial knowledge. Their parents (your client's grandparents) must have treated them the same way. Their children do not have to inherit their parents' bitterness, criticism, and harshness.

The most elegant and mind-easing way to help them is to forgive their parents for their mistakes.

1. Select a conflict with your parents for this pattern. Think of a conflict with one or both parents or caretakers. The conflict does not have to be current, and your parents do not have to be living. Pick a conflict that you would like to resolve, or that you feel is limiting you in some way. For example, it may be absorbing your mental or emotional energy.

Throughout these steps, we will work with your internal representation of a male and female parent.

If your situation does not match, you can select an appropriate childhood authority figure or influence for the missing gender parent.

2.Tune into your negative maternal representations.

Focus on the areas in your body and mental space where you find feelings and other representations related to the negative aspects of your mother figure.

Imagine these feelings and other representations flowing from your body and mind into the palm of your left hand.

Continue doing so until you have them all represented in your palm.

4. Constellate them into a shape. Invite these representations to function like energy that can coalesce into a solid, visible shape.

5. Break state. Distract yourself with an activity such as thinking about a travel route or tying your shoes in order to change your state.

6. Do steps two through five for your father's representations.

Tune into your negative paternal representations, concentrate them into the palm of your right hand, and constellate them into a solid shape. Break state.

7. Elicit your maternal and paternal positive intentions. Ask your mother-in-law what positive intentions she had underneath the negative actions that led to your representations.

Continue to solicit these meta-intentions until you feel that you have a complete sense of this. The intentions may not have been rational, but you have many hints from your childhood as to her underlying positive intentions.

You might phrase your question as:

"What good thing were you trying to do for me with these behaviors and attitudes?"

Repeat this with your father's representation.

8. Thank the parts. Directly thank the parties for participating in this pattern, and validate their positive intentions for you.

9. Encourage the parts to appreciate one another. Have the parts face each other and express appreciation for each other's participation in this pattern and their positive intentions.

10. Combine all the parts.

Tell the parts that they can become a single, more positive, and powerful force by combining into a single entity. Ask them if they are willing to proceed with this. If not, resolve any ecological issues. Then slowly bring your hands together and allow the images to merge into a single entity. Keep your hands tightly together until you have had some time to integrate this change. Then open your hands and reveal the new entity.

11. Store the new part. Discover where in your body or mental space that you would like to place this new part so that it can become an integrated aspect of your resources. Touch the area where you will store these resources. Maintain contact with it to establish an anchor as you bring the image into that area. Allow the feelings to carry you back through your childhood and into your mother's womb, infused with these positive feelings.

Now allow these resourceful feelings that are resonating throughout your body and mind to carry you through your life, literally growing you up to this present moment in your adulthood.

12. The Future Pace: Continue to touch the anchor and step into the future so you can imagine your future with these resources.

13. Test. In the coming days and weeks, notice any changes in your relationship with your parents, if they are alive, and any authority figures or other intimate relationships. Notice any ways that you feel empowered by these resources.

Mapping Across

Mapping across means transferring resources from one state to another. Robert Dilts' research into meta-programs helped us figure out how to do this. Mapping across changes the meta-program and creates different results. For example, let's say that you supervise someone who gets into a bad mood every time a customer talks to him in a certain tone of voice. The employee has difficulty making the customer happy and occasionally irritates certain customers.This is bad for business, and the employee is spending a lot of time feeling unhappy. This employee has had very good experiences with people. Pretty much everyone has This means the employee has resources he can use to change his behavior. In one state, he feels good about people. In the other state, he feels bad and acts badly, too.

Mapping across means you use the good state to change the bad one. You get the resources from that good state to map across to the situations that normally bring out the bad state. Once you have mapped it across, the employee will have an easy time responding to customers that have an attitude. He'll even enjoy having more self-mastery, happiness, and job security. The Swish and Advanced Visual Squash patterns are two important NLP techniques that use mapping as a main procedure for behavioral change.

MAPPING ACROSS WORKSHEET	
Visual Submodalities	
State 1	State 2
Bright < > Dim	
1 2 3 4 5	1 2 3 4 5
Large < > Small	
1 2 3 4 5	1 2 3 4 5
Close < > Far	
1 2 3 4 5	1 2 3 4 5
Clear < > Distorted	
1 2 3 4 5	1 2 3 4 5
Color < > B&W	
1 2 3 4 5	1 2 3 4 5
Associated < > Dissociated	
1 2 3 4 5	1 2 3 4 5
3D < > Flat	
1 2 3 4 5	1 2 3 4 5
Auditory Submodalities	
State 1	State 2
Loud < > Quiet	
1 2 3 4 5	1 2 3 4 5
High Pitch < > Low Pitch	
1 2 3 4 5	1 2 3 4 5
Tempo Speed (Fast < > Slow)	
1 2 3 4 5	1 2 3 4 5
Right Side < > Left Side	
1 2 3 4 5	1 2 3 4 5
Verbal < > Tonal	
1 2 3 4 5	1 2 3 4 5
Clear < > Distorted	
1 2 3 4 5	1 2 3 4 5
Close < > Far	
1 2 3 4 5	1 2 3 4 5

The Big Book of NLP

Mapping Subjective Experience

Source: Richard Bandler & John Grinder

Build your modeling skills with this form of analysis. This skill will dramatically improve your ability to understand the world of another person, as well as your own, so that you can influence them with excellence. In this skill, you will be finding and structuring the keys to people's subjective experience. It can be done in less than three minutes, non-verbally, using eye accessing cues.

1. Arrange things with your partner. Select a partner for the exercise. Establish that you will be creating the mind map, and that the person can best cooperate by following your instructions and without answering verbally. As you proceed with the following steps, pay attention to the person's eye movements. You may want to take notes for review. When I elicit the accessing cues, I use my five fingers:

1 for Vr (Visual Remembered),

2 for Vc (Visual Constructed),

3 for Ar (Auditory Remembered),

4 for Ac (Auditory Constructed) and

5 for K (Kinesthetic).

I then imagine key points around their heads as they speak. For example, if their eyes go up and to the left for Vr, I imagine a floating point there. Then I make an arrow between that point and the position of their Vc, and so on. This way, I can even guess the movements they'll make ahead of time.

2. Get Visual Remembered cues. Have your partner recall a pleasant memory, and then ask them to focus on the visual aspect. Prompt them to access visual cues with questions such as: Can you see yourself yesterday? What did you wear?

3. Get Visual Constructed cues. Have your partner construct a visual impression that they do not already remember, with a question such as: "Now imagine yourself with blue eyebrows. What if the room lost gravity and everything started floating around?"

4. Get Auditory Remembered cues. Have your partner recall the audio aspect of a memory. "Listen for a bit to your favorite song. How does it sound in your mind?"

5. Acquire Auditory Constructed Cues. Have your partner create an internal auditory experience, by imagining something they have never heard before. "Imagine that BMW is testing their motorcycles by asking one hundred riders to drive their motorcycles into a four foot deep reservoir of water all at once. How does that sound?"

6. Get Kinesthetic Constructed cues. We skipped Kinesthetic Remembered, because people generally do not recall kinesthetic memories, but rather re-construct the feelings according to visual or auditory cues in the memory. Try a cue such as: "Imagine that you are rolling around on an iceberg in light clothing."

7. Test. As you develop skills in this area, see how well you can observe and predict eye movements, and how well you can remember which eye movements are associated with each strategy. When you work with a partner, practicing an NLP pattern or tool, it is better if you go through the process completely as a client a few times, and then give it a few days before you change places and work on it as the practitioner. The reason is that we tend to get so caught with the need to complete steps or to work methodically through a pattern, that we may miss the important non-verbal cues of our "client."

When practicing with a fellow practitioner, work on real problems rather than inventing one. This will further your personal development, provide a more realistic "laboratory," and show you that the pattern really works.

Matrixing

Matrixing is a way to strategically plan your work. It uses NLP to generate your responses to the client on the fly. This means we can use NLP know-how, such as analyzing the client's meta-programs and repairing their meta-model violations. If you aren't 100% on top of things like meta-model violations, the processes to follow will still make sense. A "meta-program" is the set of cognitive patterns that an individual tends to emphasize in managing their mental processes. This establishes an important link between our thoughts and the sensory representations that NLP uses in so much of its work.

You could say that meta-programs are the rules that govern our thought and decision-making patterns, especially in terms of how we select from our memories and environment in triggering and constructing those patterns. Put more concisely, meta-programs constitute the rules by which we select strategies (mental, behavioral, etc.) that we use to achieve our outcomes.

One way to get a feel for someone's meta-programs is to notice what they pay attention to. An example meta-program is"toward versus away from." A "toward" meta-program derives motivation and perspective from moving toward something. A person on a diet would experience himself or herself moving toward their desired weight and appropriate foods. An "away from" strategy would emphasize eliminating fat and avoiding fattening foods or excessive eating. The meta-model asserts that we must exclude a great deal of information in order to function. When this exclusion takes place in a dysfunctional way, it can lead to problems such as overgeneralizing, as in bigotry. Such errors are called "meta-model violations."

One method of repairing such violations is to ask questions that require a more specific answer or that bring forth a contradiction. For example, If atheists are immoral, how do you explain this long list of atheists who have made great contributions to humanity?" or... You say she hates you? What exactly do you mean by "hate"? I know she did you a favor yesterday. "

Matrixing for Difficult Problems

Matrixing means being relevant to complicated problems requiring a strategic response rather than a formulaic one. This is in contrast to the common approach of NLP practitioners, which is to focus on a very specific problem and apply a specific technique to it. This is not to say that such an approach is wrong.

There can be a great benefit to the artful winnowing down of a vague problem into a specific, operational definition, and many NLP practitioners excel at this. Many of them also excel at selecting a technique from their NLP quiver to rapidly resolve the problem. However, not every person will receive adequate help if their problem must be the equivalent of a sliver in their finger, and there's no reason to limit NLP's contribution to that of a pair of tweezers. Many of the problems clinicians and coaches find are quite complicated.

Some coaching clients may seem to have buried themselves in unresourceful narratives and stories that they have become very attached to. Many clients will work with a coach on success or other life issues, but have mild mental health issues that are either left over after getting psychotherapy, or not yet bad enough to get the client to seek a therapist. The book, Shadow Syndromes, talks about the way that "subclinical" issues can disrupt people's lives without necessarily being readily diagnosable.

We often call these clients "twilight" clients, because they may benefit from psychotherapy or medication, but are not necessarily motivated to explore that route. When they are, their residual problems don't contraindicate coaching, but they can make them more challenging for the coach. Because such problems affect nearly everyone in some way, coaches should get to know enough psychopathology to help them understand their more stuck or confusing clients. This knowledge can be useful in many ways. It can help the coach respond in a more strategic way and can help them have a more realistic sense of what will be needed.

My Favorite Matrix

I'm tempted to call this a starter matrix, but it is so fundamental to thinking about problems. This matrix may look simple, but it is very flexible and can be used to formulate very complicated problems, especially if you use it in a mind map format. You can use it for an overview of all the life needs of a client or use it to zero in on a specific problem. It supports holistic and strategic planning. It helps to bring your intent and next best actions into focus. Let's start with the categories and then an example.

1. Meaning: Examples include stigma, self-concept, vision as a source of goals, and meta-model violations.

2. Context: people, things, and situations in the person's environment that affect them.

3. Behavior: The actual behavior of the person and any plans that have a strong emphasis directly on behavior, such as behavior modification, able to include desired behavioral goals and habits. able to focus on ways that developmental issues have created behavior limitations or patterns.

4. Physiology: A focus on what is affecting the client from a biological perspective. can include lifestyle factors such as exercise and diet. The more you think in terms of evolutionary psychology and the "internal pressures" that this creates, the more you may find yourself thinking in terms of physiology. As you know, NLP has plenty to say about observing and influencing your client's physiology while thinking in terms of state management. Both coaches and therapists find that they can think more about physiology as they incorporate reprocessing techniques such as EMDR and EFT into their work.

Now try this: Think of a client, or even yourself. On a fresh, blank sheet of paper (or some kind of mind mapping software), put the four categories near the center. From there, you can branch out and add the most important related issues. Continue to branch out until you have actionable items. Here's an example:

The name and some of the details have been changed to protect her privacy: Marcy is 30 and hates her job, loves her husband, hates the way they get into arguments, feels kind of untrusting and judgmental of people, is very bright, is a really good salesperson, is underemployed because her employer isn't making very good use of her, and really wants to take her life to another level. She has trouble when a lot of little tasks and details come her way because of ADD. She has had counseling for ADD and has been reticent to take medication because it seems kind of creepy to her.

Meaning: Mary is generally irked. Underemployment, being overwhelmed with details, and feeling intolerant of people that act petty, boring, or stupid, all make life less satisfying. She loves her husband, but he thinks and speaks in a very step-wise fashion. This is very difficult to tolerate for a person who thinks in hypertext. She realizes, though, that he is bright and successful, and his heart is in the right place. Coaching or counseling will need to help her find a more life-affirming and dynamic way to be a very smart person in a world that can seem pretty dumb.

Context: Her need to improve her career is important here, because her context is a major source of her complaints. The results will show up here, but this is not necessarily the category where the real action will be. Changes in her attitude (meaning) and behaviors (behaviors) may be the keys that unlock her career potential or help her convince her employer to make better use of her sales skills, which are excellent.

Behavior: Her issues with the rest of humanity show up here in the sense that she does not have very satisfying relationships in her personal life, and she is not sure how to get into harmony with her husband. In addition to working in the meaning category, behavioral strategies may be important.

Physiology: Marcy has a lot of youthful energy, but the issues are taking their toll. Nonetheless, she brings a lot of energy to her job, her relationship, and her home projects. ADD has a physiological side, of course, and she will need to learn to cope with it, even if she takes medication. ADD coping methods will go into the behavior category. The prospect of medication, supplements, and other things that address ADD from a physiological angle is discussed here.

Here is an example of a plan for someone like Marcy. She has come in for coaching. She has had psychotherapy, and it has been helpful, but she wants to focus on success and lifestyle. Nonetheless, it is very obvious that there are emotional issues and ADD symptoms that loom large.

Meaning: Goals: To get from irked to fun and strategic. Getting into harmony with people and her husband. By being fed up with her distracting judcgmentality and impatience, she will probably come up with better strategies for making her relationships more satisfying. By being less distracted by feelings of oppression and under-appreciation at work, she will probably be able to come up with better strategies for her career as well.

Methods: Metaphoric, reframing, and other counseling techniques will be helpful. Reprocessing will be more helpful if we can connect with earlier experience that helped to establish her pattern of relating. Timeline work might be very helpful here.

Context

Goals: To get from being overwhelmed and under-appreciated to meaningful challenges that draw upon her gifts and inspire her to develop even higher skills.

Methods: Sometimes it is necessary to get context changes in order to progress in coaching or counseling. In this case, it looks like the context change is a goal rather than a short-term objective. That means that the focus on methods will be in the other categories. Not that keeping an eye on the classifieds isn't a good idea.

Behavior

Goals: Complement her success with specific strategies.The first two sessions created a strong impression that the short-term action is in the meaning and physiology areas.

Methods: Coming in a close third is the area of ADD coping strategies. These strategies will probably do a lot for her attitude and feelings of resourcefulness as well. This should create an upward, self-reinforcing spiral. It is also important to enhance her intimacy skills with her husband. But her thought patterns that bind her into less resourceful ways of handling her husband come first.

Physiology

Goals: Reduce ADD symptoms and respond to old emotional triggers with new mastery.

Methods: Consider medication (via a referral to a psychiatrist), supplements, exercise, and anything else that will help her with ADD from a physiological perspective. Direct her to sources of information for this.

Do reprocessing to help her generate a more resourceful state instead of being stuck in an irked state. Whatever processes are used, NLP techniques will rely a great deal on state management.

Meaning Translator

This is a process for helping you discover new interpretations of the words of an inner voice. You will often notice that the meaning of the voice alters, either gradually or more drastically, with each step you take. There is no difference in response if a step does not provide you with any new understanding. Thus, different individuals regard some steps as more relevant than others for them.

While working alone, you'll have to take a break after each step to complete the task at hand, and then read the next one. Then you'll have to reenter your previous stage's experience before you can proceed to the next step. You can close your eyes and completely immerse yourself in each stage without interruption if someone else is reading each step to you.

1. "Recall a bothersome voice and pay close attention to what it reveals to you—the volume, rhythm, inflection, pauses, and so on."

2. Who is speaking? Is this your voice, or did you learn to talk this way from someone else? " In order to determine the part who is speaking, you need to look at their face and think about all the things you already know about them, such as their personality traits, values, needs and wants, and abilities and limitations.

3. "Can you tell me where you are? This speaker, or your own voice, is speaking to you in a bigger context, so pay attention to that. Take note of all the nearby sights and sounds, as well as the wider environment in the distance.

4. "When did this happen? " If it's a static image, turn it into a movie that incorporates previous episodes that have an impact on what's happening now, as well as imagined future occurrences that have an impact on what's happening now.

If it's a static image, turn it into a movie that incorporates previous episodes that have an impact on what's happening now, as well as imagined future occurrences that have an impact on what's happening now.

5. "Is there anything else going on right now?" When it comes to this event, what else have you noticed and discovered?

6. "How is this other person reacting to all of these circumstances, and how are you reacting to the person?" Remember to take in everything you can about this occasion.

7. It's quite doubtful that the voice's meaning hasn't changed based on all of this additional information. A few—or maybe all—of the various steps in this procedure may have modified the meaning slightly, or certain processes may have had a greater impact than others. Pause for a moment to really appreciate the significance of the voice in your life right now.

8. Future Pace what you've learned to potential scenarios in the coming weeks or months.

The Big Book of NLP

Mental Hell

There are several habitual thought processes that undermine your sense of self-worth, and one or more of them is almost certainly the reason you purchased and began reading this book. Winston Churchill famously said, "If you're going through hell, keep going." This is the polar opposite of what the majority of people will do when confronted with their fears, insecurities, and unavoidable failures. Rather than confronting the issues directly, they either freeze in place and surrender (victim mentality), fight themselves mercilessly (self-deprecating), or flee using avoidance tactics (bad habits and addictions).

The unfortunate reality is that the most emotional issues in our lives will not resolve themselves simply by ignoring them or by unnecessarily degrading our self-image. By employing these strategies, we are merely postponing the inevitable, which will undoubtedly grow in size and scope and influence our decisions and experiences in life. By avoiding confronting our most fundamental emotional issues, we place ourselves in a limbo state of mind dubbed "mental hell." If we remain there for a long enough period of time, the bonfires of this mental hell will feed off one another by tearing down our self-esteem.

The most important key to getting through this mental hell, and coming out the other side stronger, is awareness. By becoming aware of these issues, we expose inner conflicts and are able to tackle them consciously and methodically. The truth is that, as Winston Churchill suggested, the only way out of hell is straight through.

A Tour of Mental Hell Territory:

I.   Weakness: Belief in one's inadequacy, in one's inability to do anything correctly, feeling and subsequently behaving like a loser.

II. Approval seeking/Unlovable or unlikable: The conviction that one is unlovable or unlikable, that no one honestly cares about him or her, and that one is incapable of forming or maintaining friendships or romantic relationships, and being concerned with these ideas. If you are a "people-pleaser," this is the underlying fear.

III. Helplessness: The conviction that one is incapable of coping—either with a specific situation or with life in general. This underlying conviction contributes to feelings of inadequacy and worry.

IV. Worthlessness/Defectiveness: The notion that one has no value or is unworthy... or that one is "damaged goods." For some, these ideas are similar, while for others, they are diametrically opposed.

V. Abandonment: The assumption that significant people in one's life will abandon him or her or will be unable to handle being alone. Individuals who hold this belief may take considerable steps to avoid being alone.

VI. Hate and fear: Belief in the untrustworthiness of people, that they are out to get you, or that they are otherwise not looking out for your best interests. This is a fundamental concept that contributes to people becoming excessively suspicious or outright paranoid.

VII. Entitlement: who fall into this category believe that they are exceptional, superior, or more deserving of something than others. Frequently, this serves to mask an underlying insecurity (defectiveness, belief in emotional deprivation): Individuals who are insecure but do not wish to be perceived as frail put on a "tough guy" or "tough chick" persona. However, some individuals were raised with no boundaries and truly believe they are superior to others.

VIII. Vulnerability: There are various manifestations of this idea, as it is expressed in different aspects of life, but in general, it is the perception that one is unsafe and extremely prone to being wounded in some way (relationally, medically, or financially). Individuals who hold this belief perceive life occurrences as more dangerous than they actually are.

IX. Emotional repression: The assumption that one must suppress one's emotions—that one must refrain from speaking up or sharing thoughts or feelings—because doing so would be improper or detrimental in some way.

X. Inadequate self-control: The belief that generates the cognition, "I need it now." Individuals who believe in the "heat of the moment" lack self-control and the ability to restrict themselves or delay gratification. This belief may manifest itself in impulsive substance addiction, sexual promiscuity, binge eating, temper tantrums, and shopping sprees.

XI. Emotional scarcity: The conviction that one will not be able to meet one's emotional requirements, as a result of which he or she frequently does not attempt. Certain individuals who hold this belief will assert, "I have no needs," "Your needs are more essential than mine," or "It is weak to have needs."

XII. Enslavement: This is a notion about control. Certain individuals believe they must cede control of their lives to others, while others make conscious attempts to avoid being controlled or controlled. If you have "control issues," this is a factor.

XIII. Retribution: The conviction that one is deserving of punishment. Punishment can be directed towards either self or another person. As a result of this belief, our culture has become highly litigious. Additionally, sadistic, masochistic, and self-harming behaviors may be a result of this mindset.

Meta-Model

The NLP linguistic meta-model formulates specific questions that clarify deletions, generalizations, and distortions in speech. When done incorrectly, these are referred to as violations of well-formed syntax. Syntax in grammar refers to the correct order of words in a sentence. Syntax in NLP refers to the proper arrangement of concepts in speech.

The NLP meta model is important for everyone to understand because violations of well-formed syntax cause a wide range of problems, from everyday relationship issues to major political issues. However, by asking meta-model questions that clarify these violations, we also clear our thinking. They also assist us in recognizing when another person's thinking is influenced by these violations, allowing us to regain control of our own mental maps and sense of reality. We are much less vulnerable to manipulation with the meta-model.

The meta-model assists us in analyzing speech by distinguishing between two types of structure: deep structure and surface structure. The deep structure is, at its core, a collection of sensory representations (neurological connections) that come together a lot like a chemical reaction. They bubble up and come together to form thoughts, opinions, and decisions. Then we put those thoughts, opinions, and decisions into words. That's when we have the surface structure. Those words cannot possibly contain all the impressions that led you to speak them.

Generalizations

Generalizations happen when someone translates some experiences into a rule that applies to all similar experiences. Sometimes generalizations can go by without being noticed. If someone says, "Everybody at the party hated me!" you might ask, "Who else did they hate?" If she says, "Everyone had friends there, they were just mean to me," you know she is unaware of anyone else feeling uncomfortable there. If you asked, "Oh, so they were sorry to see you arrive and glad to see you go," she might start thinking of exceptions and reveal one, even though she seems to be attached to the idea that everyone hated her. This means that her poor syntax just opened the door to a more accurate internal map; that is, she realized that there were exceptions to her generalization. Now she has a resource: the knowledge that there are people that appreciate her.

Universal Quantifiers

Universal quantifiers are an all or nothing kind of generalization. If someone says, "Every time I do someone a favor, it ends up biting me in the rear," you might ask, "I wonder what it is about you that makes that happen every time, you know, since that doesn't happen every time to anybody else." Your friend might come up with an insight like, "Well, you're right, I need to quit trying to help people who are so out of control, because it spills into the lives of anybody who connects with them." In this case, he found a universal source that gave the universal quantifier at least some truth. In this case, that could be better than finding the exceptions to his generalization.

Lost Performatives

Lost performatives make a rule without anybody having responsibility for it. If a girl gets a cut on her face and a nurse says, "Now you'll never win a beauty pageant," then you have a kind of cloud of lost performatives. One is that she should care about winning beauty pageants. Another is the implication, not a direct statement, but the implication that people will think she is ugly for the rest of her life. Another is in the nurse's tone of voice, which is telling the girl that it is her fault. You had to be there to hear that part. If you consider the culture of the region where this happened, it is also connected with the idea that she won't find a man to love her. Let's just take the main one, which is that she should care about winning beauty pageants. You might respond to that with, "You idiot, she's just an impressionable, vulnerable, wonderful, young girl with infinite potential, and she's too bright to waste her time running around with bimbos who try to be beauty queens." I'm going to get you fired for being such a twisted human being. " But that's pretty confronting. How about this one: "Who is it who thinks she should care about winning beauty pageants?"

Modal Operators

Modal operators make a "must" out of a preference. Albert Ellis, the developer of rational emotive therapy, focused a great deal on this one. People cause themselves a lot of suffering with modal operators because, when the "must" is not achieved, they feel like some horrible injustice has taken place. It distracts them from finding creative solutions and enjoying life as it is. If a client says, "I must have that woman, but she likes my friend," you might say, "It sounds like something really awful will happen if you don't get her." Tell me about that. " He might say, "Well, that is a really awful thing. If I don't get her, that will be really awful. " You might say, "So if you didn't get her, you will be in a really bad emotional place, really broken-hearted." To which he might say, "Yes, I couldn't handle it." Now you can go in for an exception, asking, "I wonder how many months it would take before you get your sense of humor back." His subconscious mind would have to have an incredible amount of restrictive control over him to keep him from clicking into exceptions. You could add fuel to this. "I suppose you'd know that from how you've handled a broken heart in the past." Witty quotes charm us because they toy with our internal syntactical violations. Consider this quote from Oscar Wilde: "There is only one thing in life worse than being talked about, and that is not being talked about."

Deletions

Deletions happen when the speaker leaves something out. When a person is being too vague or manipulative, deletion may be the culprit. If someone says, "What a lousy day," you could ask, "What is so lousy about it?" If she says she has lice, you now know she really DID mean it was a lousy day, since that's how the word "lousy" got its start. Unless you need to know where she got the lice, that's probably more information than you needed to know. Simple deletions are those where information is simply left out. You can't talk for long without making numerous simple deletions. After all, if you included all the details, it would take a long time and you'd get a reputation as a crashing bore, so deletions are a necessary part of everyday speech. Unspecified nouns and verbs are deletions that leave you wondering what thing or action the person is talking about. If a powerful local criminal says, "I'd hate to see what happens to your family if you don't pay us to take care of your nice restaurant in our part of town," you'd say, "How much do I pay and to whom do I write the check?" Oh, I mean, do you take unmarked bills? " Maybe that wasn't such a good example. What if your friend hears, "I was driving and here I am with this bad head wound." While she's taking her friend to the hospital, she might say, "But, what happened?" Maybe it wasn't a car accident. Was he attacked? Was he being vague because he was hiding something, or was he being vague because the head injury affected his brain? If so, then we could say that the deep structure is the injury itself. Let's hope it isn't too deep. But seriously, it is important to remember that deep structure includes everything from manipulation to psychological defenses to pure physiology. Let's try one more, a nice plain one. Your employee says, "We'll be a little late delivering to the buyer this month." You might ask, "How late is it exactly?" With the information you need, you'll know whether it's an emergency and how to handle the buyer. Otherwise, you could really be blind-sided. Employers and other leaders often get a watered-down version of bad news from their staff. That is a good time to trot out your meta-model questions.

Lack of Referential Index

Lack of a referential index is a deletion where there's an unspecified party or an unknown "they." If someone tells you, "Everybody knows you're a liar," you could say, "Who on earth would say something like that about someone like me?" That kind of backs the person into a corner, challenging them to disclose their sources. Maybe someone does think that you're a liar or that you lied about something, but how could every single person think that? Has this person been telling stories behind your back? At the very least, your meta-model question shows them that you can't be intimidated by such a cheap shot.

Comparative Deletions

Comparative deletions happen when the speaker fails to say what they are comparing something to. If a sales person tells you, "This motorcycle gets fifty percent better gas mileage!" you may want to ask, "Better than what, my skateboard?"

Distortions

Distortions are based on real sensory data, but they twist it in some way to create the wrong conclusion. If it's extreme enough, it's a form of delusion. If someone says, "A white car followed me all the way to the gas station. Someone must be obsessed with me and stalking me," you might wonder if the driver of the white car was going to the same gas station.

Coincidences are distorted all the time. When someone hears about two simultaneous occurrences, like a few small businesses closing in town, and turns it into a pattern, they might say, "Can you believe it? The whole country is going out of business. I'm moving to Brussels. " You could say, "I'm moving to Brussels because six new businesses have opened. That means we'll be overrun in no time! Let's go before there are no English speakers left." Maybe that would be a little too sarcastic. You'd better get to know this person well before you get too carried away with your reactions, or else you'll end up alone, bitter, homeless, and frozen. Whoops, I just used some distortions., haven't I?!

Nominalization

Nominalization happens when we transform a verb or adjective into a noun. It also has to be something that isn't a real thing in the world. In other words, you couldn't put it into a wheel barrel. In fact, come to think of it, nominalization is a nominalization in and of itself.It's a noun that isn't an actual, real-world object.

Some other examples include: accuracy, righteousness, superiority, excellence, and destiny. You can see nominalization happening in old philosophy and old psychology texts quite a bit. That's odd, because philosophers have published material critical of this for centuries.

It gets more problematic when a number of nominalizations, or a chain of them, are discussed as though they were definite, real, understood things / objects. When people do this, they come to all sorts of weird conclusions. Here's an example: Someone said that atheists believe in a dog-eat-dog world. The deep structure that went on in their minds went something like this. Atheism equals evolution. Evolution equals Darwinism. Darwinism equals social Darwinism. Social Darwinism equals survival of the fittest, which means no compassion for those in need, a dog-eat-dog world. But social Darwinism is a political philosophy that only got Darwin's name attached to it because it resembled natural selection, which is a part of the theory of evolution. On each side of that weak link, the chain contains fairly good generalizations. Most atheists believe in evolution.

Social Darwinists believe in a dog-eat-dog world. But those two chains are only linked by a completely irrelevant nominalization. The verb "to evolve" becomes a noun: evolution. Then, that noun gets attached to social Darwinism only because Darwin discovered evolution. The jump to social Darwinism is only possible because of word play. This is what we mean when we say that people live in a fantasy world because they act as if words are real things. But there is often a hidden agenda behind nominalization. People who are not very introspective may not even realize that they are pursuing an agenda. The person who said atheists are dog-eat-doggers wanted so badly to feel superior to non-believers that he came up with this as a response to research showing that atheist doctors were doing more for poor people than religious ones. Outside the field of NLP, another word for nominalization is "reification."

Mind Reading

Mind reading is an irritating distortion. This happens when someone decides they know what you are thinking. For some reason, it's usually something negative and untrue. If you tell them they are projecting, they probably won't understand. If you tell them what you are really thinking, they may actually argue with you, as if they know what you're thinking and you don't. If they think you're lying, what more can you say? So you see how irritating this meta-model violation can be.

Cause and Effect Distortions

Cause and effect distortions can be sneaky. This happens when someone thinks they know what caused something simply because the two things happened together. It's like the rooster thinking that crowing makes the sun come up. He must be right. It happens every time. People do that a lot with their emotions. They'll say someone made them angry, as if they had no responsibility for their emotions. Everyone understands what they mean, but people can go too far with this. If they do it to manipulate people, as in emotional blackmail, then you might want to say something like, "Even I am amazed at the power I have over your every emotion." Or you could simply restate that you are doing what you do for perfectly good reasons and let them sort it out. After all, if you don't pay attention to emotional manipulation and you DO pay attention to their mature, appropriate behavior, you will probably have a better time, and they will respect themselves more. It's good to bring the best out in others. You could say that this is meta to the meta level, because when you produce a strategy that serves your personal well-being or higher values, then you have gone beyond coming up with cute responses to show other people that they are illogical. You have taken things to another level. It is understanding and using the meta-level that is important, not having a lot of snappy comebacks that could alienate people. This section was designed to build your knowledge and observation skills, not make you think you need to be sarcastic or directly confrontational all the time in real life.

Complex Equivalence

Complex equivalence connects two ideas that don't belong together. For example, if your client is too upset about an argument with her son, she might say, "I can't believe I told him he was lazy. Now he'll be traumatized forever." You could respond by asking questions about the kinds of stress that he has survived, and how he recovered from them, maybe even how they have helped to build his character. You could discuss ways to get over the argument and build better agreements about his responsibilities and the consequences of good and bad behavior. You could talk about how to create more consistent rules at home and how this benefits everyone. One of the best ways to help with complex equivalence is to supportively approach the issue from several factual and positive directions, as in the example above.

The Big Book of NLP

Presuppositions

Presuppositions are the hidden ideas in a statement. If someone asks you if you have stopped beating your spouse, they are presuming that you still beat your spouse. And that's assuming that you have one to beat. You could say, "You should know, or haven't you spoken to your mother lately?" but we wouldn't advise that. Maybe you could say, "I never started, but I hear it's hard to stop once you start. Have you considered a support group?"

Meta-Model Challenging

With this pattern, you will get a chance to work on a fundamental skill that will help you when modeling and ensuring that you communicate effectively.

1. Recognize meta-model violations.

When someone is speaking to you, pay attention to meta-model violations such as excessive generalization or deletion, as well as inappropriate presuppositions and assumptions. Examine whether you are able to create accurate sensory representations of what the other person is saying. During the "mapping over" into sensory representations, it is likely that you will encounter gaps in your understanding that will tempt you to "fill in the blanks" by departing from the sensory representation or by using your imagination. How well do you understand what the person is referring to and what they are trying to convey?

2. Inquire about any meta-model violations you come across.

When two ideas that don't belong together are treated as if they do (complex equivalence), then you should inquire. I'm perplexed as to how anti-war demonstrations are dividing our country. Is it possible that the individual is unaware of the fact that countries have always been divided over issues and that this has been the nature of politics throughout history? Perhaps they are aware of this, but are concerned that a military coup will result as a result of it this time. If a person becomes irritated or manipulative when you ask meta-model questions (questions that clarify meta-model violations), try to figure out what the person is attempting to prevent you from knowing or doing as a result of your questions. You can begin by directly inquiring as to why they are becoming enraged (or whatever their reaction is). It goes without saying that this should be a situation in which you are safe and do not stand to gain much by alienating this individual. After all, this is just for practice purposes.

3. Continue until you have a well-formed understanding of what the other person is saying.

4. Test your understanding by expressing it to the other person and seeing if they agree, or test your understanding by seeing if you have a clear understanding of how to respond effectively. To give an obvious example, if you were given directions by someone, did you manage to get to your destination on time?

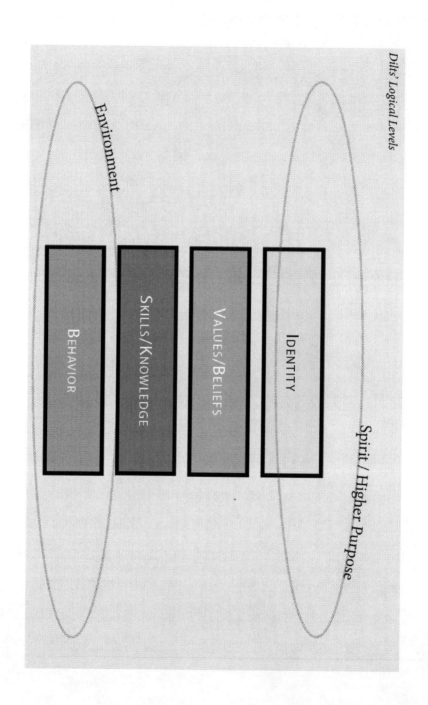

Dilts' Logical Levels

Environment

BEHAVIOR

SKILLS/KNOWLEDGE

VALUES/BELIEFS

IDENTITY

Spirit / Higher Purpose

Meta-Model: Intentional Usage

Produce constructive change as efficiently as possible with the very structured questioning of this pattern. It includes presuppositions in the course of asking meta-model questions. The purpose of this very structured questioning is to help produce constructive change as efficiently as possible.

Discuss a personal problem with someone (questions included). Ask the following questions in the specified order in the course of the discussion. Phrase the questions as you wish in order to fit the situation and the person you are speaking with.

a. "What do you believe is the problem?"

b. "What is the cause?"

c. "How have your efforts to solve the problem failed so far?"

d. "If the problem were solved, what would be different (how would you know)?"

e. Note: At this point, we flip into a positive frame that moves into a solution state. "What do you want to change about this problem?"

f. "When will you stop it from limiting you?"

g. "How many ways do you know that you have solved the problem?"

h. "I know that you have already begun to change and see things in new ways."

i. Test. Observe changes in physiology, attitude, and behavior. Note any changes that occur in the person's life in the next few days or weeks.

Meta-Model Therapy

In order to protect the therapeutic relationship between a therapist and a client, the founders of motivational interviewing created two very useful elements. Coaches can use it too. Instead of the therapist, the client makes progressive, mature statements. This removes resistance and accelerates the client's healing. The first method is "negative spotlighting."

When someone says something that defies well-formed syntax, you can exaggerate it to help the other person model their world better. "I don't need to be a purist," a drug addict might say. I occasionally use cocaine. Then say, "You have total control of cocaine now." Anyone in a recovery program knows this is absurd. "Well, uh, I guess that's just the addiction talking," they must say. Notice that it was not you who said it. You only used motivational interviewing to contradict what they said.

Although the practitioner's claim is exaggerated, it is not made in a sarcastic manner. It must be done with complete sincerity and gentleness. It is stated factually. "Oh, you think you can now control cocaine?" It's a factual statement. "You are now in total command of cocaine." You say it smoothly, as if it's new information. So the client can correct and educate you. That shows the client she's smart and has something to say. It allows the client to come to her own conclusions and control her own thoughts to change her direction. This allows the client to think more freely.This is very helpful because now the client owns the enlightened statement; they do not feel compelled to resist you because you are not trying to shove it down their throats. Any time you feel like you are pushing a client or customer, you could probably benefit from a motivational interviewing technique. The original book on this is called "Motivational Interviewing."

The other motivational interviewing technique that is a great meta-model response is what we call "positive spotlighting." Here, you highlight something very constructive or adaptive that the client says. This reinforces the constructive way of thinking and gives them credit. If the person says: "I realized that my wife left me because I was abusing drugs." You could say, "You have the kind of insight that shows real courage in the face of a tremendous loss."Isn't that much better than saying, "So you're finally realizing what a schmuck you've been!" ?

This positive approach reinforces the best qualities of the person and creates hope and strength that could make the difference between sobriety and relapse, perhaps even life and death. This is not to say that you bear total responsibility for every choice a client, customer, or employee makes, but I say it to remind you of what an important contribution you can make to people's lives when you learn the powerful insights and methods of Neuro Linguistic Programming.

Metaphors

The unconscious is always looking for solutions, but our defenses and traumas can keep us from connecting the dots. We have evolved to digest our daily experiences through REM sleep, but traumatic and other anxiety-provoking material can prevent REM sleep from doing its job. However, it is that we become stuck. One of the solutions to being stuck lies in the art of metaphor. A metaphor means creating a story or idea that symbolizes something. For example, you might write a story about a famous event in history but change the characters into various mythological or magic characters. Many of the most famous stories are actually metaphors for what was going on politically at the time they were written. Many more are love stories that resemble our own love lives in various ways. That's why we can relate to them. But Erickson contributed a great deal to using metaphors for healing. Metaphor bypasses the conscious mind and helps the unconscious process issues that are stuck. Metaphors can help us process things that we could not process on our own.

The book Little Annie Stories is a wonderful collection of metaphorical stories to tell children that are intended to help them deal with difficult issues like bed wetting. The book, My Voice Will Go With You: The Teaching Tales of Milton H. Erickson, M.D., is an excellent addition to the library of anyone interested in the Milton model and metaphor. One way to begin building metaphors is to read collections of them. That is why I recommended those books. Of course, there are others. You can begin building metaphors by picking a challenging issue and turning it into a story about animals. Whatever the challenge is, turn it into something that has similar emotional significance. For example, if the challenge is about regaining self-esteem after a failure, the story could be about the animals going to a dried up watering hole and going on a search for water. The thing that makes a metaphor healing is that there is some kind of healing message embedded in the story. In the water metaphor, the animals going on a quest for water is like someone not being stuck in low self-esteem and going for new opportunities. Being thirsty didn't stop the animals; it drove them on.

Experiencing a dramatic or hurtful failure doesn't stop people; it drives them to build the needed skills and seek new challenges. So the water is a metaphor for success and self-esteem at the same time. Since people have parts, as we have learned, Different characters in the story can match different parts. One of the animals could say, "It's hopeless. There's no point in going on. We must stay here and hope for rain." The ensuing dialogue could be a message to the unconscious to turn the voice of hopelessness into a voice of motivation.

Metaphoring

Practice using metaphors to achieve therapeutic ends. Metaphor is essentially the use of symbolic events or items to symbolize something else. Many believe that the Wizard of Oz was a metaphor for the United States' debate about going off the gold standard in the 1900's. Kafka's Metamorphosis is said to be a metaphor for the denial of self engendered by conformity to a harsh capitalist society. In coaching and psychotherapy, healing metaphors can bypass conscious filters and rally unconscious resources. Metaphors such as those in Little Annie's Stories can be used to help children navigate developmental challenges and fears.

1. Choose a situation to which you can apply a healing metaphor. Think of a situation in your own or someone else's life that is creating fear or difficulty adjusting. It can be an adult or a child.

2. Determine what is essential for healing. Jot down a core idea that would be healing or useful in this situation. Jot down some ideas that support it.

3. Create your metaphor as a situation in a story. Think of a story situation that resembles this but does not directly state it. For example, a child who is afraid of the dark could be transformed into a story about a prince who must get to the castle in order to become the next king, but he must pass through a dark forest that he is sure is full of goblins and witches.

4. Complete the metaphor for healing. Find a way to propel the story and reach a resolution with healing meaning. For example, you could enthrall your child with the prince's travels through the dark forest, with his certainty that the sounds he is hearing mean he is about to be eaten by goblins or turned into a toad by witches. He could have had close calls with things that turned out to be birds and rabbits. (The metaphor states that these fears aren't really fears of bad things; in fact, they might be cute or harmless).

5. Act out the story. Practice telling the story until it feels fairly smooth.

6. Tell the story. Tell the story to the person who needs to hear it.

7. Test. Notice if it has a positive impact on the person regarding the situation that they were having trouble with.

Meta Programs Review

The meta programs model is only briefly reviewed in this edition. If you'd like to learn how to thoroughly and properly use the meta-programs to analyze yourself and others, consider reading the book "NLP: The 57 Meta-Programs" (ISBN-8087518071).

In many NLP training programs, you'll probably hear the following statements: "Meta-Programs can be thought of as the primary programs that govern people's mental processes.", "It is useful not to think of Meta-Programs as nouns, as the name might imply." , "Rather than describing what people are, Meta-Programs help us understand how people function in any given context." Now let's try to make it really simple:

Meta-Programs Are Tendencies on a Continuum.

A person is either being pulled toward one end of the continuum or the other, and there are very few extremes in reality.

At any given point in time, a person is leaning toward one or the other, with their position in a constant state of change,depending on the environment and circumstances that are in operation at the time. Like ocean tides that ebb and flow based on the earth's proximity to the moon, a person's behavior and responses will fluctuate depending on the stimuli that they are influenced by.

Using Meta Programs is all about not labeling things or people in terms of "black and white," but instead recognizing the many shades of gray that often exist between two opposing ends of a continuum or in different types of situations.

MP1: Chunk Up / Chunk Down

People prefer to think, communicate and learn (as examples) in varying size "chunks" of information. There are primarily two types of strategies here, with a third taking a minor role.

People who prefer a global outlook can easily recall times when they were bored when someone insisted on presenting them with details they felt were irrelevant. They are more concerned with a situation's governing principles and general overview. They believe statements such as "If you keep your eyes on the dollar, the pennies will take care of themselves."

People who prefer a detailed outlook have a tendency to recall times when they were irritated by someone who was vague and failed to provide them with sufficient details. Ask: "Do you want to delve into the specifics of a situation?" Many believe, "If you focus on the details, the big picture will work itself out."

People who prefer to process information metaphorically have a tendency to think about one thing in terms of another. This is also known as "lateral thinking," which is a great tool for enhancing your creativity. You can easily use lateral thinking by first chunking up and then chunking down in a different direction, by asking: "What else could be an example of this?"

MP2: Match / Mismatch

When it comes to working with and comparing data, there are generally two ways of operating when we are first presented with new information. We can either look for what matches our existing knowledge, or we can look for what is new to our frame of reference, what differs from our existing knowledge.

People who sort for sameness are interested in how things measure up similarly to what they have experienced before. They tend to value predictability and security and find comfort in routine. They are likely to resist change and feel threatened by it. They generally adopt a conservative worldview. They can remain comfortable at the same job for years, enjoying the stability that it offers them. They tend to be stubborn and stuck in their ways.

People who sort for differences focus on how things differ from their previous experience. They value change, freshness and variety, and will easily become bored with situations that remain constant. They will notice the one picture that is hung incorrectly, and will thrive on new experiences. They are excited by terms like re-engineering and restructuring and the inevitable change that they imply. On the extreme side they tend to become annoyed by things that are rigid, and frustrated with situations that are predictable.

People who sort for sameness with exception first notice patterns of similarity, and then focus on differences. They like things to remain relatively stable, but can handle change that comes gradually. They tend to be fairly adaptable and live pretty stable lives.

People who sort for differences with exception tend to notice differences first, and subsequently focus in on similarities. They are comfortable with variety, but not really with profound change. They enjoy rearranging things, which can lead to pursuing new jobs, homes and relationships relatively frequently to indulge their need for variety.

People who sort for sameness and differences equally tend to seek out change and stability in equal measure.

MP3: Rep. System Sort

Our brains think or create thoughts by receiving information through our senses and then relaying that information back to the world around us. We "see" pictures, "hear" sounds, and "feel" sensations. In NLP, these sensory systems are known as the representational systems that form the building blocks of thought. There are two ways of discovering which sensory channel a person is using: (1) by paying attention to the direction in which their eyes move while they are communicating and (2) by noting the kind of predicates (adjectives, verbs, adverbs) they make use of.

People who represent visually usually sit with an upright posture and move their eyes upward when visualizing. They use high tones and breathe high in the chest. They observe people and want to be looked at then they are speaking. They are generally slender in build. They use visual-based predicates, for example: See, Look, Clear, View, Dawn, Reveal, Hazy, Focused, Imagine, Eyes, Take a peek, Take a look, Tunnel vision, Paint a picture, Illustrate, Picture, Short sighted, Show, Read, Dark, Glance, Crystal clear, Sight for sore, Naked eye, Bird's eye, An eyeful, Overlook.

People who represent in auditory ways move their eyes horizontally when accessing mental data. They breathe from the center of the chest in a rhythmic and stable way. They will often demonstrate impressive verbal communication and articulation skills. They tend to point their ears in the direction of the person talking to them, so as to not look directly at them. They are often of medium build. They will use auditory predicates. For example: Sound, Hear, Speak, Tell, Listen, Silence, Dialogue, Pitch, Volume, Loud, Quiet, Quote, Bang, Static, Nag, Tune, Listen, Amplify, Give me your ear, Tune in, Tune out, Rings a bell, On another note, Make music, Clear as a bell, Earful, Loud and clear, State your purpose, Unheard of, Utterly, Well informed, Word for word.

People who represent kinesthetically move their eyes downward when accessing information. They tend to breathe deeply. They talk and move deliberately and slowly, gesturing a lot. They make use of kinesthetic predicates, for example: Hard, Tough, Warm, Cold, Grasp, Feel, Solid, Touch, Catch on, Unfeeling, Scrape, Boils down to, Control yourself, Come to grips with, Get in touch with, Get a load of this, Get a handle on, Hang in there, Hand in hand, Hold it, Lay cards on the table, Know-how, Keep your shirt on, Hold on, Pull some strings, Slipped my mind, So-so, Too much of a hassle.

Some people are also known as auditory-visual representers. This representation style places a huge focus on words, causing the people who use it to practically live in a world of words. For them, pictures, sensations, and sounds go unnoticed for the most part. They have been described as "the cerebrals".

MP4: Agree / Disagree

People relate to one another in a variety of ways. There are people who look for things they can agree on with other people when they're dealing with them. Other people are always aware of the many points they disagree with when they talk to someone. They seem to be compelled to be argumentative.

People who adopt an agreeable mode value cooperation and synergy and seek ways to inspire it. They are more concerned with the common ground that exists between people than with the conflicting opinions that would separate them. They value their own opinions, but not to the degree that it causes division. They look for the positives in a communication scenario and adopt a "glass is half full" attitude.

People who adopt a disagree mode can't help but be drawn to what they perceive as glaring differences in opinion between themselves and others. They generally consider their opinion on any given matter to be the correct one and will defend it, sometimes to the detriment of the relationship. They tend to enjoy and even thrive on arguments and debates. They take the "glass is half empty" stance when it comes to areas of disagreement with others.

MP5: Uptime / Downtime

In processing information, some people tend to major in the internal realm of their own subjectivity (downtime), while others focus mainly on the external world (uptime).

People who process internally (downtime) primarily go inside themselves and are mainly aware of their own thoughts and feelings. They are, in a sense, blind and deaf to the external world. They can sometimes seem to "zone out" and be in their own private world. They tend to make little eye contact and can often be found staring off into space.

The Big Book of NLP

People who process externally (uptime) are aware of all the external things that impact their senses. They can be seen paying attention through their use of body language, eye contact, and gestures. They create little information from within and rely heavily on external sources.

MP6: Sensory / Intuitive

We can gather information from things in two different ways: we can use our senses or we can use our intuition.

People who use their intuition rely heavily on their internal judgements and tend to ignore external observation. They may take heed of external observations at a later stage when they come to their minds. They tend to think of themselves as ingenious and imaginative. They may ignore important information in their external environment that is at odds with their instincts. They can sometimes find people who they sense to be boring and uninspiring. They are able to imagine possibilities, have a large tolerance for complex things, are able to appreciate the aesthetic and the theoretical, and love to invest their energy on a creative and symbolic level. They use labelling often in their communications, as well as evaluative language.

People who use their senses prefer to rely on facts and identified meanings. They can sometimes ignore useful hunches that are in conflict with their perceived surroundings. They tend to think of themselves as real, down-to-earth, grounded, and practical. They think of those who rely on intuition as impractical and unrealistic. They primarily use descriptive language that focuses largely on the senses.

MP7: Black & White / Continuum

Some people are comfortable with, or have had more training in, working with clearly defined categories. Others are more at home with discernment in the gray areas in between the extremes.

People who evaluate in black and white are able to make clear and definite distinctions. They are motivated to respond quickly and tend to adopt a more judgmental mindset. They will use clear and definite language. They may be tempted to express themselves dogmatically. They will usually communicate in ways that suggest perfectionism.

People who work within the continuum are able to discern things at much finer levels. They tend to be more tolerant and compassionate. They can be indecisive. They will refer to gray areas and include a large number of qualifiers in their communication. They will often correct themselves as other possibilities come to mind.

MP8: Optimist / Pessimist

Optimism and pessimism refer to the way in which a person thinks about the world around them, whether those thoughts are grounded in reality or not.

People who are pessimistic have minds that are conditioned to tune into worst-case scenarios. They can therefore be highly skilled at things like quality control, problem solving, proof-reading, etc. They can easily feel helpless and hopeless if they go too far in this state.

People who are optimistic have minds that are trained to identify best-case scenarios. They can effectively present a vision and motivate people toward achieving it. They tend

The Big Book of NLP

to have an "empowerment" frame of mind. When this mode is at its most extreme, they may be unable to deal with problems decisively and honestly.

MP9: Best / Worst Case Scenario

In this meta-program (closely related to #8. pessimism/optimism), we make the following distinction: Whereas pessimism and optimism refer to general perceptions of current reality, best-and worst-case scenarios refer to thinking about a possible future event. The former describes mental processing with regard to how things currently are, and the latter deals with the matter of processing related to how things could be. Picture the scene (perhaps you are experiencing this right now): You find yourself in a job with an incredibly stressful and negative environment that makes you very unhappy, but at least the pay is fairly decent and you live close to work, so there are no travel complications. Do you find yourself motivated to explore new and better opportunities, or do you fear that things might only get worse at some new job that you accepted? For you, is it a case of "Better the devil you know, than the devil you don't?" Beyond this distinction, the characteristics highlighted in the previous section still apply.

MP10: Certainty / Uncertainty

This Meta-Program deals with the solidity of our mindsets in terms of our certainty or uncertainty in holding on to them. There are those who process ideas, beliefs, thoughts, and values in ways that are bold and assured (certainty), while the mental constructs of others are more flexible and open to being influenced by the ideas, emotions, and experiences of those around them (uncertainty).

People whose mental constructs are certain usually move through life with inflexible beliefs and opinions.

People whose mental constructs are uncertain tend to revise their beliefs and opinions in light of new experiences and information.

MP11: Focus Sorting

The process of shutting oneself off to the surrounding environment is known as "stimulus screening".

This process reduces the amount of external information that the person allows himself to be influenced by. In this sense, people fall somewhere on a continuum between not filtering out any stimuli at all, to shutting out almost everything at the other extreme.

People who are non-screeners generally sense a great deal of what goes on around them. They tend not to weigh the various elements of a situation according to relevance or importance, so often fail to shut out irrelevant or unimportant stimuli. They therefore experience environments as complex and abundant in distractions. They exhibit a high degree of understanding with others due to feeling sensitive to their emotional reactions. They consider things like serenity, peace and calm to be important, and this is reflected in their language.

People who are screeners are typically selective with regard to the stimuli that they allow themselves to be influenced by. They unconsciously rank elements of an environment in order to reduce the need to have to pay attention to everything around them. To the extreme they can often come across as non-attentive and even rude due to the large measure in which they are closed off to the stimuli around them. They are often oblivious to the emotional reactions of those around them and can appear inconsiderate. They value things that are exciting and new, and will tend to express this in their communication.

MP12: Why / How

The way a person's mind functions with regard to mental direction can either focus on "why" something may have happened, or "how" it occurred and affected things as a result.

People who initially focus on why tend to need to make sense of things through understanding the motivations or causes involved. They are prone to getting caught in a stressful state because they are constantly consumed with the question of "why". They usually develop a philosophical mindset.

People who initially focus on how want to understand how something happened or how it affects the surrounding environment. They devote less focus and energy to the motivations involved. They express themselves as pragmatists.

MP13: Origin / Solution

When considering situations or circumstances, particularly those involving problems or difficulties, some people are driven to understand how the situation came to be (its origin, or what caused it), whereas others are more focused on managing and dealing with the consequences.

People who focus on the origins of things need to know how something started or what its source is. They feel that they are able to control or master something more effectively if they understand its origin. They are inclined to adopt a philosophical attitude towards things.

People who focus on the solution to things are driven to manage the resultant consequences and seek out solutions. They tend to feel more at ease when a plan is in place to take care of the situation. They follow a more practical approach to processing information.

MP14: Static / Process

The way in which people perceive "reality" dictates how they navigate through life. Some think in terms of ideas like permanence, eternity, and certainty (static), whereas others are focused on changes, progression, and movement (process).

People who adopt the static view exist in a world that, to them, is filled with tangible things like people, things, places, etc. They use language that is rich in nouns. They tend to think about processes as things. They view things as unchanging and ascribe static identity to things or people, saying things like "Jill is annoying." or "Peter is silly." They are easily drawn into judgmental thinking and attitudes.

People who adopt the process view live in a world filled with perpetual motion and energy. They make use of language that is rich in verbs and behaviors or functions. They will often re-interpret things as processes. They tend to be more understanding and tolerant in their dealings with people.

MP15: Digital / Analogue

We encounter information in two forms: verbal and non-verbal. The verbal category is comprised of the symbols that have been developed in order to communicate. These are things like music, mathematics, language, and art. The non-verbal category includes all the visual cues that originate from our physical realm: posture, breathing, tension, eye-movement, etc. Both of these categories provide a large amount of information and messages, and people tend to favor one or the other. People who have experienced a significant amount of hypocrisy with regard to people saying one thing and then behaving differently may increasingly favor using non-verbal methods of interpretation over time.

People who favor verbal expression pay careful attention to exactly what someone is saying. They tend to be proficient in careers like law, writing, and politics, where the use of specific words is important. They tend to take an interest in the field of linguistics. They may be insensitive to visual behavioral cues.

People who favor non-verbal expression are primarily mindful of how people communicate and focus on volume, tone, pitch, etc. They are more challenging to persuade with words alone, placing more trust in what a person's physicality conveys. They tend to excel in careers like drama, sales, and healthcare or nursing. They can be guilty of jumping to conclusions regarding a person's meaning and intent. They may be interested in the practice of people-watching because they think that behavior is the best way to get the most accurate information.

People who are more balanced in their approach tend to process information using both methods of analysis in equal measure.

MP16: Emotional Coping

The specific focus of this meta-program is stress, whether it be in the form of extreme and recurring threats and dangers, or extreme and recurring overload. In the face of these kinds of stress, some people will opt to shy away and avoid them, whereas others will boldly confront them and wrestle with them. While this response may find its origin in the conscious mind, brought about by cues of danger or overload, it is controlled entirely by the unconscious mind. This meta-program readies a person's body and brain to access a heightened energy state for either confronting or fleeing.

People who adopt the fight response tend to actually enjoy challenges and pressure, as well as the accompanying opportunities to "go at" them. In an extreme capacity or with little forethought, they can exhibit violent and threatening behavior that is out of control. They can come across as highly intimidating and conniving.

People who adopt the flight response perpetually attempt to distance themselves from confrontations and challenges. They highly value peace and harmony. "Why can't we all just get along?" they ask. To the extreme, they can be easily taken advantage of, or tend to strive to please people excessively.

People who adopt a balanced approach can be described as generally assertive. They have been trained through experience to neither fight nor flee, but rather embrace skills such as negotiation and compromise. They are considered to be emotionally balanced and healthy.

MP17: Internal / External

When it comes to evaluating things, there are two primary ways of doing so. We can do so from the point of view of our own experience (internal), or without involving our reference at all (external). This Meta-Program has to do with how we position our focus of discernment for responding and evaluating, whether internally or externally.

People who focus on themselves (internal) judge things on the basis of what they consider to be relevant. They are self-motivated and choose their own path. They may be willing to consider information received from others, but in the end, they will make up their own mind. They personally own their values, beliefs, thoughts, and emotions.

People who focus on others (external) weigh information based on the opinion of others. They rely on others for motivation and allow their decisions to be significantly influenced. They tend to feel lost and overwhelmed without the input of others. They run the risk of being "people-pleasers."

The Big Book of NLP

MP18: Associated / Dissociated

Associating refers to processing information in such a way that we experience the full emotional effect. Thinking and evaluating in this way may feel like we have been transported into a movie, experiencing the story first hand, as opposed to watching it from a distance on a DVD. All the sensory experiences will be vivid. In this mode, it is like we are experiencing the information.

Dissociation means that we distance ourselves emotionally as we go about the business of contemplating and evaluating. In this mode, we adopt a bird's-eye perspective, as if we are seeing things through someone else's eyes. We have stepped outside of the relevant situation, allowing us to observe the information.

People who associate will relive the experience while being acutely aware of all the sights, sounds, and feelings. They will exhibit anything from a mild emotional state to a very exaggerated one. They tend to display increasing physiological signs as their emotional association increases. They are usually theoretically orientated and demonstrate an aptitude for facts and figures. Some people will physically move forward in order to experience more of the event.

People who dissociate will experience a bland or mellow emotional impact. They will tend to talk about an experience as opposed to about it. They operate more rationally than emotionally. They tend to adopt a mental framework that is very open and caring towards people, since they usually "see them from the side", from a more objective perspective. They come across as spiritual and social people. They are great problem solvers, since they first separate themselves as observers, watching the situation without making it personal. Some people will physically step backwards in order to gain some perspective on a situation or to see more of what's going on in some distance.

MP19: Feeling / Thinking

This meta-program is closely related to the one previously covered. When presented with a situation, there are those who deal with it with all their senses awake, feeling the experience as they encounter it. On the opposite end of the continuum, there are those people for whom it is typical to distance themselves emotionally from the circumstance at hand and employ their cognitive skills in thinking about and assessing the situation.

People who are feelers are very in touch with their senses and are very engrossed in environments that are rich in sensory stimuli. They tend to use descriptive, emotional, and metaphorical language. They are deeply impacted on an emotional level by the environment around them. They value creativity. They are spontaneous.

People who are thinkers are enthusiastic about logic and reasoning and enjoy environments that stimulate these faculties. They tend to use philosophical and analytical language. They are constantly evaluating and analyzing the world around them. They value reason and logic. They are more predictable.

MP20: Active / Reflective / Inactive

There are those who have a tendency to process information very quickly and impulsively (active mode). For other people, the approach is more slow, thoughtful, and methodical (reflective mode). Still others display little interest or capacity in processing information at all (inactive mode).

People who use the active style position themselves as doers. They directly and quickly impact and change situations. They tend to do it first and consider it later. They often assume the roles of go-getters and pioneers. They make their fair share of mistakes, but typically achieve far more success.

People who use the reflective style are prone to analyzing and studying before acting. They can therefore come across as more passive in their approach. They live by the saying, "Fools rush in where angels fear to tread." They position themselves as evaluators.

The healthy and beneficial approach is to operate somewhere between these two styles of behavior. People who tend to respond in an inactive manner prefer to neither study nor do, but attempt to ignore and avoid altogether.

MP21: Convincer

As we gain experience in evaluating information, we ascribe significance and value to different experiences and things. This in turn results in us developing different methods with regard to being certain about something's value or significance. Can we identify exactly what causes us to consider something credible? For some people, they are convinced about the believability of something based on the idea that it looks right. Others are looking for something to sound right, and then there are others who still need something to feel right or just make sense. There are two factors that are crucial in this meta-program. Firstly, how is the relevant information received and internalized (visual, auditory, kinesthetic, or auditory digital)? Auditory digital refers to specific, identifiable symbols in the form of words and language. Secondly, what process is involved as the progression is made from just a thought to a position of certainty?

People who use visual convincers make decisions based on circumstances that look right. They act when the visual factors look attractive. They are significantly influenced by visual aids like charts, diagrams, and images.

People who use auditory convincers make decisions when things sound right. They act when the audio aspects are pleasing and appealing.

People who are auditory digital convincers rely on solid language representations (self-talk) that lead to them feeling certain and confident regarding a certain course of action.

They look for details and specific facts and reasoning. They are influenced by things like brochures, press releases, courses, and reports.

People who use a kinesthetic convincer act when a choice elicits the right internal sensation and it just feels right. They value hands-on opportunities.

MP22: Emotional Direction Sort

When some people express themselves emotionally, they do so by focusing on one specific area. Others tend to direct their emotions in numerous directions. This Meta-Program has to do with the focus and transmittance of emotions.

People who are uni-directional in their emotional focus are able to harness their emotions so that they remain focused in a direct way. They are good at linking their emotions to the specific event or person that triggered them without letting them affect non-related areas of their lives.

People who are multi-directional in their emotional focus allow a powerful emotional experience to color every area of their lives. They are prone to emotional instability. They seem to be unable to control their emotions when they are in a very emotional state.

The balanced approach to this meta-program results in healthy and appropriate emotional responses that are context-focused. An unhealthy extreme can present itself in conditions like multiple personality disorders.

MP23: Intensity

This Meta-Program has been described as the boldness or timidity factor with regard to emotional expression. It manifests as surgency (high intensity) and de-surgency (low intensity) and measures a person's emotional intensity. Some of the manifestations along the continuum of this program are things like shyness, timidity, and restraint, and on the other hand, things like boldness, confidence, and tenacity.

People who adopt the surgency mode search for and thrive on high-intensity experiences (horror movies, roller-coasters, sky-diving, etc.). They often like being scared and shocked. They enjoy being the center of attention and the limelight, which further encourages their risk-taking tendencies. They tend to be the kinds of people who throw caution to the wind. They express themselves in a carefree and happy way, and they tend to be talkative, alert, and direct when they talk.

People who adopt the de-surgency mode value safety and predictability. They stick to the rules and tend to display little creativity. They avoid drawing attention to themselves and gravitate to routine lifestyles. They are prone to paranoia when taken to the extreme, and they can allow themselves to be doormats. As they carry the burdens of the world on their backs, they speak in a way that is a little more withdrawn and introspective.

MP24: Toward / Away

The focus of this meta-program is on the direction in which people tend to move in relation to the things they place value on or the things they have no desire to value at all. There are two ways in which a person can orientate themselves with regard to their desired values. There are those who move toward their desired values. On the other hand, there are those whose focus is to move away from their undesired values. We can think here in terms of pull values and push values. Pull values motivate a person's movement in such a way that it attracts them toward a desired state of being. Push values motivate movement by driving a person away from a state of being that is unattractive or unpleasant.

People with a motivation strategy base their movement on going towards what they want. They chase after desired outcomes in such a way that their goals pull them toward the future. They adopt a "go after" mindset. They thrive on achieving, attaining, and obtaining things. When they make decisions that help them reach their goals, they do well. They are less good at knowing what to avoid.

People who adopt an away motivation strategy base their movement on shying away from what they don't want. They avoid undesirable outcomes in such a way that what they dislike propels them forward.They tend to struggle with managing priorities and chasing after goals. They adopt a "run from" mindset. They are easily sidetracked by unpleasant situations. They are most efficiently motivated by pressure and penalties.

MP25: Past Assurance / Future Possibility

Following very closely (chronologically and relationally) the previously covered Meta-Program, we encounter past assurance and future possibility. There are the kinds of people who derive great comfort and security from taking the well-worn path. These are the people who value the tried and tested approach. They can be heard saying, "If it ain't broke, don't fix it." On the flip side of the coin, or rather, at the opposite end of the continuum, we find the kinds of people who thrive on taking "the road less travelled". Their words can be heard as they start their new adventure: "Nothing ventured, nothing gained!"

People who look for past assurance are drawn toward familiarity and find comfort in things that are known. They are not big risk-takers and prefer betting on a "sure thing". They do not cope well with change, preferring to stick with the status quo. They may tend to settle for circumstances that are less than healthy as opposed to facing the potential risk of making the necessary changes.

People who look for future possibilities feel most alive when they are experiencing something new and exploring new territory. They enjoy the excitement of a gamble and don't mind throwing caution to the wind in pursuit of an adventure. They handle change well, even embracing it. They may be more likely to put themselves in dangerous situations because they act too quickly.

MP26: Options / Procedures

There are two main strategies for dealing with instructions or for accomplishing tasks. Some people prefer to follow procedures, whereas others look for options.

People who operate based on options are efficient at identifying new ways of doing things. They tend to get frustrated when following a rigid set of procedures. They are constantly looking for ways to improve on existing methods. They value innovation and creativity.

People who operate based on procedures like to work with clearly defined procedures and parameters. They are most efficient when working in a pre-determined and structured framework. They tend to lack the motivation and creativity to generate their own procedures for accomplishing tasks.

MP27: Judging / Perceiving

People adapt themselves to life and to the information that influences their personal journeys in one of two general ways: they can make deliberate plans to order, influence, and control their lives, and decide on what they like or don't, and how to go about changing it (judging mode); or they can seek to understand life as it is and unfolds and just go along with the flow (perceiving mode).

People who naturally judge and control their wants and try to make life adapt to them. They tend to live life on their own terms and in their own way. They like clearly defined parameters and a structured framework within which to live.

People who perceive tend to adapt themselves to the flow of life (floating along) through observing, perceiving, and accepting. They make a few judgment calls regarding things and drift along in a pretty easy-going way. They will typically do what feels right in the moment, as opposed to adopting a long-term plan. They like to keep their options open and have room to maneuver.

MP28: Necessity / Possibility / Desire

The language that people use has a monumental impact on the way they perceive the world around them and the experiences that they have as a result of that perception. In the field of linguistics, what is known as "modal operators" refers to the specific terms or words that a person uses that identify their mindset when it comes to relating to and operating in the world. These words illustrate the kind of mental map that a person has constructed over time that he or she uses to navigate their way through life. These words also point out the motivations that drive a person's choices and behavior. Are they motivated by necessity or desire?

The Big Book of NLP

People who operate in necessity mode typically use words like "must," "no choice," "should," etc. They exhibit operation from a platform of compulsion and obligation. They tend to view life as an inescapable burden and that they are powerless to change it. They regard their circumstances as their lot in life and will lean toward behaving and understanding in that way.

People who operate in possibility mode make use of words like "can, will, could, may," etc. They tend to project an optimistic view of life. They do what feels right to them and construct reasons accordingly. They seek out new ways of increasing their options. They largely feel that they have a measure of control over their lives and they feel empowered to choose and act.

People who operate in impossibility mode use language like "can't, mustn't, shouldn't," etc. that expresses limitations and restrictions. They have adopted a mindset in which certain avenues of conduct have been classified as off-limits and unacceptable. They tend to respond passively to situations, which restricts their responsiveness in the moment. They often make psychological impossibilities for themselves, like not being able to walk on water, for example.

People who operate in desire mode use words like "love to," "want to," "decide to," etc. They tend to embrace their circumstances and opportunities with gratitude and positivity. They have adopted a mindset that allows room for human choice and the personal ownership of their conduct and direction. They are excited and motivated by their own self-talk, unless their goals are completely unrealistic, which causes them to be disappointed and angry.

MP29: Primary Interest

People are attracted to various interests based on their personal set of preferences. When we ask a person questions regarding things like their favorite music, their favorite food, or their favorite vacation destination, we will most likely see this meta-program activated.

Primary interests are made up of the following categories: People (who); Things (what); Activity (how); Information (why); and Time (when).

Those who place the greatest value on people are primarily focused on the who. They often refer to what people think, feel, say, or do. They are very easily drawn into gossip when they take this preference to an unhealthy level. They function well socially, but tend to feel lonely when they find themselves alone.

People who place the highest value on a place are always thinking in terms of location. They ascribe loads of meaning to the environment they find themselves in. They typically devote a lot of attention to the location and décor of their homes, work spaces, etc.

People who place the highest value on things direct their attention to what their environment is comprised of. They take pride in physical things like homes and cars, as well as intangible things like status, fame, and power. They tend to pursue materialism and acclaim as a means of securing happiness. They will find it easy to take care of things while devoting less attention to nurturing social relationships.

People who place the highest value on activity are interested in activities and in experiencing things. They like to get up and go and are critical of the "couch potato" mentality. They get very annoyed when bored or faced with a lack of interesting things to do. They can take an interest in any type of sport, as long as they get to participate actively.

People who place the highest value on time regard time as a precious commodity that is not to be wasted. They are focused on the duration and chronological placement of an experience. They will often ask, "When did it happen and how long did it take?" They are always on time. They get upset when someone is late.

People who place the highest value on information want to learn something valuable and seek to be able to apply it in useful ways. They are interested in deepening their understanding of things or in broadening their skill-set, in growing as individuals.

MP30: Perfection / Optimization / Skepticism

People adopt different styles of thinking and feeling and then decide to go after their goals in life. Some manage the business of setting and reaching goals in a perfectionist style. For others, an optimization style comes more naturally, and for others still, they attempt to avoid the setting of goals at all.

People who adopt the perfectionism approach never feel satisfied with their performance or achievement. They tend to frustrate themselves by setting goals that are unrealistically high. They are typically focused primarily on the end result and rob themselves of the joy and experience of the challenge as part of the process on their way toward that result. They are prone to making harsh judgments against themselves and others when their high standards are not met. They can tend to procrastinate as a defense mechanism against performing a task poorly... "Best not to attempt it at all rather than try and fail." They tend to start projects well, but then get distracted and frustrated by the flaws, or weighed down by the details.

People who adopt the optimization approach embrace a more pragmatic approach to achieving their goals. They just work on doing the best they can with the materials, skills, and time at their disposal, and they do not fret about things beyond that. They tend to break down goals into small steps so that they can enjoy incremental stages of success along the way. They appreciate the value of finding joy in the journey as much as in the result or outcome. They are good at going with the flow and tend to achieve good results because they are not overly concerned about producing the "perfect" result. They run the risk of not paying attention to real problems and limitations because they have a positive mentality that is taken too far.

People who adopt a defeatist approach prefer to avoid the business of goal setting and achieving altogether, and view the whole subject through pessimistic lenses. They don't think much about their future much and fail to take constructive steps toward bringing it about. They avoid participating in attempts to better themselves or their strategies because they expect the worst to happen anyway.

People who adopt the realist approach relate to goals only in terms of information and facts. They focus less on the dreaming and visualizing components of goal-setting and more on the bare facts involved. They do so in primarily a sensory-based manner.

MP31: Value Buying Sort

When dealing with the business of buying or deciding to buy something, there are typically four values that are in operation. These values tend to be at the forefront of people's minds when they are reaching a decision with regard to whether or not to purchase something. They are: cost, quality, time, and convenience. Different people will have different areas of focus as they make their purchases. Some people will employ a combination of these values to aid them in reaching a decision. When these values are applied to the matter of buying something, they are often at odds with each other. Sometimes a person will start out focusing on one value, like convenience, but later find other values, like cost and/or quality, impacting their decision more than they expected.

MP32: Responsibility

There are different ways in which people think about, behave, and feel with regard to the concept of responsibility. Some people want and are drawn to responsibility and therefore move toward it and think about their behavior, language, and feelings in terms of feeling responsible for things. Others have no desire for responsibility and find the notion of it very unattractive. For these people, the idea of responsibility elicits strong feelings of discomfort and even pain. People who are inclined this way move away from responsibility and even consistently shift blame away from themselves in order to not have to deal with it. They even consider other people or situations responsible for their own attitudes, feelings, and conduct.

The Big Book of NLP

People who adopt an over-responsible approach take on the role of a caretaker. They are efficient at problem-solving and have compassion and want to improve circumstances for others. They can fall into co-dependent relationships with those who are habitually irresponsible. It's possible for them to take on the responsibilities of other people and to send a message that makes people doubt their dependability.

People who adopt an under-responsible approach fail to own and accept their own actions, language, and emotions. They tend to rely on others to take care of them and be responsible for them. They tend to consider themselves incapable of taking care of themselves. They can be guilty of entertaining a victim mentality, which can overflow into being demanding and pointing blame. They can, in extreme cases, hold others responsible for their happiness and generally feel that the world owes them.

People who adopt a balanced-responsible approach are able to appropriately and effectively respond to themselves and to others. They have the capacity to maturely determine when to give and when to receive.

MP33: Trust / Distrust

Some people, when meeting a person for the first time, automatically extend a certain measure of trust toward them, believing that people are generally good, decent, and reliable, unless convincing evidence to the contrary emerges. Other people have a sense of caution and distrust when they meet new people. They think people will let them down, so they lean toward caution as a way to protect themselves.

People who are trusting are comfortable embracing strangers and welcoming them into their lives. They will come across as warm, friendly, and genuinely interested in the person they are meeting or conversing with. They can fall into the trap of extending trust towards people too quickly and impulsively, running the risk of being taken advantage of.

People who are distrusting will be cautious towards new people, carefully observing them and evaluating their motivations, behavior, and language. They can come across as cold and distant, making the stranger feel unwelcome and even threatened. They tend to keep people away with their guarded attitude, which makes them think that people are generally unfriendly and dangerous.

MP34: Extro / Ambi / Intro

As we all know, life has a way of running us down over time if we don't take care of ourselves adequately. Stresses, pressures, deadlines, responsibilities, all these things contribute to making us feel quite run down and weary over time. People have various ways, from a social and relational perspective, in which they renew their energy and vitality. Some people feel charged up when they are in the company of other people, gaining strength from their company (extroverts). Others feel the need to withdraw when feeling weary. They need to be able to close a door, or to escape to some place away from the hustle and bustle of life, and to be alone. They feel rejuvenated when they have quiet time by themselves (introverts). Then there are those who benefit from a combination of both, depending on what they feel drawn to at the time (ambiverts).

People who adopt an extrovert approach seek out company when they are in need of renewing themselves. They draw on the energy and company of others and feel energized in a social setting. They are drawn to events or parties where there are lots of people gathered; they love the energy of a crowd. They tend to become clingy and suffocating when adopting the extrovert mode to the extreme. They tend to perceive the alone-ness of solitude as the hurt of loneliness.

People who adopt an introverted approach require their space and quiet when they are in desperate need of rest and relaxation. They feel comforted and calm in the context of solitude, particularly when they need to recover from stress or pressure. They can become anti-social and disconnected when taking their introverted tendencies to an extreme. They tend to perceive the energy of the crowd as shallow and insincere.

People who adopt an ambivert approach tend to judge each need to recharge on its own merit. They can gain comfort, strength, and renewal from the company of others, or from being by themselves, depending on the occasion and the circumstances at the time. They value and see the benefits of company and solitude.

MP35: Ind. / TP / Mng

Some people prefer to stay independent, some value the process of team play, and others still prefer to operate in a managing capacity. Identifying a person's natural mode of operation within the context of this meta-program is of great benefit when it comes to assessing their suitability for working independently, working as part of a team, or managing others. Also revealed is a person's adaptability in inter-personal relationships.

Have you ever been asked to oversee a task that required delegating work to others? Did you feel that you had a good idea of what those who reported to you needed to do their jobs effectively? Did you find it easy to give people instructions and direct their efforts, or did the experience make you uncomfortable?

People who are effective and managed will answer "yes" to all three of the above mentioned questions. They are skilled at managing both themselves and others. They are very aware of the direction they and others need to take in order to achieve success and are comfortable with sharing their views boldly. They tend to want to take charge in a project-orientated environment and expect others to adopt the same strategies as they do.

People who are effective at working independently will answer "Yes, no, no." to the above questions. They are aware of what it takes to achieve the goal in question, but lack the motivation to actually lead and manage. They are effective at motivating themselves and taking responsibility for their actions. They possess a large resource of self-control and discipline.

People who are dependent workers will answer, "No, yes, no-or-yes." They tend to rely on someone telling them what needs to be done. They may not feel confident about their opinion of what needs to be done, may simply lack the intuition to recognise the correct strategy at all, or naturally function in a passive mode, waiting on instructions. They usually have no problem following instructions once they have been provided.

People who display potential to be effective managers will answer the three questions, "Yes, yes-or-no, no." They feel confident in knowing what others need to do in order to achieve their goal, but hesitant with regard to sharing their thoughts and/or suggestions. They feel threatened or intimidated by the idea of managing others.

People who operate most effectively as team players will answer, "Sometimes, sometimes, sometimes." They may feel comfortable in a manager role, or not, depending on the context and factors at the time. They may feel comfortable sharing the responsibility for driving the success of the group. They enjoy the relational aspect of working as part of a team and the energy that they draw from it. They place a high value on family and togetherness.

MP36: Satir Modes

The work of Virginia Satir has led to the identification of five distinguishable styles of communication. Satir noted that communication has to do with both information and the style in which that information is relayed. Four of these modes are considered ineffective and poor in terms of producing positive results. These are placating, computing, distracting, and blaming. Though generally unproductive, these four modes have the potential to be put to constructive use. Satir highlighted the generally healthy mode of communication as leveling.

People who adopt a placating approach are afraid of being rejected or abandoned by others, or that the people around them will direct anger toward them. They consequently use language that is intended to win the favor of others, always trying to gain approval, constantly apologetic, and never confrontational or disagreeable. They adopt an attitude that appears to suggest that they are useless and hopeless.

The computing mode refers to those who detach themselves from their emotions and attempt to respond to situations in a logical and controlled way that is not influenced by their feelings. People who adopt a computing approach are intent on delivering responses that are cool and calculated. Physiologically speaking, they tend to feel cool and dry. They keep their voices even and make use of abstract language. They have often developed a fear of and caution regarding their own emotions.

The distracting mode refers to behaving and responding in an unpredictable manner that jolts and interrupts oneself and others. People who adopt a distracting approach tend to shift between the other behavioral modes quickly and without prior indication. They are known to say or do things that are in no way relevant to the language and actions of others. They tend to feel dizzy and panicked physiologically. They use a tone of voice that is erratic and unstable, varying in pitch for no apparent reason. They can appear to have significant psychological issues, which makes relating to them challenging.

The blaming mindset refers to constantly looking for and seeing problems and faults, bossing others around, and trying to manipulate and control others. People who adopt a blaming approach believe that they are better than everyone else. They project the message that everyone else is to blame for everything that goes wrong. They generally perceive that nobody is concerned about them. They tend to feel a physiological tightness and stress that is indicative of high blood pressure. They usually have loud, hard, and abrasive voices.

Leveling refers to the healthy communication mode of expressing oneself in an assertive manner so that one's language and behavior are direct and straightforward, in keeping with one's honest and authentic state. People who adopt the leveling approach express themselves in such a way that there is harmony between their actions, words, tone of voice, and postures and gestures. They tend to be easy to understand and relate to, projecting themselves as "What you see is what you get" kinds of people. They contribute to relationships that are safe, mature, and capable of genuine intimacy.

MP37: Congruent / Incongruent

When people respond to their surrounding environment, they can do so congruently or incongruently. Their manner of response has to do with their chosen style and the energy expended in the process.

People who respond congruently exhibit behavior that mirrors their internal emotional state. They would respond with calm and relaxation, for example, in a tranquil and peaceful environment that inspires those calming emotions.

People who respond incongruently behave in ways that are in opposition to their thoughts and feelings. They would exhibit calm and relaxed behavior, for example, when they are actually feeling stressed and agitated. They tend to have a conflicting perception of their environment in their mind, asserting itself in opposition to their conduct.

MP38: Comp / Coop / Polarity / Meta

In this course, we have discussed the fact that meta-programs represent tendencies of behavior and responses along a continuum, fluctuating and changing over time depending on the situational context. We express ourselves in relation to people, data, things, and situations in a number of ways. These styles of expression include competitive, cooperative, polarity, and meta.

People who adopt a competitive response process have the relevant thoughts, experiences, and feelings in terms of competition and comparison. They tend to ask questions like, "Who do I consider to be the best, the first, the strongest, etc." They can display a sense of excitement regarding any situation, which they may be able to turn into a competition. They have a win-or-lose mentality.

People who adopt a cooperative response have an attitude of helping those around them to share the experience at hand. They tend to ask questions like, "What can I do to make this experience more meaningful for everyone involved?" They do their best to secure a win-win outcome.

People who adopt a polarity response base their choice or response on opposing those that are presented to them, flipping to the opposite end of the relevant behavioral spectrum. They will tend to respond with stress and tension in a calm environment, for example. They will find or create reasons why the situation they are presented with isn't real or cannot possibly last, therefore choosing the other direction. They enjoy competing and will often adopt a competitive mode of behavior.

People who adopt a meta response evaluate situations at a higher logical level as a result of having thoughts about the situation at hand, and not just responding to it.

How flexible we become in our behavior will help us switch between these different types of communication and emotions at will.

MP39: Social Reaction

People can respond in a social setting in one of the following ways: actively (proactively and reactively), reflectively, inactively, or both.

People who are socially active take action immediately. They can tend to respond impulsively without giving the situation appropriate thought. They make their share of mistakes, but also achieve significant successes. They speak, think, and behave quickly. They like to achieve results, preferring to strike while the iron is hot. They operate in a proactive capacity when embracing this mode in a balanced manner. They behave in a self-referential way, generally speaking.

People who are socially inactive are overtly cautious in a group setting to the point where their involvement and participation are paralyzed. They procrastinate to the point where practically nothing gets accomplished. They tend to be viewed as distant, disinterested, and anti-social.

People who are socially reflective like to assess and observe a group before getting directly involved. They prefer not to let too much time pass without taking any action at all. They tend to feel relatively insecure and unsure of themselves. They fear making mistakes and, therefore, are cautious about taking action. They run the risk of becoming inactive as a result of unhealthy procrastination. They are rarely pioneers in the realm of business. They are most efficient in environments that demand evaluation and reflection.

People who are socially balanced are confident in chasing their goals in a group context and are able to do so with a healthy amount of reflection during the process. They are open to receiving feedback before they commit to a course of action.

MP40: Things / Systems / Info / People

In the realm of work, career, vocation, etc. (the prominent activities in our lives), we have our preferences with regard to what we would like to work with. These can be things, systems, people, or information. Highlighting the factors that made a past work situation or environment very rewarding and meaningful for you will point you in the direction of which of the above-mentioned modes matters most to you.

People who value working with things use language that focuses on things as opposed to the other elements. They focus primarily on the task at hand, and less on people or emotions. They are concerned with achieving results and getting the job done.

People who value working with systems are primarily concerned with processes, procedures, the synergy between various components, etc. They pay relatively little attention to people and their feelings when weighed against the procedures and systems involved.

People who value working with other people are mindful of the thoughts, health, and emotions of those around them. They interact effectively socially and have highly developed interpersonal skills. They come across as friendly and are willing and ready to assist others.

People who value working with information are interested in the specific details and criteria that are involved in the project or task at hand. It is common for them to be analytical and to be good at working with facts and figures.

MP41: Quantitative / Qualitative

This Meta-Program sheds light on the characteristics of the comparisons people use when weighing things against one another. It surfaces whenever a person enters into the process of choosing between two or more courses of action. These comparisons are made in broad ways: quantitatively and qualitatively.

People who evaluate in a quantitative way will respond to questions by speaking in reference to rank, placing, order, measurements, and the like. They access the sensory modes (#6) as their consciousness focuses on external standards. They begin their comparative process with concrete data and therefore use inductive reasoning (#1).

People who evaluate in a qualitative way use language that highlights the quality of an experience: enjoyable, terrible, better, poor, etc. They have their consciousness focus on internal factors, such as values, meanings, etc. (intuition, #6). When they compare things, they start at a global level, so they use deductive or abductive reasoning (#1).

MP42: Knowledge Sort

This Meta-Program sheds light on how a person concludes that they are able to accomplish something and where they gather the information for that conclusion. Rather than dealing with how a person perceives and "knows" that something is true, it has to do with the source of the data that the person uses to arrive at their decision. Some people go about gathering information via modeling, some via conceptualizing, some through seeing it being demonstrated, some through experiencing it, and still others through having it validated by an objective authority.

People who gather information via modeling seek out those who have a relevant knowledge base as well as the capacity to produce results in that area.

People who gather information through conceptualizing typically have a solid internal dialogue and self-referencing approach. They seek out information by studying, discussing, investigating, thinking, etc.

People who rely on demonstrations to gather information are most impressed with what they personally observe and experience.

Those who gather information through experience feel more confident about the information at hand when they have the opportunity to interact with it through their senses. After they have had a chance to evaluate it through action, it feels reliable to them.

People who lean on an authoritative source to gather their information put a huge amount of reliance on the opinion of the relevant authority concerning the information. If the authority figure validates it and confirms it as being true, then it is true in the mind of the person who adopts this approach.

MP43: Closure / Non-Closure

When people process information, they don't always follow the process through to completion. There may be time constraints, the information may be insufficient, or the reliability of the information may be in question. This meta-program has to do with how people deal with closure, or the lack thereof. It focuses on the internal experience of coping with something that is unresolved or incomplete. Some people are highly motivated to seek closure, others less so. In the event that closure cannot be reached for whatever reason, some people are more comfortable with moving on than others.

People who operate in a closure style are more efficient at and enthusiastic about the final stages of a project. They tend to want all their business neatly wrapped up at the end of the day. They think in terms of certainty and absolutes.

People who operate in a non-closure style are more enthusiastic and focused at the beginning and in the middle of a project. They tend to be unaffected by a lack of closure. They are comfortable waiting for something that has started to eventually reach a point of finality.

MP44: Social Presentation

People who go through life with a system with regard to relating to other people or groups have been described (Cattell, 1989) as being artless, friendly, spontaneous, and naive, or artful, shrewd, and socially acceptable in their behavior and responses.

People who operate as shrewd and artful consider the impression they make on others to be very important to them. They hold things like politeness, etiquette, and procedures in high regard. They dislike revealing too much about themselves and expressing their thoughts and feelings. They tend to possess lots of social ambition, doing their best to climb the social ladder. They run the risk of behaving in a selfish, insincere, and manipulative way.

People who operate as sincere and artless are unimpressed by social presentation and regard it as superficial and hypocritical. They tend to have limited or no social ambitions and are less shaken up when disappointed by others. They can come across as crude and unrefined because of their lack of social graces. They run the risk of behaving rudely and inappropriately in public when this mode is taken to an extreme. They can develop an anti-social behavioral strategy.

MP45: Power / Affiliation / Achievement

This meta-program deals with how a person adapts to the behavior directed toward them by those who are in a position of dominance (bossiness, sarcasm, insults, etc.). It sheds light on the style a person uses in handling power and influence, or not.

People who adopt a power strategy derive pleasure and satisfaction from dominating, manipulating, and competing. They seek out the feeling of superiority that is associated with this style. They see everything in terms of win or lose. They are driven not only by their own success, but also the failure of others when the mode is taken to an extreme.

People who adopt an affiliation strategy navigate relationships by utilizing cooperation and respect. They are driven to create and nurture healthy relationships with others through consideration and empathy. They think in terms of win-win.

People who use a strategy called "achievement" are more concerned with getting the job done and getting the results they want than they are with having fun.

MP46: Value Sort

The way in which people value things takes shape from their thoughts, ideas, and comprehension of what they consider to be important. Through the valuation process, people ascribe worth to things, people, experiences, etc. Values arise when we think of thoughts of worth, value, or significance about other specific thoughts. In other words, the process of value-creation occurs at a level beyond the normal thought process regarding people, things, and situations. Here we are referring to thoughts about other thoughts. In doing so, people experience states of being that are above and beyond the thoughts upon which their values are based. They experience things like concern, appreciation, love, passion, etc. In a sense, values function on two levels. The first is the initial thought process itself, based on one of the Meta-Programs we've been discussing, and the second involves the thought process about the worth and importance of the initial behavior, feeling, or communication.

Taking this idea further, people believe in the values they have embraced (in their significance and worth) and therefore trust in their values and allow them to dramatically influence their emotions and behavior. A person will value every meta-program that they make habitual use of. The fact that they use it regularly indicates that they have attached some value or significance to it. The list of potential values is difficult to determine, because whatever a person believes to be important, they transform it into a value. These could include what could be considered fundamental values (survival, love, belonging, etc.), or things like physical fitness, alone-time, or friendship. Appealing to a person's personal values will make your interaction with them significantly more powerful and influential. After all, there are very few people (if any) who would not respond with enthusiasm and a positive attitude to their own values.

MP47: Strong-Will / Compliant / Stubborn

When people are told to do something (as opposed to being asked), they can choose to respond in a number of different ways. Some people are strong-willed, some are compliant, and others are stubborn in their approach.

People who adopt a strong-willed approach find it difficult when they are told to do anything. They will push back against any information that they are in disagreement with. They are assertive and confident regarding their own views and opinions. They may have their ability to accurately perceive information hindered by various belief filters at work within them that interpret instructions as insults, manipulations, etc.

People who adopt a compliant approach promptly accept instruction in a receptive, mature, and open manner. They can fall prey to manipulation and control when taking this program to its extremes.

The Big Book of NLP

People who adopt a stubborn approach will tend to resist instruction purely for resistance's sake. They immediately react in a resisting manner when they hear language that expects or demands cooperation. They demonstrate a combative attitude that is motivated by pride, arrogance, or laziness, rather than logic and/or values.

MP48: Conditional / Unconditional

One of the most fundamental states of awareness has to do with that which deals with our "sense of self". Our understanding, perceptions, and definition of our "self" reveal a pivotal area from which we do our evaluating, processing, distinguishing, and valuing. These ways of understanding ourselves typically take place at a level that is beyond our conscious mind. To assist in the understanding of this concept, the following terms and definitions will be helpful. Self-esteem refers to the assessment of our own worth and dignity. This ranges from feeling entirely rotten and worthless at one extreme to feeling incredibly valuable at the other. Some people mentally assess their value based on temporary and unstable factors or upon unconditional factors. Self-confidence has to do with the degree to which we feel assured of our own skills, talents, and work. It refers to the faith that we have in ourselves regarding our skill and ability at various things. Self-confidence functions conditionally and takes shape from our positive and negative encounters and experiences with regard to education, social interaction, beliefs, etc.

Self-efficacy deals with our sense of efficiency, or our capacity to use our consciousness to effectively navigate the world and all it presents to us. Self-conscience has to do with how we orientate ourselves as moral or ethical beings regarding right and wrong. When a person fails to distinguish clearly between these conceptual representations of self, identity confusions arise, which can complicate their sense of who they are as people.When a person has low self-esteem and simultaneously attempts to improve their assessment of themselves through competencies and skills, he or she inevitably steps onto the "hamster wheel" – deriving worth from their achievements.

These temporal conditions make for an unstable and inharmonious appraisal of their worth. As a result, this person will never feel genuinely confident in any kind of sustainable way. In the event that they fail the test that they have crafted for themselves too many times, they may reach a state where they feel permanently and irrevocably devoid of worth and dignity. Beyond this potential outcome, the above-mentioned process can lead to extreme states of either self-loathing or arrogance. It leads to the idea that people are not valuable simply by virtue of the fact that they are human beings with inherent and unquestionable worth. Instead, people are seen as having to earn the right to be valued. When a person is mindful and aware of their inherent value as a human being, however, they are empowered to live in a manner that is free of self-criticism and hypocrisy. Recognizing your own worth leads to a balanced center of value and dignity that makes it possible for you to live and act in a healthy way.

MP49: Self-Confidence: High / Low

Self-confidence is, in essence, our faith in, or certainty regarding, our ability to do things well. Whereas self-esteem has to do with our mental assessment of ourselves, self-confidence has more to do with an emotional or experiential fact about ourselves. Self-confidence relates to what we are capable of doing, and therefore highlights human do-ness, as opposed to human being-ness. Self-confidence can be found in the life of any person living a relatively ordinary life. Every normal person has a number of things that they feel confident about doing... from the simple and basic, to the more complex and specialized. People who adopt the behavioral mode of pessimism, or those with a perfectionist approach to life, may fail to see many of the things that they are good at doing. This only reinforces their lack of confidence and dramatically skews their perspective regarding what they are capable of. Those with low self-confidence will often express doubts and uncertainties regarding their abilities or opinions. They may come across as timid and sensitive in their language style. Those with healthy confidence, on the other hand, will sound sure of themselves and use definite and assertive language.

The Big Book of NLP

MP50: Mind / Emotion / Body / Role

Different people have different ideas regarding the concept of "self", and they also use different factors in defining themselves. The way in which a person defines him or herself (how they do it and what they conclude) plays a crucial role in driving their behavior, emotions and language. People can define themselves using any combination of the facets mentioned above. People who adopt an Associated approach (#18) will tend to define themselves based on their feelings, whereas those who Disassociate (#18) will tend to place too much of an emphasis on their feelings. A person who uses the Choice strategy (#46) in the strong-will continuum will typically identify himself or herself based on their will. And so on.

MP51: Self-Integrity

People adopt different strategies for living up to their ideals and doing their values justice, and also go about determining how successful they are in doing so in different ways. This awareness that a person has of his or her conduct as weighed against their values gives rise to a sense of internal harmony and peace, or one of inner conflict and emotional dissonance.

People who live up to their values experience a sense of inner harmony and congruence. They enjoy a strong degree of self-acceptance and of feeling centered. They exhibit behavior that matches their language and intentions. They are given additional mental and emotional resources to devote to the pursuit of their values.

People who neglect their values feel conflicted and torn on the inside. They tend to find it harder to look at their reflection in a mirror and like what they see. They display incongruence between what they say and how they behave. They direct a lot of negative energy internally as they judge and fight with themselves.

MP52: Past / Present / Future

In most cultures around the world, people identify three "time zones" as they relate to things that have already happened, things that are happening, and things that will happen in the future. These zones are referenced in the language and temporal tenses of the past, present, and future. An additional, conceptual type of "time" occurs, known as "atemporal." People tend to think of one of these "time zones" as being more important than the others in their minds.

People who focus on the "past" are mindful of past experiences and the significance that those experiences hold for them. They tend to use language that is rich in past references and tenses. They place a lot of value on history as well as tradition.

People who focus on the "present" use language that is rich in present tense and references. They may live in the present excessively to the degree that they fail to consider the future consequences of their actions or their future goals.

People who focus on the "future" use language that is rich in future tense and references. They can become excessively focused on the future, failing to take the necessary steps in the present that will create the future of their desire.

People who do not focus on "time" live outside of time consciousness.

MP53: "in-Time" / "Through-Time"

People of most cultures around the world understand historical "time" and its length from event to event as a "time-line". This understanding of time causes people to perceive time as either moving through them so that they have the sense of being immersed in it or as staying apart from them so that they live outside of time. The former refers to the "In"

Time" processing strategy (experiencing "time" in an associated way), and the latter to the "Out of "time"" processing strategy. When a person perceives "time" as being outside of them and at a distance, they have a more objective perspective on it. These aspects of a person's processing have to do with the manner in which he or she stores memories.

People who adopt a "through time" approach think of "time" as having a single directional flow along a continuum. They perceive time as occurring sequentially along a continuous line, thus giving them awareness of the duration of an event relative to another. They usually have dissociated memories. They tend to sort things chronologically and are comfortable with structure, rules, and procedures. They tackle their responsibilities and decision-making in a basic, systematic way.

People who adopt an "in time" approach tend to store their future ahead of them and their pasts behind them. They think of their time-lines as moving through them, so that they find themselves in the line. They generally use associated memories and have little awareness regarding the duration of events. They generally process things in a random fashion. They will often get caught up in their own world and lose track of time.

MP54: Sequential / Random

In this meta-program, we deal with the manner in which we access our memories. There are two primary patterns of operation: those who adopt a random access process and those who adopt a sequential access process.

People who make use of a random access pattern jump from one memory to another with ease. They store their memories in an unrelated way so that they can easily switch across boundaries separating people, places, and content. They archive their memories by comparing different events that occurred at different periods.

People who make use of a sequential access pattern store their memories in a linear and connected way. They keep asking themselves, "What happened then?" or "what happened right before?" They do not move randomly between unconnected memories. They can encounter a degree of difficulty when accessing memories because they need to begin in some place that often doesn't relate to the memory they want, and then they have to move linearly until the correct memory is identified.

MP55: Ego / Strength

"Ego has been defined as a set of cognitive and perceptual functions that serve adaptive purposes as we grow in our ability to respond to our environments. Others have referred to ego as being a problem-solving mechanism that facilitates interaction between needs and the environment. To the degree that "intelligence" is defined as the capacity to make accurate judgments, this also explains, to a degree, the core of "ego strength."

People who adopt The Instability Approach are easily rattled by the smallest problems that they encounter. They tend to perceive almost anything as an incredible pain and challenge and constantly worry and fret about it, feel vulnerable towards it, and constantly complain about it. They exhibit the kind of behavior that everyone gravitates toward in the infancy and childhood stages of life. They embrace childish coping mechanisms for responding to real or perceived problems (tantrums, mood swings, impatience, etc.).

People who adopt The Stability Approach embrace a more philosophical attitude toward life and pursue worthwhile goals while being mindful of the fact that problems will arise and that they are a normal part of the human experience. They remain calm and collected in the face of challenges and maintain an objective perspective. As soon as they have a problem, they start looking for ways to solve it. They spend very little time worrying or fretting about it.

MP56: Morality

People display different approaches when it comes to dealing with issues relating to ethics, morals, integrity, etc. Some people are always mindful of the responsibility to embrace conduct that is honest and good, whereas others seem completely oblivious to any such need (whether intentionally or unintentionally). Considering the relevant continuum in relation to this meta-program, there are those on the one hand who adopt a conscientious approach in taking responsibility for their moral and ethical failures. On the other hand, there are those who find the unconscientious approach attractive and who feel no sense of responsibility when behaving in a manner that hurts or disappoints others. The conscientious sort of person pays attention to the rightness and wrongness of situations, in particular those that genuinely go against or adhere to legitimate moral codes. That person has a well-developed sense of responsibility and is personally committed to embracing right conduct in the various situations that arise. That person has the capacity to turn away from immediate, unhealthy or harmful pleasures and to focus instead on steady integrity over time. That person tends to be too judgmental of him or herself or others when adopting this approach to the extreme. The conscientious person is guided by a strong, internal moral map. He or she is the kind of person that attempts to embrace integrity when they are in the public eye as well as when they have privacy and solitude. They believe in doing the right thing, even if that means doing the difficult thing. Their reward is the feeling of peace and inner harmony that comes from being able to look at their reflection in a mirror and be at peace with what they see.

The unconscientious sort of person tends to be blind to true guilt, or is intent on dismissing it deliberately. That person is in the habit of ignoring rules, ethics, morality, etc. That person lives in a selfish, self-indulgent way and cares little about who or what gets damaged in the process. That person develops a reputation as being untrustworthy and unreliable. That person leans toward sociopathic and criminal activities when adopting this program to its extreme. The unconscientious person is primarily concerned about one thing: looking out for number one. They are intent on pursuing pleasure at almost any cost, and don't care what they need to do in order to achieve it. They are often treated as mere objects to be used in the pursuit of chasing after their narcissistic nirvana. There are antisocial and amoral people who act only when they stand to gain something as a result.

MP57: Causational Sort

Specifically, this meta-program is concerned with how a person perceives the "cause" of a situation or an experience.

It is difficult for people who believe in no causation to comprehend the world in terms of consequences or cause-and-effect relationships. They believe that things just happen the way they do in real life.

They believe that the world operates at random because there is no evidence of any kind of intelligence intervening to influence the process.

Some believe that they live in a framed system where everything happens for a reason and as a result of something else, while others believe that they live in a chaotic system where everything happens for no reason at all. Mathematics, physics, and chemistry are among the fields where they gravitate because they deal with absolutes and certainties.

They believe that the world and people all over the world are guided by some sort of intelligent design, and they believe that it has something to do with them and their situation.

Multiple causes and effects are considered to operate in an open system by those who believe in the Multi-Cause-Effect theory.

They believe that in almost every circumstance, a multitude of causes (some expected, others unexpected) contribute to producing some kind of effect. These individuals have the ability and the proclivity to think about things that do not make sense when viewed in terms of absolute causality.

The belief in personal cause and effect causes people to be more cognizant of the ways in which they themselves influence and cause different circumstances. They have a proclivity to adopt a self-referential behavioral response as well as the approach of balanced responsibility. By taking this program to its logical conclusion, they may find themselves in the position of being overly responsible.

The Big Book of NLP

In the case of those who believe in external cause-and-effect, they conclude that factors outside of their control are responsible for the outcomes that they encounter in life.

They believe that they are at the mercy of the tides of life, and that the only thing they can do is put on their life jackets and ride along for the ride, to whatever destination and outcome the tides of life lead them to.

People who believe in the magical believe that everything is the result of forces and/or beings that exist outside of our known world and dimensions, and that they are responsible for everything. It is superstition that motivates their responses, and they are motivated by a desire to please and appease whatever "powers that be" are at work in the world.

They place their trust in the repetition of secret information that will change their lives and make them better and better over the long term.

People who believe in correlation are opposed to the belief in causation, and prefer instead to consider so-called "causes" to be merely correlations rather than causes in themselves. They are able and willing to see the connections between things, factors, people, and so on, but they don't try to figure out what caused them.

Meta Questions

This is an art form, and that is why it is an essential part of master practitioner training (when done adequately). A meta question is investigating the value of a stimulus, but not in an evaluative form, but only as a direction to enhance performance. Meta question examples

"How can this be useful right now?"

How can I reach this level of X (excitement, joy, creativity, etc.) more easily and/or faster?

"What states are the most resourceful in this situation?"

"How can I reduce the chain of states from non-useful to useful?" (e.g., from feeling devalued to feeling empowered)

How can I reframe an unfair criticism so that it reflects on the blamer rather than on myself?

"How might you re-direct that anger so that you could turn it on and off at will?"

"How can I make this skill a part of my own repertoire?"

Meta Transformation

Source: L. Michael Hall

Select a behavior for transformation.

Identify underlying intentions.

Identify related outcomes.

Identify meta-outcomes in the form of high states.

Describe your ultimate transcendent meta-state.

Step into your transcendent meta-state.

Fully experience your meta-state.

Experience this as a way of being in the world.

Test.

Create personality-wide changes by taking transformation to a meta level.

STEPs 1-4: Stepping Up.

1. Select a behavior for transformation. Choose a behavior for this pattern that you wish to change; one that is unpleasant or ineffective.

2. Identify underlying intentions. Determine what motives help to maintain this behavior. Remember that these can be the motives of a part that has positive intentions, but that makes ineffective or un-resourceful choices in pursuing those intentions. Keep an eye out

for the results that have some indirect benefit, even though they are less obvious outcomes of the behavior pattern (secondary gain).

3. Identify related outcomes. Keep asking the following question until your answers begin to loop: "What do you hope to accomplish, experience or have as a result of this behavior?" Then begin asking, "What do you want from this result, that is even more important to you?" and keep on asking until you begin to experience a loop.

4. Identify meta-outcomes in the form of high states. You are seeking meta-outcomes. You will know that you have identified them when the answers to these questions are states. When you begin looping among high states, you have completed this part of the pattern.

Steps 5-9: Stepping Down

5. Describe your ultimate transcendent meta-state. Describe the state you would experience if you achieved all of the higher states stemming from your meta-outcomes. Use all sense modalities, including self-talk.

6. Step into your transcendent meta-state. Amplify the state as much as possible, and imagine stepping into this state as if you could step into the future where you have achieved your meta-outcomes.

7. Fully experience your meta-state. Continue to amplify your meta-state, experiencing it fully, as if you could absorb it into your body as pervasive energy.

8. Experience this as a way of being in the world. Return to your immediate life situation and Future Pace into your immediate future, with this meta-state pervading all that you are and do. Experience how you express it in all your activities and way of being.

9. Test. In the coming days and weeks, discover how this experience alters how you experience your life, and how your behavior changes in the area of your life that had the undesired behavior pattern.

The Big Book of NLP

Mini-Trance Inductions

You can help a client enter a rapid TDS by asking, "What happens when you imagine X?". For example, if the client says she would like to have a better relationship with her husband, you may ask, "What happens when you imagine yourself speaking and behaving within the story of a better relationship with your husband?" What do you feel? What do you do? What is your tone of voice? What do you see, hear, and sense? " This question can also serve to further explore a person's desired outcome as a part of the well-defined outcome process. On many occasions, a client will come up with new insights as they play the scene in their mind. As they do so, it is a chance to use misdirection and hypnotic language to further strengthen the positive changes they wish to make.

Mirroring: Method

Enhance your ability to establish rapport and to model excellence. This pattern builds a useful "second position" with another person. This ability is essential for modeling others and developing intuition in understanding the internal experiences of those you model.Here's a quote about mirroring and rapport from the book NLP: The New Technology of Achievement, by NLP Comprehensive, Steve Andreas, and Charles Faulkner: "Fitting in is a powerful human need. We all have many examples of these behaviors, because we do them already. They are all based on some form of being similar, familiar, or alike. Finding ways to be alike reduces our differences, and so we find the common ground upon which to base a relationship. "

1. Select a subject (person) for a conversation. Don't tell them that you will be mirroring them.

2. Carry on the conversation while mirroring the other person.

During the conversation, ask their opinions on various topics. Mirror their physiology, including factors such as the tenor and cadence of their speech and body language such as gestures. Do this subtly. If you need help maintaining the dialog, use active listening. This involves showing that you understand what they are saying by rephrasing their contributions. Beginning with a phrase such as, "You mean..." or "So you're saying..." As you mirror, add elements such as their breathing as much as possible. Notice how you feel as the rapport between you two develops.

3. Test your intuition and understanding of the person. Assess your rapport-building skills. Test your gut reaction to what they say. Can you foresee their thoughts? To test the effect on rapport, try expressing your own opinion. If you express your opinion tentatively, the person may enjoy reassuring you of its correctness and demonstrating their mastery of the subject. This makes you a positive anchor. Highly effective rapport can learn information about the other person from their subconscious, making them feel psychic. This is great for modeling.

4. Exercise your influence by shifting your attitude and physiology. Test your ability to influence others through rapport. Try shifting your attitude and physiology (e.g., breath pace, facial expression, and body language) in what you consider to be a desirable or possible direction. For example, shifting from a resentful or angry state gradually into a more constructive or powerful state. If you do this with some care, the other party is likely to shift with you. This has enormous value in areas such as sales, leadership, and coaching.

5. Test. Explore these skills of "pacing and leading" in your relationships. Think of situations in which you could use these skills to improve your personal life or career performance. Notice what outcomes you get, and refine them as you go.

Mirroring: Behavioral

In behavioral mirroring, you match behaviors that have symbolic meaning. They are mostly subconscious. In fact, the more subconscious they are, the easier they are to mirror. After all, no one can think you're imitating him or her if you're imitating something they don't know you're doing, can they? But what about being either masculine or feminine with the opposite sex? I mean, aren't you supposed to be different? Doesn't the opposite sex expect this? Well, yes and no. Remember, you are not completely giving up on your actual personality. You are just adjusting certain things. Did you know that when men talk to women, many tend to use a somewhat higher voice? Apparently, many people already do a certain amount of mirroring, whether they know it or not. It makes sense that we would evolve with some subconscious rapport-building instincts. After all, these abilities have contributed to our ability to survive and to procreate. We know that the brain's neurons that are in charge of empathy and connecting with other feelings are called mirror neurons. Autistic people have difficulty with rapport building because they have fewer mirror neurons. Autistic people, who are high-functioning enough to be concerned about rapport-building, have to work extra hard at learning these skills because they are not as good with this kind of sensory acuity on an instinctual level. It has to start out as a much more conscious process.

Consider this, returning to the idea of gender differences. Assume a man is speaking to a lady. He is a textile mill sales rep and she is a clothing company buyer. He deduces from her demeanor that she did not get her job because she was a college graduate with a stellar GPA. Aside from her skin tone and scent, he can tell she smokes. Her accent indicates she is from a conservative and religious region. She occasionally makes judgmental remarks about people, implying that those who are different are so because they want to be eccentric, difficult, or irresponsible. You don't tell this person you take antidepressants.

The man matches her by displaying qualities she clearly admires and mentioning personal history that aligns with her beliefs. For example, he casually mentions hard-earned money. If he has a degree, he avoids big words and abstract ideas, except for ideas he can express clearly. A literary tradition of commenting on things with dry humor, like Mark Twain, exists in the south of the United States. He uses plain but insightful and cynical

The Big Book of NLP

humor. His wit is directed at the rich, not the poor, and the marginalized, not everyday people. If he attends church, he mentions it. He may talk about visiting family with his close relatives, letting her know he values family. He uses similar body movements, but with a gentleness that allows her to feel relaxed and connected. He also does other physical mirroring, such as posture and breathing.

Mirroring: Symbolic

Notice how we have gone beyond physical mirroring to include things of symbolic value. This is symbolic mirroring, and the symbolic behavior is often subconscious behavior. And we have seen that you can combine symbolic and physical mirroring. This combination of symbolic and physical mirroring is very powerful.

This same sales person probably has a wardrobe that is quite different for each area of the country that he visits. There is an engineer who happens to have autism and who works in the cattle industry. She wears western clothes, complete with the trimming and pearl buttons. This helps her have rapport with the cattle industry people that she works with. Since she is autistic, it is important for her to do what she can to improve her rapport. But it is an odd idea, an autistic person in a western getup. Yet, this person became so good at rapport skills that she was able to get the cattle industry to adopt a very stringent set of rules for the humane treatment of animals. Her name is Temple Grandin. She used her leverage with the McDonald's Corporation, which does business with so many of the vendors, as a powerful strategy for inducing change. This is a person who knows how to create well-formed outcomes. As an engineer with an analytical mind, she got a head start on how to establish a well-formed outcome. Isn't it interesting how she has serious weaknesses as well as powerful strengths?

She chose to go with her strengths to create a career and even engage in transformational leadership. Anyone who saw her as a child, unable to speak for years and throwing tantrums because of her frustrations, would never have predicted her success. We know of an individual who wanted to become more persuasive to conservative people. So he wrote a piece that expressed some of his liberal ideas, but using the same language as the conservatives. The result was that some liberals became angry with him for writing conservative rubbish. The symbolic aspect of the words he used was more powerful than the actual meaning of the words. Never underestimate the power of subconscious symbols and how they play with rep systems.

For practice in looking for subconscious symbols, look at advertisements. For example, when there is an ad for a drug on television, notice how the commercial changes when

The Big Book of NLP

they talk about the possible side effects of the medication. Notice how the music, acting, body language, colors, and other aspects change to make that portion less memorable.

Notice how they give the impression that the drug is highly effective, whether it actually is or not. In one commercial, the main character is a cartoon of a bee with large eyes. During the part about side effects, his eyes get very droopy.

Mirroring: Exchanged Matches

Not all your mirroring has to use the same parts of the body, just as your symbolic mirroring does not necessarily use exactly the same words. For example, NLP teaches that you can make a motion, such as finger taps, that matches the rhythm of the breath, rather than match the breath timing with your breath. This is called an "exchange match."

You are exchanging body parts while matching the rhythm or another aspect of mirroring.If you are a man and you're attempting to match the woman in front of you, avoid looking at her breasts while trying to figure out her breathing pattern!

You will get caught, and using the excuse, "I was trying to match your breathing." will not work in this case. By looking at her shoulders instead, those tiny movements up and down will give you a hint of the breathing pattern she is using, and by applying exchanged matching, you can move your leg or hand up and down accordingly.

You will be surprised to find out that in such a case of an exchanged match of a breathing pattern, if you increase the speed of your matched movement, their breathing becomes faster! And if you slow it down, their breathing also becomes deeper and slower.

Have you ever noticed how, when an angry person is yelling and making a scene, someone will try to calm them down by moving their hands palms-down in a rhythmic motion and saying something like, "Hey, slow down, it's okay, we can find a solution to this problem."

The Big Book of NLP

Mirroring: Wrongs

Some things you shouldn't mirror. For example, if someone is aggressively attempting to be the alpha dog, you need to be more creative. But if you show aggression towards something that the other person judges, you can form a strong bond. It's also fun to yell. If you are comfortable with your aggressive side, you can adopt an aggressive posture without displaying aggression towards the person. Adopt a team-like quality. This is similar to dealing with people who are desperate for attention and lack emotional control, such as those with borderline personality disorder.Mirroring people with very intense needs is much more of an art form and not a good place to start practicing. If you need to, though, you can do mild mirroring of body language without giving the impression that you think your needs are greater than theirs. You can also, on a symbolic level, share the kinds of resentments and other things that the person tends to focus on.

By staying within the world that they mentally live in, you do not alienate them by intimidating them with a larger world. These individuals can easily collapse into feeling very threatened or inferior, and this can cause them to go out of their way to undermine you. This can include something called "triangulation," where they put other people against you. This can even include your boss or legal authorities. It's critical to build rapport with these people and guard against any attempts to undermine you. If you want to, you can use your general rapport-building skills with people who have more intense needs than average.

This is especially true for psychotherapists, doctors, and other professionals who work with distressed people. You will learn that once you establish rapport, you can use it to influence or lead others. Pacing and leading is the pattern of reflecting and changing others' behavior.You don't mirror their suffering; you just mirror the general physical and symbolic items that make them feel comfortable with you and allow them to express themselves. If you can sense their state, that is enough to increase your empathy and let them know it. Most people can empathize with others' feelings, but some are already very sensitive. Both ways.

Mirroring is technical enough to keep you from being overwhelmed or distracted by the other person's feelings. If this is not the case, and you still feel their emotions, you have probably mirrored them too closely, and thus induced their state in you. In that case, you will need to learn to reduce your mirroring, especially in the physical sense. Better yet, you can use NLP to discover and alter your overwhelm strategy. You can start with what internal representations you have about the suffering of others. Nurses, therapists, and social workers are often people who do a lot of subconscious mirroring without any training in it. If someone feels that you are mimicking him or her, they are probably aware of NLP and mirroring. If they seem uncomfortable or offended, the best response is typically to back off of the physical mirroring but maintain the symbolic mirroring without getting carried away.

Miscarriage / Stillbirth

For many years, as a private therapist, I used grief procedures and value hierarchies to help clients deal with the loss of the life of an unborn baby, be it near the end or beginning of pregnancy. Both parents suffered in that instance. When the very same tragedy happened to my partner and me, I completely changed my approach. Given that it happened inside her body, I was the outsider, suffering the trauma but in an observer position. What worked to soothe her emotionally, and in extension, my own despair as well, was a simple reframe. Since that happened, I have only used that reframe with clients and got amazing, almost instant results. It goes like this: "Whether you believe in God or not, it does not matter to the universe, right? You could keep your old idea that this happened because of something you did or did not do, and how unlucky you are or how bad it made you feel. And it should feel bad. It's almost the most horrible thing that can happen to a person, besides losing a child who was already out there in the world making a fuss and impacting our lives. What if we take this idea and look at it from a different angle? Every baby has a body and a soul, and that soul came from somewhere. Now, just like we sometimes get a call and someone says to us, "Oh, sorry, it's the wrong number" and hangs up abruptly, that could be the situation here. That soul was sent to you, and at the last second, before it's too awkward, it realized it was the wrong number and hung up, went back up to heaven, or wherever it came from, and was sent again to the right uterus somewhere else. Maybe it's the soul that was meant for an Australian couple who struggled for years to have a baby, and right now they see the blue lines on the pregnancy test. But wait a minute-what about you? Where is your baby? A moment ago, you were expecting to give birth in February, and now you're not. You know it deep inside. Your baby's soul is on the line. It's a waiting call, and it couldn't come to you while the wrong call was occupying the line. Now it's going to be patient and wait for your body to recover, regain your strength, and heal, so that his or her soul can finally ascend from heaven, or from wherever they send new souls to earth, and make you and your husband joyful, just like that Australian couple. You just have to wait your turn, and it's coming. Allow it to come by vowing to heal as fast as you can and let go of that sadness. You did not lose a baby; it was taken away because it did not belong to you. Mistakes happen, even in heaven, and all you can do is look forward to the future."

Mistakes Into Experience

Source: Robert Dilts

Select a behavior that needs to be updated.

Elicit the limited beliefs that are part of the behavior. Think of a negative outcome of this behavior.

Compare the negative outcome to a worse potential outcome.

Identify positive things that resulted from the negative outcome that you identified in step three.

Express the positive intentions underlying the negative behavior. Discover the positive significance of the bad outcomes.

Re-experience the negative events while in the positive insight state.

Mark and store the wisdom gained from this pattern. Test.

Update a behavior that has not been re-evaluated but that is not working optimally or is dysfunctional.

1. Choose a recurring behavior pattern that causes some kind of bad outcome. An example: attracting people who violate your boundaries (like someone who shows up to your birthday drunk and starts a fight—it ends up being all about them instead of your birthday).

2. Identify the limited beliefs that underpin the behavior. What beliefs encourage this behavior, or limit your alternative behaviors or outcomes? Example: "Believing" that you should ask "Why?" over and over instead of coming up with a solution such as setting definite limits with a person who violates your boundaries.

The Big Book of NLP

3. Consider the negative consequences of this behavior. What is one bad outcome of the behavior that has a lot in common with other bad outcomes of the behavior? In other words, it is a fairly predictable type of bad outcome. For example, having a special day ruined by a person that you have not set limits with.

4. Compare the negative outcome to a worse potential outcome. Think of something that is even worse, and that actually could have happened as a result of your behavior pattern, but didn't happen.

5. Identify positive things that resulted from the negative outcome that you identified in step 3. Although the negative experience from step three was unfortunate, ask yourself what positive outcomes you can identify. For example, you may have discovered that one of your friends is the most insightful because they clearly saw what was going on. Or perhaps you have gained a lot of knowledge through experience that, once you have put it into action, will constitute tremendous wisdom that you can use to enhance your life and the lives of others.

6. State the positive intentions that underpin the negative behavior. Your behavior pattern is based on positive intentions of some sort, despite the bad outcomes that have resulted from it. Clarify these positive intentions and find a way to express them. They are worth writing down. Come up with positive intentions for the other people involved, even if they create negative outcomes or intervene in a way that you do not like.

7. Determine the positive significance of the negative outcomes. What meaning can you take from the bad outcomes that have come from this unresourceful behavior pattern? For example, you may have realized that you have some very good resources that, once they are used for the right purposes, will serve you well. You may have realized that there are limits to your stamina or capacity for boundary violations that are worthy of your respect and assertive protection. You may have realized that, once put into action, this wisdom will prevent a tremendous amount of suffering.

8. While in the positive insight state, relive the negative events. For now, connect fully with the sense of wisdom, putting any feelings of hopelessness or cynicism aside for now. Realize that this is a positive state. Imagine taking that positive state through the memories you have of those bad experiences, seeing them from a new, resourceful perspective.

9. Take all the good energy of the positive state and everything that you have learned from these experiences, and imagine transporting this to the place in your mind where you store the elements of your wisdom. Tag them in some way that makes them available to you when you encounter situations for which they are relevant, so that you can prevent bad outcomes and generate excellent outcomes.

10. Test. Over the next days or weeks, notice any ways that the problem behavior changes. For example, do you have better ways to prevent the typical bad outcomes that would come from this behavior?

Examples of strategies might include being more effective at managing the expectations of others, being more realistic about what you can do, sensing risk factors early enough to take evasive action, and responding more objectively to a situation by keeping things in perspective.

The Big Book of NLP

Modeling Excellence

Model states of excellence. This pattern requires three people: The Person Being Modeled and two Modelers.

1. Establish a pattern of excellence. Have the Person Being Modeled enter a state of excellence.

2. Model the Person Being Modeled. Have the first Modeler explicitly model the Person Being Modeled from the second position.

3. Model with how and why questions. Have the second Modeler explicitly model the Person Being Modeled.

Have them ask why questions to elicit beliefs, values, meta-programs, meta-outcomes, and have them ask how questions to elicit goals, and T.O.T.E.S. (evidences and operations).

4. Demonstrate the opposite state. Have the first Modeler choose an experience that is the opposite of the state of excellence being modeled, such as a stuck state.

5. Repeat steps two and three. Have the two Modelers repeat steps two and three.

6. Compare and contrast. Have the Modelers compare and contrast their models of what the Person Being Modeled has demonstrated, as well as their opposite, and explore what is similar and different in these descriptions.

7. Test. Over the coming weeks and months, discuss how well the participants have been coming along in learning to model and establish rapport.

Narrowing

One of the most common linguistically based self-induced suffering habits is awfulizing. "Awfulizing" is a term used to describe thinking that is characterized by exaggerating the gravity or negative repercussions of events, situations, or imagined threats in an attempt to justify feeling like a "victim" and behaving inappropriately or disproportionately to the situation. Examples:

It's always my fault. I'm always the one to blame.

I'm already 40 years old. From here on out, it's all going downhill. "

"I'm at the bottom. I can't go any lower unless I'm dead."

I will never get out of this problem. I might as well give up now.

Narrowing means reducing the width and scope of the awfulizing criteria. Instead of arguing with the illogical conclusion of awfulizing or using positive words to encourage the person, we narrow their statement of fact and transform it into a process. It is as simple as replacing the word "why" with the word "how". Feel the difference between the questions "Why are you at the bottom and can't go any lower?" To the question, "How are you at the bottom?"

The "how" question immediately reassigns the responsibility back to the subject. "Why" suggests that there are forces that keep you at the bottom. "How" suggests that there's a process, a logical succession of steps, which ends up with you at the bottom. By interfering and altering any of these steps, the end result changes. "Why" allows for any trigger or stimulus out there to be blamed for the end results. "How" narrows the options to a single linear process, and each step must be an action, therefore a choice of behavior.

Necessity Vs. Possibility

One way of knowing what something is is to understand what it is not. That is, when does something stop being itself and start being something else? This is why we have boundaries: to define when one thing stops and another begins.

But there are many different types of boundaries that serve different roles. For example, there are necessity boundaries, which are like rules for life. "You should call your mother on her birthday," or "I need to finish this paper by today," are two examples of necessity boundaries.

While some of these boundaries come from society, most of them we actually put on ourselves, as the two examples show. There are also possibility boundaries, which define what can and cannot be accomplished according to some kind of outside force. "There's no way we can improve profits this year," or "It's too expensive to have a relationship," are examples of this.

While both of these types of boundaries seem clearly defined, you can break through them simply by asking, "What would happen if you did?" and "What stops you from doing _____?"

There are also personal boundaries. These we can also divide into two groups, either when the boundaries are not clearly defined or when they are too rigid. When boundaries are not clearly defined, a person does not know when a behavior or response is appropriate. Screaming and yelling are fine at a concert, but not so much in the office.

Conversely, a person with too rigid boundaries will limit themselves to certain emotional responses, so while they might be calm in the office, they will not "let themselves go" at a concert or party. When they do break one of these rigid boundaries, they often become very upset with themselves, even if this behavior is socially acceptable. In movies, we frequently see these two types of characters paired together in "Odd Couple" situations, where one character has very loose boundaries and the other has very rigid ones.

Negotiation Model

Source: Tad James

1. Identify each of the parties' positions in the disagreement.

2. Make absolutely sure there is a chance for potential agreement. It's important to make sure that both parties can come, each, to an independent decision. It means that there are no hidden power plays involved, as in one party that can use their contacts to force the hands of the other, regardless of mitigation.

3. Start with the weakest end of the base position and work your way up (chunk up) until you've reached a point where you can no longer hold the original position. When the original position ceases to have any meaning, you've reached a conclusion.

4. Separate the behaviors from the intentions. Assert a clear distinction between the two.

5. Close with a precondition. "It doesn't matter what we do, as long as you receive X or Y."

6. Only chunk down as fast as you can keep the story on the same page.

7. If agreement cannot be preserved, chunk up the objections.

8. Test by future pacing each party and eliciting their reactions to the future fulfillment of the agreement.

Nesting

Nesting means that an idea is contained within another. That can happen in the form of a story that occurs within another story. The purpose is to enhance trance and open-mindedness. It makes the metaphors or teaching elements of the story more powerful.

"When I was learning hypnosis, one of my teachers told us about when he was in Italy, and he was seeing so much art and architecture and learning so much, that he had a dream where he was in a big Catholic church, and Mother Mary came down into the church on this sunbeam that glistened and radiated through the huge, beautiful, and colorful stained glass window. She told him about giving birth, and the exquisite joy that she felt being part of history and a new movement that promised to make a better world; that the pain of childbirth and the humbleness of her surroundings could not compare with the kindness of her people."

This is about the memories as told by someone in a dream, as told by someone in another country in a story about my training. That is four levels deep. My story (recalling training), the trainers' story (being in Italy), the dream (of the big church) and another story (Mother Mary's recollections). The story served as a container for metaphors about making changes in one's life despite the discomfort that can be part of that. The metaphor was that of childbirth.

Nested Loops

Source: Milton H. Erickson

Create a well-formed outcome.

Come up with an indirect suggestion.

Build the five stories and cue points.

Introduce the beginning of story #1.

Tell the stories, open the loops.

Embed the suggestions within story #5.

Close the rest of the loops.

influence and persuade others merely by telling them stories. This is one of the best, if not THE best, methods of conversational hypnosis. It involves no induction, no snapping fingers, and no need to get approval for a hypnotic session. It's also very easy to learn and practice. It can be used for almost any situation where you would want to implant hypnotic suggestions without being obvious (which also means almost certain failure) and without the need to induce a person into hypnosis. You can use this method to talk with your kids before bedtime and implement some positive suggestions that will benefit them and the family.

You can use it to talk with your boss about a raise (or to be precise, tell your boss when he'll give you a raise).

You can use it to talk with your employees to motivate them and to inspire creativity.

You can use it in training (just like Bandler has been doing for years and years with his stories).

You can use it in writing, like I do from time to time.

There is no end to the ways you can use the Nested Loops method.

The Nested Loops method is another classic method that Milton Erickson has created and used successfully for many years. By using this method, you're building tension, just like they do in regular storytelling. You create five interesting stories that are interesting to your audience (which you should know, of course). You open one story after the other, and at a cue point you switch to the next story (the graphic below demonstrates it). Once you open the fifth story, you include your hypnotic suggestions in it, and then you close story number five, and continue to complete and close the stories in reverse order. That's the classic application of this method, and it is thoroughly explained below. There are a number of reasons why this method works so well to influence people:

1. Your mind doesn't like loose ends, so your mind begins a TDS (Trance-Derivational Search) in order to close the open loop. Your mind looks for the completion of it, and while it waits for it, more stories are opened, overloading the mind's attempts to keep track. It is all done subconsciously, of course.

2. Concentrating on the content and entertaining details of the stories will confuse the listener and will cause his mind to drift from the structure to the details, thus chunking down. By the time you get to the fifth story, your listener's mind has less tendency to resist suggestions, and these will most likely be accepted immediately.

3. There is no "watch out" sign. When you induce hypnosis, some people will go into a defensive position, guarding their unconscious mind as though it were a precious fortress. Hypnotherapists work long and hard to bring down these defenses, and it takes a lot of energy and time. By telling a story in a casual conversational style, without even mentioning the word "hypnosis" or snapping your fingers, the defenses are down (unless that person has a good reason not to trust you).

4. The loop is habitual. Our minds pick up patterns quite fast. Once one loop has been closed (story number five), the listener's mind expects that the rest will be closed too, and

it is much more alert to pick it up. When an additional one is closed (number four or five), it forgets all about the suggestions and lets them sink into the unconscious with the stories. It is much more important for the mind to close the loops than to deal with the suggestion that has been "slipped" in between them.

1. Create a well-formed outcome.

You must firmly decide what you want to accomplish and with whom. You need to know your outcome as well as your audience's needs, wants, and desires. By knowing this information, it will be easier for you to construct your stories and suggestions in the most effective manner.

Ask yourself questions such as:

Who do I want to influence?

What do I want to suggest to them? (Don't write the suggestions yet, just your outcome.)

Who are they exactly? Is it better if I work with only one at a time?

What are their needs? What do I know about their needs, wants, and desires? If I could sum it up in one word, how would I name what they want for themselves?

What type of story would be most appealing to them? (You'll know the answer once you answer the previous questions.)

When would be the best time to sit down and talk to them without interruption?

Do they already trust me, or do I need to establish trust (and rapport, of course)?

2. Come up with an indirect suggestion:

Since we're talking about a conversational hypnotic method, it would be much more effective to use indirect suggestions. Saying something like, "and you will find yourself passionate about cleaning your room," is a very direct suggestion. Saying instead, "and you know, I felt great after cleaning my room, just like you do with yours..." provides an indirect suggestion. Since it takes time to master this method (as with every good thing), start with only one suggestion. Later on, once you learn to go through these steps without planning too much, you can use more suggestions.

3.Build the five stories and cue points.

There are very few rules for these stories:

1. They must be entertaining, since we're using five of them. If they are boring, you'll have a sleeping audience.

2. The method will work better if you use real-life stories from your own past. Do not use stories that involve the person you're trying to persuade; they have their own version of this memory. Don't even include their role, as that is too obvious. If you must, you can make up your story.

3. Learn to tell those stories in an interesting way. 4.

Record yourself before you try it out on someone else.

Fine tune your story telling until there is nothing in the content, or in the delivery, that is likely to annoy.

Craft it into an engaging, thrilling tale.

4. The length of your story shouldn't be an issue, but don't use 100 words where five would be enough.

Say it in short, but say it all, and in an interesting manner. You can repeat some key points if needed.

Once you've chosen your five stories, break each into cue points; a place where it would be appropriate to cut the story, but that does not give away the end of the story.

4. Introduce the beginning of story #1.

Now comes the tricky part: how to get them to listen to you. It's hard to tell you exactly what to do since every situation is different. The easiest situation is when you have control over the environment, as you do when you're a presenter at a training or a father putting his kids to bed. In a business meeting, where there would normally be several interactions between you and the listener, you can still use this method, but keep in mind that you will have to let the other party speak from time to time. I always introduce the beginning of story number one by saying, "You know what, I must tell you something that just popped up in my mind and reflects almost exactly what you said..." Another option would be: "Let me tell you a story..." or even better, "Did I ever tell you about the time I jumped from a bridge..." The first sentence is crucial because it is used to initiate the momentum of listening to your story. The more completely you occupy their conscious minds with interesting stories, the better you will maintain the momentum.

5. Tell the stories, and then close the loops.

It's a good idea to remember the order of the stories as you tell them. I do so by using my right-hand fingers and tying each story to a finger. I start with the thumb, and in my own imagination, I picture a keyword from the story tied into my thumb. For example, if story number one involves a monkey, I see that monkey biting my right thumb. If the second story involves a diaper, I can see my index finger covered with a diaper, hitting the monkey who's biting my thumb. That ridiculous image will definitely remind me of the order of my stories. You tell story number one up to the cue point, and then you use some linking phrases to break it up and go to the beginning of story number two. You can use almost anything here:

And the police man asked me about my uncle, who you know is a carpenter. By the way, I never told you, but I worked for him for a couple of months when I was 17. In fact, that summer, just after my birthday, he felt so sick that I had to do all of his work. In one client's house... And they have the policeman's story unfinished while hearing about your sick carpenter uncle. When you get to story number five, that's the time for the next step.

6. Incorporate the suggestions into the story # 5.

That's where the juice is. You tell story number five from beginning to end. While you're in the middle of it, right after the cue point, you slip in a few suggestions. It is so easy you won't believe me unless you try it. And you see, at that exact moment, what would you have done? I'm sure you have a good feeling about doing it, just like you would do your homework as quickly as possible to finish it the same day you get the assignment, just like I did when I went through that mission of...Your listeners won't even realize what is going on. Your previous stories have already overloaded their minds; now they are not analyzing your suggestions. Now, complete story number five smoothly, as though you had never interrupted it.

7. Close the rest of the loops.

Don't leave their minds hanging there, searching for the end of the loops. Close each remaining loop in reverse order. After closing story number five, you have a way to go back to closing story number four, because the cue point of story number four is what initiated story number five. Continue closing these loops until you reach the end of story number one. You may want to add a couple of questions to encourage time distortion. After finishing story number one, ask questions like: "By the way, you told me before that you're interested in XYZ. Tell me about it." Of course, XYZ has to be something that the person told you before you initiated the Nested Loops method.

Nested Loops: a Sample Story

"You know, this is amazing because for the last few days I didn't really get any question about this method, although it is quite an impressive and effective one. Everybody uses stories, you know, some are doing it well and some are doing it well, but not in an effective or influence or both ways down...

and see, right as I write to you, I am reminded of that first time I ever read a story that truly influenced me. I am not sure if you are familiar and know this one—the Catcher in the Rye. It is truly a lovely story that does influence you in many ways.

Two of the ways that it has impressed upon me were exactly what I thought they would be, but much more—first, I started seeing people around me that acted exactly like that kid in the story...now who wrote that one...hold on, let me use my neurons well...

Who wrote it? I believe, J. D. Salinger. What is that J. D. anyway? Is it a shortcut or is it his name? Anyway, as I was saying, I read a lot of stories. Some are good and some are not...

and you would think that all a good story needs is a good plot, but it isn't so, at least so I believe, because you see, I believe a good story challenges your beliefs...

it doesn't really matter which beliefs, or how devoted you are to them, but I think it is essential that you be challenged. Otherwise, what's the point of paying twenty bucks for 300 or 400 (how many are those today anyway?) pages of a fiction. It's not real, you know...

Just like the unconscious isn't real. It's a fiction, you probably know this by now, but let me tell you how I thought of it: I think the unconscious is a fairy tail, because you see, no one can point out exactly where in our brain or even in the whole nervous system which lies all over your body, you know, where is it then? ...can you touch your nose with your right finger and tell me whether it's there? ...

how about your eyebrows? ...

neck? ...

The Big Book of NLP

back? ...

stomach? ...pancreas? ...little piggie?...and that little piggy went to the market... my grandma did this gig to me even when I was well grown up (in fact, I was 22 years old). She kept telling me I don't eat enough, though she only saw me like maybe once a week.

A great woman she was, even as a nana (grandma) she kept telling jokes, even dirty jokes!

You'd be surprised how funny it is that your grandma is telling jokes like these...and isn't that just not only amusing but gives a sense of youth-full-ness, gratitude and relaxation...

now double that because she did tell extensively funny jokes. anyway, I miss her.

I was talking about the unconscious not being real. ...you know it isn't. ...can't point to it, can't put it in a barrel (old meta-model conspiracy)...it's a nominalization. It's actually a process, or more so—a group of processes that is just it—unconscious. In other words, it is all the processes of your nervous system that you are not aware of at this specific moment, because you can't pay attention to many different things at once as you read this. ...because you know, as you read this you have to first let your eyes catch the letters and form them into the words that I have written previously, and then let your inner voice form them into auditory conversation that is way inside your mind. ...that's consciousness. ...now, while noticing you're blinking and your ever deeper breath, and friend—you don't have many conscious options...all the rest is the 'sub' of consciousness. And because you don't pay much attention to whatever happens outside of this scope of reading these words and making sense of whatever I'm saying, it is surely important to us, I believe, to screen our reading list. Read the stories that worth reading, read things that challenge our beliefs—there, I said it again, didn't I? ...a challenge...

A story that will make you think if the way that you interpret reality is the reality itself. Harry Potter did it for many children. And Jerome David Salinger did that exactly in his Catcher in the Rye story...oh, yes, that's it. JD is Jerome David...ahhh, I remember.

Right. Now...he wrote many books, but that was the book that got my attention. Catcher in the Rye is marvelous, truly, go read it if you can.

I can still remember its main character, Holden Caulfield, a 17 year old boy, who's also telling the story...that boy is troubled with that transition from boyhood to adulthood. And he got me thinking so much, you know...

Amazingly enough, not everyone reads stories, and not everyone who reads stories is reading the right stories. And even those who are writing stories wonder why their stories are being read less than others who write even less-seemingly-interesting stories...and that's because the language the most popular writers use is more effective and compelling. And my goal here was to expose one of many methods to influence others by doing a series of stories with nested loops."

The Big Book of NLP

New Behavior Generator

Source: Richard Bandler & John Grinder

Identify an issue and the needs for a part that will handle that issue effectively.

Elicit a part for this role, eliciting an appropriate state and set of resources.

Have them create third position scenes in which they express the part.

Do an ecology check.

Edit the scenarios to address all objections. Improve motivation.

Run through the scenarios in first position and anchor the state.

Instruct the subconscious to create a highly effective part from this.

Test and refine the part.

Create a new, more adaptive behavior; a cohesive, outcome-oriented strategy.The power of parts makes this pattern effective.

1. Identify an issue and the need for a part that will handle that issue effectively. 2. Based on a key issue, come up with a part that the person needs. By part, we mean a functional, cohesive collection of strategies such as assertiveness. You can call the part by its function, for example, an assertive part.

2. Elicit a part for this role, including a suitable state and set of resources. Elicit an appropriate state that will support this part, and build up the person's connection to the specific resources needed for the part to fulfill its role. An excellent strategy to include is

having the person recall all situations in which they expressed this part in some way, even if it was incomplete. Be sure to expand this re-experience into all rep systems.

3. Ask them to create third-person scenes in which they play the part. Have the person create detailed mental scenes of how they would express this part. Have them experience the scenes from the third perceptual (dissociated) position.

4. Conduct an eco-check. See if any part of the person objects to anything about these scenes. Be sure to check all rep systems for parts for that object. This can be a good point at which to use finger signals in trance.

5. Edit the scenarios to address any objections. Improve motivation. Have them edit the movie (dissociated mental images from step three) to adapt to any objections raised until all are satisfied. As this is accomplished, repeatedly direct the person's attention to their growing sense of alignment and motivation.

6. Run through the scenarios in first position and anchor the state. Now have the person experience these new scenarios in the first (associated) position. Have them anchor the state.

7. Instruct the unconscious to create a highly effective part of this. Instruct their unconscious to extract the rules and motives from these scenes and construct a part that will be available as needed. The unconscious is instructed to build a very effective, efficient, savvy, and elegant part for this purpose, and to give it the tools and authority to do the job with ease.

8. Put the part through testing and refinement.

In the situations that need this part, you'll notice any improvements. In particular, notice any ways that this part is being expressed. Take note of any ways you can enhance this part, and refine it through this process or other appropriate patterns as you go. When working on generating "new" behavior, you want to work with parts that are natural to the person you're working with. If the person is very shy and has social anxiety, you wouldn't want to begin your change-work with him or her by generating a "socially popular" part. This will cause unnecessary anxiety and internal conflicts.

Given the last example, you would first work with behavioral change patterns such as the Swish or Anchoring, and then, when the person's feelings are neutral in regards to social settings, you can work on generating a socially popular part. In addition, do not confuse learning skills with behavior generation techniques. We try to emphasize natural human skills rather than inventing entirely new ones. You are not going to teach a person how to excel in tennis through this specific technique, but you can certainly help them become more assertive and self-confident when they step onto the tennis court (or anywhere else for that matter). For learning skills, you would need the full neuro-linguistic programming modeling process.

Nuanced Gesturing

This is a kind of pacing and leading that is much more subtle than the classic description of pacing and leading. It provides some lead time with initial pacing by contextualizing your client's words with your subtle physical responses to their words and affect. As a training aid for practitioners, this system can help you become more conscious of your more subtle reactions to your clients so that you can manage your state and body language in subtle ways toward advancing your work as a healer. Your gestures will have the most significance if they are not too restrained or too wild. Many of your clients will be easily over-stimulated or be highly sensitive about trust and boundaries. When you employ this system, you will find that many of your clients respond well to your physical gestures. You might want to watch a video of yourself to see whether you already do this unconsciously, or whether you do it as well as you think you do already.

People gather a tremendous amount of information from people through "non-digital" aspects of communication, such as tone of voice and body language. By "flattening" the "volume" of your various non-digital communications, the more subtle elements become more obvious. Also, by focusing on enhancing your state, you will have more unconscious alignment with your conscious gestures. Thus, your communication will be richer and more nuanced. To get used to this approach, practice this system in everyday conversations that are not high-stakes. Pay attention to your body language.

Do not attempt to pace your conversation partner. Instead, allow whatever body language you'd care to reveal to be expressed. However, keep your body language somewhat restrained, like water simmering instead of boiling. In order to do this, keep your hand gestures within the frame of your body. Do not allow them to move outside of your silhouette. Your gestures, whether you are reacting or expressing yourself, should be mostly very small or subtle. If you are prone to generous gestures or talking with your hands, this may take some practice. Once you get used to this, you will be able to be more selective about when and how you make bigger gestures. This will make them stand out more and have more meaning because you can produce more contrast in your movement. Also, you will not seem eccentric if your intensity and quantity of gestures tend to be too high. If you tend to sit very still, you will need to bring your reactions and self-expression out so that you actually have gestures that convey them.

Once you feel comfortable doing this, add awareness of your facial expressions and bodily positioning.

Make subtle shifts in your facial expression, such as a slight and gentle lifting of the eyebrows or widening of the eyes, or a slight shifting closer or farther from your conversation partner that expresses the amount of excitement or intimacy of the conversation. When you are comfortable with this, add more awareness of your non-word vocal expressions. This includes laughs, sighs, and exclamations of surprise. Practice using your voice instead of air sounds through your throat or nose, such as huffing or snorting. Notice that when you laugh, it is possible to project it as a very pure vocal release, a little like singing. Notice what it's like to use restraint here, with just brief but clear laughter.

Phase two of this practice is to choose responses that consciously contextualize what your conversation partner is communicating. For example, get in touch with your most positive reaction to what they are saying and subtly adjust your body language and facial expressions to convey these positive reactions. It is as if you are somehow providing background music to their self-expression, but it is with your body instead of sound. If it is a very personal communication, you might foster in yourself a very empathic and understanding state, and saturate your subtle body language with that.

Once you are comfortable with this, phase three of your practice is to bring forward the state in yourself that, as background music or context, will influence your conversation partner's state in a direction that can be productive. For example, if your friend does not feel understood in a situation and is taking it too seriously, you might exude understanding while at the same time feeling larger than the situation. If your friend is very sad, you might bring forward a combination of empathy and being resolved and at peace, as though you have experienced such losses and have found inner peace, but at the same time, feel deeply what the other person's pain means.

Phase four is to bring this system into your work with your clients. To do this, you must have a good sense of what kind of leadership will be most productive. Rather than trying to force things in a productive direction, think more short-term, as in facilitating a state in your client that will foster a feeling that will pave the way toward progress. For example, if you have a client who is obsessed with having been betrayed by a lover, you can make space for them to vent; BUT, at the same time, promote a state in them which is about how commonplace such betrayals are, how complicated people are, and how your client has the capacity to betray as well. This sensibility is useful because it makes the experience of betrayal less dramatic and self-absorbed. But what kind of state would you be in to encourage their growth? The Symbolic Somatic Priming System, an extension of the system you are reading now, has the answer. And why do you think you're paving the way for this new state? You might stop vengeance from harming someone, like your client. Helping them make objective decisions faster rather than merely commiserating or telling them to "get over it and get to work" By promoting a healing state shift, you will also help with reprocessing. State shifts can cause profound mental shifts. Changes in the state are often emphasized. It's called "top-down" thinking. But a "bottom-up" approach that emphasizes the influence of primal resources on our thinking is often more effective. By primal resources, we mean the "older" (evolutionarily) unconscious NLP practitioner of the nervous system.

The Big Book of NLP

Nurturing Inner Voice

The voice that constantly tells you that you're not good enough, that something must be wrong with you, and that you've always been and will always be a failure needs to be dealt with. Instead, we need to install a nurturing inner voice, which is indeed a path to rebalancing the critical parental messages that you have internalized. If you want to move forward, you need to replace that critical voice with a new one that is responsive and empathic, and that can help you feel calm, soothed, and encouraged in the present rather than limited in the past.

1. Initiate a downtime state.

2. Is there anyone you know who has a really nurturing quality? It makes no difference whether he/she is real or fictitious. What is its identity?

3. Once you've decided on one person, bring him or her to mind and allow him or her to come to take the form as an internal part.

4. Consider the person in his or her nurturing role. How does this person appear? What exactly is he/she up to? It could be something as simple as humming to a child or gently stroking their hair. If a child is scared, should he or she be comforted by using a soothing voice? Cooking one of your favorite foods? Reading a book? Whatever feels natural.

5. Make that nurturing scene as evocative as possible. Pay attention to what is being said as well as the tone of voice he/she is now using.

6. Now, imagine yourself as one of the characters in the scene, first as the child and then as the loving and supportive figure, and consider which one feels more appropriate for you. What would it be like to be that child or nurturing figure?

7. Anchor the nurturing voice as you assume the part. Enhance the auditory sub modalities. Anchor again. Stack the anchors.

8. Think about a time when you were harsh on yourself.Hear what you said and the sentiments those words evoked in you.

9. Fire the anchor.

10. Now, consciously shift your voice from critical to nurturing—both in words and tone. Fire the anchor again.

11. Move to the second perceptual position.

12. Consider how it feels to be met with compassion and empathy rather than criticism.

13. Move back to the first perceptual position. Play around with the nurturing voice in your head a few more times to get better.

14. Future pace. Use this more nurturing voice and words the next time you find yourself in critical voice mode.

15. Advanced version: create and switch between many different nurturing voices when practicing.

Outcome Audit

Source: Robert Dilts

This is a process that can help you strengthen your belief in the potential achievement of a desired outcome.

1. State the well-formed desired outcome in one sentence. Below we refer to this description of the outcome as X (therefor, replace X with your statement).

2. Say "X, because…" - answer: Why is this outcome important to you?

3. Say "X, and as a result…" - answer: What is the effect of successfully achieving the outcome?

4. Say "X, after…" - answer: What must happen before this outcome is fulfilled?

5. Say "X, while.." - answer: What is happening in sync with the achievement of the outcome?

6. Say "X, whenever…" - answer: In what contexts is this outcome essential?

7. Say "X, so that…" - answer: What is the intention behind setting this specific outcome?

8. Say "X, if / in case…" - answer: What constraints does this outcome present?

9. Say "X, or else…" - answer: What are the alternative options, both positive and negative, to this outcome?

10. Say "X, just as with…" - answer: What prior evidence, small or big, do I have to further enhance my belief in being able to achieve the outcome?

Out-Framing

In NLP, we use the Out-Framing approach to doubt an existing non-resourceful belief and loosen its neurological "fibers." By doing so, we weaken the belief and make room for a resourceful one. We want to question a limiting belief or assumption and consider alternative opinions. This pattern uses the law of requisite variety to accomplish this. Introduced to the cybernetics field by W. Ross Ashby, the "Law of Requisite Variety" says: "If a system is to be stable, the number of states of its control mechanism must be greater than or equal to the number of states in the system being controlled. Ashby states the law as "only variety can destroy variety."

1. Create the grid. Draw a two-dimensional grid with timeframes Past, Present, and Future on one axis and perceptual positions Self, Other, and Observer on the other.

2. Move into the first position (self). Connect to the grid's Self position, Present timeframe cell. Note any limiting beliefs pertaining to your goals that arise in this cell.

3. Get off the grid. Move outside the grid, leaving the limiting beliefs in their cell.

4. Repeat with the remaining cells. Perform steps two and three for each of the surrounding cells. Unless the situation dictates a different order, use the one offered below. Before you proceed, become familiar with the meaning of each cell.

a. First Position, Future: Treat it as a future in which the limiting beliefs and related issues are resolved.

b. Future, Second Position: Imagine a mentor that fosters your resourcefulness and totally believes in you and your ability to transform.

c. Third Position, Future: Picture a wise, compassionate being who is observing your future.

d. Present, Second Position: Imagine a mentor in the present.

The Big Book of NLP

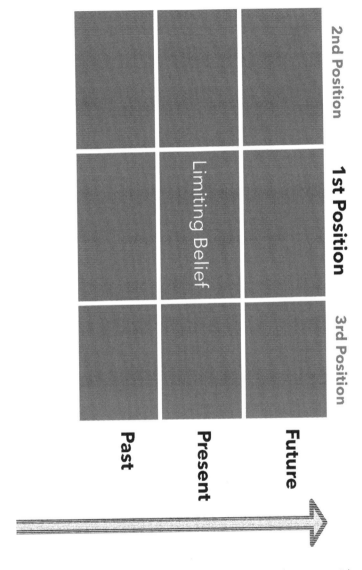

e. Third Position, Present: Picture a wise, compassionate observer with a detailed but big-picture grasp of your present.

f. First Position, Past: Imagine yourself in the past, with a positive perspective on your accomplishments, gifts, and skills, as well as the dreams that had already come true for you by that time.

g. Second Position in the Past: Think of a real or imaginary person who was a past and significant mentor. Imagine this person as having a valuable perspective on your situation now.

h. Past, third position: Think of an observer who has an objective, compassionate perspective on your past and how it is connected to your future.

5. Out of the other cells, View yourself and the limiting beliefs you discovered in the First Position, Present, but from the perspective of each of the other cells described above.each of those perspectives, provide an alternative belief or meaningful message to help the "you" in First Position, Present become better able to doubt the limiting beliefs you found in that position and to become more open to alternative beliefs.

From the first cell, integrate the valuable new information.

Associate yourself with your First Person, Present, and those limiting beliefs.This time, you will receive the alternative beliefs and meaningful messages from each cell. Notice how this alters your experience of these limiting beliefs and your state in that cell. Directly state that you are experiencing more openness to these alternative perspectives, and describe them as you receive them. "I am open to the idea that…" You will need to create the grid in order to keep track of these alternative, resourceful messages. If you are prolific, just write them as you go, preceding them with the name of the cell you were in at the time. Start with your limiting beliefs.

Pace Embed Tag

This is a popular Milton Erickson technique, that is used to cover an embedded command. It is frequently referred to as PPPL (pace pace pace lead). However, that is the least useful approach, as the 'lead' part is too obvious. The formula is: Pace → Pace → Pace → Embed → Tag. For example:

Pace: "Well, I can see that your head is resting on the top of the recliner, and..."

Pace: "you may hear the subtle hum of the air conditioning, and..."

Pace: "you might even still smell the fragrance of the essential oil in that bowl on your left, and.."

Embed: "as you do, you may find yourself deeper in trance, deeper still, and..."

Tag: "it is a pleasant feeling, is it not?"

Pacing and Matching

Pacing and matching are important to modeling and rapport-building. This pattern helps you pace their model of the world. This is a profound form of pacing.

When you practice this pattern, you will sharpen your awareness of people's unconscious communications. When you pace a person's model of the world, you can better understand their perspective and build rapport.

The other person's sense or intuition that you understand them and can relate to them improves rapport unconsciously.

Pacing involves matching elements of another person's body language and speech in order to improve rapport and your own understanding of the person.

Pacing is not mirroring because you are not simply imitating the person. Rather, you are integrating various elements of their style into your own. For example, if you use the person's vocabulary grade level, the person will feel more at ease with you. But if you fake their accent, you will offend them.

Pacing could be compared with method acting, in which the actor enters another person's reality by finding it within. This takes pacing to a higher level, in which you are able to embrace the other person's frame of reference.

Bandler and Grinder have found that you can enhance pacing by matching predicates, that is, the person's primary rep system references. If they "see" your point, you could pace their visual predicates by talking about how they "view" things. Practice pacing with people as you go about your day. Try it anywhere and everywhere.

Examples

Visual rep system pacing:

1a. "I don't like just sitting around and doing nothing, it's too boring"

1b. "I se what you're saying, waiting for someone can test your patience, obviously"

Perceptual postion pacing (and reframing):

2a. "I think we're just too different from each other"

2b. "Of course, otherwise how would two people can ever find interest in one another?"

Start by erring toward being too subtle, and work your way into more complete pacing. That way, you won't offend anyone. If you are in an anonymous situation where it doesn't matter if you appear eccentric, try more extreme pacing and see what it takes for people to actually give you a funny look. You may be surprised at how well you can pace without a problem. Instead of following the steps, you can practice this pattern by improvising from these instructions.

Dr. Milton H. Erickson tells us about a child patient of his that was autistic. As quoted in Phoenix: Therapeutic Patterns of Milton H. Erickson, by David Gordon, Dr. Erickson said:

"And she brought the girl in, and introduced the girl to me and me to the girl. And the girl made a number of weird sounds and so I REPLIED with weird sounds, and we grunted and groaned and squeaked and squawked for about half an hour. And then the girl answered a few simple questions and very promptly returned to her autistic behavior. And we really had a good time squeaking and squawking and grunting and groaning at each other. And then she took the patient back to the hospital. In the night time she took the patient for a walk. She told me later, "that girl almost pulled my arm off, yanking me down the street, she wanted to see you...the one man who could really talk her language."

Parts Negotiation

Select the behavior.

Identify the parts.

Specify the outcomes that the parts desire.

Identify the meta-outcomes that the part is contributing to. Step #5. Create inter-part understanding.

Negotiate an agreement.

Seal the deal.

Test.

Win the battle of willpower and succeed with inner alignment. Abolish self-sabotage and liberate energy for commitment and innovative problem solving. Enjoy the pleasures of life, knowing that you are leading a balanced life. This happens when your parts are working together effectively. A part is a constellation of motives and attitudes and can be largely unconscious. It may be irrational according to your consciously-held standards. It includes a state that you can recall experiencing and associate with it when needed.

1. Decide on a behavior.

Select a behavior that you feel is detracting from your success or excellence, and that represents two aspects or parts of you.

2. Identify the parts.

Determine which part primarily supports this behavior and prevents alternative behaviors. Also identify the part that creates your concern about this behavior. This second part is expressing your distress at not achieving something or at being poorly aligned with your higher values.

3. Specify the desired outcomes for the parts.

Describe what each part wants. Think in terms of outcomes. You can identify with (or associate with) a part and speak from its point of view to get a rich expression of outcomes in terms of VAK, values, and situations that trigger the part. Do this for one part at a time. What outcomes does it promote? This can include positive outcomes, even if it is failing to produce them. Don't assume that a part actually intends to produce negative outcomes. They may merely be side effects. However, if there are gains (like avoiding effort or confrontation of some kind) from the negative outcomes, then that is a clue that the part may be causing (or at least failing to preclude) these negative outcomes.

4. Identify the meta-outcomes that the part is contributing to.

As you'll recall, a meta-outcome is a higher-level outcome. For example, if a part wants an outcome of eating carbohydrate-rich food before bedtime, the meta-outcome might be that it has learned that this will reduce your anxiety from having unstructured time at night and even help you sleep. If you thought the meta-outcome was to make you fat, this is probably actually an unintended outcome. On the other hand, some people feel vulnerable when they lose weight. In that case, the meta-outcome of getting or staying fat would be to feel less vulnerable and perhaps attract less interest from the opposite sex as an immature means of being protected from child abuse that actually ended a long time ago.

5. Create inter-part understanding.

Make sure each part understands the positive values and roles that the other part is responsible for. Convey to each part how their behavior interferes with the activity of the other part and how this lies at the heart of the problem.

6. Reach an agreement.

Negotiate an agreement between the parts. Start with a question such as, "If the other part agrees to refrain from interfering with you, will you refrain from interfering with the other part?" Get an internal sense of the response. Work with these parts until they reach an agreement. The better you understand the needs that these parts fill (by understanding their positive intentions and roles), the more effective you will be at facilitating this negotiation.

7. Complete the transaction.

Ask each part for a trial period during which it will commit to cooperating. Also, get a commitment to signal you if it is dissatisfied for any reason. That will be a point at which negotiation will be needed again.

8. Test.

In the coming days and weeks, see if your problem behavior improves or if you develop new, more resourceful behaviors. Notice any ecological problems or other nuances that require you to do more negotiating. Notice if there are any additional parts that need to be involved in negotiating on this issue.

Perceptual Positions

Perceptual positions can really help you with visualization as a tool for excellence. Perceptual positions are like the people in grammar. Here is an advanced secret. When it comes to challenging situations, very few people find that their perceptual positions are aligned. This is true no matter which perceptual position they explore. This is the secret to the power of perceptual position alignment.

Once you align your perceptual position, you will have an edge that is rare for people in challenging situations. Very often, it is the misalignment itself that is the cause of the challenge in the first place. You could say that once you have aligned perceptual positions, you have drained the swamp, so you can see whether there really are any alligators to worry about.

The first position can help you feel calm or grounded. It can help you tune into your own power as a person and feel whole. This first position is seeing the scene through your own eyes. It is called the "fully associated" position because any other position is disconnected from your normal sensory experiences and your thoughts.

In the first position, your sight, hearing, and feelings are all where they should be when you are 100% in your body and in touch with your senses.

The second position can help you create a more convincing communication strategy. By walking in the other person's shoes, it can help you develop more empathy and understand people's feelings in a richer way. In the second position, you see and hear yourself through someone else's eyes, and you imagine experiencing their reaction to you.

The third position is a great way to see things more objectively without emotions distracting you. In the third position, you see yourself as if you were watching a movie of yourself. We have already performed a process from the third position.

Do you also see any other people from that more distant position?

You can build your inner resources from the third position, and you can analyze what's going on from a cool-headed point of view.

What would this conversation/event look like to someone totally uninvolved?

Imagine yourself being out of your body and off to the side of the conversation between you and the other person. You can see both yourself and the other person. The third position allows you to step back, to gain a sense of distance, to observe, to witness, to feel neutral and to appreciate both positions fully.

The fourth position can give you a view of the systems that are involved. I'm referring to systems such as the family or organizations that are part of the situation and that are connected to it in some way.

The fourth position can help you explore how the situation came to be as it is.

This perspective can open up a new channel of creative solutions for any situation, even in situations that appear to involve only one person. That's because every individual is in a cultural and social reality. Remember the NLP presupposition that every communication derives its meaning from its context? You could say that about every life as well. In the fourth position, you take on the collective point of view. It's a little like being the sap flowing through the branches of a tree; you aren't just looking at the tree.

As you look at the situation, try saying things like, "The kinds of outcomes that would work for us are..." or "The way we should discuss this is..." As you can tell, the fourth position is about us; it's about the collective good and the motives that run through the system, whether it's two people or a global corporation.

The fifth position can give you a cosmic view that is like being enlightened and beyond the whole situation.

This cosmic view comes about because the fifth position is more dissociated than any of the other positions. Sometimes it can be healed simply because it gives you a transcendent perspective that can bring a sense of peace that you have not experienced in that situation.

The Big Book of NLP

It can permanently change your experience of it and your reactions to it. Getting into the fifth position may take some practice because it is so foreign to most cultures. Experienced mediators, though, may have already been there and will appreciate seeing how it can be used in NLP.

One way to get a sense of the fifth position is to come from the God place. This is where you imagine being the source of what is going on, whether it's an argument, cancer, or a law suit. At the same time, you hold the people involved, including yourself, in pure, loving compassion. Then you beam healing and hope into the situation, where that healing and hope are resources that those involved can absorb as they are ready. If you feel that the universe is a threatening place, or you hate your idea of God, you might appreciate getting a vacation from that state of mind.

Phobia Cure

Source: Richard Bandler & John Grinder

Select the stimulus or situation, and go to the third (dissociated) perceptual position.

Run the movie once normal and then backwards.

Run the movie again in black and white.

Move into 1st position, run the movie backwards in full color.

Repeat until the person is desensitized.

Optional: Enhance the procedure with strategies such as sub-modality modification.

Re-associate, do an ecology check via future pacing. Consider additional work as needed to support continued success.

Eliminate unrealistic, habitual fears (such as the fear of flying) that can limit people's lives. It can even help with trauma recovery, reducing or eliminating symptoms of post-traumatic stress. This is also known as the visual-kinesthetic dissociation pattern. It uses dissociation, moving you to a vantage point as a spectator, to alter your reaction to the problem stimulus. Fears, also known as phobias, can be irrational and bother people for years without letting up. Psychology has various ways of working with these phobias, and medication sometimes resolves them. In one documented case, trauma to the front of the brain even got rid of a fear of social activity. But we don't recommend hitting anyone in the head; they could end up with a phobia of you.

The Big Book of NLP

Getting rid of phobias is important because phobias prevent people from doing things they need to do. Also, people with anxiety can have slower reaction times when they are supposed to deal with a threatening situation. At first, that sounds strange, because you would think anxious people would react very fast to a threatening situation as a top priority.

With too much anxiety, however, mental processing can end up being slower than normal. This means they may not handle fearful situations well. That can amplify their fear, creating a vicious circle. NLP has come to the rescue for many people with phobias. Researchers have learned that virtual reality can create the same fears as a real situation, but NLP practitioners have been using the imagination therapeutically from the beginning, and your imagination is free—it even comes with its own software. In this pattern, you will use the third perceptual position and some basic steps from a new discipline: Time Line Therapy. Keep in mind to be cautious. This pattern is designed to be easy on people. However, if you suspect that the person has a mental disorder, have them evaluated by an appropriate specialist to determine if this pattern will cause destabilization. It is possible that, in extreme cases, its focus on a negative memory could be re-traumatizing.

1. Select the stimulus or situation, and go to the third (dissociated) perceptual position. Have the person select a stimulus or situation that they react to with excessive anxiety or fear. Have the person imagine sitting comfortably in a movie theater, about to watch some video of their life. Have them imagine that the video is searching backwards for a point just before their first experience of fear pertaining to the situation.

The primary purpose of this step is to help them experience what it was like not to have the problem. That is the value of using the third perceptual position (dissociated, watching from the position of an objective observer). This can be used to create a valuable resource state. Although it is not necessary, this step may also help them pinpoint how the reaction pattern began.

2. Play the movie normally once, then backwards. Have them watch the situation play out from this dissociated position. Then have them run the movie backwards to the point where it started.

3. Replay the film in black and white. Now have them change the movie from color to black and white and run it again. This time, when it ends, have them freeze the image and fade it to black, the way some movies end.

4. Move into position, and run the movie backwards in full color. Now have the person move into the first position (seeing through their own eyes). Tell them to experience the movie first-hand and in full color, but backwards to the beginning of the clip.

5. Repeat until the person is desensitized. Repeat these steps until your client no longer has a fearful reaction. To summarize the steps, get them back into the movie theater, run the movie backwards, switch to black and white, and run the movie forwards. Finally, switch to the first position in full color and run the movie backwards to its starting point, where it freezes frames and fades to black.

6. Optional: Enhance the procedure with strategies such as sub-modality modification. If this basic version of the method is not successful enough, you can modify it with strategies such as additional dissociation. For example, you can have the person move into the projection booth and watch themselves sitting in the theater watching the video. You can also use other sub-modalities. As you know, people vary as to which sub-modalities have the greatest impact. Another strategy with this pattern is to trigger a resourceful state and maintain it while watching the video from a dissociated position. You might trigger the state by thinking of a time when you felt very secure and confident. If the memory or stimulus is extremely triggering, you can "code" the memory by turning elements of it into symbols or outlines so that your body is not imagining the actual stimulus to respond to. You can also "humorize" the memory by changing elements to make them ridiculous. For example, you could turn an intimidating person into a little bunny with a party hat and give him a child's voice. Consider doing a Swish pattern in addition to the phobia curing pattern if necessary.

7. Re-associate and conduct an ecology check using future pacing.Consider additional work as needed to support continued success. Once the phobia is gone, they can think about the situation, bring them back to the present, be aware of their surroundings, and check the ecology. How does your client feel that they will be without this reaction now that they can feel what it's like to be unafraid? What images of the future do they come up with? You may need to work with parts if the person does not feel fully aligned with this

success. That will help prevent them from sabotaging their success, and it will also help them come up with more effective and creative ways to live without this phobia.

Phonological Ambiguities

You can take advantage of the similarities in sound between words in creating ambiguity. Phonological ambiguity is the uncertainty created by similar-sounding words.

"Can you be a good s(u)pport about this new plan?" (Sounds like a good sport.)

"Relaxing from your head on down to your sole-s of your feet." (Sounds like down to your soul, spelled s-o-u-l instead of s-o-l-e.)

Physical Presence

Pain often causes us to disconnect from our body, which can also be called kinesthetic dissociation. Even when the pain subsides, as it often happens, we could get stuck in that dissociative state. This pattern can help in re-establishing a physical presence in the body.

1. Focus on one area of your body that isn't experiencing any discomfort. Even if you've been in constant pain for a long time, there is always a part of your body that is relatively free of discomfort. Although this area of your body may be tucked away, like the inside of your forearm or the palm of your hand, it is still important to pay attention to this area of your body.

2. Anchor this spot, as you feel the absence of pain, pleasure, or comfort, or at the very least the flatness of sensation, wherever it may be,

3. Take a moment to focus on a part of your body that is or has been hurting you. Take it at your own pace, and if it becomes too uncomfortable, find a less painful area where you can stay more comfortably.

4. Take a few deep breaths into this area and start to let go of any tension or pain as you exhale and trigger the first anchor. You may feel stinging, burning, warmth or hot, stiffness, hardness, piercing, or aching, among other feelings.

5. Pay attention to how your feelings change in response to your consciousness and breathing.

6. Breathe in and out, sensing what you perceive in the place in your body that is devoid of discomfort. Then release it as you trigger the anchor again.

7. Repeat steps 3 to 6 as many times as necessary. Breathe in and out, shifting between the parts of your body that are more painful and those that are more pleasurable. When you reach each one, take a moment to pause and let your breath reacquaint itself with the space.

8. Test. What have you discovered about this part of your body that you weren't aware of before?

Physiomental State Interruption

Source: Richard Bandler

Master the art of change by learning to clear a space for a new state. You can do this by breaking or interrupting the current state. States may be useful or not-useful, functional or dysfunctional. NLP makes extensive use of breaking states, and there are many ways to do it. Confusion is a guaranteed state breaker. You can guide a person to the state of your choosing rapidly from a state of confusion.

1. Identify the state you experience. Recognize what state you are in and name it. It may not be as clear-cut as depression, boredom, or anger, but you can come up with a name that captures the essence of the state.

To help you find a name, notice the feeling of the state or the direction it carries your thoughts.

2. Initiate an interruption by exaggerating a driving sub-modality. Notice how this state is represented in your sense modalities. Identify a sub-modality feature that is important to this state.

 Change that feature to make it absurd. For example, if you hear a voice that says, "I am not worthy of love," change that tone of voice into that of a cartoon character. Or if you feel a throb of depression when you have a certain thought, take a break and work through a rational procedure such as a series of 7's (7, 14, 21, 28...)

3. Test. Notice whether your state has changed significantly. If not, the problem may be in your choice of sub-modality feature. You may not have found an impactful one. Experiment with how you change the sub-modality to make it absurd.

Playing the Critic

Failure is inevitable. It's necessary for learning, adapting, and strengthening. The process of achieving any desired outcome requires continuous feedback that is both constructive and actionable. In every journey, there are milestones and forks in the road that present a challenge on one hand, but also an opportunity to advance faster. This is where the role of the critic comes in.

The critic's role is defined by several characteristics. The critic's representational preference is Logic. Its focus orientation is 'Why'. Its gravitational approach is Away. Its preferred time frame is long term past or long term future, most often both. Its communication reference is external (others). Its comparison mode is Mismatch (review the relevant Meta-Programs for more).

1. Select the active, desired, well-defined outcome you're working with. Defining the issues and obstacles you've recently encountered in the pursuit of this outcome

2. Initiate a downtime state.

3. Elicit the virtues of the critic:

a. Ask "why?" Why has this happened in this way?

b. Seek Logic: What is the source of this obstacle?

c. Physiology of the critic: eyes down, head down, tilted to the right or left, angular closed posture, one hand touching the face ("the thinking man").

4. Enter your timeline. Float above it. Lean slightly backwards (away).

5. Remain above the present, then turn around on the timeline and look towards the past.

6. Consider the issues in the context of your personal history over a long period of time.

The Big Book of NLP

a. If I hadn't done X, what would have happened?

b. If I hadn't done X, what might not have happened (that did)?

c. What bits of information seem out of place? Look for the mismatched stimuli.

7. Float higher above the timeline, dissociate, and consider other people's emerging timelines with yours, around the period when the obstacles started to bother you.

a. Who is involved? Who can be trusted?

b. Who should be avoided? Who must you be careful of?

8. Float back down to the present, turn around on the timeline, and face the future.

9. Consider the potential consequences in the future time frame.

a. If I chose to do X (a new choice), what would most likely happen?

b. If I chose to do X (my new choice), what would most likely not happen at all?

c. What bits of information seem out of place? Look for the mismatched stimuli.

10. Exit the timeline and break state.

Pleasure Installation

Source: L. Michael Hall

Make your happiness list.

Select one of the items.

Mind map your happiness values.

Place a second tier on your mind map.

Enjoy the enhanced happiness state.

Carry your enhanced happiness into other activities. Step

#7. Expand your pleasure activity zone.

Test.

Rebuild your joy. Many of us have lost touch with joy. The reason may be that we need to recover from a traumatic event or from the happiness death that occurs when we become over-invested in trivial things. This pattern can help restore that connection for whatever reason. It also helps you understand your values, which affects how you can expand your happiness.

1. Make a list of many things that bring you happiness. If you think of happiness as being what happens when you consciously enjoy experiencing pleasure, this opens up a world of pleasurable sensations that you can enjoy.

2. Select an item that is especially good. It must be one that you can clearly tie to a sensory experience. Taking a hot herbal bubble bath with Epsom salts is an example that involves several sub-modalities.

3. Create a mental map of your happiness values. You can do this in your mind, but we suggest that you take a piece of paper. In the center, place the happiness experience that you selected. Ask yourself the question, "What personal value and meaning turns this pleasure into happiness?" Draw a line from the experience and write the answer at the end of that line. An example is, "This is a time for stress management that is good for my health. I know I'll feel relaxed and flexible after this, and besides that, it symbolizes class and luxury."Keep creating answers like this until you are satisfied with this exploration.

4. Place the second tier on your mind map. For one of the answers, ask another question: "What personal value and meaning makes this answer a pleasure for me?" Draw a line from the answer and write the new answer at the end of the line. Generate as many answers as you like. Do this for each of the first tiers of answers, so that you have two layers of answers, one after the other.

5. Take a few moments to relax and take in the meanings that you have noted and that drive your pleasure state. This is a sensory pleasure expanded into happiness through your values. Carry your enhanced happiness into other activities. Amplify your pleasure state and step into it. Imagine other pleasurable activities and what it would be like to bring this state into those activities.

7. Extend your leisure activities. Arrange this pleasure state with other sensory-based experiences. Imagine doing these things in this state. Observe how it affects your participation, creativity, or other positive traits. Consider how it might improve your engagement in school, work, or relationships.

8. Test. Over the coming days and weeks, notice any ways that you are able to experience activities, situations, and relationships with constructive pleasure.

Pleasure Reduction

Source: L. Michael Hall

Select an "overused pleasure."

Determine the meta-state levels that give this meaning for you.

Repeat this to derive higher levels of meaning.

Take in the full enjoyment gestalt.

Reduce the meaning and enjoyment.

Future pace this reduced meaning and enjoyment.

Generate other sources for the highest meta-level meaning states that you identified in step two and three.

Test.

Break free from addictions, compulsions, and obsessions by reducing the pleasure they create. It is useful for behaviors that are based on real needs but have become excessive.

1. Select an "overused pleasure."

2. Determine the meta-state levels that give this meaning to you. In the center of a sheet of paper, write down the pleasurable activity.

Draw a circle around it.

Think of the pleasure and ask, "What positive meaning and values do I give to this pleasure?"

The Big Book of NLP

Write each answer briefly in the space immediately around the circle. Think of each answer as a kind of state that embodies feelings and meaning pertaining to this pleasure.

3. Repeat this process to reach higher levels of meaning. For each of the answers, ask the same question, and surround it with the answers you get.

4. Take in the full enjoyment of the gestalt. Review all the answers, experiencing them as a complete profile of the kind of happiness that drives the behavior in question.

5. Diminish the significance and enjoyment.

Determine which of the meanings is the most important in driving you to excess.

Do this by placing your hand over one answer cluster at a time.

For each cluster, ask, "If I could take away this cluster of meta-states, how much would it reduce the pleasure?"

Continue doing this until you clearly see which meanings exaggerate the importance of the pleasure and which are more intrinsic to the pleasure, that is, more essential or basic to its real meaning. For example, health is a core value for eating, while having something to do while watching television is not a core value for eating.

6. Future Pace yourself with this diminished meaning and enjoyment.

Consider what could detract from the activity's enjoyment. Seeing yourself get fat from overeating Assume you are doing the activity and say to yourself, Imagine a negative factor, such as getting fat, when another pleasure or meaning enters your mind.

7. Other sources for the meta-level meaning states identified in steps 2 and 3.

A meta state is a collection of all the high-level meanings found in steps two and three. Embrace the blissful nature of this state. Activate your creative part to show you new ways to enjoy this pleasure and to create its meaning. Convey the idea that it is possible to enjoy life to the fullest without going overboard.

8. Test. See how well this pattern reduces the selected behavior to an appropriate level and how well it helps you create pleasure and meaning through healthy pursuits.

The Big Book of NLP

Positive Contribution

What if your client could do nothing wrong?

Taking this position isn't always a good idea, but it is a skill worth practicing because it primes your clients to become more cooperative and creative in finding solutions. This experience is like a chess sequence in that it starts with a set up and is followed by additional moves. Try using these ingredients during an entire session with clients that you feel may benefit from it. This will be for them, but also for your practice. Each time your client says something that you feel you need to resist, correct, or negatively judge, look for one of the following opportunities:

1) a need to which you can relate their statement;

2) a monetary value to which their statement can be linked;

3) a feeling, either positive or negative, to which you can relate their statement, or...

4) a positive goal to which you can connect their statement

Each time you select one of these connections, also think of a second connection that will begin to create momentum in the direction of a good outcome, either in the short or long term.

For example, if the client says that his boss is a real jerk, you might connect this to a feeling such as, "You look bitterly disappointed." I know you don't want anything to get in the way of enjoying your work and really performing. "

When you decided to connect the feelings, you thought at least one step ahead, and saw that bringing the feelings into the foreground would not only show that you can acknowledge his body language and stay relevant, but you also planned to connect the feelings to his values and dreams. The client thought he was simply angry, but the words "bitterly disappointed" not only more accurately reflected his body language, but they also primed him to connect with what he was disappointed about. You may not have known exactly what it was, but it was most likely something like his career goals, his hopes for his role and contributions in the company, or his desire to function at his best (which his boss was interfering with through emotional stress). By speaking in general or vague terms in the second segment ("... enjoying your work and really performing"), you leave room for him to connect with the specifics on his own terms. In the rare situation when you are too far off the mark, the client will tell you. To bring one (or all) of these into focus, you might simply ask the client to talk about it. If the client is not good at making such connections right away, you can ask about these things more directly and make the connections for them.

Stumping the client and having them squirm while they try to make connections can simply anchor a state of confusion and helplessness, as well as interfere with the development of rapport. On top of that, it wastes valuable time. And in the field of rapid therapy, the more time you waste, the less effective you are (and the least profitable, since you're paid for results, not by the clock). Memory research has shown that staying with that "tip of the tongue" feeling when a memory cannot be verbalized does not strengthen memory power, even if the memory does eventually come into consciousness. Also, it is more important to move the treatment along than it is to give the client practice in articulating things that are not very conscious. There is nothing wrong with supplying the words for the client, so long as the client feels free to tell you how those words need to be adjusted to more accurately reflect their inner world. The more experienced you become, the more consistent you will be in providing just the right words. This creates a great deal of momentum and efficiency in this kind of interventive experience.

Now that you have the client talking about their dreams and needs, you have opened the gate to creating meaningful objectives for your work with them. This is much more productive than "trying" to "get" the client past their anger. That was just the surface emotion anyway. Now look at the kinds of goals that might be on the table, with the client's full interest.

1) Getting into a very creative, positive state when dealing with his boss, and having specific strategies to turn the situation around;

2) Increasing his confidence and resources in order to negotiate a better position and a better boss;

3) Destroying his boss with deft use of office politics and outshining his boss, and

4) Getting so attuned to his goals and confidence that his boss doesn't shake him and, as a result, is no longer a threat to your client's performance. (Or some combination of the foregoing.) Your assessment of your client and your client's self-knowledge will help you select from goals such as these.

Porn Addiction Removal

This pattern is designed to eliminate cyber-porn addiction, a widespread problem that has a tremendous impact on productivity and peace of mind. It is not intended as a judgement about pornography, but rather as help for those who are experiencing a loss of control. This pattern is not offered as a substitute for professional help. If this may be necessary, we encourage you to seek it.

1. Make an image of the unwanted associated compulsion. Think of the last time you masturbated to online porn. Step into the experience, experiencing it from the first perceptual position. That means seeing what you saw back then. Listen to what you hear and feel what you feel.Imagine it as if it is happening right now. If this step is unpleasant, please understand that this is the only unpleasant step in the pattern. Notice where exactly in your body the compulsive feeling begins. Intensify this sensation so that it tells you exactly where it is located in your body. Notice what images you see while you're feeling this. One image might be more repeatable than the rest. What sounds are associated with this image? Make sure that the pornographic media is included in this image. Make a mental note of this image and the associated sounds and feelings.

2. Break the state. Step out of feeling compelled to masturbate with online porn. To break state, stand up, move around, open your eyes, blink faster, move your facial muscles, wave with your right hand, stretch your left, lift your right knee upward, say your birthday date out loud, think of green, think about how a UPS truck looks, and think about what you ate for breakfast today.

3. Develop a more positive self-image. Now you're going to create a strong, resourceful, and positive self-image. This resourceful image will restore your self-control. Imagine how you would look if you had a better hobby, that is, a positive compulsion. The best way to destroy a negative compulsion is to replace it with a positive one so that you feel complete. You can choose any positive habit that comes to mind, preferably one that you enjoy but have neglected due to your online porn addiction.How would you talk? What would your voice sound like? How would you dress, walk, run, and drive? How would you feel in new situations if you owned that positive compulsion? That image is the near future image of you; the person who has solved that big issue of changing a negative

compulsion to a positive one. He or she doesn't care about who or what caused the porn compulsion. He or she can't tell why their past porn compulsion is gone, as they now have a favorite positive compulsion. We call this image the "near future you" to imply that you are already beginning to experience this new sense of self. Build that image right in front of you. Make it a life-sized, bright, colorful image of you as a person with so many resources, abilities, and self-esteem that you can face the hardest challenges and conquer them all. Experience yourself as a person who has plenty of choices in life and who has an amazing ability to create more choices. See yourself as a person who has a positive compulsion; the one you selected during this pattern. Look at that image, letting yourself feel its attractive power. Connect with how intensely you really need to be that way. This is important. If you cannot feel it at the moment, go back and make the image stronger. Make it larger, brighter, and more powerful. If you were to see that image of yourself in the same way that you view people that you admire, how would you appear? Imagine all the porn-addicted people in the world looking at you with true admiration because of your self-respect, self-control, and resulting success. Imagine your positive interests leading you to increased health, better sexual relationships, and greater self-respect. Put a mysterious smile on that image of yourself. Imagine you can hear yourself think, "I feel good being me." Imagine the tone of your voice. Experience the attractiveness of this person you have become. Experience the attractiveness of this way of feeling. Imagine those words, "I feel good being me." happening all around you, bathing you in these good feelings as though you could soak them up.

4. Establish the new self-image. Make a mental frame around that image of you with your new positive compulsion. Shrink it down to a tiny little picture in the open space in front of you. Don't let it stand there quietly! Make it sparkle and flash at you. Take that sparkling little dot in the distant space in front of you and jump it quickly back to its previous size. big, life-sized, and colorful. Enjoy experiencing the image (including your mysterious smile) and the words, "I feel good to be me." surrounding you. Open your eyes for a moment, then close them, thinking of a black screen. Now see that dissociated positive image again. Shrink it again so it becomes a tiny black dot blinking in the distance in front of you. Now bring it back quickly to its normal size. Continue shrinking and expanding it, really putting your heart into it.

5. Begin the change. At the beginning of this process, shrink back the dissociated positive compulsion image and place it right in the middle of the disturbing image that you discovered. Swish the images around. Simultaneously, rapidly expand the tiny dot into a

full-size image of your dissociated positive compulsion image, until it completely covers the negative image of the compulsion.Make it larger and brighter, with the stereoscopic "I feel good about me." and your mysterious smile as before. Practice doing the two movements simultaneously. Put the negative image in front of you with the black, blinking dot (the dissociated positive compulsion image) in the middle. Now quickly SWISH them: shrink the first one quickly, and as you do this, enlarge the tiny dot onto the full-size confident new positive compulsion image, along with its sounds and feelings. It helps you do this with speed and gusto when you say "SWISH!" and snap your fingers when you do it. It is critical that you do not swish the images back! Open your eyes right after you've done the swish and experience the positive image in full color and loudness, including the sound of, "I feel good to be me." Open your eyes, blink for a second, and close them again. See the negative image with the blinking dot on it? Say "swish" while you snap your fingers. Swish the images again, bringing the positive image to life. Let the good feelings from the positive image move all over your body. We're half way through.

7. Make the change! Open your eyes, move around a bit. Close your eyes. Imagine a blank screen. Do the swish ten times as fast as you can. Do this powerfully, with as much emotion, enthusiasm, and determination as you can muster. Use your desire to put an end to the negative image in your life as your source of intensity. You can generate intensity by realizing how much this compulsion has taken from you. Remember: Negative Image: Black Blinking Dot-SWISH and Finger Snap-Big, colorful and positive image, stereo, "I feel good being me," he smiles, mysteriously. Open eyes, close eyes-blank black screen-back to the beginning. Good!

8. Generate pleasure. Now, we will attach that new, pleasurable, compelling, dissociated, positive compulsion image to everything in your life. Reach out with your hands and grab the strong, dissociated, positive compulsion image like you would grab a big mirror. Grab it, lift it, and you'll notice something new: it's hiding thousands of thousands of high self-esteem, dissociated, positive compulsion images!They were hiding there all that time to surprise you! Experience images of yourself as a strong, committed, powerful, happy, thrilled, popular, excited, and successful person in everything you do in life.As you lift the image, all the other images are lifted with it. Smile at yourself, get some momentum, and throw it up high above you. Everything is spread out in the open air above your head. A split-second later, they all fall down, spreading all around you. In front of you, representing your future, are thousands of them, covering the ground. Just around you, there are a

couple thousand more. Around you, as you look back on your past time line, hiding behind your back, are thousands more.

Consider each one to be framed by a blinking, shiny frame yelling for attention!Know that it will be amazing to face challenges in your future where all that your mind can remember is how powerful and strong you are. It's almost more pleasure than you can contain. The images behind you rule the earth, covering and hiding the small, weak negative images. The images control the past now. They blink, craving attention everywhere you look. Because, as you try to find a negative memory, all the blinking positive images interrupt the search. They yell at you, "Look at me! I feel GOROOOD being me! " Play around, pick one up, see the mysterious smile, hear the stereo effect voice around you, see the image as it grows and gets brighter. Now imagine yourself waking up in the morning, eating breakfast, and seeing your positive images all over the place, blinking and yelling for your attention. You can open your eyes now and look around.

9. Test. Take a moment (not too long) and think about your computer. If you can, sit in front of your computer. Do you feel compelled to masturbate or to do something else? In the coming days and weeks, see if you experience your computer life differently. If you can't remember the negative image clearly, or you did but didn't feel off balance, then these are signs of success. If you still feel compelled to cyber-porn, seek the advice of a professional.

Positive Intention

Define the problem.

Reveal the underlying motives.

Get to the core motives.

Transform self-sabotage into success. By discovering the positive intent behind a negative behavior or attitude, you can release tremendous energy and positive commitment. Other NLP patterns, such as the Parts Negotiation pattern as well as the Behavior Appreciation pattern, depend on this insight. In his outstanding book, Sleight Of Mouth: The Magic Of Conversational Belief Change, master trainer and famous NLP developer Robert Dilts says: "At some level, all behavior is, or at one time was, positively intended. It is or was perceived as appropriate given the context in which it was established, from the point of view of the person whose behavior it is. It is easier and more productive to respond to the intention rather than the expression of problematic behavior. "

1. Identifying the issue. Briefly state the problem with enough detail so that it is clear in your mind. It may be primarily a situation, a personal problem, or a challenge. Focus on defining unproductive behavior. Get clear on why the behavior is not useful.

2. Expose the Hidden Motives. Take a few moments to relax, breathe deeply, and lie back. Now, go inside. Imagine your mind has special internal messengers. In NLP, we call them "parts." These are parts of your personality that have characteristic tendencies or habitual behaviors.

Find the part that is responsible for generating the unproductive behavior. Bring this part into awareness as though it were a complete personality. Remember that a part is an aspect of you. It is a collection of aligned motivations. A part is like a little personality inside of you. In order to be aligned and successful, you must not work at cross purposes with yourself. This requires negotiating or working with your parts. Now imagine that you can do a role-playing game with this part. Inquire of the part what it desired to have, do, or become as a result of the negative behavior or attitude.What value or benefit was to come from this? Ask directly, "What did you wish for me to accomplish by doing this?"Take as much time as you need to imagine and listen to the parts' responses.

3. Get to the heart of the matter. Keep asking "why" and "what" questions to clarify the motives. Recycle each answer into a new question. Continue this until you feel that you have gotten to the core motives. You should identify a core belief along with the core value and core reasons for the behaviors or attitudes that, at first glance, seem to be unsupportive of you.

Positive Personal Significance

Nearly everyone wants to be a hero, but people who are marginalized want it more. Why else would comic books have a hero that can't reveal his or her identity but is intensely tempted to do so in order to impress someone? You can use this experience with anyone, but loners, underachievers, or people who are feeling unappreciated especially need this in order to trust you. For them, it's a key nutrient as well. In this experience, you will show your connection with their sacrifices and positive intent.

Listen and Observe:

1) What is causing your client anxiety? The obvious stressors are external, but you are deeply listening to how the client has internalized real or imagined judgment from others, an authority figure, or "society."

2) Where is your client's drive and effort coming from? Notice what the client is doing to deal with the situation, even if it is destructive or too passive. Find out what values are driving the client and which of those are the most intensely felt. The woman recovering from drug abuse and trying to regain custody of her children may not appear to be doing what she is supposed to do, but she probably feels inside that she is working very hard and that her hard work is not being appreciated. This could even be true. Recovery from addiction can exhaust others' patience, and this is a painful situation for someone desperate to rejoin society. You might find that she is terrified of what may happen to her children because of negative stories and news about foster care. You can recognize this as coming from her love for her children and her being protective.

3) Take note of how well or poorly your client connects their higher values with their efforts. Do they FEEL that they are motivated by high values, or are they so preoccupied with the unfairness or threats in the situation that they find little inspiration? You can often predict that this is what you'll find because they exude an oppressive fatigue and weariness.

4) Notice how well they are able to see their efforts as an expression of their desire to meet an important challenge. Again, the unfavorable alternative is an overemphasis on threat and unfairness, which leads to fatigue and wear.If you find yourself becoming irritated at a client's immature lock-on to unfairness and threats, remember that they have been living this, and they have probably experienced a nasty blend of double binds and emotional shocks, if not outright trauma, that has wound them into a tight coil of perseveration. They may also have cognitive difficulties related to injuries, mental illness, or addiction. Although it may be appealing to wave your magic wand and produce instant NLP magic, never resent a client for posing a challenge that threatens your ego.

Sometimes cognitive impairment or being locked in a struggle can seem like they are not cooperating or even sabotaging the work. The intrusion of the coach/therapist's ego into the process can be sneaky. Even a hint of this can create a vicious cycle in which the practitioner and client feed into a negative relational dynamic. You can bounce out of this judgmental state by thinking of the client as a possible candidate for long-term cognitive rehabilitation, which is something that practitioners can contribute to a great deal. This is because restoring thinking occurs by preparing for and dealing with actual situations and people rather than artificial means such as cognitive computer games. By engaging them at this level, you can trigger more respect in yourself for the client. To complete the experience, you ought to repeatedly link the client's higher values as fuel for their efforts. To do so, you demonstrate genuine appreciation for how hard they work and struggle.It is important not to be maudlin here, because there must be no exaggerating or acting.

A restrained and objective comment will have a stronger impact than a more intense presentation. Then, state that you can see how the client would do this in order to pursue the higher values that you have recognized. You can also link this to something you want to see happen that you feel the client is very likely to agree with. For example, you could say:

"There are few things as difficult as recovering from addiction...Especially when you have lost so much. Not to mention dealing with all the add-on demands like all these appointments and the harsh timeline. You're under a spotlight that can really distract people and make them feel demoralized. Your love for your children must be incredibly powerful for you to be so totally driven. We really need to work on some stress management skills so you can stay in shape.... and make it obvious to the social worker and the judge what you're really about here. Just as an expert runner must avoid getting sick from being too thirsty... we need to make sure you're in good shape for all this. "

Make this a theme, especially in the first phase of your work. Look for every opportunity to produce this experience. This will contribute to your motivation as well as your client's, and it will help to keep key goals meaningful and in focus.

Pragmagraphic Swish Design

Source: Robert Dilts and Todd Epstein

Create a "map" of physical locations the states.

Step into the "Must" position.

Step backward to the "Desire" position.

Step backward into the "?" position (the trigger).

Get clear on the sub-modalities involved in "?"

Step into "Creative Choice."

Do sub-modality-work in the "?" position. Repetitions of step 7.

Test.

Resolve compulsive patterns, which are actions that a person feels compelled to perform despite knowing better.This can include addiction, blurting out things you thought only your parents would say, eating comfort food, switching on the television when you have paperwork to do, and many other behaviors.

Because it is much harder to change a compulsive behavior once your drive has reached a high level, this pattern is an opportunity to prevent the behavior before your drive becomes too strong, by helping you become aware of it on a more subtle level before it becomes strong. It weakens the connection between the drive and the triggers that activate it, and replaces it with a constructive drive.

1. Determine the physical locations of (A) "Must," (B) "Desire," (C) "?," and (D) "Creative Choice."

2. Step into the "must" position.

Choose a compulsive behavior.

Physically stand in the "must" location.

Experience the feelings you have when you do the behavior.

What does it feel like when you "MUST" express your compulsive behavior?

3. Step backward to the "Desire" position.

Move to the "Desire" position by physically stepping backward. This spot is the feeling that you have just before "must" breaks into your awareness.

4. Step backward into the "?" position (the trigger).

Step back again, this time to the "?" position. This is the trigger that comes just before (B), "Desire."

You may not have been aware of it before, but it is a feeling that triggers the "desire."

It may include thoughts, and the feelings or thoughts may be triggered by a situation, such as the smoker who always lights up in their car.

5. Get clear on the sub-modalities involved in "?"

Notice the sub-modalities that are most influential in increasing the intensity of (C). Discover which sub-modalities decrease the "? feeling.

6. Step into "Creative Choice."

Step into the "Creative Choice" location. Attend to the feelings that stem from this state.

You may have experienced this state while exploring the sub-modalities that decrease the "?" feeling.

You can think of other "Creative Choice" experiences as well. Notice which sub-modalities have little or no impact.

a. Determine the sub-modalities.

Experience the sub-modalities that give the most gusto to your "Creative Choice" feeling.

notice, which has no impact.

b. Notice the sub-modalities shared with "?"

Notice which of the sub-modalities intensified "?" and "Creative Choice."

7. Do sub-modality-work in the "?" position.

Return to your "?" spot.

Elicit the strengthening sub-modality for "what?" (e.g., bright and big), as well as the one that reduces the intensity of "creative choice." Notice how this creates a sort of pull into your "desire" location.

Gradually intensify the "Creative Choice" sub-modality. If it is dim and small, it will become bright and large.

At the same time, slowly reduce the intensity of the sub-modality for "?"

Keep going until their intensities have completely reversed.

"Creative Choice" is now low intensity, and "Creative Choice" is high intensity.

As you do this, move from your "?" spot into the "Creative Choice" spot.

8. Repetitions of step 7.

Step out of "Creative Choice" and repeat Step 7 as quickly as you can.

Repeat this process at least five times.

9. Test

Test your results by stepping back into the "?" spot and discovering which direction you find yourself wanting to move toward.

Notice what occurs when you attempt to return to your prior compulsive feelings and behavior.

The Big Book of NLP

Pre-Grieving

Source: Steve Andreas

Focus on a potential loss that is difficult to face and preoccupies your mind at times.

Explore your experience of things that you readily accept as temporary. Include your beliefs and values, and your memories of creatively moving on after these acceptable losses.

Map the balancing representations onto the anticipated loss. See yourself creatively moving forward in life after having resolved the loss.

Future pace experiencing and expressing these gifts.

Refine as needed for ecological integrity.

Install via your timeline. Test.

Resolve fears of future losses by eliminating many of them. Become more resilient by better tolerating and recovering from the losses that will occur in the future, even extreme losses such as disability.

1. Pay attention to a possible loss that is hard to face and makes you think about it at times.

Focus on a future loss or potential future loss that you sometimes become preoccupied with. It may be a person, thing, or situation.

2. Explore your experience of things that you readily accept as temporary. Include your beliefs and values, and your memories of creatively moving on after these acceptable losses.

Think of some things that you appreciate despite knowing that they are temporary. Focus on the ones that you can best accept as being temporary.

Notice the ways you have a balanced or positive experience of these things and how to manage their passing.

You may even look forward to replacing some things, as is the case when technology is improving.

Notice how your beliefs and values support your balanced relationship with these things and their nature.

Notice how you represent the temporary nature of these things through sub-modalities. Add to this the actual experiences you have had of creatively moving on with your life after the losses that you accepted or were at peace with.

Notice how you carry with you an appreciation for what the person, situation, or thing meant to you.

3.0 Map the balancing representations onto the anticipated loss. See yourself creatively moving forward in life after having resolved the loss.

Map the balancing representations that you explored in the previous step onto an anticipated loss (from step one) that can be more difficult to accept.

You can do this, for example, by adjusting the sub-modalities involved in that difficult loss so that they match the most potently balancing sub-modalities that you experienced in the prior step.

Now imagine yourself after adjusting to the loss from step one.

Picture and sense yourself from the third position (dissociated) as you creatively move forward in life after having adjusted to the loss.

Notice how you carry with you an appreciation for the person, situation, or thing that you have lost, thus honoring these memories and gifts.

The Big Book of NLP

4. Future Pace experiencing and expressing these gifts.

Generate an even more resourceful future.

Spend some time imagining future situations where you experience and express the gifts of the person, thing, or situation that you have lost.

This might take the form of sharing life lessons with another person, or creating a valuable skill from a gift that the person, thing, or experience brought forth in you.

5. Fine-tune as needed to maintain ecological integrity.

See if any parts of you object to creating this resourceful future.

Use these objections to enhance the future that you are creating.

6. Install through your timeline.

From a meta-state, view your timeline. Install your future representation at the appropriate time.

7. Test

Short of actually waiting for the projected loss to take place in order to test this pattern, you can apply it to losses that are in your immediate future, even though they may not be as serious as the one you chose this time around.

Additional Advice

You can repeat this exercise to better cope with the same thing and with additional future losses.

You can anchor the resourceful loss state in step two, and then do the exercise beginning in step three after triggering the resourceful state and recalling the most effective sub-modalities for mapping onto the new loss.

You can use this exercise to gain a more balanced state when you deal with a potential loss, so that you will remain objective when there is a risk of loss.

This kind of objectivity can sometimes prevent a loss, such as when one saves a relationship or a job because of the maturity, caring, and poise that they express.

Others may experience you as less self-absorbed and more expansive as a person.

Presupposing Trance

One known trick of stage hypnotists is to induce a trance in a subject by suggesting that a current reality observation is a "formal" indicator of the person already entering the state of hypnosis. While it may not work in a heated debate with another person, it does work when the client has already completed a TDS or is nearing the end of his presenting problem story.Well, I see you are blinking more and more, which means you are allowing yourself to go deeper into a trance; "I noticed how when you first sat down, your hand was up on that table and now it is motionless in your lap, which means you are getting more and more relaxed as you look inside and wonder if this nice comfortable feeling is you in a trance or... that you are ready for more..."; "Can you tell me, as you go into a trance, what really goes on inside, as you sit there with your right palm up and your jaws loosen...".

Problem Deciphering

We are constantly concerned with the unknown. The moving shadow in our bedroom late at night can startle us, until we turn on the night lamp and see it's only the curtain. This pattern is meant to turn a vague problem into a specific and manageable one.

1. Give the issue a title.

2. When does the issue manifest itself? Is there any pattern or regularity in the occurrence of the problem, such as only occurring on Sunday, in the early hours, or at midnight?

3. Where does the issue arise? Is there a pattern to where the problem happens and where it doesn't happen? Is it only in the house, for example, but never at work?

4. What is the issue's output? Aside from the client's words and actions, what would a third-party observer notice about the client's behavior when they were experiencing the issue? What would I have to do if I had your issue and wanted to replicate the experience of it?

5. Who is it happening to? Is the problem yours alone while you face it? With whom else? Are there any variations in terms of "spectators"? How do you interact with these people? How do they interact with you during the experience of the issue?

6. What are the issue's extenuating circumstances? Is there ever a time when the issue does not occur? What makes those times/locations/environments unique?

7. What actions does the client take differently as a result of the issue, or what elements are avoided? When it comes to activities they participate in or avoid, how does the problem impact their lives?

8. What does the client demonstrate during the session that is relevant to the issue? When you talk about a state, you remember all the physical and mental sensations that go with that state.

The Big Book of NLP

9. What are the client's explanations and frames of reference for the issue? How is the issue viewed from the client's unique point of view and background?

10. What has the client or others tried to do about the "issue"?

11. When the issue is resolved, how will we know? How will you be able to tell if the issue has been solved objectively? Putting the client's issues into words that can be seen by others makes them easier to solve because the results are already known. These results need to be based on what we know to be true.

12. What is the plan of action? What may be the first most significant step to take, in order to move from current reality to solving the issue?

13. Future pace.

Problem Definition

Source: Martin Roberts

This pattern helps you find your way out of a problem that you are stuck in. It addresses our tendency to define a problem in a way that makes it seem impossible to solve. When you approach any technique of problem solving, be sure to experience a resourceful state of mind. The best techniques for problem solving will not do much good if you aren't "in the mood" to find solutions or if you're operating under stress. Physical distance, when appropriate, can also help to quiet the mind and put you in a state of creative flow.

1. Use meta-model distinctions to analyze the problem. Think about how you have defined your problem. How would you succinctly state the nature of your problem? Look for well-formedness violations in this definition. These include vagueness, over-generalization, and distortions of meaning, causation, and presumption. Look for ways that you define the problem as being outside of your control or as being like a thing instead of a process. What happens when you take the problem and treat it like a verb? For example, "How do you deal with social anxiety yourself?"

2. Investigate the problem's ecology. Look at the ways the problem can serve you. You are looking for things that may perpetuate the problem because they act as incentives. For example, social anxiety can cause you to reduce demands on yourself. Seeing how this happens can help you turn your attention to the problems that would make it difficult for you to tolerate those demands. With this expanded awareness, you can brainstorm solutions and get help.

3. Look for dysfunctional presuppositions that you have unconsciously embedded in the problem as you have defined it. Do your presuppositions make the problem somehow impossible to solve? Do they set up a condition for solving the problem that requires an uncooperative person to cooperate with you? Notice how these presuppositions are arbitrary and unnecessary. Challenge them.

4. Generate "what if" scenarios in order to come up with new problem formulations. Since this is brainstorming, go for quantity rather than quality. Use this as an opportunity to

"massage" the boundaries that your mind has created. For example, "How would I think of this problem if I had amazingly high self-esteem?" "What if I was a highly aggressive person?" "What if I had all the compassion, wisdom, and universal connectedness of a saint or Buddha?" Look at the problem in these scenarios, and see how it seems different.

5. Test. In the coming days, see what new resources and solutions come to mind regarding this problem. Watch for new behaviors and feelings. Has this exercise led to you being more flexible in your thinking and behavior in some ways?

Problem Solving Strategy (I)

Source: Robert Dilts

This pattern is the first in a series of innovative problem-solving strategies. This one uses the power of metaphor. You will need to have a good handle on metaphor in order to do this pattern.

1. Choose the problem and step into the problem position, associating with it. Consider a problem that you feel you need to approach in a fresh way. Choose a location in front of you to step into, that you will anchor to this problem situation. Step into that position and experience this problem first hand, experiencing how it happens in first position (through your own eyes).

2. Take a meta-position. Select another position that will serve as your meta-position, where you will view the problem from a transcendent or distant position. Step into this position.

3. Experience a rich resource from a resource position. Think of a resource situation that is unrelated to the problem. The situation should help you access a very rich and compelling resource state. For example, it could be an activity that gives you a strong sense of self, mission, creativity, or passion. Step into a new position that will now serve as your resource position. Fully integrated into the resource experience.

4. Create a metaphor for the problem, but one that is based on the resource position. Come up with a metaphor for your problem situation. In other words, create a new, fantasy problem that is a symbol for your real problem. The resource activity, its context, and your resource state should all serve as inspiration for your new fantasy problem.For example, if skiing was your main resource activity, then a real problem such as difficulty concentrating could be symbolized by getting your skis crossed up. The ski problem is now a metaphor (symbol) for the concentrating problem.

5. Imagine solving the metaphorical problem. Observe the resulting changes in your experience. Maintain your distance from the problematic situation, and imagine solving

the metaphoric problem. For example, you would come up with a solution to crossing your skis by developing good coordination for parallel skiing by focusing on controlling one of the skis so that the other naturally follows. Notice how this solution calls forth changes in your physical state, internal strategies, TOTEs, and so forth.

6. From your meta-position, apply the metaphoric solution to the original problem. Now step back into your meta-position. Explore how you would take the solution that you just created (for that metaphoric problem) and think metaphorically in order to translate it into a solution for the actual problem situation. For example, focusing on body language and controlling one of your skis to get parallel skiing is like clarifying your goals and reasons for focusing your mind on your studies.

7. Step into the problem location and check for results. Step into the problem situation location and see if you have dissolved your impasse.

8. Repeat, using other resource states. Repeat this process, using other resource states applied to the same problem. This brings in a variety of your resources, so you approach the problem from very different angles.

Problem Solving Strategy (II)

Source: Robert Dilts

This pattern helps a team of two or more people resolve a problem by creating a shared experience of an appropriate resource. The idea here is that if all the involved people are aligned with each other, any conflicts they may have had between themselves are no longer a factor in their effort to solve a given problem. This pattern is not only for business teams; you can use it when working with members of the same family or even couples. When there's a problem to be solved by more than one person, their shared interest and alignment alone might give all of them a stream of creative ideas for solving the issue. Using such a strategy might also help to mediate conflicts.

1. Locate a resourceful experience. Think back to a recent time in which you've had an experience you could define as resourceful. It should be an event in which you were fully congruent and competent, where you've been acting like a master and you have achieved your outcome. Associate into this memory. See what you saw, hear what you heard, feel what you felt, and notice what this acquired resourceful feeling actually feels like. Feelings can be expressed in terms of movement, so where and from where does this feeling go/come from?

2. Pre-mirroring a shared resource. Stand up, facing your partner. Demonstrate the movement of your resourceful feelings to your partner. Show him or her how it feels. Do not speak, just move your body to illustrate the feeling. Stay associated with your memory.

3. Posting-mirroring a shared resource Remain in the first position (associated) and mirror your partner's response to your movements. That is, mimic your partner's movements.

4. Switch to the second position. Exchange places with your partner. Move to the second position and act as if you are him or her. Be sure to notice the movement you've elicited from yourself in Step Two. It will change.

5. Shift to the third position. Move to the observer position (third position), and carefully observe both of you. What is similar? What seems different? Note the similarities and differences in the expression of the resourceful feelings movement that you and your partner show to each other.

6. Back to the 1st position, facing the same direction. Return to the first position, which is fully associated with the resourceful memory. You and your partner should now face the same direction, standing side by side. Now both of you begin the resourceful feelings' movement (each on your own) and continue until you find a similar move. It can be anything, long or short, rapid or slow. This is the "we" zone.

7. For teams, repeat with pairs. If you're doing this pattern with multiple teams, work in pairs and then combine them. Repeat in the same manner so that all four, six, or eight, and so on, are eventually aligned with a shared movement that gives each his or her own subjective, resourceful experience, but at the same time, it is a shared one.

8. Test. Testing is easy. It involves the solution of the problem at hand! Team up and work on the problem; every time you face a conflict, re-group in the same direction format and use the shared movement maneuver. If you feel a sense of "we are going to solve this one together," you have accomplished this exercise successfully. If not, it needs to be repeated, perhaps with a stronger subjective resourceful experience of each team member. When working with teams of people that you don't know personally, work hard first to establish group rapport with them and your position as a leader. Even if the team's current leader (a boss, a manager, or a supervisor) is present, make sure that he or she knows in advance that you're taking this approach in order to help the group come together and not to take over his or her responsibilities or authority. The best way to initially establish leadership is to use the one-up-manship concept. That's a concept that has been used by churches for years. Notice how the priest is always standing higher than the public, always in fancier and special clothing, always looking calm and in control, always moving with intention and always speaking with confidence.

You can do the same in any setting. In business situations, dress as if you own the place and you're the richest guy around. Walk in a consistent rhythm, not too fast or too slow, look around, and speak to mere strangers with confidence and never ever apologize. Even if you're late, do not say "I'm sorry I'm late, but I had this or that." Say something like, "I know I'm late, so we'd better start now."

Problem State

Sometimes we want to define an outcome only to sort out or solve a problem state that bothers us. The well-defined outcome criteria forbids negation or removal of anything as an aim, because not wanting something necessitates keeping it considered in our mental world and distracts us from our aim. By identifying and clarifying the problem and approaching it from different angles, we can transform it into a desired outcome that can then be well formed and fit the criteria.

1. Take a few moments to clear your mind and stay in the present moment.

2. What is the problem state that you would like to solve or change? Declare it in a statement: "I experience a problem when I..." or "My problem is that I..."

3. Effective negation: What do you want to avoid, remove, reduce, or stop? "I want to stop being/doing/behaving..."

4. Polarity: What is the opposite of the problem state? "I want, instead, to do/act/be..."

5. External reference: Who do you know that demonstrates access to the desired state you wish you had access to as well? "I want to behave/be like..."

6. Traits: What personality traits and behavioral principles do you recognize in that person that you'd like to emulate in yourself as well? "I want to embody the natural..."

7. Generative: What other qualities do you already possess that would further amplify the desired state? "I want to be even more..."

8. Future tempoIf I already had natural and easy access to the desired outcome, I would

9. Now, apply what you've learned in this process to the well-defined outcome pattern.

The Big Book of NLP

Process Orientation

Clients will often use nominalization and generalization to describe problems they're facing. "I am too lazy" or "I am always late to important meetings", "I am a procrastinator", "I have a fear of driving on highways," etc. When they describe what should be a process, as if it were a permanent object, we can use a simple linguistic maneuver to challenge that perception: "If I ask you to teach me how to X, please tell me how I would do X as well as you do." This helps you pinpoint the visual and kinesthetic anchors that "remind" the client to experience the problem. After disabling these anchors, you can ask them again to walk you step by step through the process of intensifying their problem, but this time the anchors are irrelevant, so they would have a hard time explaining the logic behind the behavior, which loosens and weakens the ineffective process even further.

Pseudo-Orientation in Time

This is a classic Ericksonian maneuver. You presuppose a future occasional meeting with the client in which they present in real life the changes you've made in the session. Erickson used it on his students by suggesting to them that they run into him in 6 months and tell him how and when the problem they were facing was solved.

For smoking cessation, for example, you should not tell the client "in six months we will meet and you will not smoke," because that's a negation that places the image of smoking within the client's mental map. You might say something like, "I wonder if you will remember to call me in a month or two and tell me that you're still drinking the morning cup of water with a slice of lemon." During the session, you can introduce a potential replacement (and kinesthetic anchor as a reminder) for the smoking habit, and by suggesting that the client still use it in a month or two, it gives the impression that smoking is out of the picture.

Recently, I worked with a female client who described herself as ugly and fat. Although she wanted to get involved and get married, she strongly believed no man in his right mind would ever want to be with her. As always, it's best to orient the therapy around an easily reachable desired outcome, and in her case, it was losing weight. So once we established the daily habits for her to become thinner, I used a simple pseudo-orientation in time suggestion that knocked down both issues she came in with: "I hope that you are now aware that we have a 100% success rate with clients who want to lose weight, and now that you're in the process, you'll see many changes going on at the same time, and I just want you to be prepared that as you become thinner, you will most likely attract the attention of worthy men, so please don't get too arrogant about it in a couple of months, and I hope that you'll get an invitation to your wedding. If you do forget this promise, I will be disappointed, but I understand that being popular and thin and busy can make you forget, but then again, I am expecting that envelope on this coffee table in front of us within a year. "

Punctuation Ambiguities

You can create transderivational searches with punctuation ambiguities. One form is to blend sentences.

For example, "As you sense some of the excitement of learning, physically sensing calm alertness" is a sentence where the word "physically" does double duty in the middle of two clauses, one about physically sensing the excitement, and the other about physically sensing calm alertness. You can also add improper pauses like... this... as you experience transderivational searching, causing you to try mind reading. These pauses can help you pace the person's breath as well. Another punctuation ambiguity is created by not providing the end of the... As you do a transderivational search, into which I blend a new idea.

Punctuation Diet

In the healing process, attention, frustration, and cooperation are all influenced by psychological time. As a speaker, it is possible to create a more compelling and time-constrained experience by emphasizing certain words. As you speak, keep an eye on how attentive your audience is to your every word. It's possible that you'll need to get used to the idea of people paying close attention to what you have to say and then allowing you to finish your thoughts. In addition, you might discover that they're eager to align and contribute ideas in the same direction. Be on the lookout for a slight forward lean or head forward posture, less blinking, and an unusually wide-eyed quality in others as you practice this system. Listen to recordings of yourself and experiment with the following iterations. Be sure to record yourself speaking normally first. You can use these techniques if you have a lot to say and need to grab the audience's attention and make sure your ideas stick.

Practicing this can help you pull your emphasis away from words that should not be emphasized. WHEN you EMPHasizethe WRONG WORDS, YOU can sound PREACHY and HAVE a SING SONG QUALity to your SPEECH.

Try it this way instead: When you EMPHasize the wrong words, you can SOUND preachy and   have a SING song quality to your SPEECH. This style will actually make it seem as though you are taking up less time as you speak. Less punctuation creates more contrast, and thus, more interest.

The human mind can take in a good number of non-emphasized words, so you will not lose your message by reducing the number of emphasized words. You actually compress psychological time so that it's easier to listen to you and take in your message. You can use this for pretty much anything you say, whether it is to the media, to clients, negotiating, or in your personal life. Listen to experts that are very media savvy when they are interviewed. Practice this with things that you typically say. You can mentally rehearse, record yourself, and refine the technique to fit your personality.

Qualities Projection

In essence, this advanced pattern depicts and positively uses the psychological process of projection, in which a mentality, characteristic, or quality is attributed or transferred to a person, community, or object by another—and is afterwards rejected by the projector. In a way, it's the reason we are drawn to hero's journey stories and films. We want to be like the hero we see on screen, but we reject the idea that these admirable qualities exist within us as well.To put it another way, projection is when you perceive yourself in other people and ignore the same qualities in yourself. If during this process, you feel emotionally unstable or uncomfortable, break state and postpone this practice to a time when you can do it with a trustworthy friend or your therapist.

1. Select and write the name of a person, either from fiction or real life, whose qualities and traits you admire.

2. Make a list of all the admirable qualities.

3. Initiate a downtime state.

4. Enter your mind's theater. It's empty, and the screen is blank.

5. Take a seat in the theater. Remember that the projector in the room behind you is supplying the image you see on the screen.

6. Watch the person you named acting on the screen, either in a scene from real life or a fictional story, and exhibit the qualities you admire, one by one.

7. Anchor the feelings of excitement and satisfaction you get when that person acts on those qualities.Make sure to anchor each presentation of the trait separately.

8. Break state. Go in front of a full-sized mirror.

9. Turning toward the mirror, strive to sustain as much eye contact with your reflection as possible as you concurrently attend to your own breathing. Breathe in deeply and smile.

10. Begin to recite aloud the list of attributes you have constructed. However, instead of reading merely the words that you have penned, you will be trying these qualities on, i.e., owning each of them.

11. Own each trait with a direct "I am..." declaration. Then, fire the anchor. Do this with the entire list and repeat the process five times.

12. Make a mental or actual note of anything that comes to mind as you say each statement. It's important to be aware of and fight the urge to stop or rush through the practice.

Realist Role

The role of the realist is to keep moving forward towards the desired outcome, and to ground the dreamer's ambitions and visions in reality. The realist is the actualizer of the action steps envisioned by the dreamer, and its main function is to act in the moment, not to judge the reasons behind the decisions.

The realist's role is defined by several important characteristics. The realist's representational preference is Action. Its focus orientation is 'How'. Its gravitational approach is Toward. Its preferred time frame is short term present, exclusively. Its communication reference is external (Environmental). Its comparison mode is Match (review the relevant Meta-Programs for more).

1. Select the active, desired, well-defined outcome you're working with. Defining the issues and obstacles you've recently encountered in the pursuit of this outcome

2. Initiate a downtime state.

3. Elicit the virtues of the realist:

a. Ask "How?" How can I make this happen?

b. Seek Action: What is the next most important and immediately available step?

c. Physiology of the realist: eyes straight ahead, head straight, eyes wide open, symmetrical and centered body posture, smooth movement, hands on waist (diamond pose).

4. Enter your timeline. Float above it. Lean slightly forward (toward).

5. Remain above the present.

6. Consider the issues in the context of the next 24 hours.

a. If I did X today, what would happened?

b. If I avoid doing X today, what will definitely not happen?

c. If I did X today, what would not happen?

d. If I avoid doing X today, what will definitely happen?

e. What bits of information seem to be in sync and related? Look for the matched stimuli.

7. Exit the timeline and break state.

Recognition Expression

Naturally, it's important for clients to feel that you "get" them. However, the serious emotional binds and traumas that they experience are among the most important things for you to acknowledge. When a client mentions something that is profoundly important, such as that, you should draw upon your life experience and flash a sign of recognition that shows your client that it registered and that you are not judging them or becoming defensive in some way.

First, you must be on the lookout for these profound disclosures. Many times, a client will mention something without any emotional emphasis. Still, they are likely to look at you to see how you respond. If you missed the content, that look should signal you to tune into the profundity of what they just revealed. When you notice a profound disclosure, here are some excellent ingredients for your response:

1) Take a deep breath in while slightly extending your upper back and tilting your head up, your mouth partially open, and your brows lifted.

2) Exhale completely.When half exhaled, acknowledge this in a way that conveys an "oh that..." quality. For example,

"Ah, attorneys..." or

"With years lost, right?" or (slightly shaking head), "It's just scary how many people are going through this now." or my favorite, "Isn't that something?"

Of course, you don't want to be dishonest. If you really don't know what the experience is about, convey how important it is to you to know more about what it involves and what impact it has had. Either way, you'll probably need to learn more about what the experience means to your client, as in how it colors their challenges today.

Reconstructing Into Values

Our culture doesn't encourage people to articulate their values or even to introspect very much. Our social institutions, including our schools and major media outlets, tend to encourage thinking in cliches.

When you link their automatic thoughts and efforts to their highest values, you really help clients develop an entirely new level of self-respect and appreciation. Then they get the added benefit of seeing how they can become even more aligned. If there's anything an NLP practitioner knows by heart, it's that alignment creates more creativity and energy than most people knew they had.

When you deconstruct the client's experience through a process such as the previous one, or some other sense mode breakdown, you are in a good position to work toward reconstruction.

Example

So you really want to say these things to him, and you know that with his personality, he will start manipulating and not really let it register. At least that's his usual style. Tell me about the values that drive your desire to say these things. "

Client: "Well, it's really disturbing to know he's in this little world of his pulling something like this with no accountability." I really want to get through to him. "

Therapist: "If you got through to him, that would mean that he would be a more caring person who could contribute more to the world, I suppose."

Client: "Well, yes."

Therapist: "Oh, and you would feel very different, free to say what you want and improvise when someone plays games like that."

Client: "Yes, I have to say I feel limited with people like that. I seem to attract these idiots. Each time I'm angrier than the last time. "

Therapist: "I suppose you could say that your desire to meet a challenge like this is about making the world a better place."

Client: "Okay, yeah, that would feel good. When pigs fly,

So the therapist said, "So do you doubt your ability to communicate your values, or his ability to hear them?"

Client: "Well, I'm sure with a little work I could be ready to say what I need to say. But this guy is a real piece of work. I don't think anybody ever gets through to him. "

Therapist: "Does that mean that refocusing your efforts on your own goals would be more meaningful than this fellow's personality problem?"

Client: "Okay, yeah, you got that right. It's true. I should. "

Therapist: "Since you tense up and seem unhappy about that prospect, let's talk a little about what makes this not inspire you—because I know you get very jazzed about certain kinds of professional challenges."

Note that we are starting to trigger a more resourceful state by comparing this challenge to some that have inspired her and by reminding her of feeling inspired. From here, the work would be about resolving obstacles to letting go of people with certain types of personalities and how to strategically cope with them, perhaps in terms of office politics.

The "reconstructing into values" here means that the client is thinking in terms of pursuing higher values at the same time as communicating more effectively. This helps make the work about something better than getting revenge or obsessing.

Recruiting Internal Resources

To help you prepare for the day's duties, here is a brief practice. As a visual aid, it serves as a reminder of the abundance of resources available to you, within you. With the help of internal resources, you may be more present and responsive to current reality. You can use this technique to prepare for a discussion that you expect to be difficult. Visualize this whenever you lack confidence, do not really know where to go next, or just want to re-center yourself.

1. Take a few deep breaths, and as you tune out to the sounds and sensations surrounding you, answer the following questions:

a. Who in your life has provided you with unwavering support? You can look as far as you need to the past to find that person.

b. List the top three qualities you admire about this person.

c. Consider three to five additional persons you admire. They could be real or from another epoch. Make a list of three characteristics about each one of them them that you appreciate.

d. As you consider these persons, make a list of five qualities in yourself that you aspire towards.

2. Downtime: Close your eyes and enter your mind's theatre. You sit in the center of the stage.

3. Imagine the 5 admirable person from step 2c entering the stage from the left. They all wear matching T-Shirts, titled "Support Team".

4. Imagine your supporters coming closer, settling as a semi-circular team sitting around and in front of you.

The Big Book of NLP

5. Imagine them offering you these qualities that you admire. Each is holding a symbol of its most important (to you) quality in both hands, palms up and reached out towards you.

6. Accept the offer, and notice what happens with your posture as they are transferring their qualities and strengths to your hands.

7. Take a deep breath, open your eyes and note of your posture: how you are sitting right now.

8. Test. Think about the upcoming challenge that you felt less confident about previously. How do you feel now, with all these qualities embedded within you?

Referential Index Switch

When a client tries to establish a rule in order to justify a presupposition or mind reading, instead of arguing the illogical implications of his argument (which is useless as the client is convinced of their righteousness), we can switch it around to minimize the impact of the rule.

1. Pace the statement or rule.

2. Apply the paced statement to its most plausible implication.

3. Switch the referential index to put the client on a continuum rather than a strict measurement.

For example: the client says she feels her husband does not care about her because he doesn't give her flowers. A Referential Index Switch could be "Well, how many vases do you have to fill with flowers so that he is aware of how much he cares about you?".

In essence, we tell her that her rule for someone else's feelings is rigid and that even following it to the extreme is not going to affect the other person's state. It is her feelings that she needs to take charge of, not what someone else has or has not in their hidden thoughts.

Re-Imprinting

Source: Robert Dilts

Upgrade your deeper beliefs and your behaviors by changing the influence of role models. Improve the effect of negative role models, and create a stronger influence from positive role models. This pattern is called re-imprinting because many problems, including physical symptoms, learning disabilities, phobias and other problems can be caused or exacerbated by influences that are active during key periods in our development (developmental windows). This concept should not be used to deny genetic, toxic and other influences that form a direct biological basis for many such problems.

1.

a. Choose the behaviors, symptoms or beliefs you wish to change. Unless you are a beginner, choose behaviors or beliefs that seem to be deeply ingrained.

b. Float up over your timeline and look toward the future.

c. Pay attention to the physical expression of your target as well as in the form of beliefs.

d. Walk backwards slowly. Pause at each location that is relevant somehow to the target.

e. Continue back until you reach the earliest experience of the target (the initial imprint experience).

f. Access the state associated with this target and the experiences.

g. From that state, verbally express the beliefs that came from these experiences.

h. Speak in the first person, for example, "I do not deserve protection and compassion."

i. Move back in time to a point just before this first experience (the initial imprint experience).

j. Notice how this changes your state. You know that you have gone back far enough when you are in a very different state; one that has no sign of the imprint experiences or the beliefs that stem from them.

2.

a. Float forward to the actual present, but stay in the observer (dissociated) position.

b. Looking back over your past timeline, notice how your imprinting experiences have affected your life; how they have helped generate the behaviors, symptoms or beliefs that you chose for this pattern, and any others that you can discover.

c. Talk to yourself, as if you were narrating a documentary about yourself, speaking in third person (he/she). Describe what you were just observing about your life.

d. Think about all this with positive intentions or secondary gain in mind. How have the behaviors, symptoms or beliefs that emerged from these experienced reflected an attempt, on some level, to cope with them. Even if the results were bad, seek the underlying positive intention or presuppositions.

You may get your best results by looking for subtle feelings connected with these things, and then putting words to those feelings. If you discover that an irrational attitude has strongly affected your life, then you have found something especially important. Remember that these attitudes can range from simple to complex. They may show up in simple reactive measures such as avoiding responsibility or other fear-inducing experiences (because, for example, of an experience that lead you to believe that you would be harshly criticized any time you tried to do something). On the other hand, they may manifest as more complicated ways of managing (or manipulating, more likely) other people in the service of an agenda such as denial. For example, "I must carefully orchestrate interactions so that I am not exposed to any beliefs or ideas that would frame my pot consumption as a problem; my loss of motivation and mental clarity are not to be connected with that."

The Big Book of NLP

3.

a. Focus on any people that figured largely in these imprint experiences. Although we're talking about "imprinting," your experiences may or may not actually involve other people in a significant way. Pay special attention to any ways that you "absorbed" (modeled) another persons style or attitudes, so that you came to cope with certain situations in a characteristic, dysfunctional way.

b. For each person, associate into their perspective (the second perceptual position), and experience one or two of the most significant imprint experiences that they were involved in from their perspective. Describe the experiences in their terms, using first person (I, me, my) language in their style as much as possible.

c. Step off of the timeline, into an objective position (third perceptual position), and determine the positive intentions behind their behavior.

4.

Do the following for each person involved in your imprint experiences, if any:

a. Decide what resources that the person needed at those times, but did not have, but that you can contribute now in some way now.

b. Find a location on your timeline where you have had a very significant experience of being rich with these resources. (For example, a person dealing with drug use might recall being in a twelve step meeting that was very compelling and resulted in a period of drug avoidance and better functioning).

c. Step on that point in your timeline.

d. Amplify this rich state, and experience it as a kind of energy.

e. Anchor the state.

f. Imagine that you can transmit this resource back through your timeline to each person who needs it.

g. When you feel that you have made a good connection, float back to the imprint experience, and associate into the position of the person that received the resource.

h. Re-experience the imprint experience from their perspective, but with the resources actively in place. You can amplify the resource state in them by triggering the resource state.

i. Staying at this point in your timeline, move into your own perceptual position.

j. Notice how this experience has changed with the resources in place.

k. Experience how this upgraded experience stimulates beliefs and attitudes in you that are more resourceful.

l. Express this verbally in first person.

m. Do the previous two actions for each person that you identified as being significant in the imprinting experiences.

5.

a. Move back to your present time, into an objective position.

b. Look back over the imprint experiences, and (as you did for the significant people), identify what resources would have been valuable to you during the imprint experiences.

c. Experience these resources and access the state that they inspire.

d. Anchor this state when it peaks.

e. With these resources, and in this state, float back to a point prior to your early imprint experience.

f. Transmit or give these resources to your younger self at that timeline point.

The Big Book of NLP

g. Imagine walking along your timeline from that point toward the present, and experiencing all the changes made by all the changes (re-imprinting) from this pattern.

6. Test. In the coming days and weeks, notice any ways that this re-imprinting pattern has influenced the behaviors, symptoms or beliefs that you chose for this pattern.

Reinforcement (I)

Fear of the unknown can prevent people from leaning forward into the new and healthy choices they make in the course of therapy and halt their progress. Reinforcement of the positive changes is often needed.

1. Take a few deep breaths. Initiate a downtime state.

2. In your opinion, what else needs to happen for things to go even better?

3. Close your eyes. Imagine a person in your life that is already benefiting from the progress you've made in therapy. It could be your parents, your spouse, your children, or any other relationships that are influenced positively by your new choices of behavior and attitudes.

4. Assume the second perceptual position and the role of that person. Look at "you" from within the mental map of this person.

5. Tell X (the client's name) what the last couple of weeks have felt like because of his/her new choices. Tell them how much you appreciate their efforts and how proud you are of them for getting through the struggle and becoming stronger.

6. Break state. Take the fourth perceptual position and notice the ecology of the situation. Notice how your new choices of behavior have influenced not only that one person, but everyone else in their and your surroundings. Because of you, that person was inspired to make new, healthier choices of their own and, through that, inspired other people to do the same.

7. Break state. Assume the fifth perceptual position and notice what is known as "six degrees of separation"-the extensive network of webbed influence and how every choice you've made inspires hundreds and hundreds of better choices in acquaintances and acquaintances.

The Big Book of NLP

8. Break state. Future pace Imagine a time in the future in which random strangers recognize you somehow and tell you that this person you both know has told them about what you've done for them, how you inspired them, and how that got them motivated to get better. And they thank you for being so generous.

9. Break state. Open your eyes and answer the same question again: In your opinion, what else needs to happen for things to go even better?

Reinforcement (II)

This is a cognitive-linguistic approach to the reinforcement of positive changes during therapeutic interventions.

1. Ask: "What is going better in your life since our very first session X weeks ago?"

2. Listen to the answer, maintain rapport, and ask: "On a scale of 10 to 0, where 10 means that the problem that brought you to me has been sufficiently solved or your most desired outcome has been reached, and 0 is the worst moment you've experienced in your lifetime, where are you now?"

3. Repeat the number the client says, and ask: "What does that number stand for?" If the client hesitates, give them time and encourage them to consider broader perspectives in terms of location and time.

4. Ask, "Let me ask you this now, that you have experienced such important changes: how is it that you are already at that number?" - If the client seems confused, you may say, "You see, most of my clients take much longer to get there, and yet you've made these wonderful changes in such a short time, although you told me when we first started working together that you're weak and have low self-esteem. You have proven the exact opposite in half the time! "

We use the client's positive perceptions to embed commands, presuppositions, and future paces in them to make further positive changes.

5. Ask, "Now let me ask you this-how did you manage to remain at that number?" This is an important question because what the client describes next is the basis for the next plan of action in their therapy program.

6. Ask, "And now the obvious question-what would one step higher look like? I'm not asking you to take any risks; just fantasize for a moment what it would mean-what would you see, hear, and feel if that number was X+1 instead of X? "

If the client is not sure of the answer, ask: "How would you notice in real life that you had gone up 1 point?"

7. Ecology check: "What difference would X+1 make for you and the important people in your life?"

8. Future pace: "What do you see as the next step?"

Relationship Clarifying

Source: Robert Dilts (an adaptation of Characterological Adjective)

This pattern helps you identify characterological adjectives (CA's). Ca's encode the basic characteristics of relationships. Each CA implies a counterpart. For example, the CA of "victim" implies the counterpart of "victimizer." Getting to the essence of a dyadic relationship opens the gateway to understanding the dynamics of the relationship and how the two parties contribute to enduring patterns, including dysfunctional ones.

1. Pick a difficult person or situation to work with. Come up with a person that you have trouble communicating with or a situation that gets in the way of you being creative and productive in getting desirable results. In such a situation, you would feel stuck.

2. Find a typifying word in the third position. Imagine that you are observing the situation from a seat in a movie theater. Allow your mind to come up with a word that captures the essence of the situation, such as "obstructive" or "narcissistic."

3. Place yourself on the screen in this situation. Observe your own behavior and come up with a word that captures the essence of your reactions and involvement with this situation or person. For example, "reactive" or "gullible."

4. Isolate the CA's. Think of the two words or phrases that you came up with, such as "obstructive" and "reactive" or "narcissistic" and "gullible."

Take note of how these two words or phrases are antonyms for one another. You have gotten to the essence of the dyad by isolating the characterological adjectives.

Relationship Enhancement

When it comes to relationships, whether you've been in one for a long time or are just starting out, you may not have a clear picture of what you want from it and how you want it to feel. What is your preferred method of communication? If a disagreement arises, how do you intend to resolve it? How much time do you want to spend together?How significant is it to receive affectionate physical contact? In the absence of a shared vision, you and your spouse are more likely to react to events than to create the kind of relationship you want. Even if you're not currently in a relationship, it's a good idea to have a long-term relationship goal in mind. In this way, you'll be able to meet someone who shares your vision.

1. With your partner present, sit across from each other, face to-face.

2. Both of you initiate a downtime state.

3. Each time you reach out with your hands across your body (right to left, left to right), left hand palm up and right hand palm down, Rest your right hand on the partner's left hand's palm and allow them to rest their right hand on your left hand's palm. This is an uncomfortable and awkward position on purpose, as this will help overload the critical mind and bypass some resistance.

4. Both of you enter the timeline and go back to the very first date you had with each other. Transfer to a third perceptual position.Do not talk about the details of the date; only answer the following questions, each in your own turn.

a. How have your previous relationships made you a better partner for me?

b. How do you normally react when you are feeling hurt and sad about something important?

c. What makes you lose confidence in a partner?

d. When are you at your happiest?

e. Looking forward to a life together, what might ruin our relationship?

f. How can we help one another become the people we want to be?

g. When do you feel the most vulnerable? How can I prevent myself from hurting you at those times?

5. Take a few deep breaths. Break state. Turn around and sit back to back, feeling each other's backs of the heads, shoulders, and backs.

6. Enter the timeline again, and move forward 20 years. Turn around on the timeline, looking towards the past.

7. Ask each other, "Where and when were you unwilling to compromise?"

8. Break state. Take a short break to think about everything you have just learned about each other.

9. The key to this process is not to argue or debate the information given. Imagine you have read it in the other person's journal without them knowing, and move on with your day holding that knowledge inside.

Remember To Forget

If you can forget, and you can cause other people to forget (no matter what), you are in a very powerful position to change yourself. Your complete list of non-useful behaviors and destructive unconscious thought pattern issues can all be solved with a simple skill: forgetting. We usually attach negative meanings to the skill of forgetting.

When we forget, we are conditioned to perceive it as meaning that you didn't care enough, your brain is not functioning properly, or you did not remember it in the first place.

Most people believe that forgetting something is beyond their control, as if it is a matter of luck or coincidence or simply a lack of neurological resources regarding specific areas of memory. While that can be true at times, it is not usually the real cause. You can forget it on cue. You can remember anything you want to remember for however long you want to remember it, and then forget it again when you choose to.

Forgetting, however, is probably a new conscious skill for you if you are not a very skillful hypnotist by now. How many times have you heard the phrase, "Oh, just forget about it."? People have instructed you to forget something you were planning to remember. You sometimes complied if it wasn't important, and sometimes you didn't if you thought this person thought you weren't serious about the job.In fact, you can come to this conclusion on your own; you can remember about forgetting. If you can forget little things like your keys or where you put your latest IRS return, one more little thing won't be that hard to forget either, right? How about if you could forget that your spouse was very annoying yesterday evening? Forget everything about that event. Could it be useful for your relationship? Could it help to alleviate some of the lingering resentment?What if you could forget you had a headache? Do you really think you are not able to do so on cue? Can you recall a time when you had a headache and then suddenly needed to be very focused or occupied with something and you completely forgot about it?In fact, that headache didn't bother you anymore; it seems like it has dissolved into darkness—or forgetfulness.

The key point to remember is that there is no pain if you can't remember it. The nervous system is so sensitive that it sends a very nasty message to the brain when something isn't functioning right or when an organ is hurt. The pain is a response to make sure that you, as a whole, know that something is wrong with your body and you're going to find a remedy for it. If you didn't have the pain associated with stomach aches, how would you even know that your body was trying to deal with substances that hurt it? How much damage does your body need to absorb before you notice it? Has it not produced the pain?

Pain is useful. Pain is not your friend, but it is a trusted messenger. Once you have taken all the actions needed to help your body get on the road to healing, you can plan to forget the pain. And when you do, if you can't remember it, it is not a problem anymore. There are many war stories about soldiers that lose an arm or get hurt by flying bullets—and they do not feel the pain until hours later, when the battle is over. That is the power of being able to forget, whether for a few moments or for a lifetime. It is useful. Obviously, you should use it with care. Some people make it a point to remember every single detail of their lives. I believe, sincerely, that this is a very bad mistake. First, since you already distort reality as you experience it (basic NLP if you haven't read it yet), How can you make sure you remember your life as it truly is? You cannot. Therefore, by making it a point to remember every single detail, good or bad, you're actually making choices as to which version of the event you will keep. Since that's true, isn't it obvious that who you are today is based on the choices and distortions you have made all of your life, often subconsciously? In hypnotherapy, we call this "living a lie."

We are all living in some kind of lie. But some of us are simply living a better functioning lie/life. It is a skill worth learning and perfecting to be able to forget those things that are not extremely important but in their current version do disturb and ruin your present chances of succeeding.

Forget the number "365." Sometimes, when you are really trying very hard to forget something, you actually remember it even better. Forget the number "365." Forget it now. Many years ago, I did that trick with my niece. She was only 8 years old, but even at that age, she could not forget how many days are in a year. What was it then? You see? You can't forget it. If you live in the U.S., try to forget the combination of these 3 numbers: 911. Forget it now. That number actually has two distinctive but very powerful and permanent anchors: 911 (police) and 9/11. Is it going to be useful to forget how many days there are in a year? (What was that number again?) Not at all. Is it useful to forget that if you're in the

U.S. and need to dial the police emergency number, that is 911, and if you hear the term "nine eleven," should you forget what happened on that date?

Certainly not. It is not useful, and that is why people are not forgetting it. If it is important enough, it will stay, usually on its own. If it doesn't stay on its own (like the thick biochemistry books you need to learn for your next exam), you should make a point of remembering it.

You can plan to forget it. You can make yourself forget something. It is so easy that you don't have any idea how, within the next hour, you are going to acquire and almost perfect that skill. I considered showing you how you could forget you even read this article, but that might lead to an endless loop. How many times would you read the article, thinking it was for the first time?

Helping Others To Forget

Before you start daydreaming about having all-mighty hypnotic powers, throwing suggestions around and making people forget things, you must adopt an important ethical principle. Unless the person approves, you must not induce forgetting. They must give you permission to engage in this hypnotic communication. This is an ethical matter, because it means that you are placed in a "one-up" position. You can certainly persuade people, change their minds, and influence many aspects of their thought patterns, but to establish that authority, there must be a one-up position. That means that your client has accepted you into a position of trust. That is a position of responsibility. Violation of that trust would be a form of abuse or battery.

Helping Others To Forget Can Be Useful When:

In some cases, therapists feel that it is in your client's best interest to forget the content of a certain work so that they will not sabotage the work with their conscious minds. You are a salesman, and you want your client to ignore your competitors. You are a father or a mother, and you want your kid to forget a traumatic episode or some unfortunate argument in the family, so he won't be influenced to collect non-useful beliefs in the future. "I am bad and that's why my parents yelled at me." is not the right frame of mind for a six-year-old to grow up with. Making him forget it and implementing a new useful frame can mean a lifetime difference, literally. You were training a misguided, zealous NLP student, and you want to forget all the crap they taught that person that he or she accepted as the ultimate truth. You are a stage hypnotist and want to demonstrate the power of hypnosis to hundreds of people. By making them forget that they paid you $150 for a one-hour show. The useful examples are endless. Let's go directly to the juicy stuff. How could you make yourself or others forget whatever you wish?

Resolving Internal Conflicts

This pattern helps with the very common problem of disagreement between parts. When you struggle with yourself to do or not do something, when you procrastinate and seem to be arguing with yourself in your mind, this is the pattern to use.

1. The Struggle: Choose a personal conflict. It may be something you're ambivalent about, or some way that you sabotage yourself or cannot accept yourself.

2. A Recollection: Recall a memory of experiencing this inner conflict. View it from the observer position.

3. Choose a Side: Get into the first perceptual position with one side of the conflict. Step into the experience. Review the other side of the conflict from this position. Notice what comes up during this in all senses of the word.

4. Positive Intention: Still on that side, ask the other side to express all of its positive intentions, including any beliefs and goals that it can express to your side.

5. Switch: Now step into the other part. From this position, repeat steps three and four.

6. Repeat: Repeat this switching and receiving until both sides have a good understanding of each other. Be sure to include your beliefs, values, and objectives.

7. Meta-Position: Move to a meta-position above both parts. From there, ask the parts to propose solutions or outcomes that they expect to be satisfactory to both sides. Elicit concerns from either side about these ideas, and note any ecological issues. Do as much brain-storming as you need to in order to come up with a good collection of ideas.

8. New part: Notice how this new collection of ideas is an amalgamation of the values and higher intentions of the two parts. It is also an agenda. Experience how it could be considered a part all on its own. Bring this part into your body and accept it as an important part.

9. Pace and Test in the Future: Imagine a future with this part creating results for you. Redo this process as needed for any ecological concerns or problems. Test it out in real life and come back to this process as needed.

The Big Book of NLP

Resource Audit

Source: Robert Dilts

This is a process that can help you clarify and strengthen your belief in your learning capabilities and development of internal resources that are needed for you to pursuit and achieve worthwhile desired outcomes. An internal resource can be any trait or skill, such as: patience, creativity, memorization, negotiation, extrorevtism, public speaking, analyzing data, etc.

1. State the desired internal resource in one sentence. Below we refer to this description of the internal resource as X (therefor, replace X with your statement).

2. Say "X, because..." - answer: Why is this internal resource important to you?

3. Say "X, and as a result..." - answer: What is the effect of successfully acquiring the internal resource?

4. Say "X, after..." - answer: What must happen before this internal resource is fully integrated?

5. Say "X, while.." - answer: What is happening in sync with the development of the internal resource?

6. Say "X, whenever..." - answer: In what contexts is this internal resource essential?

7. Say "X, so that..." - answer: What is the intention behind desiring this specific internal resource?

8. Say "X, if / in case..." - answer: What constraints does this internal resource present? In which conditions and situations?

9. Say "X, or else…" - answer: What are the alternative options, both positive and negative, to this internal resource?

10. Say "X, just as with…" - answer: What prior evidence, small or big, do I have to further enhance my belief in being able to learn, acquire and integrate the internal resource?

The Big Book of NLP

Resource Fractal

Source: Robert Dilts

Enhance your problem solving, creativity, or simply your enjoyment of life by creating a synesthetic (multi-representational system) expression of an optimal state.

1. Select and access a resourceful state.

2. Initiate a related movement pattern. Find within yourself a pattern or kind of body movement that seems to somehow express this state. You may find a pattern, or the movement may evolve more like a free-form dance. Give yourself permission to do it your own way, without the burden of judgement or preconceptions.

3. Change up the movements. With care and mindfulness, make gentle and subtle variations of this pattern. Notice how this affects how you experience your resourceful state. Explore how this connects you to its deeper structure.

4. Transfer the movements. Transfer this movement pattern and quality to another part of your body. For instance, if you began with your hand, move it up into your shoulders and neck. Be gentle if you are not much of a dancer.

5. Extend the movements to more areas. Extend this movement quality to many parts of your body, perhaps the totality of your body. Even invite it to come out in your facial expression.

6. Use another rep system. Repeat this using another rep system. This time, you used the kinesthetic in four dimensions (by adding time expression through movement). You could swap that for visuals by drifting through memories and creating images that express the state. You could create an auditory expression by singing and tapping or by remembering and inventing sound environments in your mind. You can add words, impressionistically and poetically, or by describing the soundscapes. There are plenty of possibilities for your creativity.

7. Test. In the coming days and weeks, notice any ways that you are using your intelligence and creativity across rep systems to solve problems, be creative, or simply experience a richer world.

Reversed Effect

The human mind has rules and natural laws that govern its ways of functioning. One of the most important rules we all should get to know is The Hypnotic Law of Reversed Effect. This law simply states that the harder you focus on performing an action, the harder it becomes to perform it well. The opposite force would be, of course: "take it easy". For example, the harder you try to force yourself consciously (with reason, persuasion, etc.) to sleep, the more awake you'll just be. Reversed effect...you give more effort but get the reversed result. Why is it hypnotic? Because it works under the surface. You try to force a logic conclusion, like "I need an erection now" or "I have to sleep now because otherwise I'd be late tomorrow morning," and you force it on the part of your mind that understands it in reverse. The unconscious doesn't obey straight orders; it's not the army. You say, "I want an erection because there's none." and your unconscious is focusing on that fact. There's none. Here's the direction: no erection. It also works the other way around. You can formulate a suggestion according to the Hypnotic Law of Reversed Effect. However, you must use indirect suggestions to work the magic and not direct orders. Here are some examples:

"...and it seems to me you can concentrate on other aspects of the sexual experience while your body gathers the blood towards your penis. In fact, the more you concentrate on pleasing your partners, the HARDER IT BECOMES..."

"Now you may have the idea of being able to open your eyes while in Hypnosis, but it may seem strange and how so that the harder you try the harder it becomes, because there's a sense of no urgency to take care of all the things you've left BEHIND you and above you can still imagine that crystal view...and I dare you to make that poor attempt with your eyes, since the harder you try the tougher it becomes while you're keeping this sensation of coolness, freshness, relaxation... "

"No need to rush...make the attempt, and let it rest...so you told me that the anger just builds up within you and in a split of a second it bursts out with rage and you have no control over what seems to be so trivial, your emotions, your body, your sense of wholeness and calmness...and I wonder if you can force that anger right now, if you can create it with your own command, since the harder you try the harder it becomes and seems much easier to stay calm and quiet and absorb the world instead of reacting to it… nothing much left in life if not fulfillment and happiness and that anger that you have tried to build within you and seems like it's the hardest job in the world. "

"Can't even remember where it was the first time, however you can try and try and try and once you're tired of trying you let it go…there's are easier choices…"

The Big Book of NLP

Rhetorical Rapport

A good way to establish rapport with someone is to get them into a positive state of mind right from the start. We can do this by asking rhetorical questions, which means questions that can only have one response: a definite yes. This works especially well with children. The most effective rhetorical question is, "Do you like X?"

By suggesting a mental image of something the other person likes, in order to consider the answer (although it's always 'yes'), they have to imagine it first, which puts them in a comfortable and positive state of mind.

Then we can use a series of rhetorical questions to enhance rapport, pace, and then lead them towards linking the positive state with a new commitment. For example, "Do you like ice cream?", "Do you like more than one flavor of ice cream?", "Do you like sitting on a bench in the park on a hot day and licking the top of the ice cream?", "Do you like being aware and present while eating ice cream?", "Do you like learning how to feel even better with or without ice cream?"

Rhythmic Learning

Source: Erickson Institute

Here is a strategy that you can explore and adapt to your own learning adventures. It uses the power of rhythm to create attention and involvement. Rhythm exists in every cell of your body. There must be a deeper reason for our fascination and excitement when music grabs our attention so intensely. If a song does not have a catchy rhythm, we lose interest. This strategy uses that natural tendency to seek a continuous cycle, i.e., rhythm, in our absorption of knowledge. There is more to it, however, than just tapping your foot or hand.

While learning rote material, establish a rhythm that you will keep with your thumb, head, or foot, depending on your preference. Use a common rock rhythm that is a little faster than one beat per second. If the material is difficult to absorb, use a slower rhythm. Keep a rhythm that uses four beats, just like most songs, ONE, TWO, THREE, FOUR, ONE... Keeping rhythm, run the item you're learning through your mind. If it is long, use several rounds of four beats (measures).

Leave room for silence so that it soaks in and conforms to the measures. Silence is a very powerful part of music and the dramatic arts. It is literally part of the communication, and it is essential to make it compelling. Here is a rhythm learning example: If you were studying the cow's anatomy, you might want to learn all the structures around the ear, the regio temporalis. That could be three beats with one left over to complete the four-beat measure: RE-gio TEM-por AL-is (beat). A long word or phrase can take up more than one measure. For example, processus zygomaticus osis temporalis could be PRO-CES-sus-ZY-GO-MAT-i-CUS (beat, beat). The lower case syllables are on the "upbeat," which is in between the main beats. That means there are six beats for this one, plus two silent beats to finish the second, four-beat measure. That gives us eight beats, or two measures.

Once you have done the category, such as the region we just mentioned, you can chunk down to the specific structures or items in that category, maintaining the rhythm and including silences that make it complete.Stick with this for a specific set of words or concepts, and keep at it long enough to cover a defined area or topic of study, such as an anatomical region. See what effect this pattern has on your memorization ability. If you have music on that doesn't go too fast, you can experiment with keeping to the rhythm of the music for variety.

It might even give you some rhythm ideas, especially in rhythm and blues. If you are a musical person, you can add a unique melody to each item, or even bring the items together into a song or improvised melody.

Riding the Timeline

This is an advanced strategy to create a solid state of congruence.

1. Initiate a downtime state.

2. Enter your timeline. Float above the present moment and dissociate yourself from the fourth perceptual position.

3. Complete the sentence, "Today I am..."

4. Move backwards on your timeline to yesterday, and complete the sentence, "Yesterday I was..."

5. Move backwards on your timeline to at least three years ago, to any point in the past. Complete the sentence: "In the past, I have been

6. Break state.

7. Enter your timeline again. Float above the present moment and dissociate yourself from the fourth perceptual position.

8. Move forward on your timeline to the future, 3 months from today, and complete the sentence "I am becoming..."

9. Move forward on your timeline to the future, around age 65, and complete the sentence, "I define my identity as..."

10. Move backwards on your timeline, still in the future, 5 years from today, and complete the sentence: "I have worn masks and played many different roles. The ones that I have since discarded are... "

11. Move forward in your timeline to the future, a day before you pass away, and complete the sentence, "I wish I had learned earlier to..."

12. Break state.

13. Enter your timeline again. Float above the present moment and dissociate yourself from the fourth perceptual position.

14. Move forward on your timeline to the future, 10 years from today. Assume you have accomplished every well-defined desired outcome and complete the sentence, "This is how I got here..."; take as much time as you need to list all the milestones that got you to that point.

15. Exit the timeline when you're done. What have you learned?

Satir Categories

Virginia Satir was one of the first family therapists. Like Erickson, she was modeled for NLP purposes, and her work is one of the three fundamental models of NLP. She was born in 1916 and became a noted psychotherapist. Her best-known books were Conjoint Family Therapy and Peoplemaking, in which she describes her family therapy work to a popular audience. Satir wrote the book "Changing With Families: A Book About Further Education for Being Human" with Bandler and Grinder. She developed the Virginia Satir Change Process Model through clinical studies. This model has also been applied to organizational change. Satir found that people fell into five categories, each of which had its own body language, attitude, and communication patterns. They are the Blamer, Placater, Computer, Distracter, and Leveler. NLP has incorporated these styles into its training.

The Blamer

Blamers externalize blame and appear to be always ready to place the blame in a harsh or judgmental way. When things go wrong, the blamer starts blaming. The blamer also pushes their thoughts and feelings onto everyone else. In NLP, you may see blamers referred to as skunks because they spray their criticism outward. Blamers, like all the categories, have their own body language. When they're in blaming mode, they point their finger at people and have a firm, controlling style of body language. They tend to use confusion tactics to make it easier to get the blame to stick without too much resistance from others. They do this with meta-model violations such as over-generalizing, connecting ideas that don't belong together, and making claims for which there is no proof. Blamers can end up pretty lonely because their behavior is alienating. They do their best with very like-minded people and stay at peace with them by focusing their blame on the same people or groups. This forms a kind of bond. Inside, the blamer may not be nearly as confident and secure as they appear. Blaming can serve to compensate for vulnerabilities such as the fear of judgement and feeling so small as to need to align with a larger authority that justifies being blaming in service of that larger authority. Blamers generally blame in the name of a system, such as a family, church, employer, or political cause. As an employer or supervisor, they may be held responsible in the name of profit. Blame can be a strategy for office politics. Blamers use general statements, complex comparisons, and missing proof to confuse the other person, and then place the blame. Such people usually end up alone, since nobody wants to be at the receiving end of the blame.

The Placater

The placater is also one way of displacing blame, but they do it more diplomatically. The placater is much more concerned about how people view them, so much of their behavior is an escape from conflict or unwanted attention or blame. A blamer will fight fire with fire, but a placater blows the fire onto someone else's house and shares their neighbor's upset over the fire department's being slow to arrive. Their body language tends to be palms facing up and shoulders shrugging. They may also tend to slouch. Placaters hide their approach with meta-model violations such as cause and effect, modal operators, and unspecified verbs. They may get your sympathy with a poor-me attitude. When there is conflict, they go into hiding, at least by becoming noncommittal. Placaters may be found firmly sitting on the fence.

The Computer

The computer style can be pretty unemotional. They cover up possible emotions with extra words. They may sound academic or scientific. When someone else becomes emotional, they act like they are trying to become a counter-weight by acting even more cool, calm, and collected. Computers hide from their own feelings and invalidate others' feelings because they have not learned to cope with feelings, whether they are their own or someone else's.

NLP training materials have referred to them as Mr. Cool or Mr. Spock, a science fiction character from a planet where everyone aspired to be perfectly logical. They may tend to fold their arms, especially when things get too personal for them, and they are often seen in a neutral posture. Some fit the nerd stereotype, and may be physically awkward or make gestures that are a bit eccentric or un-self-conscious.

It may seem like they are drawing their energy up in their head, and that their body mostly serves to support their brain.In relationships, the computer can harm the intimacy by being too far away. Many computer-savvy people are considered to have an autism spectrum diagnosis such as Asperger syndrome. In terms of meta-model patterns, computers hide out by using generalizations and omitting references.

The Distracter

There is another style that can be a chameleon. They are seen as a mix between a blamer and a computer or placater. But there is a common thread that runs through their styles, and that is to manipulate through distraction. They may induce confusion or simple fatigue in the other person. They train others not to hold them accountable by making it very difficult to have a straight conversation with them. They are intuitive about escalating the distraction as needed. They can be quite exasperating, especially if they are not very socially skilled or if they are cognitively impaired. They may tend to gesture a great deal in an attempt to communicate their thoughts and emotions with their body, but subconsciously, this can serve to further fill up other people with excess stimuli, adding to the confusion. From a meta-model point of view, they switch topics too much, overgeneralize, and omit references.

The Leveler

Finally, there is the leveler. The leveler has high congruence and does not blanch at being factual. They do not over-dramatize, so if there is blaming to do, they are objective and fair about it. When confronted by the other styles, the most evolved levelers have a special ability to stay in touch with reality and their own agendas and self-interest. If they upset anyone, it's because their style interferes with manipulation by the other styles. What upsets people more than someone getting in the way of their attempts to manipulate? The leveler may have their hands facing down, as if they are trying to calm things down and encourage level-headedness. This is because they often end up in a mediator role because of their own level-headedness. Their ability to see both sides of an argument makes them good mediators.

Utilizing Flexibility

An important part of the Satir model is that people need to develop flexibility in their styles, so that they are not locked into one. With more flexibility, people can adapt to more situations and solve more interpersonal problems. They can certainly create fewer personal problems with that flexibility. So, while the leveler may appear to be the best style, it can be a problem if it is the only style in which you are comfortable. A good mediator knows that having various styles can make the difference between success and failure in a negotiation. The same holds true for anyone, really. For example, being a blamer may help knock someone off of their stream of thought because it is a real state interrupt. It may help level the playing field when someone else is being too high-handed.

Category Rapport-Building

Done properly, you may actually win the respect of a blamer by acting like a blamer, but this is advanced. You have to be in that style without putting the blamer on the defensive, so pacing the blamer's style means adopting that kind of critical attitude and intensity without causing the blamer to feel that they must fight with you or otherwise defend their vulnerability. Being upset about the same thing as the blamer is an excellent strategy. Remember that after pacing comes leading. The blamer is much more open to your input once rapport has been established. The problem for most people, though, is that they are too shaken up or angry to want to establish rapport with a blamer.

Since blamers may hold a lot of power in an organization, this can be a fatal mistake. It's best to see it as an opportunity to practice NLP rather than to expose your vulnerability. Which do you love more? You can gain rapport with a placater pretty easily since they really crave attention and understanding.

The trick is to get them connected to their real responsibilities without losing them. Starting with their higher values, that is, at a more general or abstract level and working down into the specifics, is an excellent strategy. Distracters are more open to rapport-building than you might think. As with most rapport-building, you must start out by being non-threatening.

Being non-threatening with a Satir category means not directly confronting the way the style acts as a defense against internal vulnerabilities. In the case of the distracter, you do not rub their face in whatever it was they were trying to distract you from. As a Neuro Linguistic Programming practitioner, you are getting used to juggling different ideas and even using confusion as a technique yourself. The trick with the distracter is to lock firmly onto the facts, position, and agenda that are important to you, and then take a detour. Go all over the place with the distracter, but keep dropping in points about how it is in the best interest of the distracter to do what must be done. It's a bit like breaking a horse. While the distracter tends to fatigue others, you are fatiguing the distracter because all of their efforts bring them back to the same spot, your agenda. On one level, you are pacing them. On another, you are kindling a state of compliance. Add Ericksonian language to the free-wheeling conversation and you will be the distracter master. Since levelers respect other levelers and your NLP skills help you see both sides of any debate, you will have the easiest time establishing rapport and understanding with the leveler. If there is a disagreement, make sure that you have a good mastery of the facts and a concise knowledge of the agendas of the players in the situation.Of course, you can use everything you have already learned about rapport-building. But now you know even more.

By learning about the Satir categories, you know not only more about what to do, but also what to avoid doing. But if you aren't sure where to start in an interaction, being the leveler is best. That's because the leveler always understands their side of the issue. The only concern is that the leveler may be persuaded by the other side. This creates an incentive for the person you are talking to to want to create rapport. If they are not skilled, or if they are stressed, they may fall into their more un-evolved category style, but that means that they will be more obvious as to what category they belong to.

You will be able to take your cues from there. It is very important to remember that when you see someone in a more stereotypical, manipulative, or irrational state, that state may not be where they are most of the time. Don't limit yourself by assuming that what you see is all you will be dealing with in the future. This insight makes it easier for you to bring out the best in people. This makes their lives, and yours, a lot easier.

❚❚ I am Me. In all the world, there is no one else exactly like me. Everything that comes out of me is authentically mine, because I alone chose it —I own everything about me: my body, my feelings, my mouth, my voice, all my actions, whether they be to others or myself. I own my fantasies, my dreams, my hopes, my fears. I own my triumphs and successes, all my failures and mistakes. Because I own all of me, I can become intimately acquainted with me. By so doing, I can love me and be friendly with all my parts. I know there are aspects about myself that puzzle me, and other aspects that I do not know — but as long as I am friendly and loving to myself, I can courageously and hopefully look for solutions to the puzzles and ways to find out more about me. However I look and sound, whatever I say and do, and whatever I think and feel at a given moment in time is authentically me. If later some parts of how I looked, sounded, thought, and felt turn out to be unfitting, I can discard that which is unfitting, keep the rest,

and invent something new for that which I discarded. I can see, hear, feel, think, say, and do. I have the tools to survive, to be close to others, to be productive, and to make sense and order out of the world of people and things outside of me. I own me, and therefore, I can engineer me. I am me, and I am Okay.

Virginia Satir

Scope Ambiguities

In scope ambiguities, you wonder which part of the sentence applies to which other part. For example, "when you are talking quietly with your child and your husband, at ease to talk more openly..."

Does this mean she is talking quietly with her child and her husband, and she is becoming more open, or is it the husband who is becoming more open?

I'll say it again, "When you are talking quietly with your child and your husband, at ease to talk more openly..." This could be part of a session intended to help her become ready for her husband to be more honest with her. In any case, consider how this ambiguity creates transderivational searching for meaning and primes a state of interest in a topic.

SCORE

Source: Robert Dilts & Todd Epstein

Solve problems more effectively by organizing information in a more useful way. The SCORE model drives this pattern with a flexible, multifaceted style of thinking. This style resolves problems and gathers the information that you need. It is called multifaceted thinking. This style of thinking allows you to think in more than one mode at the same time. This allows you to benefit from multiple perspectives and styles of thinking as needed. Flexibility in thinking is a great asset.

The SCORE model is based on the idea that we need, as a minimum for effective decision making, a grasp of the symptoms, causes, outcomes, resources, and effects at play in a given situation. This model supports the fundamental NLP skill of conceptualizing the current state, the desired state, and the bridge from one to the other by using appropriate resources.

1. Compile the information. Begin by gathering the information you need according to the SCORE model. These are as follows:

a. Symptoms: Symptoms are the more obvious aspects of a situation that cause us to define it as a problem. Once you have these, go farther, asking yourself what symptoms you have not noticed. Clarify for yourself how you conceptualize or symbolize these symptoms and how you judge them.

b. Causes: The causes are the dynamics that gave rise to the problem situation and continue to do so. The causes may not be obvious, so you may need to investigate, hypothesize, and test your conclusions. Knowing that there may be multiple causes and that not all causes are acting at any given time and that the cause may form a domino effect or sequence can be helpful. Looking for ecological NLP practitioner of the causes can be important as well. Use a brief ecological check here.

c. Outcomes: These are the goals and objectives that you desire. These can range from terminating a negative situation to creating a highly sophisticated new ecology and vision.

d. Resources: Resources are whatever will assist you in achieving your outcomes. It includes information, goodwill, inner-unconscious resources, capital, insight, and anything else that will further your efforts, even if you consider the effort itself.

e. Effects: This means the results of whatever you have done, whether you got the outcome you desired or not. It includes the direct effects of your actions and the indirect effects that you might refer to as side effects or unintended consequences. Effects become resources when you perceive them as feedback and create a loop from the effects into feedback resources and into new strategies and outcomes. Strategies can be perceived as symptoms when they are destructive or ineffective, as causes when they give rise to the situation, as outcomes when they result from new information and ideas, and as resources when they are assets for achieving the desired outcomes. Strategies are intermediary outcomes that people seek in developing mastery so that they can achieve larger outcomes and long-term goals.

2. Develop new insights Take all that you learn from applying the above SCORE analysis in order to generate new insights and strategies as described above. Note any ways that it could help you:

1) Improve your ability to visualize or define your desired outcomes,

2) get a better sense of where you are in the progress, dynamics, and ecology of the situation (while keeping potential or known resources in mind), and 3) take action.

3) What new strategies are you devising as a result of your new insight?

3. Test. Apply your new insights and strategies. Observe the results. Use the results as additional feedback while further refining your strategies. Always keep an eye out for solutions and resources that are outside of your current frame of reference. This is often where the greatest breakthroughs come, since most people and organizations have been approaching problems from within their current frames for some time. They have either been getting limited results, or the situation has changed without their updating their frame. Since your frame is, in a sense, a critical part of your strategy, it must be accounted for.

Secondary Gains

In therapy, when a client resists change work, we ought to first look for the secondary gains. When you benefit from keeping an issue or a personal problem, this is referred to as a "secondary gain." It is when you benefit from an unfavorable condition, circumstance, or limitation in your life. The advantages come from not resolving your problems. It does not imply that the problem is beneficial, but there are advantages to having it. As a result, it is more advantageous to keep the problem than solve it. For example, you may wish for more attention in your life.

So, as if by accident, you injure yourself subtly. As a result, everyone begins to pay more attention to you and take better care of you. You obtain what you desire (attention), but at the expense of something you do not desire (getting hurt). For plenty of people, these unwelcome issues produce the desired outcome. The majority of people are completely unaware that they are engaging in this behavior. This is why? Since it occurs at the unconscious level, it is below the level of consciousness. They're not trying to act. They simply know they're getting the desired results, which exacerbates the problem.

To elicit secondary gains, ask: "How would your life be different if you suddenly didn't do X? What will you lose in terms of feelings or resources? "

Selectional Restriction Violations

In the course of eliciting a state or creating a metaphor, you can ascribe feelings to things. This is called selectional restriction violation. Doing this not only furthers the metaphor, or supports the state, but it also contributes to trance and open-mindedness."Your lower back would like to absorb and store all that extra agitation you have been feeling, and create a balanced sense of your energies."

"What if your media player could tell you about all the wisdom and ideas for success that it will ever hold."

"The cactus lives peacefully in the arid desert."

Self-Anchoring

Decide what state you want to create an anchor for. For example, perhaps you would like to anchor a good state for meeting and negotiating. Whatever it is, pick one...Move into third position, as if you are watching your life in a movie.

Recall all the times that you felt some aspect of that state. Every time you feel some aspect of the desired state, amplify it and expand it. See yourself in the movie experiencing that state, and let yourself, as the observer, feel it as well. (That's a little different from the usual third position experience.)

Keep doing that until you feel the state intensely... Each time you think of a time in which you felt some aspect of that state, see what is most visually positive and compelling.

Emphasize those visual elements in the movie. Hear what is most audibly positive and compelling... Hear any words that others have said or that you have said that are mentally positive and compelling...

Feel what is most palpably positive and compelling... Feel whatever internal sensations are most positive and compelling...

See yourself now, standing in a nice place, fully feeling that state, and seeing how you look in that state--your facial expression, your posture, you can even add cosmic energy of just the right color streaming into your aura.

Now create a signal / trigger with your dominant hand, such as an OK sign, one that you would not do very often, or interlace your fingers in the opposite direction from normal, and hold that position while you imagine moving into the first position (directly in the feelings) with your eyes closed (so there are no distractions from the feelings), and savor the state...

Self-Criticism Evaluation

It is important to first understand what self-criticism means to the person. Being self-critical and self-deprecating are two different things, and it's crucial to distinguish between the two. Putting oneself down is a common form of self-deprecation. It can be done as a joke or out of insecurity and fear. Self-loathing saps one's self-esteem. It's not a tool to be taken lightly since your own self-talk has a significant impact on both how others see you and how you see yourself. The ability to distinguish between the two is essential if you want to lead a fruitful life in which your accomplishments build on each other and your setbacks are minimized. Unlike self-deprecation, which might point out flaws in your life philosophy, self-criticism focuses on identifying those problems and taking steps to remedy them.

1. Take the first perceptual position and think about the last 12 months on your timeline.On paper, write for each month, in short, the titles of major events that have happened in your life.

2. Break state.

3. Step into the 4th perceptual position and ask: "What is the one word that can describe this entire year?" -Whatever word popped first into your mind, write it down.

4. Step into the first perceptual position again, and read aloud the following statements. Mark any of these phrases with an asterisk if they "feel right," sound true, or bring back fond memories.

- *Everything that goes wrong in my life is my fault.*

- *When bad things happen, I take responsibility for them.*

- *I am far too quick to assign sole responsibility while ignoring legitimate external factors.*

- I have a negative view of myself as a whole, rather than just focusing on the unfortunate mistakes I might have made.

- "I am a failure" or "I'm a loser" are phrases I often say to myself.

- What I don't think about is what led to a problem or what I can do better moving forward. As a result, I'm filled with self-doubt and unable to believe in myself.

- I'm apprehensive about taking risks because I'm afraid of failure.

- In order to keep myself from failing, I tell myself that it will happen again and again. As a result, I've come to the conclusion that doing nothing is the safest option possible.

- As a rule, I try to keep my thoughts to myself. What if I make a dumb mistake?

- Somehow, I don't think I'm interesting or knowledgeable enough to engage in a discussion with certain people.

- I frequently fall short when comparing myself to others.

- I find that my self-criticism is accentuated when I am lacking in knowledge or skill.

- I have a habit of treating others as superior to me.

- I'm definitely never pleased with my achievements.

- Regardless of what I do, I can't help but notice flaws.

- Oftentimes, I have the tendency to think that if I can't do something perfectly, then I shouldn't bother trying.

- Even when the results are positive, I am tempted to dwell on the inevitable flaws.

- I have unbelievably high expectations of myself and others.

- Happiness is only possible if I'm really smart, pretty, or rich.

- I think in terms of "what if" quite a lot.

- *I live in fear of the worst-case scenario and obsess over it.*

- *I can't let go of my physical flaws.*

- *I'm a complete idiot who never asks for help.*

- *I do not speak up for myself.*

- *Self-harming thoughts are often running through my mind.*

- *My primary caretaker or parent was always critical of me.*

- *I'm a stickler for analyzing my failures.*

- *Do I spend a lot of time and effort trying to figure out what went wrong and how I'm to blame?*

- *I punish myself for making mistakes instead of learning from them.*

- *I'm not the kind of person who is quick to forget or forgive.*

- *I never compliment myself. I don't deserve compliments.*

- *I'm prone to defensiveness when I'm on the receiving end of criticism.*

- *Positive comments are something I have a hard time accepting.*

- *My worldview is based on the binary opposition between good and evil.*

- *Since I was a child, I've consistently underachieved in my efforts.*

5. Break state.

Self-Sabotage

Self-sabotage is s a form of self-defeating behavior when you work against your own values and expectations. In other words, you recognize that there is something out there that you genuinely want and believe is good for you, but you then do things that directly contradict that desired outcome.

When it comes to self-sabotage, it's important to note that it can be both conscious and unconscious, depending on your level of awareness. In the case of conscious self-sabotage, you are aware that what you're doing is counterproductive to one of your outcomes or value systems.

The term "unconscious self-sabotage" refers to when you do something that hurts a desired outcome or value but you don't recognize it until after you do it. Show this list to a client and ask them to put an asterisk next to any word that brings up an emotional reaction. If a certain memory pops up in their mind, they can write down a short sentence to describe it. Once they're done, you'll have a general roadmap of that person's mental map and a list of issues to work on beyond the presenting problem they came in with.

1. Addictions

2. Aggression

3. Anger

4. Anxiety

5. Arrogance

6. Attachment

7. Judgmental attitude

8. Over obsessive about own opinions

9. Reaction instead of action

10. Scattered thoughts

11. *Being too emotional*

12. *Being too intellectual*

13. *Not being grounded*

14. *Following blindly after another person*

15. *Boredom*

16. *Carelessness*

17. *Complaining*

18. *Compromising*

19. *Compulsion*

20. *Envy*

21. *Fears*

22. *Feeling needy*

23. *Frustration*

24. *Futility*

25. *Future thinking*

26. *Delusions*

27. *Greed*

28. *Guilt*

29. *Hate*

30. *Hopelessness*

31. *Humorlessness*

32. *Ignorance*

33. *Illusion*

34. *Impatience*

35. *Impulsiveness*

36. Indecision

37. Indifference

38. Inertia

39. Insecurity

40. Manipulation

41. Materialism

42. Mediocrity

43. Moodiness

44. Needing to please others

45. Negativity

46. No fun

47. Obsessions

48. Pain

49. Perfectionism

50. Poor health

51. Low self-esteem

52. Possessiveness

53. Poverty attitude

54. Prejudice

55. Pride

56. Procrastination

57. Rationalization

58. Inner conflict

59. Confusion

60. Cowardice

61. *Criticism*

62. *Cruelty*

63. *Defensiveness*

64. *Denial*

65. *Dependence*

66. *Depression*

67. *Dishonesty*

68. *Disorder*

69. *Dominance*

70. *Doubt*

71. *Egotism*

72. *Insensitivity*

73. *Intolerance*

74. *Isolation*

75. *Jealousy*

76. *Lack of confidence*

77. *Lack of creativity*

78. *Lack of discipline*

79. *Lack of purpose*

80. *Lack of trust*

81. *Laziness*

82. *Living in the past*

83. *Low energy*

84. *Repression*

85. *Malnutrition*

86. Resentment

87. Resistance

88. Ridicule

89. Self pity

90. Self sabotage

91. Selfishness

92. Shame

93. Shyness

94. Stress

95. Stubbornness

96. Suffering

97. Timidity

98. Unexpressed emotions 99. Vanity

100. Withdrawal

101. Revenge

Self-Love

Source: Suzie Smith & Tim Halborn

Explore your memories for places where you had pleasant experience.

Describe the attributes of this person.

Work with the second perceptual position, in the loving person.

Anchor this appreciation state.

Receive the loving perception.

Anchor the lovable state.

Test and future pace the anchor.

Enhance your ego strength and self-esteem by improving your ability to love and appreciate yourself.

1. Explore your pleasant memories of someone who intensely cared about you and who had a positive effect on you. This person will serve as a model for love, so it must not be a person who misuses any power or influence to harm or manipulate you.

2. To get a full sense of the elements that you feel contribute to being a loving person, describe the attributes or qualities of this person, particularly those that made them a loving person.

3. Work with the second perceptual position, in the loving person. Imagine floating over to this person and taking their perceptual position. See yourself through their eyes. Describe yourself from their perspective. What qualities about you does this person

appreciate? Notice how this expands your sense of yourself as a loving and lovable person.

4. Anchor this appreciation state. Use an appropriate image, word, touch, or other stimulus to anchor this state.

5. Be open to receiving the loving perception.

Tune in to your sense of the person who is adoring you. Imagine allowing this in as a form of energy. Fully experience your feelings as the person looks lovingly at you. Also, experience your own feelings of self-appreciation. Attend to your self-talk and how it reflects these perspectives. In any way, these experiences change how you perceive the world around you in this memory.

6. Anchor the lovable state. Filter out any distractions from this lovable state and amplify it. Anchor it with an appropriate stimulus. Now you have anchored a loving and lovable state that is also tied to qualities that you and others can appreciate about you. Take some time to enjoy any new ideas and perspectives that you have experienced for yourself.

7. Test. and Future Pace this anchor. Fire the anchor of being lovable. Future pace by imagining situations in which it would be helpful to be in touch with your own lovability. Remember that these future situations do not have to be situations in which you are guaranteed approval. In fact, some situations might involve people who don't appreciate you at all. Imagine being around people like that, but with your inner sense of your own lovability unshaken.

Think about how much more difficult it is to manipulate or intimidate someone experiencing this high lovability level that you are amplifying.

Self-Nurturing

Create a chart of your unfulfilled childhood emotional needs and the corresponding characteristics your parents or caretakers needed in order to fulfill them appropriately.

Build an ideal parent model and enhance it with any additional ideas. Visualize these parents expressing their parenting gifts.

Timeline back to the day you were born. Transfer your powerful good parenting resources into your parents or caretakers.

Watch your life move forward with magically perfect parents who fulfill your needs appropriately. Re-calibrate your prior negative experiences.

Follow the timeline into your present, in a state of receiving unconditional love.

Integrate and future pace. Test.

Accelerate your maturation and emotional strength by drawing upon your adult resources to resolve unfinished emotional development.

The value of good parenting resources, as conceptualized by NLP, drives this pattern.

1. Make a chart of your unfulfilled emotional needs as a child and the corresponding characteristics your parents or caregivers required to fulfill them appropriately.

On an imaginary blackboard or on paper, draw a line down the middle.

On the left, list the emotional needs that were not fulfilled for you as a child.

On the other hand, list the characteristics that your parents or caretakers need in order to fulfill those needs.

2. Create an ideal parent model and add any additional ideas to it.

Use these characteristics to build a mental model of ideal parents.

Use all representational systems to experience these parents.

Add anything else that you know about good parents or what you were missing.

As you think of these perfect parents, any number of ideas may come to you.

What would it be like to get help with homework in a really supportive way, or to be guided toward constructive behavior in a constructive way, or simply to get plenty of attention and desirable activity?

3. Visualize these parents expressing their parenting gifts.

Visualize these parents in action, handling situations that some parents would find challenging. I see them being very successful and resourceful as parents.

If you are working with a study group, or have friends or colleagues interested in this, discuss it with them to further enhance your model, either during this pattern, or at another time for future use.

4. Timeline back to the day you were born. Transfer your powerful, good parenting resources to your parents or caretakers.

Access your timeline and float back to the day you were born. Observe that experience as your adult self, bringing with you all the resources you have developed, including your ever-increasing understanding of good parenting.

Allow the momentum and magic of all the resources you have brought back to imbue your parents with perfect parenting abilities. See all this resource energy flooding into this time from your future, swirling as it suddenly stops at this moment, drawn to your parents as vortices for their power.

Even if you are not now connected to your parents, even if one or both of them were not present, create parents or caretakers for this scene.

5. Watch your life move forward with magically perfect parents who fulfill your needs appropriately.

Watch your life unfold forward into your timeline, but with these magically perfect parents.

Observe how they fulfill your needs as an expression of their magical, yet human, gifts.

6. Re-calibrate your prior negative experiences.

Pay special attention to experiences that have been negative and see how resourcefully your parents now deal with the situation.

Let the positive outcomes build your positive abilities and personality characteristics as you further progress.

7. Follow your timeline into the present, in the state of receiving unconditional love.

Trigger your state of experiencing your parents' new unconditional love, and tell your unconscious mind that these experiences can generalize, bringing you forward more and more rapidly to your present time.

8. Integrate and Future Pace.

Continue to hold the anchor in your state of receiving unconditional love.

Allow yourself to integrate these experiences and sensations as your momentum carries you into future experiences.

These future experiences show you how your expanded development will allow you to express wonderful resources for far better outcomes.

9. Test.

In the coming days or weeks, notice any ways that your relationships or care-taking behaviors improve, or ways that your personal boundaries become more effective.

Sequential Attention

Souce: Erickson Institute

Occasionally, people might over-identify with a particular aspect of their life experiences—certain limiting beliefs, most common being a distorted body image ("nobody likes me because I'm fat," "I'm single because I'm bold," etc.), for example. This is problematic in and of itself, but these people may also develop an unhealthy obsession with even more severely limited NLP practitioner of themselves. For instance, they may identify with behaviors or thought patterns that lead to the emergence of a victimized, dependent, or otherwise dysfunctional self. That's when they most often seek the help of a professional, such as yourself. This pattern is designed to help a person develop self-awareness and the ability to focus their attention sequentially on each of their major personality traits, roles, and so on. They then become acutely aware of and capable of examining these characteristics while maintaining the observer's perspective and recognizing that the observer is not the observed.

1. Slowly inhale and exhale through your nose while keeping your body in an upright and comfortable position.

2. Ask and wait for a nod of confirmation or an answer after each question:

Do you believe that you are greater than your circumstances, health, income, or relationships?

Do you believe you are more than your ideas and emotions?

Do you believe that you are more than your roles and responsibilities?

Do you believe that you are more than your physical body?

Are you eager to pursue these concepts further in order to connect with your higher self?

3. Now, slowly and attentively say the following truth-supporting affirmations:

"I have a body, but I am not my body."

"I have feelings, but I am not my feelings."

"I have a mind, but I am not my mind."

4. Close your eyes for a moment, recollect briefly in your consciousness the basic substance of this affirmation, and then gradually bring your attention to the key concept: "I have a body, yet I am not my body."

5. Open your eyes and break state.

6. Now close your eyes again. Make every effort to internalize this as an experienced event in your consciousness as much as you possibly can. You can internalize an abstract idea by letting the sensation that you feel within your body while thinking about it run freely and smoothly from your head to your toes and back.

7. Ask and wait for a nod of confirmation or an answer:

What does it feel like to announce, "I have a body, but I am not my body"?

How does it feel to announce, "I have feelings, but I am not my feelings"?

What does it feel like to announce, "I have a mind, but I am not my mind"?

How does it feel to announce, "I have a religion, but I am not my religion"?

How does it feel to announce, "I have a ___, but I am not a _____"?

8. As you settle into a comfortable and secure state of mind, allow the activation of a higher self willing to think timelessly about who you are.

9. Allow your higher self to take a step back and safely and objectively analyze the distinctions between your essential core and other elements of yourself. As you fully

accept those components of your former self as extensions, functions, or tools of your core self, you will discover how secure and important it is for your core self to continue with or without them.

10. Remain aware of how those developments are not synonymous with who you are at your core. Remain aware of how you can invoke those extensions, functions, or tools as needed by your higher self.

11. Solicit the brain's assistance in developing a higher self. Have you connected with the self that exists apart from your possessions, thoughts, attitudes, and emotions? This is sometimes referred to as the "viewer," "audience, "observer, or "supervisor" of what occurs in the body-mind.

12. Solicit from your brain the creation of a space for your higher self to exist. Have you obtained it? Consolidate the higher self as a permanent and self-sustaining entity.

13. Would you consent to your higher self freely observing your future thoughts, feelings, and attachments?

14. Future pace. As you consider the future of this new form of awareness, are there any parts of it that make you uneasy? Allow yourself some time to connect with your higher self while you journey into the future. Allow that to permeate your work, family, and social communication, among other areas.

Shared Resource

Source: Robert Dilts & Robert McDonald

Select a resourceful experience and express it in body movements.

Face your partner and begin imitating their movements.

Take on your partner's experience and movements.

Compare and contrast this with your own movements.

Facing the same directions, blend the two resource state movement patterns in a "we field."

Repeat with another pair, but with "we fields." Test.

Improve the value of resourceful states by using various perceptual positions to experience and explore them. This pattern uses a novel fourth position by invoking a felt sense of sameness between people that results from having been through the other three perceptual positions. We'll draw from the principles of spatial sorting, psycho-geography, and somatic syntax. (For more on this, learn about embodied cognition.)

1. Choose a resourceful experience and express it through movement. Do this exercise in pairs the first time through. Choose a recent experience that you found to be resourceful. Review it from the first position (through your own eyes, etc.).

2. Explore the body movements that somehow express that resourceful state.

2. Turn around and start imitating your partner's movements. Face your partner and do this movement pattern. Now, continuing in the first position, imitate your partner's body movements.

3. Take on your partner's experience and movements. Switch positions with your partner, and go into second position, experiencing things through your partner's eyes. Express your partner's movements as though you were him or her. Notice if there are any ways it changes how you experience these movements.

4. Compare and contrast this with your own movements. From the third position (outside observer), sense what makes your partner's movements similar to and different from your own.

5. Facing the same directions, blend the two resource state movement patterns into a "we field." Go back to the first position. Turn around to be side-by-side with your partner. Make your resource movements once more. Have your partner make their own version of the movements. Together, make small adjustments in your movements until you blend the two resource states through movement. What is it like to experience this shared space? We'll call it the fourth position, or "we field."

6. Repeat with another pair, but with "we fields." The two of you now have to find another pair and repeat the pattern. This time, start with the movement that you created together. Continue to expand these joining experiences until the entire group is experiencing this fourth position.

7. Test. Explore with the group what this "we field" is like. In the coming days and weeks, notice any ways that this pattern has contributed to your ability to empathize, create rapport, and be intuitive.

Six Step Reframe

Source: John Grinder

Select the behavior.

Establish the signal.

Elicit the positive intentions.

Produce alternative behaviors.

Solicit the signal that the behaviors are selected.

Future pace and ecology check.

Elicit unconscious resources in order to change a habit by producing alternative behaviors. The Advanced Visual Squash has a similar purpose to this pattern.

1. Select a behavior of yours that you would like to stop or change. The behavior should be one for which you can say, "I need to stop (behavior)'ing," or "I want to (behavior X) but I just can't get myself to start."

2. Create the signal. Ask the part that creates the behavior to give you a signal (such as lifting a finger) that will mean yes. If the part does not provide a signal, trust for now that there are positive underlying motives for the problem behavior.

3. Elicit the positive intentions. Ask the part to bring to mind the positive intentions of the behavior that you'd like to change.

4. Generate alternative behaviors. Ask your creative part to produce three alternative behaviors that would fulfill the needs revealed in the prior step. Solicit the signal that the

behaviors are selected. Ask your part that produces the problem behavior to give the signal when it is satisfied that there are three behaviors that will fill the needs revealed in step three. If the part did not cooperate in step two, then ask it now if it will participate by providing a yes signal. If not, then assume for now that you have come up with better alternatives that you will test in the next step.

6. Future Pace and ecology check.

a. Future Pace each of the behaviors several times.Detect and mitigate any ecological difficulties. Re-run this pattern as needed.

b. Experiment with the behaviors in real life to see if the desired behavior change occurs.If not, think in terms of ecology (such as parts conflicts) and re-try this pattern in order to refine your behavior change work.

If you would like to do a version of this pattern that is more conscious (less "new code") because of the circumstances or because you'd like to do more intensive brainstorming, then you can write down the motives (from step two) and alternatives (from step three) as quickly as possible, until you feel you have satisfied each step. As soon as you are done with the basic pattern, you should jot down the new behaviors and place the note someplace where it will remind you to try them out. Perhaps it belongs in your appointment book or on the refrigerator.

Smart Eating

Source: Connaire Andreas & L. Michael Hall

One of the key causes of excessive eating is poor awareness of when one is actually hungry as opposed to simply being tempted or using food as an antidote to stress. Another problem is that, although it can be appropriate to eat a number of smaller meals rather than three large meals per day, those small meals have excessive carbohydrates.

Students and knowledge workers use a great deal of blood sugar because the brain consumes it for thinking in surprising amounts. Thus, they must be careful to avoid snacking beyond their actual needs and to avoid the blood sugar roller coaster that is caused by consuming refined sugars and starchy foods. The current "diabesity" (diabetes and obesity) epidemic (also known as syndrome X) is directly related to the over-consumption of refined carbohydrates through products such as soft drinks.

1. How do you know when it is time to eat? Determine how you know that it is time to eat. Carefully look for the rep systems and sub-modalities involved.

Include your internal feelings, such as tension, mental fog, and irritability, in this Be sure to include the feelings in your stomach. What does "empty" really feel like?

2. What would be best to eat?

Ask your inner wisdom: What would it feel like to have eaten? That is, what would make me feel good after I ate it in the short term?

Consider the various foods that are available to you right now, and imagine that you are finished eating them.

Notice your most subtle feelings. You can experience a range of feelings, such as healthy and balanced, bogged down and sleepy, and very satisfied, but in a gluttonous way. Keep trying different foods until you find at least one that makes you feel very balanced and healthy. Inspect the rep systems and sub-modalities that tell you it is an ideal food. How do you "know" that you feel balanced and healthy? If none of these do this for you, then consider additional foods that are not available right now.

3. Compared the before and after. Compare this "ideal food" feeling with the feeling you had before you ate it; that is, the feeling that tells you it's time to eat.

Which one feels better? If the "before" feeling seems better, perhaps you should try out more imaginary foods to find something better. Or does it mean that you should simply wait longer before eating your ideal food?

4. Make a comparison with an unhealthy item. Try comparing the "after" feeling with a not-so-healthy item, such as a candy bar.

Carefully inspect the difference between these feelings. Go forward in time a few hours to see what the unhealthy "after" feeling is. Go forward a few days and feel that result. How do these sensations compare to the feelings of step three?

5. Future Pace. Once you have found food choices that make you feel balanced and healthy, see how many more food items you can think of that provide healthy, balanced feelings. Imagine making those food choices in the future. Amplify the healthy, balanced feelings and imagine them growing over time as you make these food choices. Imagine yourself as a very spry, active, bright elderly person with those healthy, balanced feelings surrounded by young people who are eager to gain wisdom from you.

6. Run a testOver the coming days and weeks, notice how this pattern influences your food choices.

Consider how those options make you feel. See how you can enhance this pattern so that it works best for you as an individual, getting the best effect on your food choices and resulting energy and mental clarity. Making it less comfortable to reach the type of food you want to avoid craving is a very easy task. Simply stop buying it. Skip it when you get to the candy section in the supermarket.

Another well-known nutrition trick for sweet cravings is fruit juices and smoothies. I don't have enough space in this book to explain it thoroughly, so just give it a try and see how it

The Big Book of NLP

works for you. Do not buy concentrated juices and always read the labels. Even when it says "100% juice," it might say "from concentrated" in small print.

Another tip that helps me a lot in the morning is to drink one glass of fresh orange juice, the squeezed type, of course. It's a rush, I guarantee it. One last piece of advice—do not give up or avoid the foods you really love. If pizza is your favorite food, go for it once a week. If your mind knows that you aren't going to become a health freak (which can be a health risk in itself), it will become more and more patient throughout the week and will let you lose weight, knowing that once a week you're going to enjoy your favorite indulgences. Of course, don't go overboard here! But don't make it a stressful change.

Softeners

In a therapy session, we often ask the client to become somewhat vulnerable and reveal unfavorable NLP practitioner of their personality or past behavior. Rapport is obviously a helpful tool to facilitate trustworthiness, and there is also a linguistic syntax we can use to soften hard questions. The formula is:

Open Softener (first perceptual position) + the hard question + Closing Softener (optional)

Open Softeners: "I am wondering...", "I'm curious to know...", I wonder if you can tell me...", "I would like to ask you..."

Closing Softeners: "... if you don't mind me asking?", "... if it's alright with you?", "...if you are ready to speak about it now?"

For example, notice the difference between the two hard questions:

1. "How did respond the moment your boss touched you inappropriately?"

2. "I wonder if you can (a deliberate pause) tell me (pause) How did respond the moment your boss touched you inappropriately (pause), if you are ready to (pause) speak about it now?"

Somatic Awareness Enhancement

This is very similar to the previous Symbolic Somatic Priming System. However, this system serves to help the person feel a sense of flow through their body, to "fill in" areas that may feel less aware and alive, or to just connect with a particular area for some other awareness purpose. This can be good for aiding the state change that is a good part of reprocessing. When they are able to tolerate it, clients who are out of touch

For example, a person who has experienced a difficult childhood may not be very aware of their heart area.

When you are at a point in your relationship where the client can begin feeling that area, you might talk about what it means to "reclaim feelings" or to "be more fully alive in your own body."

At the same time, you can gently sweep your hands upward from the abdomen up through the heart area over the sternum. Because clients with difficult childhoods are often frightened by the feeling of emptiness where their hearts should be, you can help them reclaim their awareness with such a gesture. Of course, this is just part of a larger collection of interventions.

In another example, when you're talking to a person who is prone to controlling others in order to protect his flagging self-esteem, it can be helpful to connect him to the somatic experience that comprises the knee-jerk response to feelings of insecurity. This feeling has become a reflex of anger and feels justified in punishing the person who "made" them angry. This can be a formula for domestic violence.

You might talk about how amazing it is that the body can go into a totally different state the moment someone says something that hits a nerve.

As you do that, you might tense your chest and bring your fists up toward your chest while pulling your shoulders up into a tense position.

Again, this can be a moderate or subtle gesture. There is no reason for it to be extreme, because you are directing awareness, and this is easy to do with mild gestures that do not call too much attention to themselves and distract the client from the process you are conducting.

With the client more aware of how their body reacts, it will be easier to move into working on creating alternate responses.

Somatic Fractal

Source: Robert Dilts

Select a shape.

Make the pattern with your finger.

Add body parts to create a more complex movement pattern.

Have your partner guess the original pattern.

Switch roles.

Test.

Practice intuiting deep structure, and explore how this is a useful skill for mutual understanding. This pattern draws upon the somatic syntax model.

1. Choose a shape. Do this pattern with a partner. Select a simple shape, such as a triangle or figure eight, but keep it secret for now.

2. Use your finger to create the pattern. As your partner keeps their eyes closed, make the pattern with your finger.

3. Include more body parts to make a more complex movement pattern. Keep this up, and begin adding body parts. Start small, perhaps with your wrist, and expand out until your entire body is involved as much as possible. Explore this as though you were creating some kind of new dance. Don't try to make your body express the original pattern as an imitation. Instead, you are allowing it to act as a "seed move" that inspires new movements.

4. Have your partner guess the original pattern. Ask your partner to open their eyes and try to guess the deep structural pattern (the original shape you started with) that led to your somatic fractal (the end result of your movement expansion into a more complex move). This is called a "fractal" because, metaphorically, it is a complex expression or result of an underlying formula (the original shape). Instruct your partner: Notice how you must call upon a kind of intuition in order to seek the deep structure that leads to the more complex movement. Get a sense of how this intuition lives in you and how to access it. "

5. Switch roles and do the exercise again.

6. Test. In the coming days and weeks, notice any ways in which accessing this intuition becomes easier and more useful. Notice any ways that this metaphoric way of seeking deep structure can play out in life situations and be valuable.

The Big Book of NLP

Spelling Strategy

Source: Richard Bandler and Robert Dilts

This pattern improves your spelling. We use a lot of the internal visual modality in this pattern. Even if you consider yourself more of an "auditory" or "kinesthetic" person, try this method and see how well it works for you. There's a lot to be said about people who stubbornly cling to their most favorite modality and almost refuse to be flexible about it, but we'll leave it to online arguments and discussions. Do not fall into this trap—even if your most frequently used modality has been auditory, you can still use successful strategies that depend mostly on the visual modality, such as this spelling strategy.

1. Examine the correctly spelled word on paper or on screen.

2. Relax. With your eyes closed, recall a familiar, relaxing experience. Once you have a strong sense of the feeling, open your eyes and look at the word.

3. Picture the word. Look up and left, mentally picturing the correct spelling.

4. Clear your mind. Open and close your eyes rapidly, get up, move around if you have to.

5. Picture the word and write it down. Check it. Look back up and left at your mental picture of the word. Write it down, as if you were transcribing it from that image. Check the spelling against the correct spelling. If it is wrong, go to step one.

6. Picture the word and write it backwards. Check it. Return your gaze right and left to your mental picture of the word. This time, write it backwards, from right to left. Check the spelling and return to step three if it is incorrect.

Imagine the word in the color that most fits the word. Maybe ludicrous should be purple. When you form the word in your mind, form each letter one at a time, in a font that is very different from the typical font. If there is a letter or letter combination that you tend to get wrong when you spell the word, make those letters big and bright compared to the rest of the word when you picture it. As you picture the word, build it one syllable at a time. Make sure that as you imagine the word, it fits into your mental view. You can experiment with seeing the letters form a circle and filling your view. Use your finger to trace the letters in front of you, picturing your finger actually painting the letters as if on a canvas.

Spell Out Words

This is not a technique to be used often, but it can be very effective at certain times, such as when someone you speak to seems aloof or disconnected. Spell out words are used quite often in advertising.

Spelling out an important word draws the person's attention to it, and promotes the induction of a light t-r-a-n-c-e.

Spinning Icons

Source: Nelson Zink & Joe Munshaw

Select a negative and positive state.

Get a visual representation of the negative and positive states.

Create a symbol for the negative state.

Repeat for the positive state.

Rotate the images around each other, accelerating to an extreme rate.

Blend the images into one image.

Tell a story.

Test.

Avoid or get out of negative situations. Solve problems and be creative.

1. Select a negative and positive state. One should be in a state you are in, or sometimes find yourself in, that is not desirable. If this is your first time working with this pattern, choose a relatively "weak" state. Once you get more comfortable, work on the stronger, more disturbing, ones. The other state should be a very desirable state that you might think of as an "antidote" to the negative state. For example, you could take "irritated easily when hearing a squeaky noise" as the negative state, and its "antidote" state, "hearing music in every seemingly inharmonic set of sounds."

2. Access this negative state and get a visual representation. Notice where in your sensory field it exists, and explore its sub-modalities. Be certain to explore the driver sub-modalities in the major modalities: visual, kinesthetic, and auditory. The driver sub-

The Big Book of NLP

modalities will give you the most elegant path for the change-work to be successful. Do the same for the positive state.

3. Have the person create an icon or symbol for the visual representation of the negative state. You can ask the person to, "Create a simple image that represents the negative state, such as a cartoon or icon."

4. Repeat this for the positive state.

5. Rotate the images around each other, accelerating at an extreme rate. Have the person begin to rotate the two icons around each other, as if they were two planets in each other's gravitational field. The images will exchange locations and continue. Have them gradually speed up until they reach an extremely high speed.

6. Blend the images into one image. Ask them to allow the images to blend into a single image. Ask the person to briefly describe the image. Do not get caught up in too many details here; the idea is just to get the general feeling of the image in order to work with it elegantly. Pace their description, but move on to the next step as soon as possible.

7. Begin telling a story. Pick any story from your life or anywhere else that suits you. The purpose is to break the state. If you have additional skills, such as those from the Ericksonian language, then use these advanced skills if it's appropriate.

8. Test. In the coming days and weeks, see how this process has made the positive state more accessible and how well the pattern has reduced incidences of being in the negative state.

See whether the person has begun employing more creative ways of coping with situations that had been arousing the negative state or more resourceful ways of preventing or getting out of the negative state.

State Induction

Define a desired state.

Kindle the state.

Amplify the state with more rep system kindling.

Expand the state kinesthetically (Kv).

This tool helps us induce a needed state (such as confidence), prepare for an event, or take steps in many NLP patterns. As you work with states and learn to manage them effectively, make yourself a list of your most favorite ones. Making such a list will actually encourage your mind to explore those states even further when you're on "auto-pilot."

1. Establishing a desired state. Think of a state that you would like to experience. Pick one that is positive and feels like a nice alternative to any negative feelings you've had lately. Think of how you would know you were in that state. Describe something about it in the four primary sense modes: visual, auditory, verbal-auditory, and kinesthetic.

2. Kindle the State. Recall a variety of situations in which you have felt some aspect of that state. If this state is not very typical for you, it is okay to think of a situation where you felt only a hint of it, or where you could only sense it in one modality. But remember, when people think something is only in one modality, they are usually just not aware of how it is occurring in one or two others. As you do this, encourage the feelings of the state to collect and amplify them.

3. Extend the state by adding more rep system kindling. Notice what sensory modes are beginning to "kindle" into this state. As you peruse your memories, work on collecting and amplifying the states in the weaker sub-modality. Include the verbal (auditory-digital, as it is called) mode, by saying to yourself some phrases that are in line with the state. For a confident state, it might be, "piece of cake, this is easy," or "The folks at the party really

want me to have a good time." Repeating one or more phrases for a while can help strengthen the state.

4. Expand the state kinesthetically (Kv). Once you have begun to sense the state in all sub-modalities, encourage the feelings to spread throughout your body, as though the energy is flowing through you and carrying the state through you on all of its currents. You can rate your state in terms of its completeness or intensity on a scale of zero to ten.

This can help you compare methods and get a sense of what level a state must reach to be of value. States don't have to reach nine or ten in order to be valuable. You can add constructed sub-modalities, as when you picture yourself walking or talking and gesturing in the desired state.

This can be very powerful. Adjusting sub-modalities can amplify a state. For example, turning up the volume of the verbal aspect or increasing the brightness of the visual With practice, you will become intuitive and natural at this. Discovering which sub-modality is most powerful in "driving" the state can help you use your resources more efficiently.

Strategy Elicitation

1. Can you think of a time when you were completely X? Can you think of a specific time?

2. When you think back to that time...

3. What was the first thing that made you completely X?

4. Was it something you have seen or the way someone else looked at you?

5. Was it something you heard, someone's tone of voice, or someone's presence or something's touch?

6. What happened next as you were completely X after you saw, heard, and felt that? (Y)

7. Did you have a mental image in mind? Have said something to yourself, or have you had a particular feeling or emotion?

8. What happened next when you were completely X? Did you know that you completely X after you Y?

9. Loop: circle back to step 6 and continue until the strategy is complete.

The Big Book of NLP

Stretching Boundaries

On occasion, a client will come in and say that everything is great in their lives, and that's why they are so worried and anxious. They're afraid that this goodness is only temporary and that at any second a disaster will hit them and break their lives apart.

This fear of loss, especially after a lucky strike or a string of successful achievements, can be solved by establishing a new frame of reference. The client is not afraid of losing money, for example, but of losing the emotional responses they currently feel due to that success. They might, for example, fear losing independence due to losing that money.

1. Initiate a downtime state.

2. Identify the personal experience that is at risk of being lost. If it's stated as an external resource, such as money or friends, ask the client what it means to them.

3. Access and associate into the personal experience-what does "independence" feel like? What do you see, hear, and sense?

4. Define the boundaries of the current personal experience. If you had a container in your hands, how big would it need to be to fit the current feeling of "independence"?

4. Now stretch your arms and pretend the container is getting bigger and bigger. And just how much independence can you personally handle? How much personal freedom can you stand?

5. Associate into the stretched personal experience and anchor it.

6. What came first-the thirst for "independence" (fire anchor 1) or the money?

7. Future pace-What will come next, in the coming weeks, as you shift your focus from external objects to (fire anchor 2), how much "independence" can you stand?

8. Test. Think about your limiting beliefs. Does it still cause the same emotional reaction, or how is it different?

Sub-Modality Overlapping

Source: Richard Bandler

Build up weaker sub-modalities to improve creativity and problem solving as you represent things in a richer way. The brain relies on representations that it can hold in various NLP practitioner of memory that it can move and manipulate as information.

Improved sub-modalities improve this aspect of intelligence. Also, you can make your speaking and writing more compelling by using your enriched awareness of sub-modalities to generate enhanced and varied sub-modality references.

Select a relatively weak modality that you would like to improve. Think of which of your rep systems you most favor. Describe or imagine something, relying primarily on your favored rep system.

For example, if you are primarily visual, you might think of a nearby park in as much visual detail as possible. Also, describe it verbally. refers to several sub-modalities, such as color. Switch over to the rep system you are improving.

Let's say you want to improve your auditory reflex system. In the example above, you would recall all the sounds that happened there. In the above example, you would have birds chirping, children playing, and swings squeaking.

As with the visual mode, include sub-modalities such as loudness, pitch, and sound reflections (echo and reverberation such as that which reflects from the walls). Verbally describe all of this as well.

Suspending Fight or Flight

It is possible to trigger blood flow to a specific location by utilizing a neurovascular point. Among other things, the prefrontal cortex regulates the amygdala's response to stress, organizing and judgment, and executes executive functions. The focus is on the prefrontal cortex. Think about a stressor and hold the neurovascular points to keep the prefrontal cortex engaged in leading amygdala control, thus suspending your stress reaction. It is possible to think more clearly while dealing with issues since the neurovascular hold interrupts a major component of the fight-or-flight response.

1. Initiate a downtown state.

2. Two spots can be pinpointed using your fingertips. They're located exactly above the midpoint of each brow, in the space between your hairline and your brows. Apply mild pressure with the fingertips of both hands while stretching the skin sideways, removing any slack.

3. Maintain the pressure as you inhale to a count of four.

4. Exhale to the count of four after pausing for a moment.

5. Take a moment to recall a stressful event in your life—past, present, or future. Dissociate to the third perceptual position.

6. Continue to hold the pressure as you inhale again to the count of four, keeping the stressor in mind. After a brief pause, exhale to a count of five.

7. As you inhale for the count of four, hold the pressure. After a brief pause, exhale to the count of six.

8. As you inhale for the count of four, hold the pressure. Pause and exhale for seven counts.

The Big Book of NLP

9. Maintain the pressure as you inhale once more, to the count of four. Pause for a count of eight and exhale.

10. Break state. Repeat this technique 5 times.

Swish

Recognize the automatic reaction.
Determine the trigger of the negative image.
Place the replacement.
Swish the two images.
Repeat.
Test.

The Swish pattern was developed by Richard Bandler and John Grinder. Depending on the desired outcome, it can be used to swap out a limiting behavior or automatic reaction for a more useful one.

1. Recognize and state the conditioned response.

2. Create an empowering mental scene to replace the negative one.

3. Dissociate (3rd perceptual position).

4. Enhance the scene's sub-modalities until it's as compelling as possible.

5. Break state.

6. Determine the triggers of the limiting scene - what happens right before the behavior is initiated?

7. Associate (first perceptual position) into the limiting scene, right before the behavior is initiated.

8. Note the driving sub-modalities of the limiting scene.

9. Imagine a small, postage-stamp-sized version of the empowering replacement scene in the bottom corner of the limiting scene.

10. Swish (exchange) the size and location sub-modalities of the two images rapidly, in one swift move.

11. Break state.

12. Repeat five to seven times the actions in steps 9, 10 and 11.

13. Test by trying to initiate the limiting thought or behavior again.

Symbolic Somatic Priming

Although there are many ways to convey or encourage feelings with gestures, this system highlights a style that conforms to some things that people commonly experience because of the bio-psychological sources, encoding, and interpretation of emotion.

There is some cultural conditioning in emotion, even to the point that there are psychosomatic conditions that often appear in some cultures that are not evident in others, but this approach can easily be modified for the individual client or general culture.

As you talk with your client, consider what emotions they are not aware of. Decide which ones you want to express the most. For example, a client may be trying to hold it together after a devastating loss when you know they would benefit from sharing and expressing their feelings. Say something to show you understand their situation.

Include body language and a gesture that expresses the kind of feeling you are allowing. Let's say you want to show your awareness and understanding by asking how much support she has or how she is doing. Start by expressing your shock at what happened. You may show a slight scrunching of the face and pull your head back, as if suddenly exposed to bright light or heat. This captures the shock and difficulty of first realizing a loss. With moderately open eyes and a slight nod, you might convey that you are unflinchingly prepared to discuss the loss without making the client feel responsible for your feelings or forced to be indirect. You are also preparing the client to deal with the loss in whatever way is required. Immediately after such a move, take a deep breath and relax your body, hoping that the client's chest will begin to relax as well. This can lead to feelings of grief and affection for the person with whom they are conversing. Then you could relate it to the loss. ((You go from shock to significance and challenge this way. A more intervention based NLP approach may not be appropriate in the most acute period of a traumatic or grief experience. At that point, you could make a gentle protective gesture, like cupping your hands around your heart and bending slightly at the solar plexus to show mature concern.

A slight sideways tilt of the head creates an even more non-threatening and understanding quality. You might say, "Ooh," (face scrunched and pulled back, inhale so you can do the release in a moment) you actually saw (opening back up and slight nod, relaxed chest exhale) the fatal crash. It's (heart directed gesture, slight forward fold at solar plexus, head a little to the side) hard enough to lose someone, not to mention Well, can you tell me a little about who is with you to be supportive during all this? I know your daughter brought you in today. "

Synesthesia

We can use synesthesia in order to alter the perception of a limiting belief into a learning experience.

As a reminder, synesthesia is the process of intentional representational systems overlapping, as manifested by phenomena such as sight-feeling pathways, in which a person develops sensations about what they see, and sound-feeling pathways, in which a person develops sensations about what they hear. Any two sensory modalities can be connected in this way.

1. Select a limiting belief to work with.

2. Note the physiological markers and eye position related to the belief. Determine what occurs internally in each of the representational systems (VAK) throughout the belief framework.

3. Separate the VAK synesthesia by assigning the proper EAC (eye accessing cues) position to each of the sensory representations.

4. Visualize the desired outcome by looking up and right (to visual construction). Don't get confused here, as many practitioners get this wrong-the instructions are for the subject, not the practitioner. When the instructions ask you to look up and right, it means the person's right side (if he sits in front of you, then he looks up right and you see his eyes go up left).

5. Confirm the communication (positive intention) of the emotion (single) and the words (only digital) in relation to the desired aim in comparison to past memories.

6. Consider the images of the memories associated with the belief and create a more realistic perspective on the overall issue by combining good and negative memories in the appropriate chronological sequence on your time line.

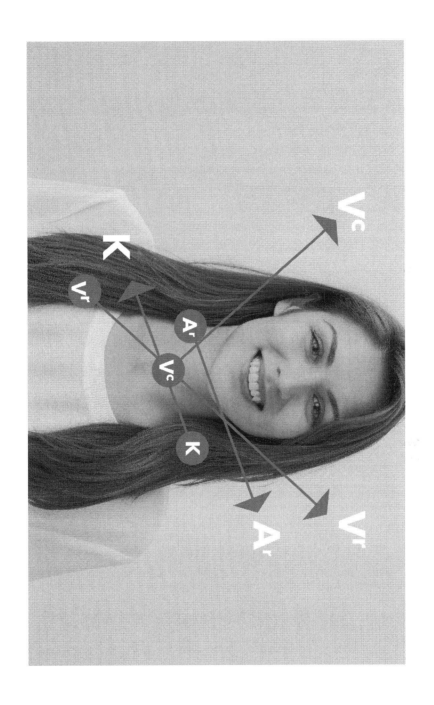

7. Observe how formerly bad recollections can now generate beneficial feedback that can bring you directly to your desired goal. You may even wish to change or augment the desired outcome in light of what you learn from the recollections. Ensure that you can visualize the steps necessary to connect the memories to the positive aim.

8. Determine a favorable, illustrative reference experience. That is, something you are certain you can accomplish in the future.

9. Continue by establishing an anchor for the experience.

10. Make the targeted goal's VAK sub-modality attributes identical to those of the positive reference experience. To aid in this process, fire the anchor for positive reference while focusing on the desired goal.

The Big Book of NLP

Syntactic Ambiguities

You can create ambiguity through violations of syntax. Now we're talking about actual grammar syntax, meaning word order. Syntax ambiguity means that the meaning of the statement is not readily clear because the syntax does not do the job it normally does of clarifying meaning. You can easily create examples by taking a participle, that is, the "ing" word, and a verb. For example, "Deeply comforting psychotherapy clients causes success." What do you think? Am I saying that clients become successful by developing comforting personalities? Or is it that learning to self-sooth creates success through greater emotional stability? Or is it simply that when you comfort them, this leads to success? Add to that, the -ing word, "comforting," could be a verb or an adjective. Consider all the transderivational searching packed into that simple, short sentence. And as for state elicitation, all three of these interpretations have to do with comfort and success, and the pathway to success. If you want your client to develop a state of mind and a mental direction that is about that, then this technique should help create those things.

Tag Questions

Tag questions are phrases like "Can't you?" that are added to the end of a statement. They help the statement bypass the conscious mind by occupying the mind with the tag question. Since the question elicits some transderivational searching, it also helps with the trance. Drug companies do something like this in their advertising in order to make the information about the side effects of drugs less noticeable. That is an unfortunate use of a valuable tool. Here are some example statements with tag questions: As you think of these successes, you can let your mind go to early memories of success, can't you? You have memories of special things you can do, do you not? And this strong foundation of early learning and success is part of how you feel, isn't it? As you read this (hear me speaking), what are you ignoring? What sounds, sights, and sensations are you not paying attention to?Can you now become aware of the toes on your right foot? Were you aware of it before I mentioned it? When you're challenged, are you 'going at it' or 'getting away'? Are passive people just lazy? Or do they act within their comfort zone alone? You cannot **not** learn, can you not?!

Taming Bitterness

Bitterness means the refusal to assimilate and integrate a situation that is happening, or has happened recently, into the current reality. By simulating and integrating a situation by processing the stimuli provided and by resolving internal conflicts and problems that exist only within the person's mental maps, not necessarily in real life.

1. Elicit the person's eye accessing cue locations for all modalities.

2. Select and recall a past experience that represents the bitterness state.

3. Elicit the sub-modalities at the exact moment the bitterness starts to emerge.

4. Use synesthesia to place each modality back in its proper EAC location.

5. Work through the driving sub-modalities in each modality, and reduce their level. For example, if in the bitterness experience, the tone of voice of the other person involved elicits a negative emotional response, reduce the volume and slow down the tempo. Do that several times.

6. Dissociate to a third perceptual position and imagine yourself as an observer in the same scene.

7. Go through the experience right from the beginning, but twice as fast in tempo, remaining in the third perceptual position, and remember to keep the modified driving sub-modalities.

8. Break state.

9. Enter the timeline, and float to the moment right before the past experience begins.

10. Since the bitterness did not yet emerge, you say, "Notice that before this event began, you had no knowledge of becoming bitter, and therefore you are aware of not finding bitterness in your body. Can you notice that?"

11. Anchor the moment of realization that bitterness did not exist at that moment.

12. Move back to the present and fire the anchor.

13. Exit the timeline.

14. Test. When you think about that original experience now, do you notice new insights and realizations about the situation, maybe things you have ignored previously? "

The Big Book of NLP

Temporal Disassociation

When a client first comes up with a statement that presents ownership of a limiting belief or non-useful state, we can use temporal disassociation to weaken the validity of the statement. The formula is:

"How do you know?" →

Dissociate to third perceptual position →

Anchor the Vr dissociated image →

Separate old 'self' from current reality.

Example:

Client: "I am really stupid"

Therapist: "How do you know?"

Client: "I failed my math exam last month"

Therapist: "Think for a moment about who you were at that moment in time, back then, right as the exam ended. See yourself sitting there after giving the teacher the paper, and step back from the scene for a moment" (anchor the client)

Client: "ok. It feels better."

Therapist: "We're not done just yet. Now that you know that this person sitting there in class is the old you, because we humans are evolving all the time, we are never always stupid or always smart, and as you think about this old you failing that exam, see if the present you can answer a better question..."

A moment of silence for the client to prepare to answer.

Therapist: "How does not excelling a single match exam, over a month ago, makes the new you stupid, while the fact remains that you are smart enough to evaluate the reasons that have lead up to that singular failure, over a month ago?"

Reinforcing the disassociation: "In fact, it would be accurate to say, that given you are a new you today, it is unfair to judge how much you are smart today, based on what this other version of you, back then in the past, did not do on time, like preparing for the exam, that would be unfair, would it not be so?"

Client: "I suppose"

Therapist: "So let's make your assessment of your old self more accurate, so that it can be useful. You were stupid at one point in time, over a month ago, but it was not during the exam. You were stupid by not preparing ahead of time, which means there was only a single moment in time in which you have made the decision not to adequately prepare for that specific exam... and that means..."

Client: "that I was stupid for one moment only and it does not mean I am always stupid".

Therapist: "Exactly so. What are you going to say from now on when you think you're stupid?"

Client: "I don't think this way now. But if it comes up, I will find that moment of decision and say it was a one time thing, the old, not who I am now".

The Big Book of NLP

TDS Manipulation

TDS stands for "Trance-Derivational Search." This is a natural phenomenon that is evident in children when they play or learn. It is also very obvious in adults while they meditate or daydream. The concept of manipulating the TDS phenomenon is relatively simple, but a bit more complicated in action. In terms of persuasion and influence, you expand the trance-derivational search of another person by asking questions that must be answered by "searching" the mind from within.

"What is the color of your eyes? I can't really tell." Brown, no TDS here since it's very common knowledge for any person. "When she said she loves you, in which direction did her eyes go?" That's a TDS question, since normally the other person wouldn't notice the direction of the eyes (unless he studies NLP, of course).

"Think about the most exciting experience in your life that happened at least five years ago." That's a deeper TDS request, since our short-term memory still keeps significant experiences from the last few years in order of priority. However, if you in advance ask for an expansion of the time frame, there are numerous experiences to be considered. Hence, a deep search must be performed in order to give you the answer.

How can you tell if someone is in a TDS?

The signs of hypnosis are the same as the signs of a trance-derivational search. To hypnotize anyone, you would encourage a trance derivational search that goes in the direction of "From Outside To Inside." To wake a person from hypnosis, you would still use TDS but in the opposite direction, from inside to outside, while at the end of the outside statements, you just use directions for physical perceptions.

The signs of hypnosis and TDS are generally:

A change in the breathing pattern—usually they'll breath deeper and slower.

A change in skin color—the general rule (since we are people of different colors) is from darker to brighter or shinier.

A change in the size of the lips—the lower lip would probably be more swollen. The upper lip may move upward and appear to be drier.

A change in eye movements—the eyes would either close naturally or become glazed, or they would fixate on a specific point with very slow movements.

A slower moving pace of the body, something that resembles a slow-motion scene,

A slower pace of responding to direct orders—in one case, when I said "move your right finger," it took four minutes before it happened.

Less sensitivity to pain—don't test it unless you're hypnotizing them, though. You never know how strong the other person's brother is.

To use that phenomenon in persuasion, you must first determine whether or not the other person is in a TDS.If he is, then your job is easy; just use truthful or false statements.

"Doesn't it hold true..."

"Wouldn't you agree that..."

"How often do you really see..."

If you get caught being aggressively persuasive, use the Remember to Forget technique. Even resisting individuals within a TDS, those who guard their mind as if it were a precious castle, are unable to keep up with the Binary Code of Forgetfulness or some of the simpler TDS questions.The practical uses of manipulating TDS are endless.

You can induce a trance derivational search in anyone, with anyone, in any situation, and anywhere.are less influenced by that effort. The reason is that their TDS is so fast that it's you who needs to keep up with their thoughts and might end up being influenced yourself.

Thought Virus Inoculation

Source: Robert Dilts

Establish the following spaces on the floor. Step into each one and elicit the corresponding state.

Test the spaces.

Process a toxic thought by taking it through this sequence.

Step through each space with the new belief.

Future pace, checking the ecology of the new belief.

Test.

This pattern creates a defense against destructive (toxic) thought patterns, conceived by Dilts as "thought viruses."

1. Establish the following spaces on the floor: Step into each one and elicit the corresponding state.

a. Neutral Space: An objective state from which you can review the process.

b. Prior Limiting Beliefs Space: Experience a belief that you no longer have and that was limiting or childish, such as believing in Santa Claus.

c. Initial Doubt Space: Experience the time at which you begin to doubt a limiting or childish belief that you no longer have.

d. Old Beliefs Museum Space: Get in touch with all of your prior limiting or childish beliefs.

e. Empowering Belief Space: Think of a belief that is functional and ecologically appropriate. Experience the sense of empowerment that comes from this kind of belief.

f. Open to Belief Space: Connect with something that you previously were not open to believing, but are now open to believing. Get the sense of openness to belief.

g. Sacred Space: Elicit the congruent and committed feeling of being fully connected to your mission in life.

2. Test the spaces. Have the person step into each space from the meta-position space. Amplify and re-anchor the state for any spaces that do not trigger the corresponding state.

3. Process a toxic thought by taking it through this sequence.

a. Create a toxic belief to guide you through the process.

b. Have the person take this belief through each of the states in the sequence above.

c. Continue cycling through this sequence until the person is ready to deposit the toxic belief in the Old Beliefs Museum Space (part d).

d. Take the meta-position and create an empowering belief to fill the void left by the old, toxic belief.The new belief must be functional and ecologically sound.

4. Take the new belief with you as you walk through each space. Follow the sequence of steps as before, but this time with the new belief. If the person begins to experience any confusion, have them step into the meta-position and clarify the belief so that it can function in the state where the confusion developed.

5. Future Pace, Checking the Ecology of the New Belief. Take this belief into imaginary future situations and look for any ecological problems to address. Refine the thoughts in any way that is necessary.

The Big Book of NLP

6. Test. In the coming days or weeks, notice any ways that this new belief influences your attitude and results in life. Notice any limitations or problems, and refine the belief as needed.

Too Much, Not Enough

How do you prevent future remorse for not following through on your responsibilities today? You feel regret and remorse when you realize you were not careful enough, judicious enough, or disciplined enough. You slack off in class, avoid exercise, or don't put in the effort at work. You prioritize immediate gratification above long-term benefits. Dessert first, please! The consequences always arrive. For every cause, there is an effect, and often times, we are shocked at how severe and bothersome the results are that our carelessness has caused. Let's prevent it from being our future selves.

1. Think about your most desired outcomes, the ones you're most excited about right now.

2. Make sure your outcome fits the criteria of being well-formed:

Realistic

Positive

Self-Reliant

Observable

Context-Dependent

Measurable

Access to Resources

Ecological

If your outcome is not truly well-formed, use the Well-Defined Outcomes pattern before continuing.

3. Recall an experience from your past that is still causing you to feel regret or remorse for something you haven't done but could have. Regret for a missed opportunity or procrastinating on an important task that resulted in failure

4. Anchor the remorse experience.

5. Recall a rewarding experience in your past in which you used your discipline to achieve a worthy goal, such as studying for an important exam and doing your best, or training for and then running a marathon, or attending a network event despite feeling tired and uninterested in socializing, and ending up in new prosperous relationships with interesting people.

6. Anchor the satisfying experience.

7. Establish two physical locations on the floor-one for Remorse and one for Satisfaction.

8. Stand on the Remorse spot, close your eyes, take a deep breath and enter your timeline.

a. Fast forward your timeline to the same day as today, a year ahead.

b. Turn around on your timeline, facing the past and looking at the present day.

c. Fire the Remorse anchor.

d. Say, "If only I had done the work!"

e. Allow the images and conclusions of the work you supposedly haven't done to come up on the timeline, showing how you slacked off instead of working on your outcome. Consider real-life present-day distractions that can realistically interfere with your plans.

f. For each one of those images, associate them with them and describe and declare them this way: "I did too much X and not enough Y." For example, "I spent too much time on social media and not enough time on reaching out to potential clients."

g. Fire the anchor again, for each of the images, and see if you can enhance it and increase the emotional impact.

9. Open your eyes, take a deep breath, and tell yourself that you would rather never feel these feelings again.

10. Now take a step back, out of the Remorse spot, and reorient your body to face the Satisfaction spot. Tell yourself that this is the moment of decision to select a path that is not even remotely related to the horrible feelings you experienced a moment ago.

11. Step into the Satisfaction spot, close your eyes and enter the timeline again.

a. Fast forward your timeline to the same day as today, a year ahead.

b. Turn around on your timeline, facing the past and looking at the present day.

c. Fire the Satisfaction anchor.

d. Say, "Wow, I am so relieved I did the work!" Enhance the auditory sub-modalities to match excitement and joy.

e. Allow the images and conclusions of the work you have supposedly done to come up on the timeline, showing how you actively and consciously chose to do important work instead of falling for distractions. Consider present-day potential distractions that may have interfered with your productivity.

f. For each one of those mages, dissociate (third perceptual position), and describe the moment of useful choice this way: "I'm really glad I chose to do X instead of Y! I am so much better off today because of it." For example, "I'm really glad I chose to email 10 more potential clients instead of wasting time on social media looking at other people's fake, make-believe adventures. I am so much better off today because of it."

g. Fire the satisfaction anchor again and again, for each of the better choice images, and enhance the visual sub-modalities to increase the emotional impact. Remember to keep the images dissociated so you can see yourself in them but not experience being in them. This is a crucial distinction.

The Big Book of NLP

12. Open your eyes, take a deep breath, and tell yourself that these are the feelings you would rather feel a year from now.

13. Now take a step back, out of the Satisfaction spot. Tell yourself that this is the moment of decision to select a path that is most likely to get you closer to realizing your dreams.

14. Close your eyes again, and enter your timeline for the last time. Fast forward your timeline to the same day as today, a year ahead. Turn around on your timeline, facing the past and looking at the present day. Fire the satisfaction anchor.

15. Turn around on your timeline, facing the future, and the present day is a year behind you. Move backward rapidly on your timeline, stopping for a brief moment at each of five general "milestones" that signal your progression towards satisfaction. End the movement in the present day and exit the timeline. Open your eyes, take a deep breath and break the state.

16. You ought to repeat steps 14 and 15 once a day for the next 3 weeks. If you feel discouraged about your progress towards your outcome or somewhat lazy, repeat the entire pattern.

Tracking Life Transitions

> *Identify your current major transition issue.*
>
> *Spatially anchor the Dragon (transition issue), and place a series of archetypes around it as specified in this step.*
>
> *Determine from which archetype you are experiencing the Dragon.*
>
> *Step into that archetype and explore its somatic syntax.*
>
> *Move through each archetype and then step into the most appropriate one.*
>
> *From the meta-position, process your experiences.*
>
> *Test.*

This pattern uses archetypes to help us come to terms with a major change or perceived threat, and to leverage that new relationship in the service of our well-being. It applies NLP processes known as spatial sorting, somatic syntax, and characterological adjectives. It uses them in relation to archetypes associated with mystery and danger.

1. Determine the nature of your current major transition issue.

Identify the transition issues that you are facing that this time. We will call them the "dragon."

Think about the aspects of the dragon. This can include changes in your status, relationships, environment, and so forth.

2. Spatially anchor the Dragon (transition issue) and surround it with a series of archetypes as specified in this step. Choose a spatial anchor for the Dragon archetype. Place the following archetypes to form a circle around the Dragon.

a. The Innocent: Does not yet have a conscious experience with the Dragon.

b. The Orphan: Experiences the Dragon as an overwhelming threat.

c. The Martyr: Experiences the Dragon as persecution.

d. The Wanderer: dislikes and avoids the dragon.

e. The Warrior: Experiences the Dragon as an adversary to engage in battle.

f. The Sorcerer: Experiences the Dragon as powerful, but as having its own meaning and destiny, and even as a potential resource.

3. Determine the archetype from which you are experiencing the Dragon.

Access an objective state (a meta state) and discover from which archetype you are experiencing your dragon. If you find it hard to accomplish, go through perceptual positions #1 to #2 and then to #3, which in essence is an objective, yet close enough to notice everything, position.

4. Enter that archetype and investigate its somatic syntax.

Step into the spatial location occupied by that archetype.

Explore the somatic syntax (the associated body movements and posture, gestures and voice tones, expressions and stance) of that archetype. Take your time here, it is important to work slowly.

5. Go through each archetype and then step into the one that is most appropriate for you. Work your way through each of the archetypes in this way, discovering their experience vis a vis the dragon.

Once you have completed this circuit, step into the space that feels most appropriate for your relationship with your dragon. Note that this tells you what steps in transition are coming up next, based on the sequence of the archetypes provided.

6. Process your experiences from the meta-position. Return to your meta-position and think about your discoveries and lessons from this experience.

7. Test. Over the coming days and weeks, notice any changes that you are experiencing in regard to this major transition.

Post the archetypes where you can see them, with the current one marked. This will inspire your thinking about how to develop the most resourceful relationship and strategies for this chapter and your next chapter.

The Big Book of NLP

Transformation Archetype Identification

Continue the Life Transitions Tracking pattern (above) by determining which process archetype is most important in your development at this time. Before working through this exercise, try The Life Transitions Tracking pattern.

1. Choose three items that represent your core. Pick three items, one from each of the three categories. It must represent something that you want to be and will always be.

We'll call this your core.

a. Animals

b. Famous historical figures

c. A legendary figure

d. Plants

e. Natural phenomena

f. Automobile

h. A portion of the body

h. Other

2. Discuss in a small group. Have each member share their three symbols with the other members. Use this format: "I am like the (item) because (reason)."

3. Decide on your hero archetype. Select from the following the hero archetype that represents the person you are becoming during this step in your personal development.

a. A wise elderly man or woman

b. Mother/father

c. Wizard

d. Queen/king

e. Healer, teacher, storyteller, etc.

In your group, have each member share their hero symbol in the format, "I want to be more like (symbol) because (reason)."

4. Select your archetype of transformation. Your hero archetype presupposes an archetype of transformation. Select a symbol that represents that process archetype from the following:

a. Enlightenment

b. Rebirth

c. Resurrection

d. Metamorphosis

e. Transformation

f. Incremental evolution

g. Transcendence

h. Quantum leap

i. Other symbol

Have the members of your group share their symbol using this format: "The process of my next step in my evolution will be like (symbol) because (reason)."

5. Create a metaphor in which, through your archetype of transformation, you become your hero archetype.

Review the three archetypes that you have chosen. Create a metaphor that is strong on imagery, like a storyboard for a movie or a comic strip. In this metaphor, your core must transform into your chosen hero archetype through your archetype of transformation. Have your group members share their metaphoric stories.

Trembling

An important part of this procedure is connecting the body with its innate ability to heal itself. Using this approach, you will learn how to properly release your body's psychological distress sensations. The idea is to put a stop to any internal monologue and redirect attention to the physical reality. Trembling is a normal reaction that the body has to help it recover after a fright or disturbance. Your active states can be trained back into calm conditions using this method.

1. Doing this while seated or reclining on your back is fine. Put your feet on the ground if you're going to lie down. Knees bowed and feet firmly planted on the ground.

2. Ask yourself, "Where do I feel the tension?" to get a sense of where it is in the body. "What is the nature or pattern of the trembling sensation?"

3. At all times, be aware that your back is being supported by the ground at all times. Then, ask: "Can I now recognize the ground's protection?" Allow yourself to be held by the ground.

4. Let the trembling feeling move into your feet or the ground by exhaling slowly.

5. Allow your body to naturally inhale and exhale. Keep your body and breath in the present moment, and let the breath slow down gradually. The best thing to do if you're having trouble staying awake is to open your eyes and reposition your body.

6. By gently pushing on the feet, you'll create a rocking motion throughout your entire body. There should be less shaking after doing this step, as it is a soothing activity. Back and forth: Allowing the trembling, and then going back to the soft rocking might be what you notice. A few tries will be necessary to get into the groove. As a means of calming the nervous system, the trembling should be transformed into body rocking.

7. Allow the movement to happen naturally by expecting your breath to assist you in the process. Instead of squeezing air out of your lungs, let it flow naturally with your movements.

The Big Book of NLP

8. As you begin to build a mild movement pattern, concentrate solely on the rhythmic movement.

9. Test. Take a breather and pay attention to the outcome. What parts of your body can you actually "feel"? What body parts are conscious? Is there any movement in your body? How does that feel? How would you characterize the sensation in your body at this moment? Enjoy the feeling of having your body back in a condition of equilibrium.

Tunnel to Peripheral

Neurological drivers are the major subjective distinctions that are directly hard-wired to the neural system. Peripheral vision has a collection of neurological drivers that make it distinct. Tunnel vision feels like a trap because it is based on sympathetic nervous system arousal and it is detailed (chunked down). Peripheral vision, on the other hand, is contextual and its manifestation is based on the parasympathetic nervous system. While tunnel vision allows us only to notice a fraction of the stimuli we unconsciously perceive, peripheral vision is panoramic.

1. Initiate a downtime state.

2. Select an issue, a problem that is context dependent or has an object of reference (a person, a memory, a future event).

3. Practice peripheral vision:

a. Focus gaze.

b. Expand your awareness to the panoramic sub-modality.

c. Loosen your jaw.

d. Calibrate your body and posture to a physiological shift.

4. Anchor the peripheral vision state.

5. Move to the first perceptual position, associate to the problem context.

6. Fire the anchor.

7. Break state.

8. Repeat five times steps 3 to 7.

9. Eco-check.

10. Second ecology check via perceptual positions: Self (first, peripheral vision); Other (second, re-integration); Other (third, observer).

11. Future pace.

Undercut Presupposition

Source: Tad James and John Overdurf

Learn to expand your client's mental model by undercutting their presuppositions through this procedure.

1. Find out what the most basic assumptions are. 2. How is this a problem right now?

2. Identify all of the argument's presuppositions.

3. Determine which one or ones will have the greatest impact on the problem.

four.Frame your response as a question, and include a solution in the message.

5. Recognize your presuppositions and restate the problem.

6. End the process by posing the question.

Example: A client says he takes the frustrations he experiences at work home with him and takes them out on his wife and kids.

Presuppositions: He is unhappy at work; he does not express his frustrations at work, nor does he try to resolve the issues that lead to these frustrations; he uses repression at work and explosions at home; he is aware that his wife and kids are not causing his frustrations at work; he wants to stop taking it out on his wife and kids.

Undercutting the presuppositions:

"How pleased will your wife be if you ask her to assist you in finding a new job that will relieve you of the frustrations you are experiencing in your current one?"

"Wouldn't your wife and kids be willing to manage with your earning a little less money in a less stressful workplace, rather than seeing you filled with guilt and shame for taking out your work stress on them?"

"Who is the one person in your job that deserves your fury?"

Undetermined State Integration

Help your subject describe his or her state. Sometimes people simply can't connect with their state to describe it. They will say things like, "I'm not sure what I'm feeling," "It seems vague," or "I feel dull" (indicating that they are becoming physically or mentally fatigued).This pattern comes to get a clearer statement that will enable you, as their practitioner, to set a well-defined outcome for the session.

1. Put your finger about one foot from the subject's eyes. Position yourself in front of the person and at eye level. Put your right hand about one foot in front of his eyes with your finger pointed laterally (not toward either of you).

2. Guide the eye's movement and blinking pattern. Ask him to take a few deep breaths and then close and open his eyes, matching your finger's movement rhythm. Start very slowly, moving your finger from 90 degrees to about 45 degrees (a downward motion), and then back up again.

3. Alter the movements as directed, and then break the state. Repeat 5-6 times with a faster rhythm until normal blinking rhythm is restored.Then keep the finger motion, but move the hand to access cues for Visual Constructed (up left) and later for Visual Remembered (up right). The purpose here is to activate the person's brain through controlled eye movements. Now let him stretch and move freely, blinking quickly several times and breathing normally.

4. Ask the questions in the manner indicated. Ask the following questions and wait only two seconds for the reply. If he or she doesn't respond immediately, offer the possible answers provided in the parentheses. Speak at the same rhythm as you notice his eyes are blinking. Questions

a. What would be the best feeling you'd like to have right now? (Curiosity, passion, calmness, excitement, decisiveness, relaxation, security, etc.)

b. How would you know if you felt it?

What would be evidence for you, on the inside, that you're really feeling X (the state they chose)?

c. What would happen once you felt X?

d. If you felt X, in which situations would it be most useful for you? (At work? With your kids? With your spouse? While you're waking up?)

e. In which situations wouldn't it be useful for you to feel X? And with what feeling would you replace it?

5. Constant fatigue state: If your subject is still feeling fatigued and dull-minded, ask the following elicitation questions: Was there a time in your past when you recalled feeling X? How did you know back then that you felt X? Could you show me how you would look if you were feeling X right now? What was it like to have that feeling? Can you feel it now?

Make sure your hand is not so close that it makes the person uncomfortable. Different people will have different comfort zones. If there is a possibility of epilepsy, such as when there is a family history, then refrain from using eye movement exercises. Have the person discuss with their physician whether such exercises are appropriate for them. The first set of questions should be asked and answered fairly quickly. If you give the person time to think, their own self-criticism is likely to inhibit them. If the person is agitated, this is not the right pattern to use. Consider using next the "State Chaining" technique or "Collapsing Anchors."

Useful Stress

Stress, when controllable and well timed, is not a disease or a foe you need to battle. When we get clients who tell us they want a stress-free life, we immediately ask, why do they want to go into a coma? As long as you're awake and aware, a healthy portion of stress is your ally, and it is useful not only for survival, but mainly for productivity and performance enhancement. This pattern can help if you view any kind of stress as a problem, and can readjust your unconsciousness to use the emotion as a driving force instead of an emergency break.

1. When stress happens, acknowledge the feeling: "I am experiencing some level of stress."

2. Define the boundaries, rules, and contexts of the feeling: "I am experiencing some level of stress as a result of being asked to give a 15-minute PowerPoint presentation at the next board meeting, on Tuesday morning at 10:30 am, in front of 12 executives and staff members, and talk about my department's recent IT upgrade."

3. Dissociate: "This is stress." Allow the sensation to have a form, a container, as if it's an airy and flexible object that was inserted into your body. Notice the kinesthetic boundaries of the stress.

4. Imagine a suitable symbol to represent the stress container.

5. Now allow yourself to notice the stress without verbalizing it, including how it affects your body.

6. Now that you're getting used to having it around, with its boundaries and familiar visualization (symbol and container), welcome the stress by recognizing that it's a response to something you care about.

7. Ask yourself: Can I locate the positive motivation behind the stress? What is at stake here? Why is it so important and why does it matter to me?

8. Now expand the stress container, enlarge the symbol, and make use of the energy that it gives you, instead of wasting that energy trying to manage your stress. What can you do right now with this energy to move forward towards your outcomes and fulfill your highest values?

For most people, it's counterintuitive to enlarge a stress response. We humans like to feel comfortable and take it easy. The problem with that approach is that nothing worthwhile is achieved by sitting idle and fantasizing or by being too calm and in a persistent "nirvana" state. The waves of stress, once you use them to propel your life's ship forward, will get you faster to that deep, calm blue water. And soon enough, you'll get tired of the quiet and boredom and seek a new adventure. There is no adventure without some level of healthy stress.

Values Discovery

This is a simple way to expose deeper emotions, the hierarchy of values, and explore the new motivations for the client's desires and attachments to specific outcomes.

We do this by asking, "What would that give you that you wouldn't otherwise have?" For example,

Therapist: "What do you want?"

Client: "Start my own business"

Therapist: "And what would that give you that you wouldn't otherwise have?"

Client: "money, obviously"

Therapist: "And what would money give you that you wouldn't otherwise have?"

Client: "Well, freedom for a change..."

Therapist: "And what would freedom give you that you wouldn't otherwise have?"

Client: "the people's respect"

Therapist: (meta model) "and whose respect do you wish to feel the most?"

Client: "my wife"

From wishing to start a business to earn more money, we discover the client's internal propulsion system (self-motivation) is linked to the respect he feels his wife is giving him. Now we have a deep structural reference for future change work.

Values Hierarchy Identification

Values are the honest answer to the question, "What is most important to me?" Values define and refine your "intuition," the feeling of what is right and what is wrong. Values provide the high-level direction for your decision-making. Not knowing your values and their relative hierarchy can get you into a lot of trouble. Frustration and destructive behavior, self-sabotage, and even crime are only a few symptoms of a simple, yet unconscious, problem: dis-alignment with your highest values.

Not knowing and not conforming to your highest values does not have to lead you to prison. Consider the times of making hard decisions, or hardly making decisions at all! If you knew your highest values, and what is most important to you—and in which order it is important to you—the decisions would make themselves.

You would only have to choose the actions and strategies that align with your values. That would make you, naturally, feel aligned, satisfied and confident. Identify the values you're holding currently and the hierarchy in which they are organized.

1. Getting into a state of relaxation: Whenever working with a higher level structures, such as beliefs or values, it is always advisable to do so in a state of relaxation and having positive expectations. You do not work here with strong negative emotions, and having any random emotional storm might cause a conflict and hinder your exploration of your true values in life.

First things first—do anything you have to do to become relaxed and comfortable. If you work with a client, induce a light trance, use some relaxation script (progressive relaxation is good, but remember to wake your client up before proceeding). Your client should be wide awake and not in hypnosis while working with this pattern.

2. Complete a list of values by answering the 3 to elicit existing values:

What is most important to you?

If you had your 80th birthday tonight, celebrating with relatives and friends, what kind of words would you most appreciate them saying about your life?

If you had to give up on everything you have, but got to keep one characteristic of your "old life," what would it be?

Refer to the list of common values below to get some ideas.

3. Establish the hierarchy by comparing each value to another. At this stage, you take each of the values you selected in the previous step and rank their importance. You do so by taking each value, in order, and comparing it to the other values.

Is "health" more important to you than "affluence" (most likely)? So now "health" is bumped up the list, before "affluence". Is "health" more important to you than "faith"? If so, it goes up the hierarchy again. And so on. You take each value and compare it to each other value in the list. It takes time and patience. But when you're done, you will feel a very unique emotion: decisive composure.

4. Conduct an eco-check. In many NLP patterns, we have a "Test" step as the last one. In this pattern, we prefer to do an ecology check since you cannot really test your values. Either you feel right about a value or you don't. But your current values and the hierarchy in which they are organized might not be very useful for your current outcomes. Values and their hierarchy are changeable.

Perform an eco-check by asking: "Does any of the challenges in my life seem logical now that I look at this list?" "Is there a better way of organizing my values so that they would fit my current needs?

Common Life Values:

Health, Love, Freedom, Contribution, Fun, Creativity, Family, Growth, Passion, Carefulness, Affection, Accomplishment, Decisiveness, Wisdom, Service, Talent, Simplicity, Virtue, Reliability, Friendship, Respect, Resolve, originality, Openness, Mindfulness, Longevity, Leadership, Intimacy, Generosity, Gentility, Faith, Grace, Enthusiasm, Experience,

Uniqueness, Endurance, Dominance, Direction, Commitment, Security, Balance, Beauty, Care, Courage, Encouragement, Fitness, Agility, Helpfulness, Hospitality, Mastery, Impact, Modesty, organization, Peace, Power, Privacy, Reason, Realism, Serenity, Sympathy, Toughness, Trust, Youthfulness, Wonder, Punctuality, Productivity, Perseverance, Intuition, Independence, Flow, Discipline, Self-actualization, Charm, Certainty, Awareness.

Values Lines Elicitation

Source: Tad James

1. Initiate a downtime state.

2. Identify the elements of the dichotomy meta-program (black-or-white; if you haven't mastered the meta-programs yet, refer to the Personality Profiling with NLP book for details).

3. Elicit the general lifelong values: "What is absolutely most important to you?" (Refer to the Values Hierarchies Identification pattern).

4. Establish a hierarchy of values and prioritize the most important ones.

5. Identify the containing / storage location of each highly important value: "What image do you have in the context of considering this value? Where is that image stored in your mental space?"

6. Enter the timeline, advance 15 years, and repeat steps 2 through 5.

7. Break state.

8. Enter the timeline, move backwards 15 years into the past, and repeat steps 2 to 5.

9. If necessary, change a value in the values hierarchy by moving it along the timeline.

The Big Book of NLP

Verb Finder

This punctuation system, which is related to the Carlin and Bi-Lateral methods, is useful for gaining someone's full attention when their minds are drifting as you speak.

Once you've practiced this, you will not want to use it all the time, but it will inform your word punctuation. (Remember that these are practices that build unconscious skills and discrimination that will enhance your verbal impact and control.) As you SPEAK, only EMPHASIZE the verbs, except for the verb "to be."

You might be surprised to FIND that is doesn't SOUND as odd as you'd exPECT. Once you get used to this in practice, you will find it easier to improvise, emphasizing whatever words your intuition tells you to improvise.

Viable Animosity

Animosity over a past incident or current rage can be dealt with using the following strategy.

1. Think about a past experience for which you still harbor resentment and anger.

2. Associate into the experience. Run the mental movie as it happened originally.

3. Anchor your feelings of rage and frustration.

4. Transform the anchor into a visual symbol.

5. Break state.

6. Hold the symbol in your hand. Make a fist with your hand and tighten it firmly. This could be interpreted as a way of expressing a deep-seated rage.

7. You might even wish to name the resentments, irritations, and rage you're aware of, and feel your hand gripping more and tighter to hold onto the fury.

8, Now slowly open your hand and extend your fingers so that they're basically straight but also form a cup.

9. What happened to rage? Because the energy of anger is altered as it is released from the body, the message here is that you may adapt to letting go of it and witness it disintegrate or even cease to exist.

10. Make a fist with your hand once again, and then open it slowly. As your hand continues to open, what feelings are you able to perceive? List all of the emotions you're currently dealing with. As you get more comfortable expressing yourself through the language of sensation, what do you notice?

The Big Book of NLP

Vision Communication Protocol

All too often, the stereotype of the male becoming overwhelmed and withdrawn or angry when his mate confronts him with more emotional issues than he is prepared to cope with at one time plays out in relationships. Of course, males don't have a complete monopoly on this trait. But, more commonly, women find it difficult to cope with the male "Mr. Fixit" approach to problems, which women say squeezes out their need for process and deeper understanding.

This protocol directly resolves this problem on several levels. It sets up a framework for a new approach, provides mental and temporal space for the protocol to do its magic, and grounds the participants in a manner that greatly reduces the anxiety that is the cause of so much communication dysfunction.

The Protocol

Frame the situation by explaining to the woman that the male has a very small emotional bladder in his brain. Women find this amusing because they or one of their friends may have complained of having a small urinary bladder. If you're talking to a man, explain that females are not usually as good at mechanical reasoning as men, and can have trouble designing their emotional issues into a workable arrangement.

Men find this amusing because they have seen their mate or other women have trouble with mechanical reasoning of some kind, perhaps something concerning the physics of operating a motor vehicle. I hope you'll forgive the appeal to stereotypes, but I'm more concerned with what works and what maintains rapport and momentum in the therapeutic relationship rather than being completely politically correct at all times.

This framing works just as well when working with homosexual partners since both genders are typically able to take their own peccadilloes lightly. For your ill-humored clients, you may want to use a very neutral way to introduce this protocol. Explain that the protocol allows people to bring up very serious issues in a positive way that does not tend to alienate or overwhelm people and avoids coming off as a "Mr. Fixit" mentality. Describe the protocol as follows: The client is to select the most important emotional issue rather than overwhelm or confuse their partner by daisy-chaining the issues.

Daisy-chaining happens when a person thinks of a disturbing issue, develops a state that causes them to think of one related issue after another, verbalizes them as they come to mind, and overwhelms, confuses, or antagonizes their partner as a result.

With this single most important issue in mind, have the person think of what the relationship would be like if the issue was resolved in a meaningful, generative way. Then, have the person describe the values that make this outcome meaningful to them.

Work with your client to think up the kinds of steps that would move their relationship toward that vision. These steps must be realistic, practical, and as attractive as possible. They should be worded in the most inspirational way possible. They should then be reworked so that they appeal to the mindset and speech style of the partner. This step can feel pleasantly subversive to your client, who is used to feeling some futility and frustration because they have confused being genuine with limiting their speech to their own frame of reference. Breaking out of this self-imposed habitual limitation can seem somehow like cheating. It's important to keep the process fun so the person does not lose momentum by thinking that they are really cheating in some way.

Now work with your client to come up with a single step that would move the relationship into this plan. It should be something that can be done almost immediately.

Note that by doing this step last in formulating the plan, your client is more likely to come up with a meaningful item than if they start out with an effort to come up with the step. This is because they have stepped back to look at the big picture, thinking of their long-term desires and their overarching values, even if only briefly.

Now ask them to try communicating this in the following sequence:

1) The set up: "I know you know how important you are to me, and the kind of vision we share for our relationship. I mean, I see us (vision goes here). "

2) "This means so much to me, because I value (one or two values go here)."

3) "And I know we can create this by doing things like (one to three steps go here)."

4) "I'd just love it if you could join with me in moving us closer to that by (a very easy initial step goes here; your client is asking for a simple behavior that would mean a lot to him or her in the relationship, and it must be something the partner is definitely able to do)."

Here is a real-life example with a client (real names were changed, of course):

"Bill, I know you love me. There are so many ways that you can show me that. Even the little things you do, like the way you make breakfast on Saturdays. And I know you want to see us have our talks be easier and get to positive places without a lot of hassle."

Note that the client, Ellen, is reframing very hard in the direction of her mate's perspective here. Otherwise, she might be saying she really wants their discussions to be more productive and for him to show that he really understands and cares about what she is bringing up, etc.

"I think if we worked out at the gym together a couple times a week, this would be great for us, because we don't want to let our work and money issues get to us. You know how much sharper we are and how much more stamina we have when we get on our game that way? "

If she were not framing this in his terms, she might be saying that they need to spend more time together and work through issues more; the sex would be better if he were in better shape and she's embarrassed about getting flabby, and she knows he doesn't really like her body these days; in the car, they could talk back and forth from the gym and get closer; she really has a hard time just going to the gym on her own and needs support to exercise regularly; she's been feeling kind of depressed and needs him to be more positive and uplifting so she can feel better about doing more things, etc. You could really help me if you could schedule your appointments so we can rely on Wednesday nights and Saturdays later in the morning. I know you want to keep Saturday afternoons and some evenings open for work. How does that sound? " (Face relaxed with a little smile, head tilted a little to the side.)

Please note that this is in no way intended to suppress discussion of serious issues such as depression, weight loss, mutual support, the emotional tone of a relationship, sex quality, body image, working through issues productively, and discussing issues adequately—all things that were brought up in the parenthetical remarks about the client reframing what she might have said.

The point is that, at this point in the relationship, her approach and his response have been disastrous, while this protocol has saved many couples by giving them a structure to work on issues productively and without becoming too triggered. If you think of a relationship as something that requires conditioning over time, like an athlete's body or a scientist's mind, then working through issues of quality in a step-wise fashion that is tied to big picture values and vision can be a positive experience.

A counter-argument might be that relationships must be approached holistically, so pulling out a single desire fails to address ecology. But remember, the single desire was derived after looking holistically at the relationship, and was the highest priority out of a number of things that would be supportive from a holistic perspective.

Success with one item can galvanize the couple to continue this process over time, with additional successes adding up to the vision they are pursuing together. On the other hand, when this gambit fails, it will be much clearer where the problem lies or what dynamic is taking place, because of the way the issues have been isolated and framed. For example, if the partner has too much dissociation and regression to tolerate even a single request that is framed positively, that partner requires mental health care that addresses this problem. The same would apply to a partner who is too compromised by drugs or alcohol to follow through adequately, even if the discussion went well at the time.

Vision Down

This simple method has produced some really marvelous results in relationships that have become strained and alienated. It is a great way to cross a gender or personality gap between nearly any two personality types. You already know about the importance of establishing a secure base for pretty much anything to happen in a relationship. You also know that alignment means that your values are lined up with your behavior. At least that's one good version of alignment.

This approach to communication involves creating a secure base as well as alignment. It also adds in some good old-fashioned sales sense. This approach to communicating is to be taught to your client. You can also use it to get important ideas across to your clients. The people who respond best seem to be the types who are moved by vision and values, and the types that think like engineers, who like to see the plan in an organized way. However, it is good for almost any type of person.

How To Proceed

Ask your client to tell you about the problem that they need to communicate with their friend (or their spouse, employer, or whoever). Have them describe the point of being concerned about this. Instead of trying to get them to say what they are "really" trying to say, have them describe what would happen if they got it across and the other person responded well.

We don't mean the short-term outcome of ending the conversation on nice terms. We mean the result of a collaborative relationship that got meaningful results regarding the issue at hand. For example, if your client is tired of walking on eggshells around her husband, ask how she would know that the issue was collaboratively resolved. Go beyond the obvious matter of her being able to speak her mind freely. Have her describe some of her husband's behaviors in this ideal future scenario. Next, ask what vision and values this outcome would express. She might say that she would feel more relaxed and loved, and that the things they wanted to do together would work out better because there would be more (and more effective) communication. They would collaborate more, so there would be a more constructive effort, producing results in their lives. To make this more motivational, have her tell you about some of these results, because they will reflect the dreams she has for the relationship in terms of the lifestyle and activities she longs for. Now help her compress this down into specific values that are more abstract. They might be the following:

1) Expression (knowing that the other person will make every effort to understand the positive intent behind what you say);

2) Mutual respect (being confident that your contribution to the relationship will be valued and supported);

3) Constructive collaboration (joyfully collaborating);

4) Fulfilling our ambitions (being able to achieve and experience the things we desire).

It really doesn't matter if client after client comes up with pretty much the same values for their relationship. These needs are universal. Often, spelled out, they sound a little like parts of the U.S. Constitution. Now have your client describe the medium-term goals that would be aligned with the long-term vision and values. And next, have her tell you what she'd like to see happen in the short term, especially in terms of how her husband can help her begin moving toward the medium-term objectives. Okay, now we have the vision and values aligned with the objectives and tasks. That is, the big picture and the worm's-eye view. Now help her practice initiating the conversation with her husband. These things always go better if a person can start with canned material. It gives them some confidence and momentum, and helps them command attention and interest because they will express themselves in a more grounded way. Finally, have her try this out with her husband, and work with her based on the results she gets. By the way, we are talking here about a reasonably functional relationship. If her husband is a highly manipulative person, we would not necessarily try this. We might choose to focus more on training the husband with behavior modification.

The Big Book of NLP

Visual Cues Elicitation

To build and maintain rapport with people whose primary representation system is visual, watch for and match the following cues:

• They usually sit with an upright posture and move their eyes upward when visualizing.

• Use high tones and breathe in deeply into the chest.

• Use visual-based predicates, for example:

See, Look, Clear, View, Dawn, Reveal, Hazy, Focused, Imagine, Eyes, Take a peek, Take a look, Tunnel vision, Paint a picture, Illustrate, Picture, Short sighted, Show, Read, Dark, Glance, Crystal clear, Sight for sore, Naked eye, Bird's eye, An eyeful, Overlook.

• Pay attention to people and want to be looked at when they speak.

• They are generally slender in body build.

Visual Rep System Development

Much like the Auditory Rep System Development pattern, this pattern will help you refine the subtleties and perceptions of your visual representational system. It will improve your ability to distinguish sub-modalities, which is a necessary skill when working with NLP patterns. It will also freshen up your creativity and problem-solving capabilities.

The visual rep system is memory-based. Visualization, in essence, is a fancy word for saying that you remember what a certain item looks like.

1. Hold up an onion in front of you. In many traditional and old-fashioned visualization guides, you will find the instruction to imagine an orange or a banana. We believe that this is no test of your imagination, and it does not provide any value in imagining something you've seen 10 thousand times in the past.

Normally, you wouldn't take an onion and observe it intensely. You would do so with an orange just before you're about to peel and eat it.

Concentrate now on the onion and try to grasp the big picture: how it looks, the colors, the shades, and so on.

2. Close your eyes and visualize the same onion. Now, with your eyes closed, just keep the image you've seen with your eyes open in your mind's eye. That's all. It's easy, and it takes almost no effort to see something and recall it the same second you close your eyes.

3. Reopen your eyes and look at the onion again. What you do now is confirm that the image in your head matches, more or less, the image your eyes are getting from the surroundings.

The reason for this step is that further on in this pattern, we will manipulate the mental image in the same way you subconsciously manipulate other images that affect your emotions. This will also persuade you of your imagination's power and control.

The Big Book of NLP

4. Close your eyes again and multiply the onion's size. Now you're doing some image manipulation. Your brain is better than any version of Adobe Photoshop and much faster than any quadruple Intel processor on the most elegant Mac computer.

Close your eyes and imagine the same onion.

As you do so, double its size. You could simply "bump" the image closer to you; when things are closer, they seem bigger. Here's a more complicated request—double the size again. If the onion was much closer now, it would probably be "in your face." If it isn't close enough to make your eyes tear, double the size again!

5. Change the colors and return to normal size.

Open your eyes and look at the onion again.

Close your eyes and imagine the same picture you've seen with your eyes open. The onion is now back to its normal size. As you look at the mental image, imagine that the onion is changing colors.

Choose randomly and fast. Choose any color you wish, and for 30 seconds or so, keep changing the color every second. Go beyond the usual colors like blue, black, yellow, white, green, or red. Try purple, army green, beige, cinnamon, coral, lavender blue, orange-peel, pink, yellow-green, smooth violet, Tyrian purple, teal, tangerine, spring green, sapphire, salmon, rose, rust, pale blue, and so on.

6. Change the structure and return to the original color. Now open your eyes again and take a good look at the onion. Close your eyes and imagine this normal-looking image. This time you are going to manipulate the onion's structure, or "physics." Imagine the onion becoming elongated, thin, and long.

Now back to normal.

Imagine it becoming fat or chubby. Now back to normal.

Imagine it becoming like the digit 8, fat on the edges and very thin in the middle.

Now back to normal.

Imagine it with a huge hole in its middle, big enough so you can look through it.

Now back to normal.

Imagine the onion having a chunk taken off it, much like the Apple logo.

Now back to normal.

Imagine the onion becoming flat, completely flat.

Now back to normal.

You can keep these mental experiments going as long as your creativity takes you.

7. Repeat. One crucial element to any skill development outcome is repetition. If your visualization skills are not as good as you'd like them to be, repeat this pattern every day or every other day.

Uptime

When your awareness is directed outwardly, meaning outside your mind to your physical body and current reality, we call it "uptime." This state is useful for learning, acquiring new skills, accepting constructive criticism, being intimate with someone else, and peak performance in sports.

Questions to elicit an uptime state:

What is the position of my body?

Am I moving or still? How exactly?

What are the spatial positions of my limbs—arms, legs, hands, and feet?

Am I breathing with conscious awareness? If I am, is my breathing fast or slow, vibrant or weak?

Is my heart rate rapid or slow, even or uneven?

Am I breathing from the upper chest, the middle diaphragm, or my stomach?

Which muscles are active? Which ones are relaxed?

Utilization

Utilization is a technique that has opened up entirely new vistas in mental health treatment and personal development.

Utilization happens when you transform an existing resource into a tool with a meaningful purpose. Where this can be surprising is when things that seem very negative or inappropriate are used. Often, the negative behavior is just a dysfunctional attempt to get a good outcome, as when a child misbehaves because it gets them some attention.

When Erickson was working at a mental hospital, there was a patient there who claimed to be Jesus Christ. The patient spent quite a bit of time rubbing his hands together while he was spaced out. It also happened that the hospital had a wood shop where patients could do projects.

One day, Erickson approached the patient and said, "Sir, I understand you are a carpenter." Since Jesus is well-known to have been a carpenter, Erickson knew that the patient would have to say yes, that he was a carpenter. Erickson got him to cooperate by having sand paper and a wooden block attached to his hands so that, instead of merely rubbing his hands together, he would sand and work on the block of wood.

In time, this sensory experience created familiarity, and his skills and interest became stronger. In time, this patient, who had seemed to be a hopeless case, was making furniture. So what was it that Erickson utilized?

He used the two most serious symptoms, which most other professionals would have tried to eliminate: the delusion that he was Jesus and the longer periods of being spaced out and uselessly rubbing his hands together.Erickson used these symptoms to link the patient to valuable resources: identity, motivation, engagement, and experience, as well as the real-world resources of the wood shop.

The next time you are concerned, disturbed, or just irritated by something that someone else is doing, put your creative hat on and see what creative forms of utilization you can come up with.

The Big Book of NLP

Brainstorm with other people who are also concerned about even more ideas and practical ways to put them into action. You can do utilization with difficult or troubled children as well.

Walt Disney Strategy

Source: Robert Dilts

Create four locations for states.

Step into location #1, Dreamer.

Step into location #2, Realist.

Step into position #3, Critic.

Select an outcome that you really want to achieve.

Step into position #2, Realist. Associate into your scenario of realizing the important goal.

Step into position #3, Critic. Is anything missing or off track?

Step back into position #1.

Repeat this cycle a few times.

Continue repetitions

This pattern helps you use the creative idea-generating talent of the famous animator, Walt Disney.

1. Create four locations for states. Start with your meta-position and step into it. The main three will be "dreamer," "realist," and "critic."

2. Step into location # 1, "Dreamer." Think of a time when you freely and creatively dreamed up some great new ideas. Relive this experience.

3. Step into location # 2, "Realist." Think of a time when you were in a very realistic frame of mind and devised a clear, realistic plan that you were able to put into action. Relive this experience.

4. Step into position #3, Critic. Think of a time when you criticized a plan in a constructive way. You had criticism that would be put to use in a positive or even an inspired state.

Relive that experience. It helps to have position # 3 far enough from the other positions so as not to interfere with their anchored states.

5. Select an outcome that you really want to achieve. Step into position #1, Dreamer. Imagine from a third position (watching, dissociated) that you are achieving this goal. Experience and think about it in a free-wheeling way.

6. Step into position # 2, "realist." Associate into your scenario of realizing the important goal.

Experience, one at a time, the perspective of each person in your scenario of success.

Now, experience the events leading to your success as a storyboard (a series of images that are in order of occurrence, as in the pictures used to prepare for a movie).

7. Step into position #3, Critic. Is anything missing or off track?

Turn any criticisms into questions for the dreamer (the you that you are observing).

8. Step back into position No. 1. Answers to your critic's questions should be brainstormed.

8. Repeat this cycle a few times.

Once you are satisfied, finish by thinking of something completely different that you enjoy and are good at.

While you do this, walk through the three positions again.

9. Continue with repetitions.

Continue cycling through steps five, six, seven, and eight until your plan feels fitting at each of the locations. It is somewhat useful to use the perspectives of the realist, the dreamer, and the critic in other NLP patterns.

However, make sure not to identify yourself with any of them.

Keep all perspectives as resources, not as belief systems. The reason is that you do not want to be a dreamer most of the time, or a realist most of the time, or worse, a critic most of the time.

You want the freedom and flexibility to use any of these perspectives according to whatever is suitable for the outcome you're pursuing.

Walt Disney is known to be non-judgmental when it comes to crazy ideas. The strangest stories and the strangest, most outrageous ideas can bring to life a new idea that will be successful. So do not put an X on any of your thoughts. You can use Edward De Bono's "Po!" strategy to come up with outrageous ideas.

Simply step into the dreamer's perspective, think about the problem or challenge you're facing, and say, "Po!" + the strangest visualization you can come up with. Oh, no! What if every person on earth could learn all of the NLP ideas and methods for the price of a book instead of five certification seminars? Oh, wait a minute, that gives me an idea!!! What if there was an NLP sourcebook of all the successful methods?! There you have it, in your hands!

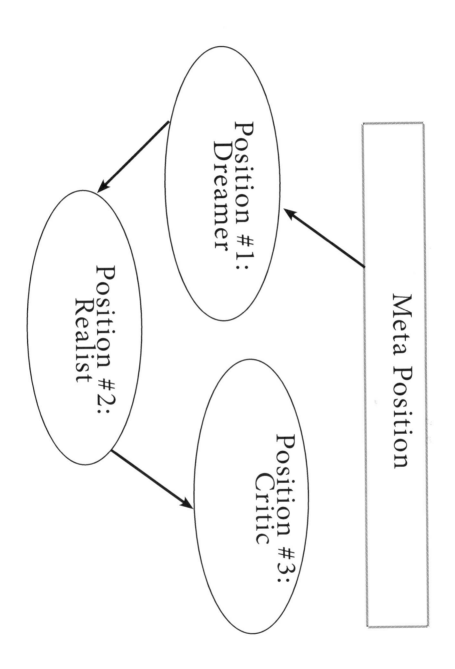

Well-Defined Outcomes

Criteria:

1. *Realistic*

2. *Positive*

3. *Self-Reliant*

4. *Observable*

5. *Context-Dependent*

6. *Measurable*

7. *Access to Resources*

8. *Ecological*

Any sequence of behaviors will result in a predictable outcome, and the value of that outcome depends on the person's wants and needs. Outcomes happen to us while goals are pursued by us. When we set well-defined desired outcomes, we do not set "goals," but a specific future scenario that, by following a predetermined sequence of behaviors, is unavoidable.

A goal is an imagined future condition, situation, or entity you wish to acquire or achieve. Goals can be detached from reality to the point of being unattainable, but they are always positive in nature. Goals can only be set by a conscious decision. An outcome is the unmistakable future that results from a particular set of behaviors, actions, or circumstances. This is what we mean by an outcome.

Conscious or unconscious choices have no bearing on the outcome, because an outcome is unavoidable. Every effect has a cause. The effect is the "outcome" of the cause. Because all of our choices of behavior cause specific outcomes (desired or undesired results), it is critical that we clearly define these outcomes before we initiate consistent behavior. It's easier to create accurate maps if you have an idea of where you're going. The best part is that you'll be able to devise new, more efficient routes to your destination. Preparation is key to ensuring that you get the best possible results from your investment. By setting well-defined outcomes, you're exploring an important and even critical aspect of NLP called "ecology," in which all of your desires, values, and needs are aligned and none of them contradicts any other.

Criteria for Well-Defined Outcomes:

Realistic: Can happen in reality within a specific time frame.

Positive: Stated in terms of what you want, rather than what you wish to avoid.

Self-Reliant: Depends on your own actions and behaviors, not on other people's compliance.

Observable: Can be experienced with your senses (seen, heard, felt).

Context Dependent: Defined within the limits of specific situations and times, not generalized.

Measurable: Is predictable as the unmistakable result of a predetermined and consistent sequence of behavior.

Access to Resources: All necessary resources are available at your disposal, including skills, contacts and money.

Ecological: The achievement of the outcome supports your highest values and is in harmony with other important outcomes.

Questions To Ask:

What do you want? What is possible? Is it realistic? What is the payoff? What specifically will you do (behavior-wise) to make this outcome a reality? Does the achievement of the outcome depend on other people's unpredictable decisions or generosity? How will you know that the outcome was achieved? What will you see, hear, and feel when it does? What are the performance criteria? What skills and abilities do you need to work on before the outcome becomes possible in reality? How will you test your performance criteria? Where wouldn't you want that behavior to be acted upon? (Context) Who are the people who can assist you? What, exactly, should you ask them? What information will be important? What questions must be answered ahead of time? (Resources) What might be interfering with your plan of action? Are there any values, other goals, people, or laws that may be challenging? How might you accommodate or mitigate now in order to make your dream a reality? (Ecology)

Wholeness

Source: Robert Dilts

Access a contemplative or spiritual state.

Imagine, from third person, experiencing an ideal state of health.

Observe your symptoms and their associated feelings and judgments.

Fully access this awareness, and flow the feelings and representations into your left hand and become an image.

Thank the symptoms and elicit its positive intentions.

Thank your symptoms and recognize them for communicating.

Focus on your inner healer and its associate body area and feelings.

Flow the inner healer feelings into you right hand, and allow an image to emerge. Thank the aspect.

Learn of your inner healer's positive intentions.

Appreciate your symptom's communications and positive intentions.

Merge the two parts, encouraging their mutual acceptance.

Encourage the states to form a cooperative relationship in service of a larger vision and their own initial higher intentions.

Get the parts to agree to this.

Visualize healing energy as you integrate the two parts.

Affirm for yourself the significance of this new wholeness.

Move into a new state of wellness through the healing powers of your body-mind.

1. Enter a contemplative or spiritual state of mind.

2. Imagine yourself in an ideal state of health from the perspective of a third person.

Imagine being completely physically healthy, with a clear mind, emotional balance, and grounded in physical strength. See yourself in this state from the third position.

3. Observe your symptoms and their associated feelings and judgments.

Switch your focus to your symptoms, noticing exactly where in your body you feel their presence. Notice that emotional feelings accompany that awareness. Identify what those emotions or judgments are.

4. Flow the feelings and representations into your left hand as you fully access this awareness.Allow them to form an image. Raising your awareness of the symptoms to a full or intense level, along with their emotional or judgment aspects,

Allow these feelings and representations to flow into your left hand as you allow your hand to open. Notice this flow with all the rep systems. Allow an image of the symptom and its feelings to form an image in your left hand.

5. Express gratitude to the symptoms and elicit their positive intentions.

Offer thanks to your symptom for revealing and offering itself. Ask your symptoms what they are trying to communicate to you. Inquire as to its positive intention and its purpose. Open your mind to a quiet, passive, listening state and notice what inner messages come through for you. If no positive intentions come through, you may be experiencing a "thought virus" expressed as symptoms.

To test this, get in touch with an aspect of yourself that harbors this symptomatic state. One way to get in touch with this aspect of yourself is to kindly tell the symptoms that you are no longer a home for them, and that it is time for them to move into pure and useful energy. If any part of you is attached to the symptoms, then you may find that it becomes present and you can inquire as to the positive intentions that have led to this aspect harboring or encouraging the symptoms. If this is the case, do not be alarmed. We are going to work through it.

6. Thank your symptoms for communicating with you. Once you have discovered these positive intentions, thank your symptoms for communicating with you.

Recognize that they have been committed to the positive intentions that your harboring aspect has revealed to you.

7. Focus on your inner healer and its associated body areas and feelings. Shift your focus to the aspect of you that wants health and wellness. We'll refer to this as your inner healer.

Notice exactly where in your body this aspect most obviously resides. Notice how this area feels to have this aspect present.

8. Flow the inner healer feelings into your right hand, and allow an image to emerge.

9. Thank you for your consideration. Increase your sense of your inner healer to a higher or more intense level. Allow these feelings to flow into your right hand.

Allow an image of this healing aspect to emerge. Thank this part for being present and connecting with you.

9. Learn of your inner healer's positive intentions. Ask your inner healer what its positive intentions are for you now.

Access an open, receptive state of mind and receive whatever messages are available now.

10. As you return your attention to your symptom, thank it for communicating with you. Offering appreciation for its commitment to its positive intentions

11. Combine the two parts, promoting mutual acceptance.

Imagine now that your symptom image and inner healer image are turning to face each other.

Ask them to access states of understanding and appreciation, and to experience the other parts of value, but from their own perspective.

Encourage this until you feel that each part accepts the other state's positive intentions.

12. Encourage the parts to form a cooperative relationship in service of a larger vision and their own initial higher intentions.

Now explain to these parts that they need to work together in new, meaningful ways in order to produce value that expresses their highest intentions.

Help them to discover their common mission in a spiritual sense. Convey how wonderful it feels to be part of a team, to build trust, and to begin to realize a great vision.

13. Get the parts to agree to this.

Recognize the abilities and resources of each part and how they can contribute to this vision and to realizing the higher positive vision of each part. They gain an ecological and congruent agreement from both parties to form a teamwork relationship that supports them in pursuing their individual and collective aims.

14. Visualize healing energy as you integrate the two parts. Return to your contemplative or spiritual state, and experience energy flowing into you that is the perfect color and quality for harmonizing and balancing you. A

djust the energy so that it is the perfect intensity, vibration, and quality to maximize your healing experience.

Imagine your unbalanced energies being brought into this flow and converted into pure and useful energy.

Turn your palms to face each other, and then slowly begin to bring them together. Encourage a healthy integration of your inner healer and symptom aspect.

Watch them merge, bathed in your healing and balancing energies. See which new image emerges from this.

15. Affirm to yourself the significance of this new wholeness. Tell yourself that you are creating personal wholeness as you join important NLP practitioner of yourself.

Pay attention to your motives that are aligned with this; this tells you that this is what you truly want.

Take time to notice how this is congruent for you, as it creates a new level of true alignment. If you find anything incongruent or non-ecological about this, you can work forward from step three to process any remaining issues.

Combine the issues together as a symptom for the purpose of the pattern.

16. Now bring the image of these integrated NLP practitioner into your heart as you notice the quality of energy or aura emanating from this new part.

See it being emitted as another quality of healing energy that you can breath in with the rest of the healing energies that you are experiencing.

Allow these energies to carry you back through time, prior to your birth, experiencing your being in the womb, and experiencing the dynamics through your lineage that led to your birth, back to the beginning of time that contained your destiny from the beginning.

From that point, allow the forces of the universe to roll forward, bringing your healing and balancing energies through life, through your lineage, and into your present moment.

Notice these forces bringing energy into your mind's power, projecting a fully healed, physically capable, mentally clear, and calm state from which you can savor life.

Observe as this wave of energy flows into your future.

17. Share this experience and a metaphor for it with people you trust, and ask them to share a healing experience and metaphor for their healing. Take some time to share this experience with others who you know to be able to talk about experiences of healing from a fairly aligned place. Ask them to share with you a brief metaphor that they feel represents a healing experience of theirs, and do the same for them.

The Big Book of NLP

Bibliography

Alpha Leadership: Tools for Business Leaders Who Want More from Life, Anne Deering, Julian Russell, and Robert Dilts, 2002

An Insiders Guide to Sub Modalities, Will Macdonald and Richard Bandler, 1989

An Introduction to NLP Neuro-Linguistic Programming : Psychological Skills for Understanding and Influencing People, Joseph O'Connor, 1998

Awaken the Giant Within : How to Take Immediate Control of Your Mental, Emotional, Physical and Financial Destiny!, Anthony Robbins, 1992

Beliefs: Pathways to Health and Wellbeing, Robert Dilts, Tim Hallbom, and Suzi Smith, 1990

Changing Belief Systems With NLP, Robert Dilts, 1990

Change Your Mind-And Keep the Change : Advanced NLP Sub-modalities Interventions, Connirae Andreas, Steve Andreas, Michael Eric Bennett, and Donna Wilson, 1987

Dynamic Learning, Robert B. Dilts and Todd A. Epstein, 1995

Encyclopedia of Systemic Neuro-Linguistic Programming and NLP New Coding, Robert B. Dilts and Judith A. Delozier, 2000

Frogs into Princes: Neuro Linguistic Programming, Richard Bandler, John Grinder, Steve Andreas, and John O. Srevens, 1979

From Coach to Awakener, Robert Dilts, 2003

Get the Life You Want: The Secrets to Quick and Lasting Life Change with Neuro-Linguistic Programming, Richard Bandler, 2008

Giant Steps : Author Of Awaken The Giant And Unlimited Power, Anthony Robbins, 1997

Heart of the Mind: Engaging Your Inner Power to Change with Neuro-Linguistic Programming, Connirae Andreas and Steve Andreas, 1989

Jay Haley On Milton H. Erickson, Jay Haley, 1993

Magic In Action, Richard Bandler, 1982

Mindworks: An Introduction to Nlp: the Secrets of Your Mind Revealed, Anne Linden, 1998

Manage Yourself, Manage Your Life: Vital Nlp Techniques for Personal Well-Being and Professional Success, Ian McDermott and Ian Shircore, 1999

Modeling With NLP, Robert Dilts, 1998

My Voice Will Go With You: The Teaching Tales of Milton H. Erickson, M.D., Sidney Rosen, 1991

Neuro-Linguistic Programming: Volume I (The Study of the Structure of Subjective Experience), Robert Dilts, 1980

NLP at Work, Second Edition: How to Model What Works in Business to Make It Work for You (People Skills for Professionals), Sue Knight, 2002

NLP: The New Technology Of Achievement, NLP Comprehensive, Charles Faulkner and Steve Andreas, 1996

NLP Workbook: A Practical Guide to Achieving the Results You Want, Joseph O'Connor, 2001

Patterns of the Hypnotic Techniques of Milton H. Erickson, M.D. (Volume I), Richard; Grinder, John Bandler, 1975

Patterns of the Hypnotic Techniques of Milton H. Erickson, M.D., Vol. 2, John Grinder, Judith Delozier, and Richard Bandler, 1997

Persuasion Engineering, Richard Bandler and John LA Valle, 1996

Presenting Magically: Transforming Your Stage Presence with NLP, Tad James and David Shephard, 2001

Personality Selling : Using NLP and the Enneagram to Understand People and How They Are Influenced, Albert J. Valentino, 1999

Precision: A New Approach to Communication : How to Get the Information You Need to Get Results, Michael McMaster and John Grinder, 1993

Reframing: Neuro-linguistic Programming and The Transformation of Meaning, Richard Bandler and John Grinder, 1982

Roots Of Neuro Linguistic Programming, Robert Dilts, 1983

Skills for the Future: Managing Creativity and Innovation, Robert Dilts and Gino Bonissone, 1993

Sleight Of Mouth: The Magic Of Conversational Belief Change, Robert Dilts, 2006

Sourcebook of Magic: A Comprehensive Guide to NLP Change Patterns, Michael L. Hall and Barbara P. Belnap, 2001

Strategies of Genius, Volume One, Robert Dilts, 1994

Strategies of Genius, Volume Two, Robert Dilts, 1994

Successful Selling With NLP: Powerful Ways to Help You Connect with Customers, Joseph O'Connor, 2001

Success Mastery With NLP/Cassettes, Charles Faulkner, 1994

The Enneagram and NLP: A Journey of Evolution, Anne Linden and Murray Spalding, 1994

The power of compassion, Dalai Lama, New York: HarperCollins, 1995

The Spirit Of NLP, L. Michael Hall, 2001

The Structure of Magic: A Book About Language and Therapy (Structure of Magic), Richard Bandler and John Grinder, 1975

The Structure of Magic II: A Book About Language and Therapy (Book 2), Richard Bandler and John Grinder, 1975

The Wisdom of Milton H. Erickson: The Complete Volume, Ronald A. Havens, 2005

Tools of the Spirit, Robert Dilts and Robert McDonald, 1997

Training With NLP, Joseph O'Connor, 1994

Training Trances: Multi-Level Communication in Therapy and Training, John Overdurf and Julie Silverthorn, 1995

Trance-Formations: Neuro-Linguistic Programming and the Structure of Hypnosis, John Grinder and Richard Bandler, 1981

Transforming Your Self: Becoming Who You Want to Be, Steve Andreas, 2002

Turtles All the Way Down: Prerequisites to Personal Genius, John Grinder and Judith Delozier, 1995

Uncommon Therapy: The Psychiatric Techniques of Milton H. Erickson, M.D., Jay Haley, 1993

Unlimited Power : The New Science Of Personal Achievement, Anthony Robbins, 1997

User's Manual for the Brain, Vol. II: Mastering Systemic NLP, L. Michael Hall and Bob G. Bodenhamer, 2003

Using Your Brain—For a Change: Neuro-Linguistic Programming, Richard Bandler, 1985

Virginia Satir: the Patterns of Her Magic, Steve Andreas, 1999

Visionary Leadership Skills: Creating a World to Which People Want to Belong, RobertB.Dilts,1996

Appendix A: Examples of Reframing

Here are a few examples of reframing. When you read the conversation below, notice how one simple shift in perception can change a person's belief or opinion.

George: "I can't imagine living in China, everything there is disgusting!"

Natasha: "What do you mean, disgusting? Have you been there?"

George: "No, but I read a touristic article about China, and they had quite a lot of warnings on the Chinese strange habits."

Natasha: "What kind of strange habits?"

George: "Well, they spit everywhere, in front of you, on the street, in restaurants, on the bus…"

Natasha: "They spit everywhere. And do you know why?"

George: "The article didn't say."

Natasha: "I've been in China. I lived in Beijing for about a year. I started spitting everywhere myself after a few weeks."

George: "WHY?!"

Natasha: "Too much rapport, I guess." (laughing)

George: "No, seriously, why do they spit? That's a disgusting manner, certainly not something tourists would be happy to experience."

Natasha: "Well, I'm sure your article mentioned the extremely polluted air in China. Yes, the Chinese government is the source of this hazard, but the Chinese people are there to

The Big Book of NLP

suffer it. In such a highly polluted environment, you get quite a lot of mucus in your throat… what should they do, swallow it?"

George: "There's no Kleenex in China?!"

Natasha: "There are more than 1,500 million people in China! Can you imagine how many tissue papers they would consume in a day this way?! There would be no trees left after a year!"

George: "Alright, so maybe that's reasonable… still disgusting, but reasonable. I guess that's why they don't use diapers…"

Natasha: "Exactly why! You'd have million of dirty diapers standing around."

George: "Alright, toilet paper is one thing. But, the article said they eat blood! And bones!"

Natasha: "Of animals, George! Not of human…"

George: "Yes, of course, but why?!"

Natasha: "Same reason as before, it's really economical. Imagine how many animals would have to be butchered if they only ate the animal parts that we eat…they use the blood, by the way, for hot-dogs, and they don't really eat the bones, they put them as an extra flavor in soups."

George: "Yes, I can imagine how it saves money, and it's probably better without all the biological waste."

Natasha: "Indeed. Did you change your mind yet?"

George: "A bit. Still strange though. They don't have normal toilets…they have holes instead of a bowl?"

Natasha: "Yes, and this is for hygienic purposes. This way, even the public toilets are relatively safe because there is no contact between your skin and the toilet. You don't need to worry who was there before you. Even the handle for water is operated by foot."

George: "Alright, so many it's not that disgusting there."

Did you take note of the simple reframing Natasha used here? She didn't even use "facts" as the basis for convincing George. She used known shared values, such as saving the environment, reducing excessive waste, and so on. Did you notice the presupposition Natasha gave George in the middle of their short conversation?

The Big Book of NLP

Appendix B: 55 Hypnotic Phrases

Milton Erickson had a way of forming hypnotic suggestions that didn't even seem hypnotic at all. He used to combine numerous hypnotic suggestions while he spoke to his patients (and later on, after Bandler and Grinder did their research, it was known that he used hypnotic suggestions with almost anyone!). The best way to use and practice these hypnotic phrases is the simplest way: say one and complete it with whatever suggestion you want to apply. Now, please remember that these are not magic tricks. You cannot simply go to strangers on the street and say something like, "... and wonder if you can wonder what it would be like to have me as your boyfriend." You'll get slapped, kicked, scratched, or worse. Be careful. If the listener did not agree in advance to either receive therapeutic intervention or be hypnotized by you, hypnotic phrases will not work.The only other option is that the listener is someone very close to you who has a lot of trust and dependency feelings towards you. It can be your daughter or son, your husband or wife, or your parents. But that also depends on the situation and the manner in which you use these hypnotic phrases. Let's start with a

#1: "And you can wonder, if you would, that…" You can complete this one in many ways. For example, you could work with a client on smoking cessation and apply this line near the end of the session. "…and you can wonder, if you would, that you have left the old smoke-inhalation habit behind you. If you do, you may also wonder how far it may seem as if it happened in a different life. " Quick tip: When I worked with people on smoking cessation, I never said, "You don't smoke anymore," because this line is like saying, "Smoke! Smoke! Smoke some more! " I used to rephrase the habit 'smoking' to smoke-inhalation, which almost never heard of in real life. This way, it becomes an unknown, something to be alarmed about.

#2: "Can you pay attention to…" Get creative here. This is a great induction phrase. "Can you pay attention to the sound of the air conditioning zooming, to the air breeze, to the smell of the fresh flowers on my desk, to the fabric of the recliner you're sitting in, to the depth of your breathing? And did you notice how, little by little, it may get deeper, as with each breath that you take even more air comes in slower than before as a sense of…." Got the idea? While their mind is waiting for the question mark in order to respond, their unconscious mind has taken the suggestions and acted upon them.

#3: "And you can allow yourself to be pleased about…"

#4: "…it might be a way that meets your needs, when…"

#5: "…and I wonder if you can enjoy the following experience, starting with…"

#6: "…and don't be surprised when you get into…"

#7: "…and you may begin to wonder when…"

#8: "…certainly I have no idea what's going on inside of your mind right now, but may I guess that you ask yourself how powerful would it be to imagine that…"

#9: "…and you may be amazed to find out how much pleasure you can squeeze from…"

#10: "Now I would like you to have a new experience…"

#11: "With your permission…"

#12: "…and you most probably discover what it's like when…"

#13: "…so sooner or later, I just don't know exactly when, you…"

#14: "…and I was just wondering if you will be surprised as…"

#15: "…how curious would you be if you'd know that…"

#16: "Perhaps it's time to take a little bit of joy on your way to…"

#17: "…now, you already know how to…"

#18: "…and maybe you wouldn't (sounded out—would ENT) mind noticing how…"

#19: "…and I wonder if I can ask you to, DISCOVER something…"

#20: "…and I would like you to take note of the physical sensations that are taking place right now in your body, from the tip of…"

The Big Book of NLP

#21: "...first, XYZ, but then later ZYX..."

#22: "...now, have you begun to notice that..."

#23: "I wonder if you'd allow yourself to enjoy how naturally and easily..."

#24: "I just wonder if you'd find joy in..."

#25: "...and that thing that makes you curious right when..."

#26: "...will you be surprised to find out that..."

#27: "...and while you notice..."

#28: "...and perhaps you begin to notice that..."

#29: "I wonder if you have ever noticed..."

#30: "Will you be surprised to find out that your arm is not even near your face anymore? Because..."

#31: "...and I wonder if you can begin allowing your..."

#32: "...that only a decision you're about to make just when..."

#33: "...most likely, you'd notice a few changes in the way you..."

#34: "...now it's very likely, no actually, most likely..."

#35: "...would you be willing to experience how..."

#36: "...now don't be concerned if you don't go as fast as others into trance, because you see, some people take their time to ENJOY their time and we have as much time as you'd ask for, even if before you know it..."

#37: "...it's so nice to notice..."

#38: "...and you shall know as you knew before, that..."

#39: "…it may be the time you felt that joy with…"

#40: "…and it appears to me that you are already in that place where…"

#41: "…give yourself that opportunity to…"

#42: "…perhaps sooner than you would expect…"

#43: "…and if you wish you would…"

#44: "…and I wonder how soon you can wonder…"

#45: "There's a famous children's song that I have forgotten about, and you may be able to record it, with the spider on the wall that…"

#46: "…it's most amazing when you find out how…"

#47: "…now you know better than anyone that…"

#48: "…and it's comforting to know…isn't it…"

#49: "…you might have a strong compulsion to act more…"

#50: "I would like you to appreciate how wonderful the…"

#51: "…can you remember a time when…"

#52: "…and while you remember, I want you to hold another sweet memory of…"

#53: "…so it's almost like knowing, really knowing…"

#54: "…and you know you're going to learn, really learn, how it is, when…"

And the last one for now, which is also one of my favorites:

#55: "…and isn't it just amusing…"

The Big Book of NLP

Appendix C: Visual Sub-Modalities

Movie / Still Picture

Is the thought represented by a still picture, such as a photograph, or by a moving picture, such as a mental movie?

The majority of people I've worked with say that a photograph is less emotional than a mental movie. In a mental movie, you can see the event happening again, whether you're in it or not (watching from the side); you can hear the words being said and feel the tension in the event.

A mental still picture is most often used to understand a concept or to remember a visual object, such as a face, a name, or a date.

Color / Black and White

Is the thought being represented as a black and white still picture or movie, or is it in color? The continuum here, obviously, would be how strong the colors are, for example, or if it's black and white imagery, are there shades of grey or a complete distinction between the 2 colors?

Location: Above or Below

When you think inside your head, there's always a location where you can point out the image you're making up. If you keep your head straight and consider your field of vision to be the "screen," where is that picture or movie located on the screen? Is it above your eye level, forcing you to look up? Is it below your eye level? Is it exactly at that point?

Left/Right Position

The same as with Above/Below, where on that continuum stands your picture/movie. Normally, the image or movie itself, as a whole, won't be running around – it works quite the same as with your TV. It would be hard for you to watch it if someone were to move it left and right constantly. So in your field of vision, on the screen, where is that picture or movie? How far to the left, how far to the right?

Light Intensity - A Driving Submodality

For most, if not all, the people I worked with, this specific sub-modality proved itself to be one of the strongest. When one specific sub-modality drives so much change in an emotional response, we call it a "driving sub-modality."

It means that when you change that sub-modality (yes, you can change them, I'll show you how), and move it on its continuum, it creates a new emotional response to that image you're working with.

Light intensity means how dark or bright the image or movie is. Is it dim? Is it brighter than "reality"? Is it too dark to notice some important details?

It works the same as in the film industry. You will notice that in order to grab your attention to a specific item, the director will distort or dim the background and sharpen the image of that item. Yes, you know it already! They do that in advertising all the time.

Perhaps because it IS a driving sub-modality, which "drives" us to drive our cars and take their products for a test-drive... OK, enough word-games with the word "drive." Let's drive forward...

Size - A Driving Submodality

Size in terms of visual modality is measured in relation to your field of vision. Is that picture or movie "bigger than life" size?

Is it small and compact?

Can you look above it, below it, around it?

Is it "in your face," preventing you from noticing actual sensations from the outside world? Is it too small to realize what's going on exactly?

Quality of Focus

It could have been a part of the intensity modality, but it also has an effect of its own. If your actual physical vision is blurry, you get anxious. You might even become a bit paranoid. It works the same with your mental images or movies.

If you think of something important and it becomes blurry, you will experience the same emotions as if it were your eyes that got blurry.

A change of focus also changes the way you pay attention to that specific scenario. You might suddenly ignore it completely just to deal with that "vision issue." Or you may become really obsessed with making it clearer. And that can cost you in energy, time and relationships.

For example, you might find yourself upset with someone you care about just because they "drew" an unclear mental picture for you. When people speak in words that only they understand, they paint a hazy picture.And that unclear image drives you crazy, because you want to understand, you want to be able to solve it, you want to be a good friend, father, lover, etc.

Thought Speed

The rate of images is also important. A movie is nothing more than slightly changed images, presented at light speed to create the illusion of movement. Of course, this sub-modality only refers to the internal movie and not to a picture that does not present any action.

Speed has action potential. It is also quite a strong sub-modality, although it works much better when the size of the movie is also large. Small, fast movies are not so effective.

We use speeding up for motivation and slowing down for relaxation or analysis. For example, if you imagine yourself riding on a roller coaster (remember that distinction?) as if you are there in that moment, the only difference is that it is all in slow motion. You see the movie "Turn Pages," the picture running slowly, like in the old movies (with the black and white strip in between them)... That's not so scary suddenly. It's even boring! How could a roller coaster, a first-person experience, be so emotionless and boring? If it's too slow to drive your emotions,

We call this sub-modality "Speed of Thought" because there are so many useful ways you can use it to benefit your life instantly. In our seminars, we teach our students to do it automatically (since most of our thinking is in patterns, anyway), and their results are amazing. All the way from creativity sparks to motivational boosts, anger management, addiction busting, and so much more. Again, if you feel you want to grab this set of tools and own it for real, give us a call or drop us an email; we'll make it happen for you too.

Discrimination by Changing Focus

We will talk about the master operative filters soon, but for now, this specific sub-modality is quite a strong one. By discriminating details in your mental picture or movie, you actually create a whole new meaning.

A great example is one that I also give in my seminars: two people go to the same Christmas party but have two different opinions on how good it was. The first person was focusing on the happy faces of people around him, while the other person was focusing on the tiny red wine stain on his white shirt... The first had a great time, while the second spent the same time thinking about the red stain.

Even though the party was going on around them in the same manner, since they shared the same time, location and social interactions, the only difference was the discrimination each of them used by focusing on a specific detail of the experience.

Later on, if you ask them both how they enjoyed the party (considering you aren't the host, so they don't have to lie to you), how do you think each of them will react?

Changing your focus by discriminating details and zoning in on one specific, even if it's only "in your mind," changes your experience.

Panoramic Frame

This sub-modality represents a continuum between a picture and a movie that resides in a frame, just as if you were watching a movie on your television screen (which must have a frame) or glancing at a picture on your wall, which might also have a (wooden?) frame.

For most people I've met, the difference in the experience is that they consider the panoramic type (the movie or picture stretched across your field of vision without a distinct border) to be more "realistic" and the framed type to be more metaphoric. In addition, I did notice that many people use the framed mental picture or movie for planning the future and the panoramic for most of their memories.

If you do that differently, though, there is nothing wrong with that! I will be happy to hear your discoveries on this subject of sub-modalities.

Dimensions

Another very distinctive feature of a mental image is the number of dimensions it occupies. I like to compare this to the cartoons I watched when I was a child (Ok, I'm still watching some, but so do you!).

The continuum of the dimensions This sub-modality lies between a two-dimensional and a three-dimensional picture or movie. Disney's cartoons from the 50's, such as the older Micky Mouse, were made in a 2D world. They were flat on the page, and while watching the movie, you could tell there was only one flat dimension they lived in. They didn't seem to have depth inside the picture, even if they used different sizes to create that illusion.

The three-dimensional cartoon, however, did have a whole lot of depth. You get the illusion that there's not only one stretched canvas from left to right, but as if there's a world going inwards and outwards towards you as the viewer. 3D graphic artists and mathematicians call this the z-axis.

This sub-modality is usually flat when you explore subjects you are bored with and feel no excitement what-so-ever. You might find that you think of "math" or "history" or "your wife's make-up routine" as being black and white, a still picture in a frame... and in 2D! Well, that's one boring thought right there! If it has depth, the depth tends to move out into fog, darkness, or downward like a funnel.

You could do this to the dimension of sub-modality of an exciting memory in order to make it boring. Perhaps you have a memory that is too exciting and this would be good. This would be a lot like the fast phobia cure, where a troubling memory or a fearful future scenario would be manipulated so that they don't trigger a negative state.

Perspective

Let's look at it from another angle, shall we?

You need to take a more global view on this one.

"If you saw this from MY side..."

We use perspectives all the time, numerous times a day. You can't really get through your day without using a whole lot of different perspectives.

And here's a clue: the perspective you use to think and visualize a situation might be crucial for the understanding and conclusions you draw. Perspectives, in many cases, are the ones you use to make decisions.

You change your mind when you change your perspective. We have all had those arguments when we finally were brave enough to look at the situation from our rival's point of view... and we felt they were right. We were wrong because we took a certain perspective which was not congruent with reality.

There are many useful ways for you to explore the visual sub-modalities. You could choose, for example, to take the global view, as if you're a bird flying up there and seeing it all from above... You could get out of your own body (mentally, of course) and go around your mate's shoulders and see the interaction from that perspective.

You might decide to take a more distant point of view, a closer one, a higher one, a lower one, etc. Whatever creative perspective you can come up with, the more angels you use to look at a serious situation, the more choices and information you get.

Visual Triggers

This is not a specific sub-modality, but it is an inner visual stimulation that is very important for our memory management topic. Visual triggers are what we call "anchors." It could be anything from your experience - it could be a face or the features of a face, for example.

I had a client who was attacked in her childhood, and ever since she has had a very strong reaction towards people who share the same facial characteristics as her attacker.

A complete stranger who had nothing to do with her past could be getting some hateful (and disturbing) looks from her just because he had the same type of nose, same facial hair arrangement, same eye patterns, etc.

Anchors are very important for two reasons: one, you have registered in your mind numerous anchors (literally, millions); and second, many of those anchors trigger unconscious processes that can change your emotions, your thoughts, and your decisions without any conscious awareness.

Appendix D: Auditory Sub-Modalities

Self-Talk vs. Other People's Voices

The voice you hear inside your head, whether it is your own voice or someone else's (even imaginary or generic) voice.

Actual Content

We put less emphasis on content since the words you use are not as important as the form in which you express them. But the syntax your choose for your words can describe a lot of your internal experience.

Emotional Expression

The emotion is obvious through the voice; an angry voice and a sexy voice do not sound the same.

Volume

How high, how low, how strong a voice is – a weak voice doesn't cause as much effect as a strong voice.

Tonality

The tonality of your voice.

Tempo / Speed Of Speech

The tempo or speed of your voice.

The Source Location

From which point in space does the voice originate?

Harmonic / Disharmony

Is it a pleasant "rhythmic" voice or is the speech full with breaks and "umm" or "ehh?" Yes, we do that on the inside as well.

Regular / Irregular

Hearing Dracula's voice or Clinton's voice is not equal. Does the voice has an irregular distracting quality or is it "normal"?

Inflections

This one is also related to content and context – In which points of the text does the voice change quality? Is there a reason?

Length / Duration

For which periods of time do you hear that voice? Does it use long sentences or short ones?

Key Words

Also related to content, these are key words, kind of digital "anchors," that trigger an emotional reaction in you. For example, for many people the syntax "nine eleven" drives a whole set of very strong emotions. It would be a different reaction for a New York citizen and a Taliban militant…

Appendix E: Kinesthetic Sub-Modalities

Temperature

Perhaps the most frequently noticed sub-modality is that our temperature rises when we're excited and lowers when we are bored. We use terms like "hot blooded" or "cold bitch" to describe behaviors.

Since all behavior is a result of thoughts, and most thoughts are the conclusion of memories, you feel what you think due to what you remember, and that has an effect on your perceived body temperature.

Your actual physiological temperature (normally at 37C) might not change at all, although you may feel "hot" or "frozen" inside.

Texture

Our world is experienced mostly in 3D. Texture as a kinesthetic sub-modality is the fabric of that memory - What do you sense it could be if you touched it? Rough? Smooth? Bumpy?

Degree of Adaptability

That is also a mental attitude and not only a visible piece of information. Could you change the movement of emotions you feel inside, or is it too rigid and "out of your control"? Road rage is often described as a total lack of flexibility in a specific context and time frame.

The Big Book of NLP

Vibration

The familiar sensation of shivering (with excitement, or due to cold). How rapid and intense is it?

Pressure

When you remember a memory, it might cause a certain pressure in your body, usually felt above the eyes or on the lower lip (notice that many people who spend time in emotional day fantasies, their lips are swollen and their lower lip especially is dropped).

Tension

Tension is felt similar to pressure, but it is a definite uncomfortable feeling that causes the desire to "release the tension." Also, tension can be described by its location in the body.

Movement

Emotions move. Emotion can be described as energy in motion. At most times, if you feel a strong emotion, it does not just lie motionless. It moves around, up and down, left and right, in crosses, in circles, in half-moon circles, or an infinite spiral…

If you feel the movement, you can also find a pattern. In NLP seminars, we work a lot with this sub-modality, because it is a very effective modality for gaining control over fears and phobias.

Breathing

The breathing pattern is a kinesthetic sub-modality. How deep, from where to where, how low, or shallow is your breathing?

Weight

Here we don't refer to your body's weight, but to the "weight" of the experience. Does it feel heavy, unbearable, or light?

Confinement

We can also define some feelings as "confined," which means they are not only manageable and light-weighted, but we can block them to a specific location, usually between our hands. These are the kind of emotional experiences that we can turn on and turn off almost on cue, without being overwhelmed. Sadly enough, in most cases we found that "love" or "passion" gets confined while "rage" and "anger" do not.

Change of Size or Shape

That is related to the Movement Submodality, since sometimes as the sensation moves through your body (or beyond it), it might change its size and shape accordingly. You may be able to "confine" it if it's a foot ahead of you and feels like it's less than the length of your shoulders.

Direction

Where did it go? Where is it going? From where?

Triggers

Just as certain words can trigger emotions, a certain touch can also be an "anchor" for an emotional roller-coaster. It is physically observable in rape victims, when a certain movement and touch can send them into a trance and a fearful internal experience in less than a brief second.

Appendix F: Modalities Abbreviations

While this might seem like a strange word, the four-tuple is just a phrase for the four primary representational classes: auditory, visual, kinesthetic, and olfactory (A, V, K, O). For each of these classes, we can add a subscript "i" when we want to describe an internalized experience, that is, an experience we remember or imagine, and a subscript "e" when we want to describe an externalized experience, that is, an experience that is currently happening.

The four-tuple system is not widely used in NLP today, and it has also been expanded to include consciousness and a person's most highly valued representational system. But the concept of the four-tuple is a good one to keep in mind when studying a person's representational systems.

Try having someone tell you about their weekend, paying close attention to their four-tuple. This should tell you a lot about their coding system and their different cognitive strategies.

V - Visual

V_e - Visual external (physical perception of sight)

V_i - Visual internal (imagery, mind's eye)

A - Auditory

A_e - Auditory external (physical perception of sound) Ai - Auditory internal (inner voice, thoughts)

A_t - Auditory tonal (tone, sound, music)

The Big Book of NLP

A_d - Auditory digital (the words)

A_{di} - Auditory digital internal (self-talk)

K - Kinesthetic (Physical Sensations)

K_v - Kinesthetic visceral (inside feeling, e.g. "butterflies" or warm stomach)

K_t - Kinesthetic tactile / touch, skin sensation

K_e - Kinesthetic perceptions - emotions

O - Olfactory

Appendix G: Code of Ethics

Most people, including NLP practitioners, feel that we are ethical people. But it's one thing to be successful and have your heart in the right place, and it's another to have the understanding of ethics that you need in order to take on challenging cases—or even not-so-challenging cases. Here's why:

1. Too many well-meaning people are getting into trouble. Most of us have a few ethical blind spots—areas that we just haven't thought about. Yet these blind spots can have serious consequences if we happen to run into a problem.

2) Innocent misunderstandings about ethics and related laws may result in serious legal consequences.

3) Coaches must be knowledgeable about the law and ethics.

There are laws and regulations that apply to coaches (or that can apply, depending on the circumstances) that you may not know about. Generally, coaching and NLP training give ethics little, if any, attention. However, coaches do sometimes come under the authority of mental health licensing boards when they get into trouble. You should know how to avoid this.

4) Even though you try to screen out clients that are not appropriate for your practice, it is inevitable that you will occasionally find yourself working with someone who has some serious issues that you are not prepared to work with. You need to have policies and procedures for evaluating, screening, referring, and transferring these people. A lot of coaches do this by the seat of their pants. Sometimes, this causes problems for them.

5) It is possible that we will cause significant problems for clients if we are unsure about one or two key ethical points.A bad result can cause the client to shy away from getting the help that they need in the future, or worse.

6) So much thought has been put into ethics and how to explain laws to therapists and others that they may apply to, that it would be crazy not to dip into this information on a

regular basis in order to be informed, stay up-to-date, and have the proper policies in place.

A little history: Laws, regulations, and ethical guidelines have been evolving for a long time, and they are continuing to undergo changes. Laws and ethics pertaining to therapy are dramatically different from those of forty years ago. Generally speaking, we're talking about vast improvements, not a mindless intrusion of bureaucracy.

Did you know that ethical standards for healers date back to the Hippocratic Oath, developed roughly 2,500 years ago, and even farther back to the Nigerian healer's code? As you can imagine, much of the impetus for regulating professionals has come from problems with the professionals' conduct. Enforcement actions range from letters of warning or other sanctions to punishments, not to mention civil liability that can result in lawsuits.

Speaking of licensing boards: Coaches are not regulated as psychotherapists by licensing boards. But if a board comes to feel that a coach is practicing psychotherapy, there may be a problem. Although boards, at least in the U.S., are not actively looking for coaches that might be crossing that line, there are ways that coaches can come to the attention of licensing boards. This happens when a dissatisfied client files a grievance with such a board.

Clients are especially likely to file a grievance with the state licensing board when there is a conflict over money, disappointment with services, or the client feels they have been used in some way, such as through a sexual relationship. When a coach or therapist tries to pull out of a sexual relationship with an ex-client, the ex-client may become quite vindictive.

One way clients can be disappointed is if you charge an unusually high fee and create unusually high expectations. Another way is if you create expectations that you are like a psychotherapist and then miss key moves that a therapist might make. The coaches that are the most vulnerable to making a mistake like this are the ones that began creating a defensive style during their childhood in which they tended to cultivate a fantasy of elevated competence in order to protect against feeling socially marginalized and inadequate. That comment sounds pretty harsh, but it is about a common occurrence. Take care not to give the impression that you are providing psychotherapy or treatment for mental disorders. Coaches can come under the purview of licensing boards if the board thinks that your promotional materials or actions put you in the position of providing a service that they license. If you look at the legal definition of psychotherapy in your state or other authority, you will see how this could happen. In some states, the definition of psychotherapy is vague.

Mental health land mines: A key concern is that the coach will end up with a person whose hidden mental health issues can cause problems for the coach, if not an outright bad outcome for the client.

Coaches should become familiar with signs of mental and emotional issues that may lead to problems, specifically because these coaches (by the scope of their professional responsibility) are not performing mental health assessments and clients may not disclose mental health issues, even if they are aware of them. Ask about previous mental health problems and treatment, and determine whether there are outstanding issues that may not have been adequately treated.

All coaches should be prepared to refer to trusted mental health professionals. Besides, networking with mental health workers may yield clients for your coach's services. Therapists should refer people seeking success coaching to someone like you, unless this is one of their specialties already.

Licensed clinicians have their blind spots, as research into the art and science of diagnosis tells us. Many therapists tend to have a pet diagnosis that they use more than the average therapist. Very common areas where therapists fail to appropriately treat or refer are sleep problems, domestic violence, substance abuse, cognitive disabilities, dissociation, and subtle brain injuries.

The takeaway message for therapists is: get deep into assessment issues and stay current. While we're at it, stay up on the legal landscape as well.

I have provided ethical guidelines above. If you review them, you will probably think of various situations where they can have some relevance and wisdom. Although coaching programs tend to provide little or no training in law and ethics, we feel that this deserves your attention. I hope you will absorb and consistently apply these guidelines. This code of ethics is adapted from models of major organizations representing licensed psychotherapists.

However, it is written specifically for coaches and consultants who are not necessarily members of such an organization. It is necessary to understand the following guidelines in order to function in a truly professional manner. This is because these guidelines can help to protect your reputation and safety, help you avoid trouble, help protect the public, and help protect the reputation of NLP coaching and consulting as professions.

These guidelines won't cover every situation you encounter, but they are very well-rounded, representing millions of person-years of professional practice. Although these guidelines are not intended as legal advice, the codes that they are modeled after have evolved hand-in-hand with the evolution of laws intended to protect the public and ensure the usefulness of the practitioners those laws regulate.

Following these guidelines can help you avoid problems such as practicing medicine or psychotherapy without a license or violating the boundaries of clients.

Do not hesitate to contact a lawyer and review relevant laws and liability issues when potential legal issues arise. When there is any doubt, it is always better to call sooner rather than later. Compared to the attitudes of many coaches, these guidelines may seem strict.

In fact, where success coaching between peers is involved and mental health issues are not being treated, you may find that the guidelines concerning dual relationships can be relaxed without creating an ethical breach. However, it is very easy to err in this area, so we recommend additional consultation and training specifically in this area for all coaches. Another good example is name-dropping and client testimonials. In psychotherapy, this is considered unethical. Getting a client to agree to this is considered imposing on a client in a manner that is not in the client's best interest because it means publicly acknowledging a mental health problem.

As you know, mental health problems are subject to a great deal of social stigma and discrimination in areas as serious as employment and health insurance coverage in countries that do not provide national coverage. In coaching for success, a client testimonial might not be of much concern, because there is no admission of having a disability or disorder. My advice is to always put the welfare of your client first, making sure that any testimonials do not convey any traits that could result in stigma or discrimination. To summarize, it is better to be safe than sorry. So be safe.

Code of Ethic

I. Basic Responsibilities

NLP practitioners support client welfare and rights, and the ethical and constructive use of their services. When clients are not physically present during sessions, as in phone sessions, NLP practitioners take extra measures to meet their responsibilities to clients as needed.

1. NLP practitioners support **non-discrimination**, and provide equal consideration regardless of race, gender, religion, national origin, age, sexual orientation, disability, socioeconomic, or marital status. NLP practitioners take reasonable measures to accommodate clients with physical disabilities.

2. NLP practitioners understand that their clients trust them, and so they **refrain from exploiting** that trust. They also understand that dual relationships can become more complicated than expected and result in bad outcomes or the perception of an ethical breach.

NLP practitioners **avoid creating any relationships with their clients that are at all likely to impair their judgment** or tempt them to exploit the client. This is especially important where there are ongoing sessions, as opposed to one or a few sessions that are not highly personal.

3. It is questionable to have a **"dual relationship,"** meaning one in which the practitioner and client engage in a different relationship at the same time, such as by also being business partners. Before considering an additional relationship, the practitioner should allow a reasonable amount of time to elapse after the sessions are complete.

When you cannot avoid a dual relationship, as may occur in a small town, the practitioner will take precautions and create limits for that relationship to ensure that they maintain good judgment and refrain from any exploitation. In any case, sex and dating are inadvisable when in a practitioner-client relationship, and for a reasonable amount of time afterwards.

Where there is significant likelihood of a dual relationship, the practitioner will consider referring the person to another practitioner.

Examples of dual relationship actions include borrowing money, hiring, engaging in a business venture with, or engaging in a close personal relationship with a client. This may also apply to the client's spouse, partner or family members.

4. NLP practitioners honor their **professional commitment** to clients. This includes refraining from abandoning or neglecting clients whose sessions are not complete.

To this end, NLP practitioners maintain procedures to support this, such as providing contact information and instructions as to what to do in case of an emergency or in case the NLP practitioner is away, and by terminating sessions properly. This should include a professional will with instructions as to how to transfer, maintain or properly dispose of any confidential or important records.

5. NLP practitioners **stop seeing clients for appropriate reasons only**, and do so in an ethical manner. These reasons may include the client not benefiting adequately, there is not a good reason to continue, the NLP practitioner is experiencing some kind of impairment such as mental illness, or the relationship has developed a significant ethical problem. for clinically sound reasons and in an appropriate manner.

When ending sessions, the NLP practitioner makes sure that any referrals for services or other arrangements are made promptly.

6. NLP practitioners **do not continue sessions with clients purely for their own financial gain**, but it is ethical to discontinue when fees are not paid.

7. NLP practitioners **are not gurus, and are not adamant about any advice they offer** except where safety and emergencies are concerned. NLP practitioners respect the right of their clients to make their own decisions in all areas of their lives, including personal relationships.

At the same time, the practitioner will help clients understand the consequences of their decisions, and will give them enough information that clients can make informed decisions about NLP. This information includes the potential risks and benefits of NLP based on the client's situation and capacities.

8. NLP practitioners **inform clients all key policies in advance**. These include the extent of their availability for emergencies and for other contacts between sessions, as well as issues such as fees, no show charges and other fee-related

policies. These include whether extended sessions cost more, and how the client will be enabled to decide on whether to accept an extended session.

9. NLP practitioners **obtain written consent before making any kind of media recording** of sessions. The consent will include the conditions in which the recording can be played and who will experience it.

10. NLP practitioners will explain to their client that the content of their sessions will be kept **confidential**, and the practitioner will honor this into perpetuity. In the event of a court order or safety issue, the practitioner is not required to maintain confidentiality. The client should understand this in advance.

11. NLP practitioners inform clients of their **qualifications and experience** prior to providing services. This can be in the form of a written summary.

12. If there are to be **electronic communications**, NLP practitioners inform their clients of the potential risks to confidentiality, what to do if there is no response (there may have been a technical problem) and how emergencies communicated electronically will be handled.

13. **If the client sees another practitioner** of some kind, such as a mental health provider, the NLP practitioner will provide all useful information when requested by the client. The practitioner will not withhold this information because fees have not been paid. The NLP practitioner will collaborate with practitioners as needed for the welfare of the client, when given permission by the client.

II. Scope of Practice and Referrals

NLP practitioners do not work with clients who have problems that the practitioner does not have **qualifications and skills** to work with, and they **refer** to appropriate professionals as needed.

1. The NLP practitioner will **refer clients** to appropriate medical or psychotherapy treatment providers when there is a concern that **assessment or treatment of symptoms of medical or mental disorders may be needed**.

2. The NLP practitioner is as **aware of the limits of his or her skills** as they are of their abilities. This is called **scope of practice**. As a result, the practitioner **prevents harm by knowing when and how to refer** clients for treatment of possible medical or psychological disorders.

3. The NLP practitioner **learns to recognize symptoms** that may indicate medical and psychological disorders so that they will be effective and timely in making referrals.

III. Confidentiality

NLP practitioners take their clients' privacy seriously. They understand that clients may divulge personal information that they would not want shared with anyone else. Personal information can harm peoples' careers, relationships, and other important life areas. Except for urgent safety concerns, NLP practitioners do not make moral decisions that would lead them to violate the privacy of their clients, and they never indulge in gossip. Practitioners have unique confidentiality responsibilities because the "patient" in a therapeutic relationship may be more than one person. The overriding principle is that NLP practitioners respect the confidences of their patient(s).

1. NLP practitioners are best known for providing coaching that enhances success and well being, and do not treat mental illnesses, therefore, so long as no coercion is involved, the practitioner may solicit permission to use client's recommendations and names in communications and advertising, and in teaching or presenting.

The client must clearly understand the potential consequences and nature of the use of their name, and give permission in advance and in writing on a form that includes this information. This can prevent serious misunderstandings later. **The NLP practitioner avoids this practice if there is any doubt about the client's objectivity**, such as occurs if the client feels dependent upon the NLP practitioner or confers authority to the NLP practitioner in some manner.

2. NLP practitioners **maintain the total privacy of their clients**, including their names or any information that could identify them. **The only exceptions** to this are a) any legal requirements, such as a court order, b) the need to use specific information to defend themselves in a court action (and the release of information is limited to what is necessary only), c) as needed in order to pursue fees in a legal action (and this is limited to the name of the client, the dates of the sessions, the amount owed, a signed form showing that the client has agreed to fees or policies but that does not contain information about the client's problems, and the service provided, d) as permitted by the client.

3. NLP practitioners **maintain client records in a safe and secure manner**. They are aware of the risks and limitations of any technology used, and take appropriate steps to prevent breaches.

They take extra cautions when transmitting or receiving client information. They dispose of records, including any hardware containing them, such as computer memory devices, in a manner that fully protects confidentiality.

4. NLP practitioners ensure that their **employees, contractors or other personnel maintain confidentiality**, and that they only have access to information that is necessary for the conduct of business and in a manner that the client understands and accepts.

IV. Professional Competence and Integrity

NLP practitioners **maintain high standards** of professional competence and integrity.

1. NLP practitioners **maintain records** of their sessions as needed for competent practice, for maintenance of any signed agreements, for reference in case there is a time lag between sessions, for consulting with other helping professionals, billing, and for any other purposes as needed.

2. NLP practitioners **seek professional assistance as needed** for any problems that may interfere with their performance or judgment.

3. NLP practitioners as teachers or presenters, **present accurate information** from reputable sources.

4. NLP practitioners develop the understanding necessary to work with **people of other cultures**. The identify the cultural and ethnic background and related needs of their clients so that they may provide effective services.

5. NLP practitioners **stay up-to-date in their field** through ongoing educational experiences. They also get ongoing continuing education that expands their knowledge pertaining to psychology and health, because of the diverse issues that clients bring.

6. NLP practitioners **maintain a reputation for honesty, fairness and ethics** in their lives. They refrain from any kind of harassment, exploitation or illegal activity.

7. NLP practitioners **do not provide any services that are outside of their abilities and legal scope** of practice. Unless qualified and legally sanctioned, NLP practitioners do not treat or offer to treat mental or physical illnesses. While people may improve in these areas as a result of NLP, the practitioner does not promote his or her services as a form of treatment. Promoted services may include training on NLP, including self-NLP, stress management, coaching, and stress management, (barring any legal or ethical concerns).

8. NLP practitioners make sure that **any new types of clients they see or skills they use are appropriate from a legal and ethical point of view**, and will be performed competently as a result of having the proper training, supervision, consultation or experience as needed.

9. NLP practitioners **do not provide services that will conflict with a person's psychotherapy**. The practitioner uses special caution and consideration with a potential client who is receiving psychotherapy. This is because the person may have a mental disorder that places special needs upon any relationship that may result in focusing on memories or goals, or that may induce emotional awareness or deep relaxation. Generally, the practitioner is advised to consult with the psychotherapist before starting sessions. It may be appropriate to proceed when the client is fully able to indicate that they are stable and can tolerate the activities listed in this section, such as experiencing increased awareness.

10. NLP practitioners take reasonable steps to **prevent the distortion or misuse of their approach** and knowledge, particularly by the media and influential persons. This includes steps such as letters to the editor, personal communications, and collective communication from practitioners.

11. NLP practitioners want to **affect people and their community in the most positive way possible**, and they want to generate and preserve respect for their approach, so they **exercise care in their public statements**, live or in any medium. As part of their ongoing education, NLP practitioners learn how to recognize and engage in rational and ethical rhetoric, debate and public discourse. This includes understanding and avoiding logical fallacies.

12. NLP practitioners **only engage in research when they have adequate support, skills and knowledge** to do so. NLP practitioners do not make public statements as to the results of their research unless they are adequately trained and competent to carry out reliable research. NLP practitioners gain the

The Big Book of NLP

knowledge pertaining to research, and will only talk about the results of others' research when they can do so competently and credibly.

V. Responsibility to Students

As with clients, NLP practitioners **do not exploit the trust** of their students.

1. NLP practitioners apply the **ethical guidelines in their conduct with students** as with clients. This refers to exploitation, dual relationships that may impair judgment, sexual contact, and sexual harassment.

2. NLP practitioners take reasonable measures to **prevent their students from holding themselves out as able to perform services and skills that are beyond their actual skills and experience**. This is reflected in the standards and testing related to any certifications or references provided.

4.3 NLP practitioners who act as teachers or who supervise students that are gaining experience **maintain and enhance their teaching or supervision skills, and get consultation** as needed.

VI. Responsibility to Colleagues and Other Professionals

NLP practitioners **treat colleagues and other professionals with courtesy, respect and fairness**. They cooperate with their colleagues in order to support the well being of their clients and community.

1. NLP practitioners **respect their colleagues privacy**, and maintain any confidences that their colleagues share with them, except where a clear ethical or legal need requires disclosure.

2. NLP practitioners make reasonable efforts to **help colleagues who are impaired** by problems such as substance abuse or mental illness.

VII. Responsibility to NLP

NLP practitioners work to **advance the goals of NLP and respect for the professionals involved** in NLP.

1. NLP practitioners continue to act in accordance with the ethics of their profession, **without being compromised by their employment or membership** in an organization.

2. NLP practitioners **give credit** to people who contribute to their publications in proportion to the contribution and according to traditional publication practices. This includes giving attribution to the people who came up with original ideas and contributions.

3. NLP practitioners **take responsibility for the marketing and promotion** of their work, training offerings, and publications, ensuring that it is done accurately and honestly.

4. NLP practitioners recognize the importance of **contributing to a better community and society**. They engage in practices that support this, such as devoting a portion of their professional activity to services for which there is little or no financial return.

5. NLP practitioners recognize the importance of **supporting laws and regulations that pertain to NLP and that serve the public interest**, and of fighting or altering laws and regulations that do not.

VIII. Responsibility to the Legal System

NLP practitioners recognize and understand their role **in the legal system** and their duty to remain objective and honest.

1. NLP practitioners who have questions or concerns about a case or practice that may have legal repercussions consult a qualified attorney in order to ensure that their conduct is in compliance with the law. They never assume that they know the law through using common sense, their impression of what is fair, or information that is not from a legal authority or that they do not fully understand.

2. NLP practitioners who give testimony in legal proceedings **testify truthfully** and avoid making misleading statements.

3. NLP practitioners **understand laws that have a bearing** upon their practices, directly or indirectly, and comply with those laws.

4. NLP practitioners **do not publicly express professional opinions about an individual's mental or emotional condition**, unless they clearly state the limitations of their knowledge of the situation and that they are offering a personal opinion. This is to help ensure legally appropriate testimony, and to avoid making statements that may legally compromise the practitioner or other people.

IX. Financial Arrangements

NLP practitioners make **financial arrangements** with clients and students that are understandable, and conform to accepted professional practices and legal requirements.

1. NLP practitioners **do not offer or accept payment for referrals**. This prevents a loss of objectivity in making referrals that could exploit and bring harm to clients or divert them from a more appropriate referral.

2. NLP practitioners **do not financially exploit** their clients.

3. NLP practitioners **disclose in advance** their fees and how they will be computed. They make sure their clients understand matters such as charges for canceled or missed appointments and any interest to be charged on unpaid balances, at the beginning of treatment. They **give reasonable notice** of any changes in these policies or amounts.

4. NLP practitioners give **reasonable notice** to clients with unpaid balances of their intent to sue, or to refer for collection. Whenever legal action is taken, therapists will **avoid disclosure of clients' personal information** such as their problems. If the practitioner refers to a collection agency, they avoid disclosure of clinical information and select an ethical agency.

5. NLP practitioners **normally don't accept non-monetary remuneration** such as goods or services for their services. This is because it can create conflicts of interest and lead the client to feel exploited. This can harm the therapist-client relationship.

X. Advertising

NLP practitioners enable potential clients to **make informed choices** regarding their services.

1. NLP practitioners are **honest about the current nature** of their skills, training and experience.

2. NLP practitioners **advertise honestly**.

3. NLP practitioners display their name, credentials and business name in a way that **does not mislead** potential clients in any way or create any unjustified expectation.

4. NLP practitioners **correct, wherever possible, false, misleading, or inaccurate information** about their qualifications, services, or products.

5. NLP practitioners **use great care in using any testimonials** in a manner that is in compliance with their existing agreement with the client or ex-client, and refrain from soliciting or using testimonials in any way that interferes with the best interests of that person.

6. NLP practitioners don't use NLP or other initials after their names to give the impression of a license or academic degree that they do not have.

One Last Note

People tend to adapt to the mastery of NLP in phases. The ones that follow are fairly typical. Many other people do not gain mastery of NLP, and that's because they do not go beyond phase two or three. Most NLP practitioners appear to feel that NLP mastery begins to develop at phase four. I hope that this article inspires you to go for all phases of development and to understand why I feel that mastery is actually in phase six.

1) Getting oriented to the core ideas of NLP: Many people start by reading various books and articles, and perhaps attending some talks or watching online presentations.

2) Recognition of patterns and practice: Many of us started by applying NLP techniques to ourselves. This gives us a good feel for the patterns and more insight into how to use them with others. This also gives us the personal benefits of the patterns, making us even better practitioners. Our own issues will be less likely to get in the way of NLP practice, and we will become more observant and responsive.

3) Gaining a better understanding of the models from which patterns emerge: This gives you a more functional understanding of the patterns—when to use them and how they can be arranged strategically in setting up additional change (larger-scale syntax and strategy). This helps you become more than a parrot that can reproduce various patterns, but someone who really understands the patterns and underlying principles. With this, you can use patterns while your conscious mind is thinking ahead or managing the relationship with the client in other ways.

4) Using NLP for personal success: This means challenging yourself to apply NLP in ways that bring you into better relationships and success as you define it. It can even mean succeeding in ways you didn't realize you could, or discovering definitions of success that are fresh and rewarding. As a result of these successes, I have a lot more faith in NLP, a lot more dedication to using it, and a lot more personal charisma while using it. You become better able to sell your services and have an impact on your clients.

5) Modeling: You begin by modeling excellent people so that you can develop additional models for your own benefit, the benefit of your clients, and the benefit of the NLP

community. This can be in mental health, personal development, business, sports, politics, parenting, or any other area of human endeavor. Your understanding of NLP allows you to improve upon established models.

6) Taking on more challenging clients and situations: Such as corporate or social change, depending on your path and career, as your mastery deepens. You continue to learn new models and patterns.

Flexibility

Milton Erickson said, "Until you are willing to be confused about what you already know, what you know will never grow bigger, better, or more useful." If the ultimate goal of NLP is excellence, then flexibility is the ultimate way of achieving it. Each person is unique—they have their own experiences and understandings of the world around them—so in order to reach an individual, we have the seemingly impossible task of trying to understand them. The only way something like this is possible is to be flexible. Flexibility might seem to contradict the fact that NLP has designed techniques to combat specific problems, because a technique is supposed to be a specific way of doing something.

This is true to a point, but it misses the larger point that for every way of doing something, we can almost always modify it to fit the person or group we are dealing with. Perhaps it is best to think of the human mind not like a car, which can only work in one way, but instead like a meal that we can cook in different ways with different ingredients, and we can cater the flavor to the individual or group we are cooking for.

In practicing NLP, flexibility can be a tricky thing. First of all, you can be presented with all types of unique and unfamiliar challenges that you need to begin working on immediately. This implies the second important part, which is that in order to be flexible, you have to be willing to use all of your knowledge and experience to tackle an issue. Even your experiences from a part-time job you had as a student could be useful in dealing with a current problem.Also, being flexible means being willing to completely give up on a plan if it is not working, no matter how much time and effort you put into making this plan.

A good guiding principle for flexibility is that for every plan you have, make at least two other different plans as back-ups just in case. If someone comes to you with a problem and a unique set of circumstances, you obviously don't want to tell them to come back in a week when you have thought of a plan, nor do you want to force them through your own plan just because it has worked in the past. Being flexible means being able to make both big and small changes. Big changes mean learning and using new techniques that you might not even believe in. Small changes mean making adjustments to what already works, not because it doesn't work, but precisely because it does; adjustments can make it more effective or applicable to more situations.

Flexibility also means adjusting things so your target audience can understand, not the target audience so they can understand. How you explain modeling to an athlete should be different from how you explain it to a fireman-the examples you give and the words you use should be a reflection of them, not of you.

Cognitive Maps

You have probably heard the expression "born yesterday" to describe someone as naive, or even a little bit stupid. This is an interesting phrase because it tells us just how much we value experience for giving us knowledge. This is important because our experience provides a guide for how we live in society. This guide is, in NLP terms, a cognitive map.

In humans, there is no single cognitive map, but rather a series of them, a bit like when you get a road map of a country or area; each map tells you about a specific area, and that map overlaps with several others. Our cognitive maps are based on packages of information that can be visual, verbal, or even kinesthetic (based on movement).

You can think of these packages as the key concepts, words, actions, and things that individually express some aspect of the cognitive map.

For example, your map for work might involve your visual representation of your office, desk, and faces of colleagues, a kinesthetic representation of driving to the building and walking inside of it, and a verbal representation of the sounds of phones ringing and the voices of your colleagues. The specific details we find in our cognitive maps are called "reference experiences," and these are what give practical meaning to our cognitive maps.

Beyond Models

For hundreds of years, philosophers and later psychologists have been dealing with what exactly constitutes a "mind". We could easily write 1,000 pages on this subject and still not have a definite picture of the mind. However, Gregory Bateson wrote in 1979 about six points that can help us understand what the "mind" is. We can call these the "criteria of mind".

1. The mind is made up of different, interacting parts that are not themselves the mind. For example, the eye gives visual information and thus is part of the mind, but the eye alone is not the mind.

2. These different and interacting parts are actually triggered by "difference," and this difference is not something that exists in the physical world. Furthermore, it is how we react to this difference that causes our behaviors and actions. For example, if you see an alligator in your kitchen, you phone the police, but there is no actual law of nature or physics that says a kitchen alligator means the police should come (unlike the law of gravity, which says objects travel towards Earth at a constant rate).

3. All mental processes require some kind of collateral energy, and a stimulus may provide that energy, or the energy can come from within the person. This means that you might be motivated because your boss might fire you, or because you personally want to be a very good worker.

4. These same mental processes also require a cyclical or even more complex set of ascertainments, very often in the form of a cause-effect chain. So our minds do not work in straight lines, but rather in wide arches and circles that connect different events.

5. In these mental processes, the results of the differences are transformed so that they fit into the events that happened before them. How they transform should be a relatively stable process, but this can also be transformed. This means that our experiences fit into

The Big Book of NLP

our understanding of the world, but we can change this understanding. The messages we receive from external experiences are coded.

6. We have a hierarchy of logical types which are described and classified by the processes of transformation, and this is the most important of all. So basically, the most important thing is that it is most important to understand how we understand something, not what it is we understand.

On Culture

There are many different types of culture. For example, the culture at work can be a "business culture", how countries perceive threats to their security is a "strategic culture", and so on. Despite all of these different types of cultures, we can break down culture into two different components: hard and soft. Hard culture is the physical results of a culture; the artwork, annual reports, weapon systems, pottery, etc.

From the NLP perspective, we are more interested in the soft culture, the ideas, values, criteria, and behaviors of a group. For example, the Kingdom of Bhutan in Asia has decided to measure gross national happiness instead of gross national product, so we can say that it is a culture of happiness instead of material wealth. This means that the behaviors, values, ideas, etc. of Bhutan will reflect the goal of happiness, not wealth. As a result, it would not be surprising to find Bhutanese people not only poorer than those from countries that prioritize GDP over GDP, but also happier.

What is more, when one person from a culture goes into a different culture, they may find many of their core beliefs and values suddenly and very openly challenged. This is the basic premise of the term "culture shock."

Research on NLP

The anarchic nature of NLP does not lend it to research, and there is no substantial body of research that tests the effectiveness of NLP. However, there are studies that look at aspects of NLP. They are mostly small studies, so they do not constitute proof, and there is definitely no scientific consensus regarding NLP. Better put, there is no significant scientific interest in NLP. Much of what research has taken place has shown a poor understanding of NLP, and suffered from methodological problems as well. Thus, it is unfair to say that research disproves NLP.

This is a ludicrous idea, anyway, since NLP is no single thing that can be proved or disproved. One of the more impressive studies took place as the Active Ingredients Project carried out by Professor Charles Figley. He became interested in rapid acting therapies, that he called power therapies at the time. This took place in the early 1990s. He compared several therapeutic approaches that are used for people with symptoms of trauma. The approaches included NLP's visual- kinesthetic dissociation (V/KD), more commonly known as the fast phobia cure. It stacked up well against other approaches, including Thought Field Therapy and eye movement desensitization and reprocessing (EMDR).

The study was not intended to be a highly sophisticated one, but more as a means of generating initial interest in researching such approaches. Figley's interest began when he discovered that trauma counselors who were the most well-adjusted were those who were trained in at least one rapid-acting approach such as V/KD. Figley developed this interest when a trauma counselor committed suicide. A couple of small studies support the NLP spelling strategy of looking up and to the left while visualizing the words being learned. Subjects had significantly better recall and forgot much less over time, to the point that their recall greatly exceeded what is normal for people memorizing things.

Several small studies support the value of the NLP phobia cure. It was not only helpful for phobias, but anxiety and depression in connection with phobias. It was also helpful for individuals reacting to psychological trauma. There is some research on sub-modalities (the aspects of how we represent things in our minds) that lends support to its use in NLP, but this has not gotten enough attention. However, cognitive psychotherapy is often practiced with elements of NLP, including sub-modality work. It depends on the therapist's background.

Anchoring is an important part of NLP. This is the ability of establishing a sort of signal (such as touching a specific area of the client's arm) that can later be used to help evoke the state that the person was in at the time the signal was established. This can be used to help get a person past their resistance to change by triggering a state that will carry them past their fear, for example. I don't know of research directly on this, but there are countless studies on behavioral conditioning, which is what anchoring is based on.

There is a great deal of research that has implications for NLP, or that, at least in theory, supports some NLP ideas and interventions. One area of research that stands out in this regard has to do with allergies. It suggests that the NLP allergy process is plausible and deserves attention from researchers.There are studies that suggest that allergies can be modified through behavioral conditioning. This is what the NLP allergy process is said to do. Also, there are some small studies of the actual NLP allergy process that are very promising.

Since NLP draws from others' work, it is no surprise that there is much research on methods that NLP has modeled, such as the hypnotic work of Milton Erickson. There is a good deal of very positive research on hypnotic communication.

Very compelling results have come out of a study on using the NLP timeline approach for asthma. Again, the study was fairly small (30 experimental subjects with 16 controls), but impressive. There were substantial improvements in lung function in a people with asthma. This is especially impressive, because people with asthma tend to lose lung function over time, not improve it. The allergy process helped them in their personal lives as well, giving them feelings of energy and empowerment in many cases. Sleep improved as well for many subjects.

Since many therapists have been influenced by NLP, possibly without even realizing it, there is no telling how much of the research on cognitive therapy has been affected by insights and training provided from NLP that has propagated into the mainstream in one way or another.

For the most part, NLP was developed outside of an academic or scientifically informed process. Thus, many of the contributors to NLP developed their patterns without necessarily knowing about existing interventions or information available to clinical or research communities. Ironically, though, NLP developers are responsible for perspectives and techniques that many psychotherapists now take for granted. These developers either originated them, or developed systematic training to make them accessible, but do not receive credit from the mainstream for their revolutionary contributions.

NLP Today

Richard Bandler said at a seminar, "The reason people have problems is that they have too much time to think." Much of NLP training and writing today resembles the early formulation of NLP. Over time, patterns and ideas have been added, but this is mostly window dressing when compared to the core of NLP that first developed.

Some of the more influential additions to NLP techniques include Core Transformation and Eye Movement Integration (similar to EMDR, and allegedly predating EMDR) from Connierae Andreas, and Timeline Therapy from Dr. Tad James.

Since the two founders of NLP have gone on to write more books and evolve their work, I'll briefly mention their more recent activities. In the mid-1980s, John Grinder and Judith DeLozier began creating new ways of doing NLP that focus more on leveraging unconscious resources. He calls this "new code." He continued working on this and publishing materials with Carmen Bostic St. Clair.

This approach often has the coach and subject producing change without knowing what solutions will spontaneously emerge from the work. An interesting feature of the new code work is that there is an overall, generic pattern used. Grinder claims that it can surpass the more specific interventive patterns that NLP is known for. One of the ways this is done is to use a game or activity of his design to produce a positive, flowing state in a person, and then have them connect that state with the problem. Grinder also continues to work with modeling, and would like to see more emphasis on modeling in the NLP community. He has also criticized NLP developers for not putting more effort into creating solutions for society and organizations, and he has focused much of his subsequent professional work on organizational excellence.

Bandler coined the term "design human engineering" (DHE) and, having learned from his loss of control over the NLP moniker, applied trademark protection to his new term. The approach emphasizes the creating of powerful states that "propel" people to excellence. It uses a variety of "mental tools" to achieve this. Although it makes use of subconscious resources, it includes a clear, conscious understanding of the states and outcomes desired. Thus, he is keeping the idea of NLP "well-formed outcomes" alive. Unlike Grinder, he is continuing to focus much of his efforts on the struggles of individuals, rather than organizations.

Now It's Your Turn

The primary objective of any truly effective therapeutic methodology is not simply to make you "feel" better in the short term. Ultimately, its goal is to help you transform into a person who can handle the inevitable hardships and sufferings of life and emerge stronger from every challenge.

You need more than a simple motivational speech. In order to be truly successful, you must go above and beyond the norm. To do so, you really do have to take care of your mental and physical health before you can support others. In summary,

Take good care of yourself. You deserve it.

Erickson Institute Books

Advanced
NLP
Techniques
Therapists
and
Coaches

Erickson Institute

- Recognition
- Curiosity
- Significance
- Contribution
- Values Elicitation
- Holding Attention
- Punctuation
- The Bi-Lateral
- The George Carlin
- The Verb Finder
- The Punctuation Diet
- Movement
- Symbolic Somatic Priming
- Somatic Awareness Enhancement
- Essence
- Somatic Leading
- Vision Communication Protocol
- Matrixing in Problem Formulation and Planning
- Matrixing for Complicated Problems
- Favorite Matrix
- How a Treatment Plan Would Look
- Deconstructing into Modalities
- Reconstructing into Values
- Future Now
- Vision Down-Stream
- Reprocessing

- Reprocessing in the field
- Think Physiology
- Targeting
- The State Shift
- Cognitive Work
- Body Scan and Future Pacing
- Recovery (Longer-Term Status)
- Time Line Therapy and Reprocessing
- Bad Code
- Good Code
- Code Triggers
- Source Event
- Echo Events
- State-Initiated Reprocessing
- Working With The Time Line
- Challenges to Reprocessing
- Post-Mystical Hyper-Structuralism
- Five Examples: Responding to Deletions
- The Action Filter
- The Intention Filter
- The Context Filter
- The Originator Filter
- The Source Filter
- The Essence Filter
- Presuppositions

Self-Analysis is a workbook, that will help you:

1. Establish Your Life's Timeline, and learn deeply about your past, discovering hidden triggers and anchors that "tick" your nerves.

2. Identify Your Core Beliefs - learn how to expose your self sabotage patterns. Most often, the very act of exposing these limiting beliefs and bringing them up to consciousness, resolves long term issues.

3. Figure Out Your Future - stop pursuing goals! The frustration and stress are not worth your time and energy. Learn how to set the right outcomes for your future, which means - the highest untapped potential you can achieve - and make that success inevitable. No "motivation" needed.

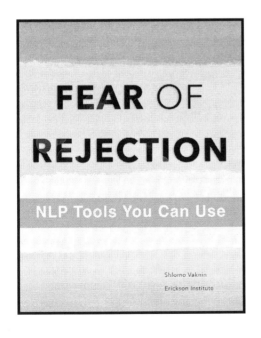

NLP

57

Meta
Programs

Erickson Institute   Shlomo Vaknin

- What are Meta-Programs?
- Where did the idea of Meta-Programs come from?
- What do Meta-Programs do?
- Does everyone use them in one way or another?
- Can a Meta-Program be altered?
- Are some Meta-Programs more common and influential than others?
- What are the benefits of studying and practicing Meta-Programs?
- How can I know what Meta-Programs are primarily relevant to me?
- Can I learn to adopt and use new Meta-Programs?
- Are these the only Meta-Programs that exist?
- Can I directly change another person's Meta-Programs?
- Can the wisdom of Meta-Programs guarantee my success in life?
- Will this knowledge change me?
- Can I use the Meta-Programs to "read people's minds"?
- Should I memorize the Meta-Programs?
- Are the questions given in the examples the only ones I can use?
- Does a Meta-Program always work the same, in any situation?
- What do you mean by "Continuum"?
- What else should I know about the "fluidity" of a meta-program?
- Is it better to be a "matcher", a "mismatcher", etc.?
- Is the way a person speaks more important than the words he or she uses?

Learn everything you need to know about each of the 57 meta–programs in NLP in order to communicate, persuade and influence yourself and others around you. It's an essential skill for coaches, therapists, teachers and parents.

"I have no intention of dying. In fact, that will be the last thing I do!"

— Milton H. Erickson

Made in the USA
Middletown, DE
15 January 2024

47892708R00459